Politics as Social Text in India

This book explores the emergence of the Bahujan Samaj Party (BSP) as an alternative political force in Uttar Pradesh, India. It focuses on the historical continuity of Dalit social justice movements and organizational politics from pre- to post-colonial India and its subsequent institutionalization as a political force with the rise of the BSP in the state since the 1980s.

The volume discusses the new age Dalit–Bahujan politics and its ethnicization of caste groups to create a bahujan samaj. The book analyzes the focused political leadership of Kanshiram and Mayawati, the strong party organization, and how they evolved an empowered Dalit ideology and identity by grassroots mobilization and championing Dalit icons and history. The author also explores the party's strategies, slogans and alliances with other political parties and communities and its political manoeuvrings to retain its influence over the electorate. The book also effectively identifies the reasons for the political marginalization of the BSP in present times in the context of the phenomenal rise of the Bhartiya Janata Party (BJP) in the state.

The book will be of great interest to researchers and scholars of political science, sociology, Dalit and subaltern studies, exclusion studies and those working on the intersectionality of caste and class. It will also be useful for policy makers, think tanks and NGOs working in the domain of caste, marginality, social exclusion and identity politics.

Jayabrata Sarkar is an associate professor teaching at the Department of Political Science in Deshbandhu College, University of Delhi, India. He has researched and worked on the Bahujan Samaj Party in Uttar Pradesh extensively and on the Bodos, a plain tribe in Assam, India, and their struggles for rights, entitlements and ethno-cultural autonomy. His areas of interest include issues related to social exclusion, marginality, identity politics and the relational context of studying these themes within the process of globalization and international politics.

Politics as Social Text in India

The Bahujan Samaj Party in Uttar Pradesh

Jayabrata Sarkar

Routledge
Taylor & Francis Group
LONDON AND NEW YORK

First published 2021
by Routledge
2 Park Square, Milton Park, Abingdon, Oxon OX14 4RN

and by Routledge
52 Vanderbilt Avenue, New York, NY 10017

Routledge is an imprint of the Taylor & Francis Group, an informa business

British Library Cataloguing-in-Publication Data
A catalogue record for this book is available from the British Library

Library of Congress Cataloging-in-Publication Data
A catalog record has been requested for this book

ISBN: 978-0-367-34757-4 (hbk)
ISBN: 978-0-429-32771-1 (ebk)

Typeset in Sabon
by Deanta Global Publishing Services, Chennai, India

For my father Professor B.B. Sarkar (1934-2010)
A Humanist and an Inspiring Teacher

Contents

Illustrations

Figures

Tables

Acknowledgements

This book is the culmination of decade-long research that grew out of my Ph.D. awarded by the University of Delhi in 2010. In the course of my research, I have incurred the debts of many, whose assistance at various stages has proved immensely valuable.

I am very grateful to Professor Ashok Acharya, who kindly agreed to act as my supervisor for this research. Conversations with him greatly refined several ideas that now appear in fuller form in this book.

Early on when I started thinking about doing research on the Bahujan Samaj Party (BSP) Mr. Ashok Verma, then a senior functionary of the BSP at the central headquarters in New Delhi, was very gracious and helpful with his time and engagement. He put me in touch with several people in the BSP, which helped me conceptualize the magnitude of research that lay ahead for me. Manoj was critical to the early stages of my research: from his trunk-filled books and booklets, CDs and VCDs on North Indian dalit history, literature and politics, he was always prompt in servicing my 'book orders', which helped me greatly to get this research underway. I also want to thank Mukesh, the enterprising salesman of Gautam Book Centre, Shahdara, Delhi, who made available a growing body of bilingual books and related source material. Mr. Dhananjay Singh, the then Delhi Secretary of the BSP, assisted me with acquiring and accessing books that are not available. Along with him, I also want to mention my gratitude to a few others associated with the BSP, both in Delhi and in Uttar Pradesh, who have requested anonymity but interactions with whom were extremely helpful for me to gain an in-depth understanding of the BSP. And Dr. Sutapa Saryal (Chandigarh) helped me with important references in the initial stages of my research, for which I am very grateful.

I would also like to thank Professor Mahesh Rangarajan (Ashoka University). Conversations with him helped me sharpen my ideas. I would like to thank Professor Priyavadan Patel (Maharaja Sayajirao University, Baroda) and Professor Chandrakala Padia (Banaras Hindu University), for their constructive comments as external examiners for my doctoral dissertation. Professor Patel went out of his way to give me a detailed analysis of how I could develop the arguments in my dissertation and turn it into a monograph. I hope he will be pleased to see how I developed the ideas he so generously shared with me.

Of particular interest for this book were three seminars where I presented parts of this research: the first at Nehru Memorial Museum and Library (NMML) in April 2012; the second, an ICSSR-UGC National Seminar in March 2017 in New Delhi; and the third at the University of Sydney Business School, University of Sydney, in July 2018 — audiences of each engaged me in thoughtful discussions and helped me expand the parameters of my research on the BSP.

I have immensely benefitted from the collections and archival resources of NMML, the Indian Council for World Affairs (ICWA), the Centre for the Study of Developing Societies (CSDS), all in Delhi, and the Ratan Tata Library and the Central Reference Library in the University of Delhi. At ICWA I would like to put on record the gratitude of Mr. Qureshi and Mrs. Sherwani, who helped me look through a mass of newspaper articles. I was privileged to be able to visit London and use materials relevant for my research in the library of the School of Oriental and African Studies (SOAS) and the British Library.

Ansar Ali, Rabindranath Basu, Rana Behal, Seema Bose, Ritu Kohli, Satish Jha, Pralay Kanungo, Sharmishtha Lahiry, Sujit Lahiry, Lalit Mohan, Seema Narain, Rajnish Saryal and Krishnan Unni were always encouraging, and my brother Dr. Nilanjan Sarkar (London School of Economics) assisted me whenever he could with his acute sense of technical and editorial details.

Finally, I would like to thank Dr. Shashank Shekhar Sinha, Antara Ray Chaudhury, Shloka Chauhan and Rennie Alphonsa of Routledge for assisting me through the various stages of the publication of this book and for answering my numerous queries related to it. A special thanks to Pratap who made the maps. This book has also benefitted from the comments from anonymous reviewers to whom Routledge had sent the manuscript.

To Saswati, my wife, Arindam, my son, and Manju, my mother – I owe a colossal sense of gratitude. They are a source of joy and inspiration, nudging and encouraging me in my academic journey.

Jayabrata Sarkar
January 9, 2021
Delhi

Maps and Table

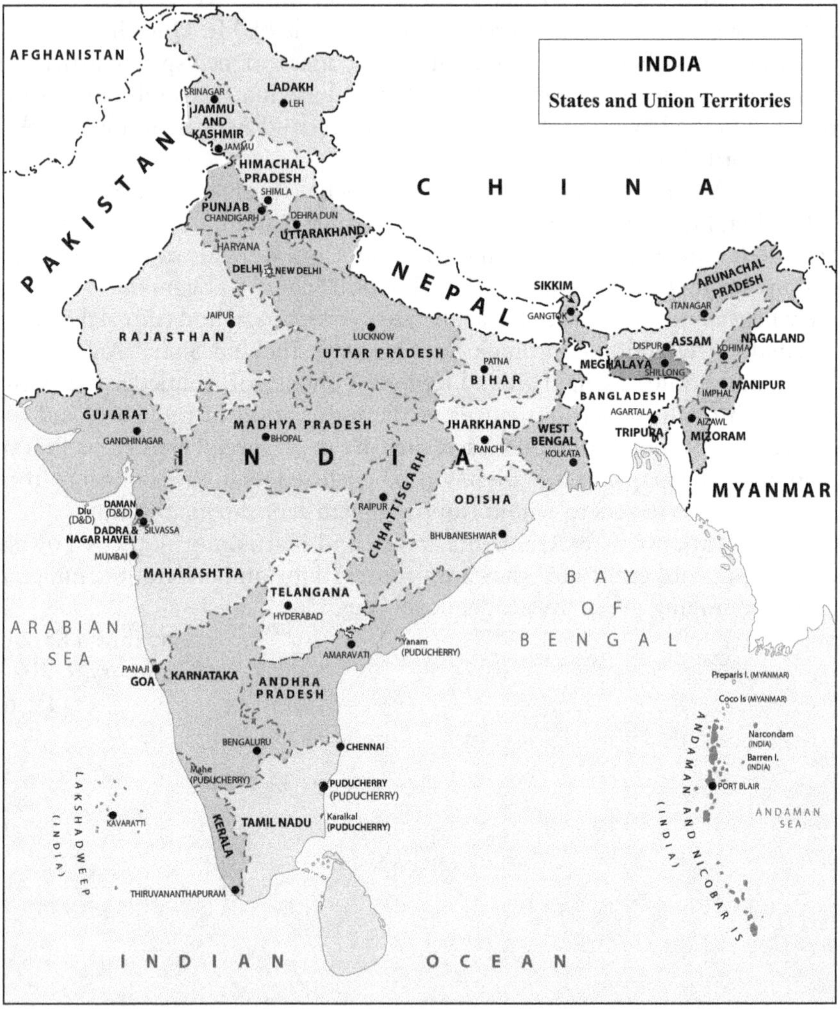

Political Map of India (States and Union Territories). Source: Author.

Parliamentary Constituencies of Uttar Pradesh. Source: Author.

Assembly Constituencies of Uttar Pradesh. Source: Author.

Assembly and Lok Sabha Constituencies of Uttar Pradesh

#	*Assembly Constituency*	*Lok Sabha Constituency*	*Reserved*	*ID*	*District*
1	Agra Cantt.	Agra	Scheduled Caste	87	Agra
2	Agra North	Agra		89	Agra
3	Agra Rural	Fatehpur Sikri	Scheduled Caste	90	Agra
4	Agra South	Agra		88	Agra
5	Ajagara	Chandauli	Scheduled Caste	385	Varanasi
6	Akbarpur	Ambedkar Nagar		281	Ambedkar Nagar
7	Akbarpur – Raniya	Akbarpur		206	Kanpur Dehat
8	Alapur	Sant Kabir Nagar	Scheduled Caste	279	Ambedkar Nagar
9	Aliganj	Farrukhabad		103	Etah
10	Aligarh	Aligarh		76	Aligarh
11	Allahabad North	Phulpur		262	Allahabad
12	Allahabad South	Allahabad		263	Allahabad
13	Allahabad West	Phulpur		261	Allahabad
14	Amanpur	Etah		101	Kasganj
15	Amethi	Amethi		186	Amethi
16	Amritpur	Farrukhabad		193	Farrukhabad
17	Amroha	Amroha		41	Amroha
18	Anupshahr	Bulandshahr		67	Bulandshahr
19	Aonla	Aonla		126	Bareilly
20	Arya Nagar	Kanpur		214	Kanpur Nagar
21	Asmoli	Sambhal		32	Sambhal
22	Atrauli	Aligarh		73	Aligarh
23	Atrauliya	Lalganj		343	Azamgarh
24	Aurai	Bhadohi	Scheduled Caste	394	Bhadohi
25	Auraiya	Etawah	Scheduled Caste	204	Auraiya
26	Ayah Shah	Fatehpur		241	Fatehpur
27	Ayodhya	Faizabad		275	Faizabad
28	Azamgarh	Azamgarh		347	Azamgarh
29	Babaganj	Kaushambi	Scheduled Caste	245	Pratapgarh
30	Baberu	Banda		233	Banda
31	Babina	Jhansi		222	Jhansi
32	Bachhrawan	Rae Bareli	Scheduled Caste	177	Raebareli
33	Badaun	Budaun		115	Budaun
34	Badlapur	Jaunpur		364	Jaunpur
35	Bagpat	Bagpat		52	Bagpat
36	Bah	Fatehpur Sikri		94	Agra
37	Baheri	Pilibhit		118	Bareilly
38	Bahraich	Bahraich		286	Bahraich
39	Bairia	Ballia		363	Ballia

(*Continued*)

Continued

#	*Assembly Constituency*	*Lok Sabha Constituency*	*Reserved*	*ID*	*District*
40	Bakshi Kaa Talab	Mohanlalganj		169	Lucknow
41	Balamau	Misrikh	Scheduled Caste	160	Hardoi
42	Baldev	Mathura	Scheduled Caste	85	Mathura
43	Balha	Bahraich	Scheduled Caste	282	Bahraich
44	Ballia Nagar	Ballia		361	Ballia
45	Balrampur	Shrawasti	Scheduled Caste	294	Balrampur
46	Banda	Banda		235	Banda
47	Bangarmau	Unnao		162	Unnao
48	Bansdih	Salempur		362	Ballia
49	Bansgaon	Bansgaon	Scheduled Caste	327	Gorakhpur
50	Bansi	Domariyaganj		304	Siddharth Nagar
51	Bara	Allahabad	Scheduled Caste	264	Allahabad
52	Barabanki	Barabanki		268	Barabanki
53	Barauli	Aligarh		72	Aligarh
54	Baraut	Bagpat		51	Bagpat
55	Bareilly	Bareilly		124	Bareilly
56	Bareilly Cantt.	Bareilly		125	Bareilly
57	Barhaj	Bansgaon		342	Deoria
58	Barhapur	Moradabad		19	Bijnor
59	Barkhera	Pilibhit		128	Pilibhit
60	Basti Sadar	Basti		310	Basti
61	Behat	Saharanpur		1	Saharanpur
62	Belthara Road	Salempur	Scheduled Caste	357	Ballia
63	Bhadohi	Bhadohi		392	Bhadohi
64	Bhagwantnagar	Unnao		166	Unnao
65	Bharthana	Etawah	Scheduled Caste	201	Etawah
66	Bhatpar Rani	Salempur		340	Deoria
67	Bhinga	Shrawasti		289	Shrawasti
68	Bhognipur	Jalaun		208	Kanpur Dehat
69	Bhojipura	Bareilly		120	Bareilly
70	Bhojpur	Farrukhabad		195	Farrukhabad
71	Bhongaon	Mainpuri		108	Mainpuri
72	Bidhuna	Kannauj		202	Auraiya
73	Bijnor	Bijnor		22	Bijnor
74	Bikapur	Faizabad		274	Faizabad
75	Bilari	Sambhal		30	Moradabad
76	Bilaspur	Rampur		36	Rampur
77	Bilgram-Mallanwan	Misrikh		159	Hardoi

(*Continued*)

Continued

#	*Assembly Constituency*	*Lok Sabha Constituency*	*Reserved*	*ID*	*District*
78	Bilhaur	Misrikh	Scheduled Caste	209	Kanpur Nagar
79	Bilsi	Budaun		114	Budaun
80	Bindki	Fatehpur		239	Fatehpur
81	Bisalpur	Pilibhit		130	Pilibhit
82	Bisauli	Budaun	Scheduled Caste	112	Budaun
83	Biswan	Sitapur		149	Sitapur
84	Bithari Chainpur	Aonla		123	Bareilly
85	Bithoor	Akbarpur		210	Kanpur Nagar
86	Budhana	Muzaffarnagar		11	Muzaffarnagar
87	Bulandshahr	Bulandshahr		65	Bulandshahr
88	Caimpiyarganj	Gorakhpur		320	Gorakhpur
89	Chail	Kaushambi		253	Kaushambi
90	Chakia	Robertsganj	Scheduled Caste	383	Chandauli
91	Chamraua	Rampur		35	Rampur
92	Chandausi	Sambhal	Scheduled Caste	31	Sambhal
93	Chandpur	Bijnor		23	Bijnor
94	Charkhari	Hamirpur		231	Mahoba
95	Charthawal	Muzaffarnagar		12	Muzaffarnagar
96	Chauri-Chaura	Bansgaon		326	Gorakhpur
97	Chhanbey	Mirzapur		395	Mirzapur
98	Chhaprauli	Baghpat		50	Baghpat
99	Chharra	Hathras		74	Aligarh
100	Chhata	Mathura		81	Mathura
101	Chhibramau	Kannauj		196	Kannauj
102	Chillupar	Bansgaon		328	Gorakhpur
103	Chitrakoot	Banda		236	Chitrakoot
104	Chunar	Mirzapur		398	Mirzapur
105	Colonelganj	Kaiserganj		298	Gonda
106	Dadraul	Shahjahanpur		136	Shahjahanpur
107	Dadri	Gautam Buddha Nagar		62	Gautam Budh Nagar
108	Dariyabad	Faizabad		270	Barabanki
109	Dataganj	Aonla		117	Budaun
110	Debai	Bulandshahr		68	Bulandshahr
111	Deoband	Saharanpur		5	Saharanpur
112	Deoria	Deoria		337	Deoria
113	Dhampur	Nagina		20	Bijnor
114	Dhanaura	Amroha	Scheduled Caste	39	Amroha
115	Dhanghata	Sant Kabir Nagar	Scheduled Caste	314	Sant Kabir Nagar
116	Dhaurahra	Dhaurahra		141	Lakhimpur Kheri

(*Continued*)

Continued

#	*Assembly Constituency*	*Lok Sabha Constituency*	*Reserved*	*ID*	*District*
117	Dhaulana	Ghaziabad		58	Hapur
118	Dibiyapur	Etawah		203	Auraiya
119	Didarganj	Lalganj		350	Azamgarh
120	Domariyaganj	Domariyaganj		306	Siddharth Nagar
121	Duddhi	Robertsganj	Scheduled Caste	403	Sonbhadra
122	Etah	Etah		104	Etah
123	Etawah	Etawah		200	Etawah
124	Etmadpur	Agra		86	Agra
125	Faridpur	Aonla	Scheduled Caste	122	Bareilly
126	Farrukhabad	Farrukhabad		194	Farrukhabad
127	Fatehabad	Fatehpur Sikri		93	Agra
128	Fatehpur	Fatehpur		240	Fatehpur
129	Fatehpur Sikri	Fatehpur Sikri		91	Agra
130	Fazilnagar	Deoria		332	Kushinagar
131	Firozabad	Firozabad		97	Firozabad
132	Gainsari	Shrawasti		292	Balrampur
133	Gangoh	Kairana		7	Saharanpur
134	Garautha	Jalaun		225	Jhansi
135	Garhmukteshwar	Amroha		60	Hapur
136	Gaura	Gonda		301	Gonda
137	Gauriganj	Amethi		185	Amethi
138	Ghatampur	Akbarpur	Scheduled Caste	218	Kanpur Nagar
139	Ghaziabad	Ghaziabad		56	Ghaziabad
140	Ghazipur	Ghazipur		375	Ghazipur
141	Ghorawal	Robertsganj		400	Sonbhadra
142	Ghosi	Ghosi		354	Mau
143	Gola Gokrannath	Kheri		139	Lakhimpur Kheri
144	Gonda	Gonda		296	Gonda
145	Gopalpur	Azamgarh		344	Azamgarh
146	Gopamau	Hardoi	Scheduled Caste	157	Hardoi
147	Gorakhpur Rural	Gorakhpur		323	Gorakhpur
148	Gorakhpur Urban	Gorakhpur		322	Gorakhpur
149	Goshainganj	Ambedkar Nagar		276	Faizabad
150	Goverdhan	Mathura		83	Mathura
151	Govindnagar	Kanpur		212	Kanpur Nagar
152	Gunnaur	Budaun		111	Sambhal
153	Gyanpur	Bhadohi		393	Bhadohi
154	Haidergarh	Barabanki	Scheduled Caste	272	Barabanki
155	Hamirpur	Hamirpur		228	Hamirpur
156	Handia	Bhadohi		258	Allahabad

(*Continued*)

Continued

#	*Assembly Constituency*	*Lok Sabha Constituency*	*Reserved*	*ID*	*District*
157	Hapur	Meerut	Scheduled Caste	59	Hapur
158	Harchandpur	Rae Bareli		179	Raebareli
159	Hardoi	Hardoi		156	Hardoi
160	Hargaon	Dhaurahra	Scheduled Caste	147	Sitapur
161	Harraiya	Basti		307	Basti
162	Hasanpur	Amroha		42	Amroha
163	Hastinapur	Bijnor	Scheduled Caste	45	Meerut
164	Hata	Kushinagar		334	Kushinagar
165	Hathras	Hathras	Scheduled Caste	78	Hathras
166	Husainganj	Fatehpur		242	Fatehpur
167	Iglas	Hathras	Scheduled Caste	77	Aligarh
168	Isauli	Sultanpur		187	Sultanpur
169	Itwa	Domariyaganj		305	Siddharth Nagar
170	Jagdishpur	Amethi	Scheduled Caste	184	Amethi
171	Jahanabad	Fatehpur		238	Fatehpur
172	Jakhanian	Ghazipur	Scheduled Caste	373	Ghazipur
173	Jalalabad	Shahjahanpur		132	Shahjahanpur
174	Jalalpur	Ambedkar Nagar		280	Ambedkar Nagar
175	Jalesar	Agra	Scheduled Caste	106	Etah
176	Jangipur	Ghazipur		376	Ghazipur
177	Jasrana	Firozabad		96	Firozabad
178	Jaswantnagar	Mainpuri		199	Etawah
179	Jaunpur	Jaunpur		366	Jaunpur
180	Jewar	Gautam Buddha Nagar		63	Gautam Budh Nagar
181	Jhansi Nagar	Jhansi		223	Jhansi
182	Kadipur	Sultanpur	Scheduled Caste	191	Sultanpur
183	Kaimganj	Farrukhabad	Scheduled Caste	192	Farrukhabad
184	Kairana	Kairana		8	Shamli
185	Kaiserganj	Kaiserganj		288	Bahraich
186	Kalpi	Jalaun		220	Jalaun
187	Kalyanpur	Akbarpur		211	Kanpur Nagar
188	Kannauj	Kannauj	Scheduled Caste	198	Kannauj
189	Kanpur Cantt.	Kanpur		216	Kanpur Nagar

(*Continued*)

Continued

#	*Assembly Constituency*	*Lok Sabha Constituency*	*Reserved*	*ID*	*District*
190	Kanth	Moradabad		25	Moradabad
191	Kapilvastu	Domariyaganj	Scheduled Caste	303	Siddharth Nagar
192	Kaptanganj	Basti		308	Basti
193	Karachhana	Allahabad		260	Allahabad
194	Karhal	Mainpuri		110	Mainpuri
195	Kasganj	Etah		100	Kasganj
196	Kasta	Dhaurahra	Scheduled Caste	143	Lakhimpur Kheri
197	Katehari	Ambedkar Nagar		277	Ambedkar Nagar
198	Katra	Shahjahanpur		131	Shahjahanpur
199	Katra Bazar	Kaiserganj		297	Gonda
200	Kerakat	Machhlishahr	Scheduled Caste	372	Jaunpur
201	Khadda	Kushinagar		329	Kushinagar
202	Khaga	Fatehpur	Scheduled Caste	243	Fatehpur
203	Khair	Aligarh	Scheduled Caste	71	Aligarh
204	Khajani	Sant Kabir Nagar	Scheduled Caste	325	Gorakhpur
205	Khalilabad	Sant Kabir Nagar		313	Sant Kabir Nagar
206	Khatauli	Muzaffarnagar		15	Muzaffarnagar
207	Kheragarh	Fatehpur Sikri		92	Agra
208	Khurja	Gautam Buddha Nagar	Scheduled Caste	70	Bulandshahr
209	Kidwai Nagar	Kanpur		215	Kanpur Nagar
210	Kishni	Mainpuri	Scheduled Caste	109	Mainpuri
211	Kithore	Meerut		46	Meerut
212	Koil	Aligarh		75	Aligarh
213	Koraon	Allahabad	Scheduled Caste	265	Allahabad
214	Kunda	Kaushambi		246	Pratapgarh
215	Kundarki	Sambhal		29	Moradabad
216	Kursi	Barabanki		266	Barabanki
217	Kushinagar	Kushinagar		333	Kushinagar
218	Laharpur	Sitapur		148	Sitapur
219	Lakhimpur	Kheri		142	Lakhimpur Kheri
220	Lalganj	Lalganj	Scheduled Caste	351	Azamgarh
221	Lalitpur	Jhansi		226	Lalitpur
222	Lambhua	Sultanpur		190	Sultanpur
223	Loni	Ghaziabad		53	Ghaziabad

(*Continued*)

Continued

#	*Assembly Constituency*	*Lok Sabha Constituency*	*Reserved*	*ID*	*District*
224	Lucknow Cantt.	Lucknow		175	Lucknow
225	Lucknow Central	Lucknow		174	Lucknow
226	Lucknow East	Lucknow		173	Lucknow
227	Lucknow North	Lucknow		172	Lucknow
228	Lucknow West	Lucknow		171	Lucknow
229	Machhlishahr	Machhlishahr	Scheduled Caste	369	Jaunpur
230	Madhaugarh	Jalaun		219	Jalaun
231	Madhuban	Ghosi		353	Mau
232	Mahadewa	Basti	Scheduled Caste	311	Basti
233	Maharajganj	Maharajganj	Scheduled Caste	318	Maharajganj
234	Maharajpur	Akbarpur		217	Kanpur Nagar
235	Mahasi	Bahraich		285	Bahraich
236	Mahmoodabad	Sitapur		151	Sitapur
237	Mahoba	Hamirpur		230	Mahoba
238	Maholi	Dhaurahra		145	Sitapur
239	Mainpuri	Mainpuri		107	Mainpuri
240	Majhawan	Mirzapur		397	Mirzapur
241	Malhani	Jaunpur		367	Jaunpur
242	Malihabad	Mohanlalganj	Scheduled Caste	168	Lucknow
243	Manikpur	Banda		237	Chitrakoot
244	Manjhanpur	Kaushambi	Scheduled Caste	252	Kaushambi
245	Mankapur	Gonda	Scheduled Caste	300	Gonda
246	Mant	Mathura		82	Mathura
247	Marhara	Etah		105	Etah
248	Madihan	Mirzapur		399	Mirzapur
249	Mariyahu	Machhlishahr		370	Jaunpur
250	Matera	Bahraich		284	Bahraich
251	Mathura	Mathura		84	Mathura
252	Mau	Ghosi		356	Mau
253	Mauranipur	Jhansi	Scheduled Caste	224	Jhansi
254	Meerapur	Bijnor		16	Muzaffarnagar
255	Meerganj	Bareilly		119	Bareilly
256	Meerut	Meerut		48	Meerut
257	Meerut Cantt.	Meerut		47	Meerut
258	Meerut South	Meerut		49	Meerut
259	Mehnagar	Azamgarh	Scheduled Caste	352	Azamgarh
260	Mehnaun	Gonda		295	Gonda
261	Mehroni	Jhansi	Scheduled Caste	227	Lalitpur
262	Meja	Allahabad		259	Allahabad

(*Continued*)

Continued

#	*Assembly Constituency*	*Lok Sabha Constituency*	*Reserved*	*ID*	*District*
263	Menhdawal	Sant Kabir Nagar		312	Sant Kabir Nagar
264	Milak	Rampur	Scheduled Caste	38	Rampur
265	Milkipur	Faizabad	Scheduled Caste	273	Faizabad
266	Mirzapur	Mirzapur		396	Mirzapur
267	Misrikh	Misrikh	Scheduled Caste	153	Sitapur
268	Modinagar	Bagpat		57	Ghaziabad
269	Mohammadabad	Ballia		378	Ghazipur
270	Mohammdi	Dhaurahra		144	Lakhimpur Kheri
271	Mohan	Unnao	Scheduled Caste	164	Unnao
272	Mohanlalganj	Mohanlalganj	Scheduled Caste	176	Lucknow
273	Moradabad Nagar	Moradabad		28	Moradabad
274	Moradabad Rural	Moradabad		27	Moradabad
275	Mubarakpur	Azamgarh		346	Azamgarh
276	Mughalsarai	Chandauli		380	Chandauli
277	Muhammadabad-Gohna	Ghosi	Scheduled Caste	355	Mau
278	Mungra Badshahpur	Jaunpur		368	Jaunpur
279	Muradnagar	Ghaziabad		54	Ghaziabad
280	Muzaffarnagar	Muzaffarnagar		14	Muzaffarnagar
281	Nagina	Nagina	Scheduled Caste	18	Bijnor
282	Najibabad	Nagina		17	Bijnor
283	Nakur	Kairana		2	Saharanpur
284	Nanpara	Bahraich		283	Bahraich
285	Naraini	Banda	Scheduled Caste	234	Banda
286	Naugawan Sadat	Amroha		40	Amroha
287	Nautanwa	Maharajganj		316	Maharajganj
288	Nawabganj	Bareilly		121	Bareilly
289	Nehtaur	Nagina	Scheduled Caste	21	Bijnor
290	Nighasan	Kheri		138	Lakhimpur Kheri
291	Nizamabad	Lalganj		348	Azamgarh
292	Noida	Gautam Buddha Nagar		61	Gautam Budh Nagar
293	Noorpur	Nagina		24	Bijnor
294	Obra	Robertsganj		402	Sonbhadra
295	Orai	Jalaun	Scheduled Caste	221	Jalaun

(*Continued*)

Continued

#	Assembly Constituency	Lok Sabha Constituency	Reserved	ID	District
296	Padrauna	Kushinagar		330	Kushinagar
297	Palia	Kheri		137	Lakhimpur Kheri
298	Paniyara	Maharajganj		319	Mahrajganj
299	Pathardeva	Deoria		338	Deoria
300	Patiyali	Etah		102	Kasganj
301	Patti	Pratapgarh		249	Pratapgarh
302	Payagpur	Kaiserganj		287	Bahraich
303	Phaphamau	Phulpur		254	Allahabad
304	Pharenda	Maharajganj		315	Maharajganj
305	Phephana	Ballia		360	Ballia
306	Phoolpur Pawai	Lalganj		349	Azamgarh
307	Phulpur	Phulpur		256	Allahabad
308	Pilibhit	Pilibhit		127	Pilibhit
309	Pindra	Machhlishahr		384	Varanasi
310	Pipraich	Gorakhpur		321	Gorakhpur
311	Powayan	Shahjahanpur	Scheduled Caste	134	Shahjahanpur
312	Pratapgarh	Pratapgarh		248	Pratapgarh
313	Pratappur	Bhadohi		257	Allahabad
314	Puranpur	Pilibhit	Scheduled Caste	129	Pilibhit
315	Purqazi	Bijnor	Scheduled Caste	13	Muzaffarnagar
316	Purwa	Unnao		167	Unnao
317	Rae Bareli	Rae Bareli		180	Raebareli
318	Ram Nagar	Barabanki		267	Barabanki
319	Ramkola	Kushinagar	Scheduled Caste	335	Kushinagar
320	Rampur	Rampur		37	Rampur
321	Rampur Karkhana	Deoria		339	Deoria
322	Rampur Khas	Pratapgarh		244	Pratapgarh
323	Rampur Maniharan	Saharanpur	Scheduled Caste	6	Saharanpur
324	Raniganj	Pratapgarh		250	Pratapgarh
325	Rasara	Ghosi		358	Ballia
326	Rasulabad	Kannauj	Scheduled Caste	205	Kanpur Dehat
327	Rath	Hamirpur	Scheduled Caste	229	Hamirpur
328	Robertsganj	Robertsganj		401	Sonbhadra
329	Rohaniya	Varanasi		387	Varanasi
330	Rudauli	Faizabad		271	Faizabad
331	Rudhauli	Basti		309	Basti
332	Rudrapur	Bansgaon		336	Deoria
333	Sadabad	Hathras		79	Hathras
334	Sadar	Sultanpur		189	Sultanpur

(*Continued*)

Continued

#	*Assembly Constituency*	*Lok Sabha Constituency*	*Reserved*	*ID*	*District*
335	Safipur	Unnao	Scheduled Caste	163	Unnao
336	Sagri	Azamgarh		345	Azamgarh
337	Sahajanwa	Gorakhpur		324	Gorakhpur
338	Saharanpur	Saharanpur	Scheduled Caste	4	Saharanpur
339	Saharanpur Nagar	Saharanpur		3	Saharanpur
340	Sahaswan	Budaun		113	Budaun
341	Sahibabad	Ghaziabad		55	Ghaziabad
342	Saidpur	Ghazipur	Scheduled Caste	374	Ghazipur
343	Saiyadraja	Chandauli		382	Chandauli
344	Sakaldiha	Chandauli		381	Chandauli
345	Salempur	Salempur	Scheduled Caste	341	Deoria
346	Salon	Amethi	Scheduled Caste	181	Raebareli
347	Sambhal	Sambhal		33	Sambhal
348	Sandi	Hardoi	Scheduled Caste	158	Hardoi
349	Sandila	Misrikh		161	Hardoi
350	Sardhana	Muzaffarnagar		44	Meerut
351	Sareni	Rae Bareli		182	Raebareli
352	Sarojini Nagar	Mohanlalganj		170	Lucknow
353	Sawayazpur	Hardoi		154	Hardoi
354	Sevapuri	Varanasi		391	Varanasi
355	Sevata	Sitapur		150	Sitapur
356	Shahabad	Hardoi		155	Hardoi
357	Shahganj	Jaunpur		365	Jaunpur
358	Shahjahanpur	Shahjahanpur		135	Shahjahanpur
359	Shamli	Kairana		10	Shamli
360	Shekhupur	Aonla		116	Budaun
361	Shikarpur	Bulandshahr		69	Bulandshahr
362	Shikohabad	Firozabad		98	Firozabad
363	Shivpur	Chandauli		386	Varanasi
364	Shohratgarh	Domariyaganj		302	Siddharth Nagar
365	Shrawasti	Shrawasti		290	Shrawasti
366	Sidhauli	Mohanlalganj	Scheduled Caste	152	Sitapur
367	Sikanderpur	Salempur		359	Ballia
368	Sikandra	Etawah		207	Kanpur Dehat
369	Sikandra Rao	Hathras		80	Hathras
370	Sikandrabad	Gautam Buddha Nagar		64	Bulandshahr
371	Sirathu	Kaushambi		251	Kaushambi
372	Sirsaganj	Firozabad		99	Firozabad

(*Continued*)

Continued

#	*Assembly Constituency*	*Lok Sabha Constituency*	*Reserved*	*ID*	*District*
373	Sishamau	Kanpur		213	Kanpur Nagar
374	Siswa	Maharajganj		317	Maharajganj
375	Sitapur	Sitapur		146	Sitapur
376	Siwalkhas	Bagpat		43	Meerut
377	Soraon	Phulpur	Scheduled Caste	255	Allahabad
378	Sri Nagar	Kheri	Scheduled Caste	140	Lakhimpur Kheri
379	Suar	Rampur		34	Rampur
380	Sultanpur	Sultanpur		188	Sultanpur
381	Syana	Bulandshahr		66	Bulandshahr
382	Tamkuhi Raj	Deoria		331	Kushinagar
383	Tanda	Ambedkar Nagar		278	Ambedkar Nagar
384	Tarabganj	Kaiserganj		299	Gonda
385	Thakurdwara	Moradabad		26	Moradabad
386	Thana Bhawan	Kairana		9	Shamli
387	Tilhar	Shahjahanpur		133	Shahjahanpur
388	Tiloi	Amethi		178	Amethi
389	Tindwari	Hamirpur		232	Banda
390	Tirwa	Kannauj		197	Kannauj
391	Tulsipur	Shrawasti		291	Balrampur
392	Tundla	Firozabad	Scheduled Caste	95	Firozabad
393	Unchahar	Rae Bareli		183	Raebareli
394	Unnao	Unnao		165	Unnao
395	Utraula	Gonda		293	Balrampur
396	Varanasi Cantt.	Varanasi		390	Varanasi
397	Varanasi North	Varanasi		388	Varanasi
398	Varanasi South	Varanasi		389	Varanasi
399	Vishwanathganj	Pratapgarh		247	Pratapgarh
400	Zafrabad	Machhlishahr		371	Jaunpur
401	Zahoorabad	Ballia		377	Ghazipur
402	Zaidpur	Barabanki	Scheduled Caste	269	Barabanki
403	Zamania	Ghazipur		379	Ghazipur

Source: https://en.wikipedia.org/wiki/List_of_constituencies_of_the_Uttar_Pradesh_Legislative_Assembly

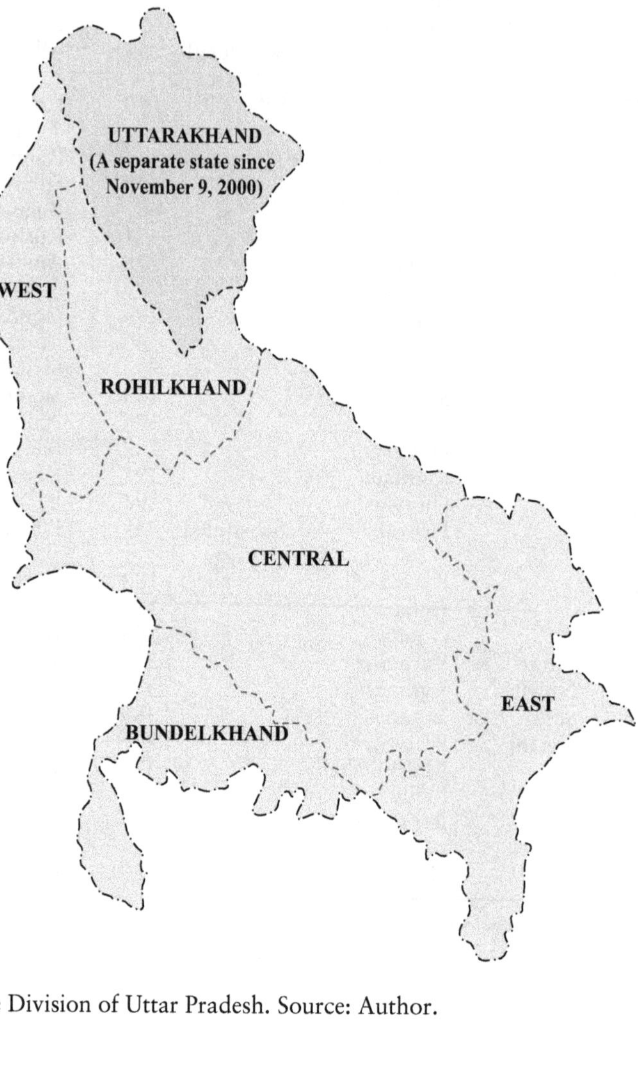

Regionwise Division of Uttar Pradesh. Source: Author.

Introduction

In the context of diverse and plural developing societies, where people engage with differing sociocultural norms and values, the perception of social justice can often expose the conflictual and contested claims among multiple groups. A varied range of social groups are inclined to seek the predominance of one's own community interests and/or rights, so that, apparently, the 'ends of social justice' are properly achieved. In a significant way, the penetration of democracy in the social life world of developing societies has seen the political advocacy of community interests through a variety of patterns of social mobilization of the in-group(s) – that has often led to participation in elections to legitimize the protection of a range of civic and political rights. However, to a substantial extent, the emergence and consequent legitimacy of a variety of social movements in the public sphere and a political regime's approved strategy or policy of accommodation, assimilation or outright acceptance depends on the character of the state (from democratic to authoritarian), including even those which are 'democratic-type', with their respective cultural and political traditions.

In post-colonial India, values and methods of democratic politics based on 'legitimate authority, representative power and the notion of social justice' have transformed the 'hybrid nature of caste associations that have appeared as both ascriptive and voluntary' and made it possible for 'caste to continue to shape identity politics as it has found new and creative ways to define itself and act collectively in political arenas'. Notwithstanding subaltern caste-based social protests that have their political roots in colonial India, lower castes, the 'bahujan' Indian electorate, have acted collectively through caste associations which have fostered a 'channel of communication and bases of leadership and organization' for the affected groups to participate in electoral politics. Mobilized around caste, affected social groups have sought to use the resulting political power to chart a political course to access increased availability of benefits and patronage and 'gained a seat at the table and earned social respect'.[1] Therefore, caste in its modern sense is a normative identitarian category to outline a democratizing politics of representation. However, a question remains: whether varied types of anti-caste/identity-based struggles/movements have been able to foreground and imbue a causative effect to the interplay between a subjective experience of the world and the cultural and historical settings in which the fragile subjectivity of the socially disenfranchised is formed.[2] Further, have these social movements effected even a semblance of material advancement in the social lives of the affected group?

It is in this regard that this book seeks to outline the socio-ideological frames of political activity of the Bahujan Samaj Party (BSP) in the electorally significant north Indian state of Uttar Pradesh. BSP's anti-caste strategized 'ethnic-electoral politics' was ideologically conceived by it as a 'type of resistance' contextualized in an 'unequal social world' – an exploitative social ordering of caste where materiality, acquisition, wealth and power are highly skewed, where the severity of caste-class hierarchical relations and inequality of social and economic dominance in a pre-capitalist economy have been reinforced by prolonged periods of state domination through laws, policies and practices.[3]

The Bahujan Samaj Party was formed in 1984 in Uttar Pradesh (UP), coinciding with a brewing decade and a half old political crisis of the Congress Party in Uttar Pradesh. In the context of UP, three political factors have had a significant bearing on the future prospects of the Congress Party: First, a populist regenerative programme for the poor propagated nationally which was ineffective in terms of delivery of public resources and goods to the marginalized sections of society, while being effectually considered as a new form of political mobilization of India's vast population of the poor. Second, the political impress of Congress Party's politics of the early 1970s coincided with the consolidation of the middle castes landholding gentry through the centrally planned Green Revolution in parts of the UP. Despite being economically prosperous, the middle castes faced representative blockage in state politics that was largely monopolized by the upper caste elites. The Congress consistently set aside any demand for state quotas in government services etc. for the middle castes and instead officially approved quotas for the most backward castes in the state. Third, by the end of the 1970s and the beginning of the 1980s the Congress Party's vote base among the poor in the state began to fragment, notably, the low-caste Other Backward Class (OBC); the dalits, especially the populous and dominant Jatavs competing for state sector jobs with upper castes and being discriminated and who were simultaneously seeking political avenues to address their concerns. This became evidently clear as the early 1980s witnessed intense caste atrocities against Scheduled Castes (SCs) by the nouveau-riche middle castes in tandem with the upper castes in the state. This is also the period when the Congress Party, forced by extenuating circumstances of political survival in UP, outlined a series of fiscal and agrarian policy measures that would wholly benefit the rising middle caste, though in the know that they were not a vote constituency for the party and were already affiliated to certain agrarian-based political parties in the state that had begun to emerge during that period. By the end of the 1980s, larger sections of the new landholding castes were supporting the Janata Dal, an emerging political force in the state which promised to alter the 'status quo' and 'majoritarian politics' of the Congress Party and the Bharatiya Janata Party (BJP), and in the process claiming to usher in an 'alternative' politics. The political decline of the Congress Party in UP coincided with the mid-1980s 'temple movement' in Ayodhya, which had gathered political momentum under the auspices of Hindu nationalist organizations with the BJP focussing on carving a Hindu majority vote. As the 'Ram Janmabhoomi (birthplace of Lord Ram) movement' gathered a feverous pitch, the arrival of significant portions of upper-caste voters of the state to the BJP dealt a political blow to the Congress Party: already denuded of subaltern voting constituency, including Muslims now at an even greater pace, the latter, post-temple movement, attracted to the Janata Dal (and with the fragmentation of the Janata Dal in UP in the early 1990s becoming a core vote base of the Samajwadi Party and only then showing political allegiance to the BSP), it signalled the end of a broad aggregative party system of the 'Grand Old Party' in Uttar Pradesh.

The BSP can be traced a decade prior to its inception to the formation of 'union-type' associations, the Backward and Minorities Communities Employee Federation (BAMCEF) and the Dalit Shoshit Samaj Sangharsh Samiti (DS-4), that conjured Kanshiram's vision for conceptualizing a possible bahujan samaj (majority society) politics. BAMCEF was founded in 1973 in Pune, and in three years, in 1976, an office was opened in Lucknow, in a state undergoing social and political change. Apparently, BAMCEF's non-political associational front to foster a 'unity of purpose' for a variety of subaltern castes was a critique of the Poona Pact (1932) and 'its consequences': the legitimacy of the 'Brahminic Social Order' (BSO), a weak and enervated Dalit movement in India and more specifically that Kanshiram experienced in Maharashtra, considered the centre of Dalit politics, where the Republican Party India (RPI) and the Dalit Panthers (DP) were split into several factions. BAMCEF defined in terms of it being a useful prop to launch a political party in future, in a sense, outlined the incremental preparedness of a 'motivated' Dalit leadership. They comprised primarily the 'quota-based' office staff of central government offices and departments, who were to find 'time, intellect and (resources) money' to lead the 'fragmented, poor, exploited and disunited' Dalit-Bahujan class. Activities of the association-type unit found its political worth in Uttar Pradesh, considered by Kanshiram the 'nucleus' of Brahmanism, where a 'future political experiment' could be conducted. There the organization spread into urban localities and even engaged in casual and informal chats to create political awareness in rural areas. On an all-India level (1978–1983), Kanshiram engaged in constructing the cultural resources for a 'new age' bahujan consciousness: the 'subjugated' yet 'glorious histories' of low-caste groups were retrieved in innovative ways: seminars, conferences, slide shows of Dalit icons, cheap handbooks of jati-purana, posters, cycle marches that connected important cities across India. However, Uttar Pradesh would remain the centre of Dalit-Bahujan politics.

In 1981, Kanshiram founded the Dalit Shoshit Samaj Sangharsh Samiti, a quasi-political organization, staffed by students and youth activists who were directed to mobilize rural bahujan masses. They were specifically advised not to pursue confrontational politics as it could lead to a violent casteist backlash by local structures of power operating within social contexts of inequality, oppression and powerlessness. The DS-4 carried out provocative programmes and forged crisp political slogans particularly in rural hinterlands with the purpose of determining the magnitude of support of marginalized social groups.

The consummate ease with which Kanshiram founded the BSP underscores the political belief for a new-age 'revised' Dalit politics in UP considered as the 'laboratory' for the experimentation of BSP's brand of anti-caste politics: to upturn the BSO that has had a pervasive control over all spheres of life. Despite constant emphasis on the 'bahujan' aspect of politics, the political vision was reposed to the dominant and populous Chamar/Jatav caste elite of the state. Much before the post-1990 'Mandal politics' that took political effect, the BSP was already contemplating a 'party-based opposition', which traditionally has been labelled as 'single-caste' movements, whose political assessment in post-1947 India leading to the decade of the 1980s had been its inability to forge a broad-based socio-political struggle. The RPI is an example of this. Yet, BSP was going to change that predicament: 'Chamar elites' were to 'unofficially' take a leading political position in the party as Kanshiram outlined a 'set of favourable political circumstances' in the early 1980s that would relate them to the precise 'historic and political role' they were entrusted to perform: as core supporters of the party with a large number of activists, privileges of government control were to be utilized howsoever modest for the sectional benefit which would create opportunities for political action to challenge caste oppression in society and politics. The Chamars (known by other caste names across north and central India) were ideologically sourced by Kanshiram as being privy to a 'historical struggle of Dalit mobilization and politics in colonial and postcolonial India' for equality and political power. However, evidence suggests that the UP Chamar elite operated through various caste-based associations in the colonial and post-independence period till the end of the 1960s and their preponderant objective was 'defence of caste interests' and legislative reforms for certain political and administrative concessions. Kanshiram further observed that under oppressive caste-ordered society in UP, a large body of poverty-stricken bahujan 'landless and victims of caste violence' and the rural and urban jobless poor youths were 'ready-made electoral capital' for the new political party.

For a party that called on Ambedkar's social justice objectives, termed by Kanshiram as 'fraternizing principles' – while critiquing state 'Dalit' political outfits (Uttar Pradesh Republican Party of India or Bharatiya Dalit Panthers) of gross political failures – and 'bahujanwad' that resembled Phule's egalitarian vision and social politics, the actual political course belied any broad similarity either in essence or in style of politics. Clearly, the political ideology of BSP was interpolated: a contentious 'fraternity-bahujanism principle of ethno-electoral politics' that would 'cut out intermediaries' for the benefit of the subaltern majority by pursuing the goal of a 'Bahujan State'. There was no question of leading a mass-based political movement to project an ethnically conceived samta-mulak (equality-based) bahujan samaj howsoever different it would be from its philosophic conceptualizations by past Dalit-Bahujan reformers and political thinkers alike. Thus, to resurrect the politics of the marginalized 'differently', the BSP was disinclined to engage with humiliation and deprivation, the central question that deeply impacted the inner core of dalits and lower castes psyche and selves; mindful of the fact that it was humiliation and deprivation which fostered political mobilization and a spate of subaltern movements among lower castes in the late 19th and early 20th centuries which questioned exploitative caste hierarchies by reaffirming their identity of community and history. For a party that equated the political success or failure of a bahujan-based party only on electoral outcomes by withholding a political exploration into the more subjective dimensions of Dalit-Bahujan politics, the post-independence period that represented an evolving dynamism and complexity of subaltern politics did not hold political appeal. Take for instance the manner in which the notion of social justice which sought to confront the dual imperatives of 'abolition' and 'redress' for the dalits and low-caste groups through state legislations developed a specific relationship between 'types'/categories used in government practices and the character of 'identities' that began to govern historically subjugated groups and lower backward castes. It led to a 'consolidation of narratives beyond the objective criterion' into an overarching narrative about social suffering and oppression, human rights and social justice.[4] Admittedly, there was a question for the BSP to politically comprehend the changed character of caste consciousness among the disenfranchised, and thereby perceive a broader social justice narrative. Yet, by default, albeit knowingly to 'cut intermediate thoughts and agency out of purview', the BSP stayed clear of such gainful discursive debates, disinterested to evolve a socio-political public space to conceptualize rights, claims and responsibilities or confronting values deeply inimical to human and social rights in society.[5]

Based on ideological perceptions of 'failed Dalit movements', the forging of a 'priority principle' for the BSP rested on authoritative 'Dalit' leaders Kanshiram and Mayawati, considered to be most effective in 'vision casting', who would maximize the commitment of the marginalized groups to the political goals of the BSP. They would maintain a relationship of formal and informal – symbolic and organic – power through a tightly controlled party structure conveying to the poor subaltern masses that they had to be led for the 'unity of the movement' towards a 'greater altruistic mission'.

Yet, how would the 'unified Bahujan struggle' materialize? Kanshiram had observed that since 'individuals represented hierarchically ordered castes, the primary objective of the party was to 'equalize caste', that is, of the 'exploited' with 'dominant' castes in terms of power, resource and hegemony, to fulfil the potential of an equality-based society. Apparently, caste would be used against caste to weaken caste mindset.[6] Tactically, the justified logic to uplift Dalit politics from the present social and political morass required 'not a moral or ethical position' but a malleable political space to manoeuvre expedient Dalit politics to map electoral nodes that defied common political logic: often taking a political gamble by losing in party's electoral strongholds and winning in regions where earlier the party had no political presence.

Can the BSP be categorized as a mainstream social movement considering that the party seeks a 'social transformation from above'? Clearly, it is difficult to conceptualize the BSP into a single mainstream category of social movements: but it appears to be reformative. This becomes clearer if the political objectives of a bahujan state are known: to 'gain access and exclusive control over state structures to accomplish the administrative and political potential within the state necessary towards the emancipation of the Bahujan by altering and effecting the implementation of existing government policies rather than the enactment of new legislations in favour of the poor'.[7]

The early years that coincided with BSP's steady popularity among sections of Dalit-Bahujan groups was reminiscent of Kanshiram and Mayawati touring certain north Indian states, holding political rallies. During this period, 'prestigious electoral contests' in Uttar Pradesh and Punjab thrust upon the party to scheme the weakening of vote share of national political parties (such as the Congress Party) to support regional parties. It underlined the mobilization of dalits, OBCs and Muslims across electoral constituencies to vote as a cohesive political unit as to orient the revised Dalit politics. On the other hand, a 'righteous' ideological 'political discourse' was also being scripted by Kanshiram and Mayawati to build a political context needed to correspond to the bombast of emerging 'electoral goals' of the party. Abrasive ideological narratives for the 'awakened bahujan mass' posed reasonable arguments: exhorting the bahujan constituency to 'acknowledge their social plight' in an exploitative caste-based society and state; and further, since the bahujan class had 'no source of information about their plight or social inequality' across India, they were 'unable to comprehend their struggle-based history and their present position of a marginalized existence'; that Brahmins and other upper caste sections of the society, the ruling political elites and the 'savarna' parties epitomised a 'degraded (manuvadi) character of the social and political system', and through 'mean political tactics like vote bank and money power, weakened the resolve of the oppressed majority and false promise'. Bahujan samaj exists in binary opposition to socio-political control legitimised through state, that is, it is in sufferance of social violence, economic insecurity, social exclusion and powerlessness; that BSP was the political axis around which the 'looted and beaten bahujan community with a negated and effaced persona' will have to mobilize through caste-based unity on its own by taking 'more responsibility of its rights by voting for themselves and use it as a political resource to deny space to manipulate elections', which is the actual (and the only viable) terrain of political opposition for the bahujan samaj.

It is difficult to fathom what degree of political success BSP would have achieved in terms of ethnic-driven politics of the bahujan class if it was not for the impact of 'Mandal' politics in the post-1990 period. The political effect in north India was significant as major political parties required a readjustment of their ideological and political objectives. Mandal polity endorsed a cleavage-based politics as political parties, both established ones and new political entrants, began to represent not broader and more inclusive aggregation of social groups but narrower identities and interests. It opened the possibility of the polity growing accustomed to several leading ideological discourses on Indian politics, shifting the arena of contestation for power towards state politics.

One of the significant aspects of Mandal politics was that it exposed the irreparably upper-caste governing elite of the Indian state to the realistic prospect of losing power to politically assertive economically powerful backward castes. In Uttar Pradesh, a fervent political mobilization of numerous caste groups began coinciding with the rise of the Samajwadi Party (SP) with an intact social base of Yadavs and Muslims, a major contender for power in the state. Yet post-Mandal politics opened political space for victims of social discrimination, significantly expanding the participatory base of Indian democracy. It represented a greater vote potency and a raised level of expectation and validity for the democratic system among these groups compared to more privileged sections of society. Irrespective of the historical closure of the '(Mandal) democratic upsurge', which did not bring any new demands or claims on the system,[8] the BSP adjusted its brand of ethnic politics to the possible social division of votes across other contending political parties – SP and BJP – in the state. Uttar Pradesh of the 1990s would usher in an era of coalition politics that for nearly two decades shaped the political outcome of BSP's claimed goal of 'transformative' politics. The institutional space that Mandal politics generated organized the form and character of BSP's politics. To leverage governmental power in a divided polity, the BSP outlined the principle of 'majboor sarkar, not mazboot sarkar' (a dependent government not a stable government), termed as 'guru-killi' or innovative politics with which every lock, whether social, economic, political or cultural, could be opened. The analogy was self-explanatory: that an 'unstable' government in a political alliance with the BSP would be forced to consider its (Dalit-Bahujan) agenda of social justice. A 'stable' government would marginalize the bahujan class and assert dominant hegemonic interests of the governing elite. Therefore, by the mid-1990s, at the height of coalition politics, BSP's ideological props to build a 'bahujan state' was eased out in favour of a single-minded target to achieve an increased space to leverage for power vis-à-vis other political parties in the state. Electoral politics of that period institutionalized a sense of permanency reminiscent of 'political rally' speeches by Mayawati, who read out staid prepared 'tactics-based' scripts to voters.

The communally charged atmosphere that preceded and followed the demolition of the Babri mosque in Ayodhya in December 1992 had left no option for the Narasimha Rao-led Congress Party government (with 'outside political support' from the BJP) to promulgate president's rule. After a year, the November 1993 state polls were held. Yet electoral outcomes in UP post-Mandal politics would depend on the capacity of the political parties to wean away 'plus votes' from contending state actors. In order to keep the BJP out of power, Kanshiram fashioned a plebeian alliance between the BSP and the SP. The tenuous pact underlined by irreconcilable social divisions, between the exploiters (middle caste landowning Yadavs) and the exploited (landless dalits), was two-pronged: to keep a national political party (BJP) out of power; also, with the emergence of a SP-led ruling coalition, the BSP would take advantage of its 'political support' to the SP to push ahead with a 'Dalit agenda'. However, politics of negativity and internal schisms dominated the unfinished term of the SP-BSP coalition government. Mayawati personalized a style of leadership that increasingly began to represent as one who was the 'benefactor and protector' of Dalit interests; acting authoritatively to intervene and change the 'upper caste' character of state administrative officers with Dalit officers; launching a tirade against a poorly managed coalition led by Mulayam Singh Yadav, who on his part had turned state recruitment of police personnel on its head by only selecting candidates belonging to the Yadav caste. The Yadav-dominated state police across various districts of the state meant that 'physical security' of Dalit-Bahujans had been compromised. There was a distinct possibility that Yadav political activists with tacit support from the local police could run amok against local BSP party workers at the slightest provocation. The two political parties appeared not keen to address critical economic and social programmes that were part of a 'common programme' when the pact was finalised ahead of the state polls. The intensity of friction between the two coalition party leaders increased as Mulayam Singh made all-out efforts and was successful in creating political factions within the BSP. At the ground level, spread over numerous districts, 'symbolic' politics of building Ambedkar statues on government land as a mark of Dalit assertion was met with several incidents of caste violence. The infamous Guest House incident of June 2–3, 1995, when Mayawati and seven of her MLAs were locked in without food, water or electricity only to be rescued the next morning epitomised the personal struggle of Mayawati, the 'victim of oppression' embodying the bahujan collective against the 'oppressor' Mulayam Singh Yadav and his 'Yadav' dominant political party.

As a coalition partner of a 'backward caste-Dalit' front with the SP against upper-caste status quo, the BSP after the collapse of the coalition expediently set aside its political creed from a general review of the 'failed historic opportunity' of the November 1993 state election. The BSP considered the political fallout not a 'loss'; instead, it was looking ahead to fulfil a new political role – that it had with clarity and purpose set out to pursue. In June 1995, the BSP, a 'minority coalition partner', headed a coalition government with the BJP, a 'majority coalition partner'. Based on the principle of 'dependence syndrome', it was BJP which was invested with the task of running the 'majboor' (dependent on BSP's support) coalition government.

The BSP-BJP ruling coalition governments in 1995 (a minority party–led coalition government), 1996–1997 (a six-month rotational chief ministership that ended after the BSP completed its tenure in March 1997) and 2002–2003 (BSP had more seats than BJP in the 2002 state polls) were marked as much by the incompleteness of the term as by the potency of palpable political instability of the ruling coalition, which provided political space for the BSP to direct the coalition government. Mayawati, the three-time CM, in a coalition pact with the BJP (1995–2003), endorsed a series of patronage-driven pro-Dalit legislations, economic and educational initiatives inclusive of costly Dalit iconography. This period occasioned an increased tempo of a vengeful ideological turf war between the BSP and the SP as the 'Dalit chief' used tough administrative measures to contain SP political activity in the state. Perhaps it was at this juncture that Mayawati's personal stature, both symbolically and materially, as the indefatigable Dalit-Bahujan icon elevated.

Underlying Mayawati's assertive Dalit politics were a set of political truths that the BSP had to contend: the idiom of 'percentage politics' to incrementally expand new 'voter base' to augment traditional social constituency 'nationally' was being impressively conducted by the BJP: for instance, the state polls and Lok Sabha elections in UP in 1996 and the 1998 and 1999 Lok Sabha elections, the latter culminated in a BJP-backed NDA alliance at the Centre for a full five-year term in office. Yet, what led to the political downfall of the BJP in Uttar Pradesh (1999–2002) was the intense intra-factional rivalry between 'OBC, Brahmin and Thakur caste groups', which led to three caste-based choices of Chief Minister in as many years. Clearly there was a disjuncture between national-level upswing of votes and fragmentation of vote base in UP. Aware of the internal strife the 'central command' of the party gave clear directives to the state unit to keep the ruling coalition with the BSP intact in the larger interest of an 'anti-SP' front. In a general sense, BJP's cautious approach towards an unpredictable coalition partner was to be viewed in a long-term context for the party: cultivating a 'national' image by transcending its majoritarian style of politics to portray itself as a party that catered to the interests of the poorer castes and weaker sections of society. It paid political dividends for the BJP in a series of state polls held during that period. On the other hand, in marked contrast, the BSP leader Kanshiram's tour across states in 1993–1994 to forge bahujan coalitions with like-minded parties was a political failure as was the participation of the BSP in numerous assembly polls thereafter. To the BSP, clearly proven a 'UP-based political party' by the mid-1990s, the percentage politics of 'caste' votes in the state became the most important political preoccupation as it served to mobilize 'plus votes' against the SP and the BJP. Yet, 'percentage' caste-oriented politics to increase vote share posed a political challenge for the BSP in its quest to realize the objective of a broader stream of bahujan votes in the context of a restrictive ethnic model of mobilization which was in operation to achieve it. It is noted that between 1996 and 2004, the party with its approved ethnic electoral model had begun to downplay the image of a Jatav-dominated party by the inclusion of a substantial number of non-Jatav bahujan castes and Muslims as candidates for state and Lok Sabha polls. In fact, a minimal number of upper caste Brahmins were also given assembly 'tickets'. The inherent weakness of the BSP was a structural inadequacy to adhere to a representative political model of accommodating diverse social groups. An assessment of the BSP post-coalition pact with the BJP in 2003 suggests an intact ethnic-political interlinkage of caste elites led by Jatavs despite the need for a broader institutional support of multiple caste groups with the party at the grassroots level. The mere inclusion of candidates from different castes or religious backgrounds for election was no guarantee for a high proportion of votes for the party. The BSP was solely relying on the crystallization of a favourable social context for a 'windfall of bahujan votes'.

Yet the contours of a two-party electoral contest in the state, the 'encouraging political atmosphere', was set not in the depths of electoral strategizing by the BSP but in the context of deep fissures that arose in the state unit of the BJP which fragmented the vote capital of the party with disastrous political consequences in the state polls of 2002 and the 2004 state Lok Sabha elections. The BSP and the SP began cultivating BJP's fragmenting traditional vote base, notably the Brahmins and the Thakurs.

The poor election result for the BJP in the 2004 Lok Sabha elections in Uttar Pradesh also set the political stage for BSP's experimentation with a 'sarvajan' (for all castes and groups) poll strategy for the 2007 assembly elections. It was a question of politically outmanoeuvring the SP as both the parties realized that the quantity of free-floating electoral capital was substantial. The SP in a coalition with the Congress Party, after the collapse of the BSP-BJP coalition in August 2003, was completing the unfinished five-year term of the 2002 state polls. The BSP, free from the political responsibility of running a cash-strapped poorly governed state by 2005 had outlined the rudiments of the sarvajan electoral model. The sarvajan model was considered as an innovative method of reorganizing grassroots politics of the party. The core feature of the electoral scheme was to accommodate dominant and/or upper caste voters, primarily the 'anti-SP' Brahmins and to a lesser extent the influential Thakurs across several constituencies of the state who could be mobilized to find 'refuge, identity and self-respect' within the BSP. Brahmins were central to sarvajan politics as their support for the 'Dalit party' would ensure legitimacy and enable diverse bahujan groups to cling together. The 'model' would operate on the premise of a caste arithmetic based upon mobilization of Brahmin and Dalit castes through apex social engineering and Brahmin jodo sanmelans (integration conferences) and bottom social engineering through bhaichara (brotherhood) committees. Likewise, component parts of the bahujan samaj and Muslims would be individually, that is caste or community-wise, mobilized and conscientized to vote tactically for Brahmin BSP candidates to increase the party's vote share by 2–3%. There was no guarantee that Brahmin voters would vote consistently for bahujan candidates of the party. The bahujan samaj would have to transfer votes to one another to further consolidate the party's vote share. About a year before the state polls, the BSP had finalized its list of candidates and intensified its carefully organized electoral campaign even as SP's credibility of running the government was going down. Acrimony and tussle for assembly tickets and internal schisms significantly affected the poll prospects of the SP. In the state elections, a low winning margin in triangular and certain quadrangular electoral contests worked to the political advantage of the BSP. The BSP won 206 seats and formed the first majority 'sarvajan' government led by a dalit Chief Minister in post-independence period and also the first 'stable' state government in more than one and a half decade with impressive vote share from the Most Backward Castes, the Muslims and the non-Jatav castes. The 'high-value' upper caste (Brahmin and Thakur) votes were a contributory factor in increasing the number of seats of the party, with the BSP representing a winning social narrative 'defector' seats, and a large number of 'reserved constituency' candidates also won.

BSP's new and successful 'sarvajan' electoral scheme became the governing ethic: with the apparent reverse of the existing upper-caste social order, the dominant castes would in the present disposition receive patronage and not the dalits who would control the dynamics of state power. It was expected to be an inclusive and non-sectarian governance model.

The 'sarvajan' government of 2007 was to be seen as representing all sections of society, where ideologically opposed groups and those low in societal hierarchy could form alliances with their 'social oppressors'. It was meant to broad-base the party at the cost of diluting even a formal adherence to 'protecting the interests' of the marginal social groups. The 'governance model' incapacitated the 'bhagidari' (partnership) framework of ethnic politics, considered as the determinant of political participation, represented by social groups based on their comparative demographic position. As an identity-based political party in state power, the weakening of the 'core' bahujan interests by a new credo of electoral-cum-governance style would cast a pervasive effect on the political fortunes of the party. Overt political representation of Brahmins in state administration and governance; lack of access of grassroots BSP activists to critique a non-performing lower level bureaucracy; growing frustration of multiple bahujan groups to failed expectations from the party; and the inability to access and receive public delivery of goods and resources compounded the political difficulties of the party. In the 2009 Lok Sabha elections in Uttar Pradesh, the BSP was not able to reproduce the proportion of vote share, and perhaps more that it polled in the 2007 state elections across diverse social groups, into Lok Sabha seats. In fact, a comparative analysis of BSP's earlier stints in a coalition government and the implementation of 'Dalit agenda' despite its avoiding consequences was significantly better than the first two years under the sarvajan government. Reactively, in the remaining three years, Mayawati outlined policy directives 'proclaiming' and 'inaugurating' innumerable social, educational and economic programmes for the marginalized poor. Yet, by that time, the BSP government was mired in bad governance and mega-project corruption even as Mayawati became aloof, assuming a halo of supreme-ness among fleeting bahujan voters of the party.

Clearly, the sarvajan governance model had failed in its political objectives. With the 2012 state polls approaching, populist social schemes to a fragmenting vote base inclusive of hastily earmarked bhaichara committees hastened the discredit of the BSP among the voters. The 'bahujan face' of the BSP, which required an ideological rallying call, had been set aside much earlier in favour of flexible electoral schemes in BSP's pursuit of state power. The BSP was now faced with a political paradox: a search for the 'votes of the poor' to which was attached the primary identity (purpose) of the party by availing an electoral model that ran counter to it.

The 2012 assembly election was a political contest between the BSP and SP, not between two ideological and caste-opposite state actors which defined the 'oppressor-oppressed' syndrome of identity politics. Unlike the BSP, which post-election loss felt defeating the SP was a mere re-working of caste politics, the SP, under Mulayam Singh Yadav's son, Akhilesh Yadav, the CM candidate, successfully incorporated an election campaign based on development, employment, electricity and education. It set aside SP's two-decade-old election campaign set on emotive religious issues and ideological contests between a neo-Brahminical Hindutva, plebeian caste consolidation and minority insecurity. The SP won 231 assembly seats, an electoral result that bore a significant shift in upper caste votes towards it and a young class of Dalit (inclusive of young Jatavs), OBC and Muslims.

The re-emergence of the BJP in India under Narendra Modi since 2014 has had deeper political consequences for the state of Uttar Pradesh. A nation-wide political campaign on a new narrative of (anti-corruption) development appeared as a highly successful ideological crusade against the 'corrupt and tainted' Congress Party-led United Progressive Alliance II government. The talisman slogan of development 'Sabka Saath, Sabka Vikas, Sabka Vishwas' (Together with All, Development for All, Trust of All) based on the maxim 'Minimum Government Maximum Governance' had an immediate political impact in Uttar Pradesh. Since BJP's massive 2014 Lok Sabha verdict (71 seats) in the state, consolidated in 2017 state polls (312 seats) and the 2019 state Lok Sabha elections (65 seats), the party has outrightly dominated India's most populous and electorally significant state. A tribute to BJP's success has been the fulfilment of target-oriented development goals that have grown exponentially, providing a re-assurance to rural and urban voters of a guaranteed public delivery of programmes despite questions raised about the estimates, figures and the success rate. BJP's political dominance in the state has been based on a continual success of a micro-managed electoral strategy infused with a socio-symbolic space of majoritarian politics to successfully mobilize the state's '60% non-core (that is non-Jatav, non-Yadav and non-Muslim) electorate' – a term that came into common parlance during the 2019 UP Lok Sabha elections when both BSP and SP teamed as 'coalition partners' against the BJP but were defeated.

Three successive electoral failures of the BSP requires a thorough introspection.

After three and a half decades, it is fair to suggest at the present moment that the BSP is no longer a 'party that wins', a term Kanshiram had used in a context to suggest the means that the party must possess – new tenets of anti-caste Dalit politics – to unseat the BSO in contemporary India. By the mid-1990s, the BSP became distinctly inclined to territorialize power to a particular region – Uttar Pradesh. A decade of poor electoral outcomes has put paid to BSP's political future in the state.

Certain presumptions which hold BSP's social justice politics must undergo review: first, a 'coalition era mentality' of a 'dependent' not 'stable' government in present-day Uttar Pradesh is a wrong political assumption to begin politics in a post-coalition era; second, did the BSP in essence pursue the objective of equalizing oppressed castes and weakening caste mindset through ethno-identity politics? – a question that can be answered in the negative. Rather than the goal of a 'social transformation from above', BSP ardently requires a political transformation at the level of leadership which is oligarchic, neo-patrimonial and less participatory. How can the BSP rejuvenate itself? There is a need to explore a genre of popular democratic politics: the bringing back of an ideology of subaltern politics which must frame programmatic goals and outline measures to generate popular activism. A decentred-from-party politics and its brand of ethnic politics must centre the notion of Dalit subjectivity and the associative concept of a fair and more equal society in the context of achieving political power.

Notes

1 Norman. P. Barry, *An Introduction to Modern Political Theory* (2nd edition), London: Macmillan Publishers, 1989, p. 150; Andrew Heywood, *Key Concepts in Politics,* USA: Macmillan Publishers, 2000, p. 135; Adi. H. Doctor, *Issues in Political Theory*, New Delhi: Sterling Publishers, 1985, p. 170; Jeff Goodwin

and James Jasper (Eds.), *The Social Movements Reader: Cases and Concepts*, USA: Blackwell Publishers, 2003, p. 3; Lucia Michelutti, *The Vernacularization of Democracy: Politics, Caste and Religion in India,* Routledge, 2008, pp. 19, 5–6, 1; Lloyd Rudolph and Suzanne Hoeber Rudolph, 'The political role of India's caste associations', *Pacific Affairs*, 33, 1, March 1960, p. 5; Suzanne Hoeber Rudolph and Lloyd Rudolph, 'Caste associations to identity politics: from self-help and democratic representative to goonda raj and beyond', *Pacific Affairs*, 85, 2, June 2012, pp. 372–74.

2 Yoshefa Loshitsky, *Identity Politics on the Israeli Screen*, Texas, USA: University of Texas Press, 2002, p. 1.

3 Daniel Rothbart, *State Domination and the Psycho-Politics of Conflict: Power, Conflict and Humiliation*, UK: Routledge, 2019.

4 Deepa Reddy, 'The ethnicity of caste', *Anthropological Quarterly,* 78, 3, 2005, pp. 555, 561–62; Ajantha Subramanian, 'Making merit, the Indian Institute of Technology and the social life of caste', *Comparative Studies in Society and History,* 2015, 57, 2, p. 297.

5 Valerian Rodrigues, *Dalit-Bahujan Discourse*, New Delhi: Critical Quest, 2008, pp. 17, 27, 29, 30; Anupama Rao, *The Caste Question; Dalits and Politics of Modern India*, 2010, Ranikhet: Permanent Black, p. 27.

6 Sudha Pai, 'Dalit question and political response: Comparative study of Uttar Pradesh and Madhya Pradesh', *Economic and Political Weekly*, 39, 11, March 11, 2004, pp. 1141–50; Sambaiah Gundimeda; *Dalit Politics in Contemporary India*, 2015, New Delhi: Routledge, p. 116.

7 PAI, '*Dalit question and political response*: Comparative study of Uttar Pradesh and Madhya Pradesh', *Economic and Political Weekly*, 39, 11, March 11, 2004, pp. 1141–50.

8 K.K. Kailash, 'The more things change, the more they stay the same in India: the Bahujan and the paradox of the democratic upsurge', *Asian Survey*, 52, 2, March/April 2012, p. 322.

1 Landscaping Dalit Consciousness

Colonial Rule and Dalit Consciousness

British colonial exploitation in India endorsed the 'traditional brahminical caste and community relations', which led to further exploitation of the toiling masses who were now burdened with 'caste duties' for new forms of surplus production for the imperial rulers. Colonial rule operated through the vigorous implementation of caste relations and depended on the native elite and the intermediary social class which eventually led to a 'collusion and convergence' of interests between the imperial and indigenous elites. It is within this new colonial system of expropriation and exploitation that community consciousness among lower castes emerged. It manifested in the form of various types of 'activities, protests and organization'. Low-caste and/or Dalit struggles took different political forms in different spaces and locales by 'attempting to throw out all civic-religious-educational and administrative disabilities imposed upon them by indigenous elites'.[1]

There is enough evidence to suggest that Dalit[2] organizational politics between the late 19th century and early 20th century began to underscore its 'subjective character by challenging in substance dominant oppressive characterizations of caste and other associated forms of social injustices.' It questioned and rejected categories like 'untouchables', 'depressed classes', 'scheduled castes' (SC) and 'harijans' (Mahatma Gandhi coined the term to mean 'people of god' to identify untouchables in 1933) that were formulated by colonial and or Hindu/nationalist discursive practices. The intention was not merely to contest dominant ascriptions of their 'social' identities but more importantly to question notions of impurity and pollution attached to their community, identity and history. Various Dalit castes[3] in different parts of India raised this critical issue independently by 'claiming that they had discovered a pure past and a pure identity, either within Hindu religion or outside it'. Familiar examples of scattered and sporadic Dalit movements are the assertions of the Adi-Dharmis and Balmikis of Punjab; Malas and Madigas of Andhra Pradesh; Ezhava and Pulayas of Kerala; Shanars, Nadars and Parayas of Tamil Nadu; Dheds and Bhangis of Rajasthan; the Satnamis of Chhatisgarh; the Kaibarta, Rajbangshis and Namasudras of Bengal; the

Chamars, Pasis and Bhangis, Koeris, Kurmi and Ahirs of Uttar Pradesh (UP) and Bihar; the Shilpakars of Kumaon; and Mahars, Chambhars, Malis and Kunbis of Maharashtra.[4]

Themes of Social Protest: The Satya Shodhak Samaj and the Self-Respect Association

Yet, in the late 19th century and early 20th century, there were those 'emancipatory movements' which acquired a more distinguishable region-specific character contemplating a broader political struggle by foregrounding the critical notion of social reform which encapsulated identifiable political goals. Two distinct types of low-caste struggle captured the ideological and political imagination of the poor: the Satya Shodhak Samaj in Maharashtra and the Justice Party (1916) in Tamil Nadu succeeded in 1926 by the Self-Respect Association. The Satya Shodhak Samaj founded by Jyotirao Phule in 1873 fought against ignorance, exploitation and slavery that were based on religious and financial exploitation. Natural rights of the deprived were upheld to re-establish human values, economic independence, social justice, humanity, intellectuality and independence of women. Phule held that if the Indian National Congress was to be 'truly national', it had to take a more active interest in the welfare of the vast multitude of lower castes. Phule engaged in what can be termed as 'ethnicisation of caste' of the toiling masses, the 'bahujan' – a broad category of people ranging from the peasant castes to untouchables. His ideas were wedded to principles of equality and fraternity, resisting the brahmins who were identified with 'Aryan invaders' responsible for bringing in the culture of an obnoxious caste system to subjugate autochthones and destroy the 'bahujan-based civilization' of India. Phule's critique of the 'brahminical tyranny and conspiracy, which reduced the bahujans to shudras/ati-shudras and women to a state of servility and misery', provides a wider social context within which the germane ideas of various 'Dalit liberation movements' in the late 19th and early 20th centuries finds a political location. The Satya Shodhak Samaj's objectives cast a profound influence, particularly, on the Namashudra movement in Bengal, the Adi-Dharma movement in Punjab and Pulaya Mahasabha in Kerala, and later on under the leadership of M.C. Rajah in the Madras Presidency through the Depressed Classes Federation by Ayyankali in Travancore and Dr. B.R. Ambedkar in Maharashtra. However, by early 1930, non-brahminism's initial 'political cradle' Satya Shodhak Samaj withered away in the face of growing Indian nationalist mass mobilization. 'Samaj representatives' in large numbers joined the growing pan-Indianist parties – Indian National Congress and the Communist Party of India (CPI). Nevertheless, it is evident that the outcome principle of social justice advocated by the Satya Shodhak Samaj 'got ontologically linked to such Dalit-Bahujan leaders and (organizations) who were (seeking) to define social justice against the local configuration of power that involved domination by brahminical and imperial-capitalist forces.'[5]

If the Satya Shodhak Samaj was seen as a political statement against social oppression and customary caste hierarchies and held out a source of inspiration for anti-caste movements, the anti-brahminical movement in South India, by the second decade of the 20th century, had begun the process of transforming the upper caste character of the ruling elites that was dominated by brahmins. In the Madras Presidency (particularly present-day Tamil Nadu and Andhra Pradesh) by the early 20th century, 'a powerful non-brahmin movement had taken root based on a call for social equality arising in opposition to the barriers to social mobility which resulted from traditional Brahmin[6] status and modern professional dominance'. The opposition of 'non-Brahminism' to brahmin dominance had the potential of serving as 'a banner for subordinate non-brahmin groups'. Eventually, the powerful non-brahmin class became the dominant actors of the 'Dravidian[7] agenda'. The Justice Party is a classic example of dominant non-brahmin backward class elite 'utilizing the avenues of representative politics in the 1920s to create public spaces of political opposition against the Brahmins and wrest caste quota-based jobs in the government'. The Justice Party did feel the effect of a nationalist Congress and many party members became parallel members of the Congress. However, it was the Self-Respect Association (1926) that took the Dravidian agenda to the masses consisting of 'students, women, new urban lower middle class, small landholders, labourers, non-brahmin backward caste and untouchables'. The Association 'adopted the personality of Erode Venkatappa Ramasamy', commonly known as 'Periyar', the cultural advocate of anti-brahminism and his configured ideological position of 'shudra primacy' that would outline the contours of political struggle of Dravidian political parties in the post-independence period. While the Justice Party voicing the concerns of the non-brahmin class supported British rule for their professional and socio-economic mobility, the Self-Respect Association opposed Gandhi's notion of 'varnaashram dharma', and hence Congress' position on the underprivileged social classes, which decisively failed to interrogate the local configurations of power in its quest for a 'national' anti-colonial struggle against British colonialism. Under such circumstances, the 'Association' supported the continuation of British rule. The process of social churning that was witnessed in south India provided the context for the emergence of new political forces in the region, notably the formation of Dravidian political parties that fitted into the category of non-upper caste-based political organizations. However, thereafter, the 'Dravidian political movement' powerfully began to advocate a 'new' Dravidian agenda peripheralizing the critical narrative of the popular 'shudra primacy' thesis propounded by Periyar. It began with the political tilt towards regionalism in the late 1930s and a decade later with the opposition to the imposition of Hindi, brought by the Congress government in the Madras Presidency. The 'anti-Hindi movement', the axis of the linguistic autonomy cum regionalism based political struggle, was spearheaded by the new non-brahmin political leadership of the Dravida Munnetra Kazhagam (DMK) that came into existence in 1949 after having split from the Dravidar Kazhagam founded in 1944 by Periyar, who had simply changed the name of the Justice Party, which he led between 1939 and 1944. Periyar was seeking to transform the Dravidar Kazhagam into a social organization by withdrawing from electoral politics. The DMK was now increasingly identified by a vernacular political elite representing the landowning backward castes who began to dominate local patronage network, mobilizing disparate non-brahmin social groups while still retaining a 'non-brahmin' shudra/subaltern caste identity. In the 1967 assembly and national elections in Tamil Nadu, the DMK did exceptionally well, winning 137 assembly seats and 25 Lok Sabha seats.[8] Thereafter, the DMK became a significant regional party in Tamil Nadu.

The Satya Shodhak Samaj and the 'anti-brahminical movement' in the Madras Presidency contested ascribed notions of dominant social hierarchies, and through their political struggle justified the liberation from a socially inferior position. The 'Samaj' focused on fighting low caste exploitation and humiliation before being humbled by the consolidation of pan-Indian parties in the 1930s, while the Self-Respect Association, operating within the paradigm of casteless and egalitarian philosophy seeking to defy dominant modes of social inequality, eventually gave an ideological fillip that translated the potential aspirations of the rising merchant non-brahmin class into political advancement against brahmin monopoly in social and political spheres. Both the anti-status quo-based movements at the onset, with presumed socio-political objectives to be accomplished, adopted a configuration of prescriptive values of justice and equality with the intention to overturn the privileged position of an established discriminatory social order towards a more equitable distribution of power and resources within society. By their resistance to a status-based order, the two 'anti-caste movements' brought a convergence of dominant themes of social protests into an enclosed colonial secular-modern space that was transforming the character of society, economy and polity in India. Operating within different sociocultural milieu, the broad typology of two major anti-caste movements correspond, and in fair measure act as political supplements to Ambedkar's pioneering struggle to institutionalize an all-India Dalit, Bahujan–low caste socio-political activism against a graded, exploitative caste-based Hindu samaj (society).

Ambedkar and the 'Idea' of Social Justice: Experimenting Strategies for Political Action

Before proceeding to explore Ambedkar's thesis on social justice, it is pertinent to put in perspective the modern genealogy of the Congress Party's viewpoint on social justice. Gandhi as the mass leader of the Indian National

Congress was genuinely interested in anti-untouchability issues as he was 'personally convinced' of the need to eliminate obnoxious caste practices. However, his attempts to moderate his struggle against untouchability could be interpreted as his efforts to produce a 'historical conjecture' to bring about national solidarity among different encrusted caste groups. Gandhi's thesis was intertwined with two related themes: one, 'colonial modernity generated a sense of social justice among different groups' through the introduction of limited social, economic and political opportunities made available at different levels in a traditional caste-based society; and two, that 'upper castes sought to define justice in terms of discrimination that these elites faced during colonial regime in India'. These elites articulated their sense of injustice in terms of their 'relative inclusion or exclusion from the opportunity structures' that came up as part of an imperial design and eventually found a 'resolution of injustice in their limited accommodation into the opportunity structures'. Consequently, the sociological base of the 'concept of social justice', defined in terms of fair treatment from colonial rulers, 'remained primarily middle class in nature expressed in terms of collaboration and competition'. It was 'inward looking and did not look beyond its own narrow interests'. Thus, for the Congress Party, the substantive aspect of social justice outlining the deeper concerns relating to the welfare of the lower caste groups and the deprived, inclusive of women facing multiple levels of discrimination and exploitation in a hegemonic caste order, could be 'supported as an idea during freedom struggle', or be treated as an operational category. However, it definitely could not be allowed to transform into a political concept to avoid a fragmenting impact on national solidarity against British colonial rule.

Ambedkar's structured debate on the emancipation of the marginalized took root in the midst of his scepticism towards the question of social justice displayed by the Congress Party that was 'gearing to prioritize the over-centralizing category of swaraj' (self-rule). Throughout the period of colonial rule, and beyond, as India achieved independence, and till his death in December 1956, Ambedkar's thematic exposition of social justice 'centred on elevating the notion of dignity and recognition into a meta-evaluative concept', that is the 'elevation of the principle of moral or cultural good, of one man one value' as the defining concept of social justice. Ambedkar not only applied 'cultural justice as the assessing standard, but (went) beyond it applying justice as a standard evaluator in the sphere of larger social relationships where claims of equal worth (would be) framed and articulated'.[9] To achieve this, Ambedkar continually strategized an alternative political vision to centrepiece the goal of social justice.

Ambedkar's thesis on the social liberation of the depressed classes was clearly spelt out in the objectives of the Bahiskrit Bharat Prakashan Sanstha and its newspaper '*Mooknayak*' in 1927 to

> awaken the untouchable, to rouse their consciousness and the manner in which this shared sense of injustice could become the rallying point

> in an oppressed group; to break down the social dialectics of caste, (and become) ... the nucleus of pride and defiance around which the new identity as 'rebel' could be built.[10]

Ambedkar held a predominant political position that 'so long as they (untouchable) were treated as separate, they (had) a right to see themselves as separate people, as a "political minority" and that they had separate needs. Those "needs" (were to) be represented in the government by the untouchables themselves'.[11] Thus, the untouchable 'question' was posited as a struggle for power and resources within the context of social inequality. In the 1920s, the untouchable struggle undertaken by Ambedkar chiefly revolved around symbolic acts of resistance such as 'direct action' – Chavdar water tank episode in 1927 – intended to create a 'crisis' against the caste-based customary code of conduct.[12] It was followed by the public burning of the Manusmriti[13]; the declaration of rights for 'rightless' untouchables and 'adoption of fundamental rights' to restructure the unequal and exploitative social order.[14] Simultaneously, Ambedkar was arguing the need for political rights for untouchables witnessed in the arguments that he made to the Southborough Committee on Franchise in 1919 and the Simon Commission in 1927 which advocated joint electorates for depressed classes and Muslims with adult suffrage and reserved seats, as well as special attention to education and employment of depressed classes in government positions.[15]

The late 1920s and early 1930s witnessed a concerted attempt by the colonial state's deliberate policy to 'enumerate and categorize' depressed classes ostensibly to bolster the question of the untouchables somewhat discomfortingly for the Congress-led national struggle. Further, 'high caste fears' about Hindu vulnerability to Christian missionaries and a strong Muslim nationalism presented the untouchables with companion opportunities[16] which could be utilized to bring a social emancipatory discourse into the sphere of nationalist politics. It is within this context that Ambedkar evolved the political course that the untouchable struggle would undertake in two significant directions. One, to put renewed effort to negotiate political rights and constitutional guarantees for the untouchables with colonial rulers; two, a sustained political struggle carried out by political parties committed to social equality strategized to increase Scheduled Caste and 'bahujan' representation in elected bodies.

In the 1930s, Ambedkar's struggle took a distinct political form as he began to seek an inherent political solution invested to secure a better future for the depressed classes. In 1932, the notion of separate electorates for untouchables acceded by the Communal Award (1932), in the aftermath of the Round Table Conferences (RTC) held in London, became a contentious issue between Ambedkar representing the untouchable 'cause' and Gandhi convinced that separation of untouchables from mainstream socio-political life was tantamount to British efforts to weaken the Congress 'nationalist' movement. The dilution of the clauses on separate electorates through the Poona Pact (1932) that emerged as a compromise formula post-Gandhi's 'fast unto death' undermined what Ambedkar had considered in the 1931 Round Table Conference, the opportunity for a true, independent (depressed classes) political representation for taking part in the process of government to reorganize the degraded social life of the depressed classes. In the opinion of Ambedkar, separate electorates would have ensured autonomy for depressed class candidates to be elected by the depressed class population, and consequently be legitimately reorganized as a political minority in government. Importantly, it would have also provided easier access to jobs in colonial government.[17]

The Poona Pact incidentally changed the direction of Ambedkar's 'politics of the subjugated' towards organization and electoral politics. Post-Poona Pact Ambedkar increasingly began to address the notion of transforming the depressed classes into a 'ruling political community' that could be achieved in two complementary ways, viz., securing jobs in administration and expecting from the British government 'token representation' of SC in political affairs. Ambedkar believed that the opening of administration to the untouchables would encourage them to acquire the education needed to 'win high positions' and create leadership opportunities to launch an attack on the barriers of the caste system. Additionally, the presence of untouchables in the administration was a mandatory corollary to legislation because it would allow for the effective implementation of laws. Access to administrative services of the state for untouchables was not merely a decisive step towards altering the role of the state but a means that inevitably led to political power. In one of his speeches Ambedkar had declared: '[O]ur object is not fighting for a few jobs or a few conveniences (but) to see that we are recognized as the governing community, for if we have power, we have social status'. Here, Ambedkar stressed that political power cannot co-exist with 'the ignorance of our people who do not know the value of organization for achieving political results'. Yet Ambedkar was circumspect about the 'organizational pressure and unity (which would) lead to action'. Ambedkar outlined two significant challenges that the untouchables and other poor/lower castes faced. First, as Ambedkar said:

> [T]here was a lamentable lack of resources at our command. We have no money. We have no press. The cruellest of tyrannies and oppressions, to which our people are subjected, day in day out all over India, are never reported in the press. Our problems on social and political questions are systematically suppressed by an organized conspiracy on the part of the press.

In this regard, Ambedkar forewarned against 'agents of other political organizations and political parties who decoy (bahujans) by false blandishments, by false promises and by false propaganda'.[18] Second, that there were obstacles in uniting disparate castes under an organization. In this context Ambedkar remarked:

> [O]ur difficulty is how to make the heterogeneous mass that we have today taken a decision in common and march on the way which leads to unity. Our difficulty is not with regard to the ultimate; our difficulty is with regard to the beginning.

Thus, the growth of bahujan unity would 'not be fully appreciated unless the tremendous difficulties' of organizational unity have been acknowledged. In fact, with a sense of disappointment he added 'that the untouchable is (actually) completely isolated', in his political struggle, 'he is opposed by the very classes who ought to be his natural allies'.[19]

In a bid to build a 'political organization' to strengthen the consciousness of the 'Dalit-Bahujan' masses and widen the social base to accommodate and give them their 'true' representatives, Ambedkar founded the Indian Labour Party (ILP) to contest the 1937 assembly elections. The electoral platform represented Ambedkar's ideological slant towards a socialist-centrist outlook with a commitment to address education, industrialization and to find remedies to an inherently complex nature of inequality on land that addressed the Dalits and the lower castes. Despite winning seats reserved for the SC in the Bombay Presidency (portions of Gujarat, Sind and Karnataka, as well as sections of Maharashtra), the ILP's electoral performance to Ambedkar represented the 'impotence of the minority'. The ILP was expected to operate as a political platform of constructing a Dalit core constituency that would include a broader united front with other impoverished sections of society.

In 1942, Ambedkar would briefly experiment with a political strategy to cultivate the core Dalit constituency by launching the Scheduled Caste Federation (SCF). The formation of the SCF contextualized the sense of disappointment and exasperation that Ambedkar had shown towards the 'failure of Marxism in India to open itself to fertilization of theory and practice' by the anti-caste movements as the communists adopted the expedient habit of leaving aside all discussions on the issue of caste and cultural change and simply accepting identities such as harijans and 'Hindu'. On the other hand, Gandhism failed to go beyond 'a spiritualistic and Hinduistic interpretation' of a 'decentralized and village-based development that left the anti-caste movement in a vacuum'. In the same vein Ambedkar suggested the futility of a socialist-Dalit political alliance as the untouchables would 'have to pool all their strength into the fight against untouchability, without expecting much socialist help'. It is within this political context that Ambedkar launched a political crusade against the Congress Party characterizing the leadership as 'brahminical and capitalist' – the main enemies of the Dalits. Congress Party, he felt, did not represent all sections of the society, and its claim as a 'united front', in reality, appeared 'reactionary' and 'Hinduistic' (that is brahminical). It was a statement that reflected the growing frustration of Ambedkar, inadequate in coping with the dominant political discourse of the Congress in absorbing disparate political ideologies and social forces and stigmatizing its opponents as 'pro-British' and borrowing the language of the Left to characterize both itself and its political opponents. In October 1939, at the Bombay Legislative Assembly, Ambedkar stated, with an obvious reference to the 'machinations of Congress politics', that 'we shall fight tooth and nail against politics being perverted for a purpose of establishing a clique of brahmin-bania (upper caste-trader) oligarchy of the ruling class'[20]; and further that 'the Congress party was and will be (in post independent India) a government run by the governing class'.[21]

The period between 1942 and 1951 witnessed Ambedkar make several attempts to advance the interests of the Dalit-Bahujan class. The SCF fared badly in the 1946 provincial assembly elections. Shortly thereafter, Ambedkar mooted the idea of 'separate settlements', a fact that he had explored as early as between 1926 and 1929, as a legal provision for the Dalits, which would create through settlements, a 'demographic Depressed Caste majority', not only in numbers but also in political intent sending 'real representatives' of the depressed classes to the legislatures. It would bypass the 'reserved constituency-joint electorate' system of representation that 'completely disenfranchised the Scheduled Castes'. Despite political setbacks, Ambedkar continued his search for the right political combination that would bring the SC and the OBCs closer. He would state that the SC and OBC had needs that were common but did not join together. Ambedkar reasonably argued that even if the backward classes and SC 'remain separate social identities', there was no reason as to why a political party, to remove their 'backward position', could not be fought together considering that they 'formed a majority of the population of the country'. The electoral manifesto of the SCF in 1951 focused on the need to promote backward classes through education and reservation, and advocating land reforms that would benefit the untouchables and the 'poor' backward classes in the countryside.

Ambedkar's last political experiment to forge a united front of the Dalit-Bahujan population was the Republican Party of India (RPI), which was formally christened four months after his death on December 6, 1956. The RPI epitomized Ambedkar's new 'caste-class' approach to the liberation of the marginalized. The party was to position itself between the 'defence of the untouchables alone on one side and a politics of class on the other', by itself a politically delicate balancing act. The latter was to be achieved by way of a horizontal federation of oppressed populations of castes and tribes that were discriminated because of their ascribed status, and which in time could form a 'block' against the governing elite. The dilution of Dalit identity would allow for 'alliances' to be struck with other political parties.[22]

What would give political mileage to the RPI would be Buddhism conceived by Ambedkar as essential for establishing equality and social democracy, a 'social reconstruction movement', engaged in re-creating India. It would advocate an 'untouchable social identity', both in demographic and religious terms and be a source of political leverage for the Dalits and the lower castes. Buddhism would be seen as a corrective to brahminical Hinduism transforming the democratic political process under the pervasive influence of the caste system.[23] In 1947, Ambedkar, as Chairman of the Drafting Committee to prepare the Constitution of India, outlined legal provisions to 'secure adequate representation and protection of depressed classes' interests by creating a specific policy arena in which, 'with the creation of reserved seats a new cadre of (SC) political representatives and leaders would emerge'.[24]

Congress and the De-Radicalization of 'Mass' Politics

Shaped by the contours of Congress' nationalist phase of political struggle, in the post-1947 period, an exclusively demarcated parameter of consensual politics emerged. Consensual politics, or 'consensualism', was a political paradox of sorts, an arrangement of power sharing in 'new' India between the modern intelligentsia, industrialists, political leaders and the powerful rural gentry – characteristic of what Ambedkar would refer to as 'shetji-bhatji' (economic and religious/brahmin elites) configured Congress Party. The 'consensual model' began to give a definite shape to a political framework, which, informally, came to be known as the 'Congress system'. The 'system' would help the party to win successive state and national elections till the early 1970s. The concrete question concerning the 'form of society' and the material allocation of 'advantages' envisioned for various sections of the populace, especially the need to 'equalize the disadvantage' of the historically exploited and disenfranchised at the onset by 'securing symbolic goods and some material guarantees through access to education and employment', was to be carried out by an expansive, interventionist bureaucratic state. The legitimacy of the new post-colonial 'weakly socialist state' that upheld a normatively redistributive vision was based upon the political belief that the nation required a 'fast track' process of modernizing society and economy. This dominant developmental discourse negated a possible early radical popular challenge to its government. A heavy industrial development, notable for creating a sound infrastructure that led to economic growth and a moderate level of urban employment, was nevertheless unbalanced and unequal. On the other hand, the new upper caste leadership of the rural gentry crucial to forging electoral victories through caste alliances maintained their 'privileges and dominance' through a combination of 'feudal resistance, conservatism and connivance' within the traditional caste class structure. As a result, land reforms were abandoned, and so were the 'income-generating schemes and provisions for resources for collective action' for the poor that was critical to the notion of distributive justice.[25]

Uttar Pradesh: Reviewing the Consensual Model of 'Party' and 'System'

What then were the political ramifications for a consensual model of Congress politics in Uttar Pradesh?

In the electorally significant north Indian state of Uttar Pradesh, the Congress Party produced a winning caste-community alliance in the initial decades through an upper caste–controlled exploitative client-patronage system that existed from the countryside at the lowest level, to the wider, national-level politics at the centre. The Congress, operating through the pattern of clienteles and political patronage, ensured the vertical aggregation of Dalit/lower castes under the dominant brahmin-Thakur leadership clique. These dominant caste(s) would not only dispense patronage benefits, but also, critically, for the Congress Party, operate in the area of their dominance and broker the relations between state-level politicians and village people. A political aggregation of Dalits enabled the Congress Party to retain a durable vote bank for nearly three decades after independence, which was further legitimized through the selective 'insertion' of SC elites in the state party machinery at the district level. This was part of a larger political design of the Congress Party in keeping with a policy of selecting members of society who belonged to prominent or numerous castes throughout UP or in one of the sub-regions such as the brahmins and Rajputs as much as the Chamars/ Jatavs (SC) and Banias, the latter more prominent in urban centres of the state. Outside the 'winning coalition' of castes and communities, a degree of political support existed for the Congress party among the landholding Other Backward Classes (OBC) such as the Jats, Kurmis, Yadavs, Gurjars etc. Despite growing economic power in land, these classes of emerging 'middle caste' tenant sharecroppers who acquired excess landholdings and ownership rights faced a 'representational blockage' denied access to power, resources and privileges due to a monopoly of upper-caste dominance in the Congress Party machinery.[26]

Over decades, Congress Party's machinations effected a 'dual policy' of the ruling upper caste governing elite: one, as a consequence of their political hold over state politics, the consequent consolidation and unification of intermediate castes on the basis of 'politicization' of caste; two, the policy of promoting the 'differentiation' and 'polarization' to divide the Dalits from 'other oppressed groups', notably the non-Dalit lower castes. It had the effect of confining Dalit struggles to a narrow focus limited to seeking economic and political aims of the most articulate and dominant Chamar-Jatav group among the Scheduled Castes. As a result, Chamars in comparison to other Dalit castes in the state, due to their demographic strength across the state, were 'over-represented' in government and public sector jobs in comparison to the 'marginalized Pasis, Kureels and Balmikis'. Thus, from the late colonial period to the early decades after independence, 'Dalit struggle' in UP has inevitably meant the prominence of a 'single-caste' political movement among the Chamars traced to their 'strategy of reformism' through the Uttar Pradesh Scheduled Caste Federation (UPSCF) in the 1940s and electoral politics of the Uttar Pradesh Republican Party of India (UPRPI) in the post-1947 period.

In November 1969, the Congress Party faced a crisis of political legitimacy following the fourth general elections as a united opposition under the Samyukt Vidhayak Dal won several 'Hindi belt' states. Facing a challenge from a majority of the political leadership, Jawaharlal Nehru's daughter Indira Gandhi created a new party. Subsequently, the Congress Party split into 'Old Congress', or Congress (O) led by Kamaraj, and the 'new' Indian National Congress (Requisitionists) INC (R), The INC was also known as 'Real Congress' or the 'New Congress' and by the late 1970s as Indira's Congress or Congress (I). Indira Gandhi's ascent to power began in the 1971 mid-term Parliamentary elections when her newly created Congress faction won an overwhelming majority of 352 out of 518 seats in the Lok Sabha. However, she centralized political power through a top-down hierarchical chain of command which was proliferated by sycophants and 'fixer' politicians with dubious credentials. The impact of an 'overtly centralized' INC (R) coincided with a political realignment of dominant social forces in Uttar Pradesh, a gradual shift in foci of power and political authority wielded by dominant upper castes in the village-district level to the 'middle caste' landowners. In the early 1980s, as the Congress' broad aggregative model began to fragment, the state witnessed a spate of caste atrocities and rural violence against an increasingly conscious low caste poor. Caste atrocities and violence were indicative of the rising economic clout of the 'new' middle caste landowning class. On the other hand, for the graduate-educated SCs, a significant number of whom belonged to the Chamar caste, the issue of 'reserved jobs' in public employment became an object of violence by the upper castes and the rural intermediate caste landed elites, the latter frustrated in their ability to realize urban state jobs despite increasing 'political voice' in state politics. The middle castes would continue to pressurize successive state governments by demanding greater quota of caste-based reservation in government jobs in the state that was poorly industrialized with a dominant semi-feudal land economy.

Notes

1 Braj Ranjan Mani, *Debrahminising History: History, Dominance and Resistance in Indian Society*, New Delhi, Manohar, 2005, p. 293; Stuart Corbridge and John Hariss, *Reinventing India*, United Kingdom, Polity Press, 2000, p. 212.

2 The term 'Dalit' is open to debate. A 'non-Dalit' meaning of the term 'Dalit' may mean burst, split, broken, torn, etc.

John. T. Platts, *A Dictionary of Urdu, Classical Hindi and English, Digital Dictionaries of South Asia*, London, 1884 (Updated in February 2015), p. 524 URL: https://dsal.uchicago.edu/dictionaries/platts/frontmatter/platts.pdf (accessed on Sept 18, 2016).

On the other hand, a 'Dalit meaning' of the term 'Dalit', according to the Dalit Panthers manifesto (1972), refers to 'a symbol of change and revolution for the SC/ST, neo-Buddhists, working people, landless, poor peasants, women and all those politically, economically and in the name of religion exploited'.

3 Ramnarayan Singh Rawat, 'The Problem', *Seminar*, no.558, February 2006, p. 12.

4 Rawat, *The Problem*, p. 12.

5 Francine Frankel, M.S.A. Rao (Eds), *Dominance and State Power in Modern India: Decline of a Social Order,* Delhi, Oxford University Press, 1990, p. 488; Platts, *Digital Dictionary*, p. 536.

6 The 'special' relationship of the dominant landholding castes and major mercantile and trading communities with the brahmins had earned them the elevated rank of 'satvic shudra' (clean shudra). However, brahminization of law under colonial administration brought in a 'creeping Aryanization of the caste system'. There was a change in the nature of property rights, that is the material base of the brahmins became 'independent of patronage from dominant non-brahminical castes' that spurred 'satvic' groups, 'like the Vellalas', to provide leadership for all non-brahminical movements.

Francine Frankel, M.S.A. Rao (Eds), *Dominance and State Power in Modern India: Decline of a Social Order,* Delhi, Oxford University Press, 1990, p. 488; Platts, *Digital Dictionary,* p. 536.

7 The 'Dravid people' and their country, that is properly the coast of Coromandel from Madras (Chennai) to Cape Comorin (Kanyakumari), or the country in which Tamul (Tamil) is spoken; in a general sense, the name is applied to four other (regions in India), viz., Karnataka, Gujarat, Maharashtra and Telangana.

Platts, *Digital Dictionary*, p. 510.

8 The Dravidar Kazhagam had criticized the colonial state for using the system of caste to control the masses and demanding a separate Dravidian state based on a casteless and egalitarian philosophy in 1949.

Stuart Corbridge and John Hariss, *Reinventing India*, UK, Polity Press, 2000, pp. 212–13; Mani, *Debrahminising,* p. 294; Ramnarayan Singh Rawat, 'The Problem', *Seminar,* no. 558, February 2006, p. 12; Christophe Jaffrelot, *India's Silent Revolution: The Rise of Lower Castes in North India,* New Delhi, Permanent Black, 2003, pp. 153–54; Narendra Subramanian, *Ethnicity and Populist Mobilisation: Political Parties, Citizens and Democracy in South India,* New Delhi, Oxford University Press, 1999, pp. 124, 83, 89, 96, 102, 103; Paranjoy Guha Thakurta, and Shankar Raghuraman, *A Time of Coalitions: Divided We Stand,* New Delhi, Sage Publications, 2004, pp. 176–77; Rajeev Bhargava (Ed.) *Politics and Ethics of the Indian Constitution*, New Delhi, Oxford University Press, 2008, pp. 234–35; Ishita Banerjee – Dube, *Themes in Indian Politics,* New Delhi, Oxford University Press, p. 218; Pauline Kolenda, *Caste in Contemporary India: Beyond Organic Solidarity,* California, Benjamin/ Cummings Publishing Company Incorporated, 1978, pp. 119–20.

9 Bhargava, *Politics and Ethics*, pp. 244, 232; Oliver Mendelsohn and Upendra Baxi (Ed.), *Rights of Subordinated People*, New Delhi, Oxford University Press, 1994, pp. 68–72.

10 M.S. Gore, *The Social Context of an Ideology: Ambedkar's Political and Social Thought*, New Delhi, Sage Publications, 1993, p. 199.

11 Thomas Pantham and Kenneth Deutsch (Eds.), *Political Thought in Modern India,* New Delhi, Sage Publications, 1986, p. 174.

12 Valerian Rodrigues, *The Essential Writings of B.R.Ambedkar,* New Delhi, Oxford University Press, 2002, p. 362.

13 The Manusmriti is a work of Hindu law in ancient Indian society. It is also known as the Laws of Manu. It is one of the 19 Dharmasastras which are part of

Smriti literature. It explains itself as a discourse given by sage Manu. There are 2,684 verses divided into 12 chapters.

The interpretation of the Purusha Sukta is one of the central aspects of the discourse provided by Manu, where the exclusion of the shudras on the basis of their ritual impurity and the purity of the brahmanas is clear. Manu is not only content to exclude them, rather it exhibits a hostile attitude towards them, indicating the shudras role in service preferably to the brahmana class.

For further reading see Archana Parashar and Amita Dhanda, *Redefining Family Law in India*, New Delhi, Routledge, 2008, pp. 23–24.

14 Radhakanta Nayak (Ed.), *The Fourth World: Appraisal and Aspirations*, New Delhi, Manohar Publishers, 1997, p. 58; Rodrigues, *Essential Writings*, p. 362; Pantham and Deutsch, *Political Thought in Modern India*, pp. 162–63.

15 Pantham and Deutsch, *Political Thought in Modern India*, p. 74.

16 Rajeev Bhargava (Ed.) *Politics and Ethics of the Indian Constitution*, New Delhi, Oxford University Press, 2008, pp. pp. 244, 232; Oliver Mendelsohn and Upendra Baxi (Ed.*), Rights of Subordinated People*, New Delhi, Oxford University Press, 1994, pp. 68–72.

Both the brahmins and the rising mercantile non-brahmin groups were demanding the transfer of power from the colonizer to fuel their own political and economic aspirations. While the brahmins were demanding a much greater power with an intact hierarchical social structure, the non-brahmin class wished to overturn the dominance of the brahmins in the social sphere. These two antagonistic classes were in competition with one another to fulfil their own sociopolitical goals collaborated with the imperial state.

Sambaiah Gundimeda, *Dalit Politics in Contemporary India*, New Delhi, Routledge, 2016, p. 35.

17 Radhakanta Nayak, *Fourth World*, p. 58; Gore, *Social Context of an Ideology*, pp. 209, 214; Christophe Jaffrelot, *Dr. Ambedkar and Untouchability: Fighting the Indian Caste System*, New York, Columbia University Press, 2005, p. 97.

18 Jaffrelot, *Ambedkar and Untouchability*, p. 82; Aruna Asaf Ali, *Words of Freedom: Ideas of a Nation*, Penguin UK, 2010, p. 32.

19 Gore, *Social Context of an Ideology*, p. 213; Ghanshyam Shah, *Dalit Identity and Politics: Cultural Subordination and Dalit Challenge*, Vol. 2, New Delhi, Sage Publications, 2001. p. 33; D.N. Sandanshiv, *Reservations for Social Justice: A Socio-Constitutional Approach,* Bombay, Current Law Publishers, 1986, p. 35; Neerja Gopal Jayal, *Democracy and the State,* New Delhi, Oxford University Press, 1999, p. 40.

20 Gail Omvedt, *Dalit and the Democratic Revolution: Dr. Ambedkar and the Dalit Movement in Colonial India,* New Delhi, Sage Publications, 1994, pp. 251, 226, 228; Jaffrelot, *Ambedkar and Untouchability,* p. 91.

21 Rodrigues, *Essential Writings,* p. 43.

22 Corbridge, Hariss, *Reinventing India*, p. 213; Jayal, *Democracy and the State*, p. 489; K.C. Yadav (Ed.), *From Periphery to Centre Stage: Ambedkar, Ambedkarism and Dalit Future,* New Delhi, Manohar Publishers, 2000, p. 143.

23 Nayak, *Fourth World*, p. 59; Yadav, K.C. (Ed.), *From Periphery to Centre Stage: Ambedkar, Ambedkarism and Dalit Future*, New Delhi, Manohar Publishers, 2000. Yadav, pp. 135-36; Shah, *Dalit Identity and Politics*, p. 149; Gore, *Social Context of an Ideology,* p. 222.

24 Vinita Damodaran and Maya Unnithan-Kumar (Eds.), *Postcolonial India: History, Politics and Culture*, New Delhi, Manohar Publishers, 2000, p. 127; T.V. Sathyamurthy (Ed.), *Region, Religion, Caste, Gender and Culture in Contemporary India*, New Delhi, Oxford University Press, 1996, p. 356; Mani, *Debrahminising,* p. 296.

25 The colonial land tenure system in Uttar Pradesh enabled the Congress to harness the local rural gentry – the zamindars – the 'tax collecting intermediaries', to vertically integrate the low castes and Dalits to the party. In the 1920s and 1930s, landowners actively mobilized the poor peasantry to serve the cause of the Congress-led anti-colonial struggle. Thus, in the post-1947 period, the 'position of landowners was protected'. In UP, the Zamindari Abolition Act and Land Reforms Act 1951, in essence, ensured that there was no major transfer of land rights to tenant cultivators. The act focused on 'abolition of various taxes enacted by landlords on their tenants', a far less radical measure than the actual redistribution of excess plots. This set the trend for the continued penury of the poor tenants. By the 1960s, a new class of peasant proprietors, who had bought excess landholdings of big landowners, began to emerge. These 'non-elite' social groups, the middle castes, steadily grew in economic power, and subsequently they used their caste identities to challenge the dominant landowners for better political representation in the party. The political tussle between the upper caste landowners and middle castes continued through the 1970s and the better part of the 1980s, with better consequences for the latter following major social and political alignments in UP politics. After the declaration of the Mandal Commission Report in August 1990, the Other Backward Class (OBC), or, more specifically, the landed middle caste gentry, used their economic position and steady rise in political power to access employment quotas in central government administrative institutions.

Source: Tariq Thachil, *Elite Parties, Poor Voters: How Social Services Win Votes in India*, CUP, UK, 2014, pp. 200–01.

Neera Chandhoke, 'Three Myths about Reservation', *Economic and Political Weekly*, June 10, p. 2289; Bhargava, *Politics and Ethics*, pp. 231, 232, 235; Partha Chatterjee (Ed.), *State and Politics in India*, New Delhi, Oxford University Press, 1997, pp. 56, 57, 60; N. Jayal, 'Affirmative Action in India: Before and After the Neo-Liberal Turn, *Cultural Dynamics*, 27(1), December 31, 2014, pp. 117–18; Partha Chatterjee, *Wages of Freedom: Fifty Years of the Indian Nation State*, New Delhi, Oxford University Press, 1998, pp. 13–14; Mani, *Debrahmanising*, pp. 291–92.

26 The Congress had a policy of selecting members of society which belonged to specifically prominent groups, namely, castes, either numerically important throughout the whole of Uttar Pradesh or in one of its subregions, or castes whose 'socioeconomic weight is heavy'. In the first category fell Chamars, Pasis, Dhobis and Bhumihars. In the second were brahmins and Rajputs. Banias, also largely represented in the Congress ranks after independence, were between those two categories, especially prominent in urban centres.

Christophe Jaffrelot and Sanjay Kumar, *Rise of the Plebeians? The Changing Face of Indian Legislative Assembly*, New Delhi, Routledge, 2009, p. 30; Mary Searle-Chatterjee and Ursula Sharma, *Contextualising Caste: Post Dumontian Approaches,* Jaipur, Rawat Publications, 2003, p. 64; K.S. Pathy and Jayashree Mahapatra, *Reservation Policy in India,* New Delhi, Ashish Publishing House, 1988, pp. 48–49; Jitendra Mishra, *Equality versus Justice: The Problem of Reservation for Backward Classes,* New Delhi, Deep and Deep Publications, 1996, pp. 46–47, 69–70; Zoya Hasan (Ed.), *Parties and Party Politics in India,* New Delhi, Oxford University Press, 2002, p. 391; Corbridge, Hariss, *Reinventing India*, p. 204; Lucia Michelutti, *The Vernacularization of Democracy: Politics, Caste and Religion in India*, Routledge, 2008, pp. 20–21.

2 Political Architecture of Social Justice

Kanshiram: Conceptualizing a 'New' Dalit

It is interesting to note that the rise of the Bahujan Samaj Party (BSP) in Uttar Pradesh, in the early 1980s, can be traced to the disappointing state of Dalit politics in Maharashtra. It was in Pune and then briefly in Mumbai that Kanshiram, the founder and the chief architect behind the popularity of the BSP in Uttar Pradesh, began to evolve a political ideology to 'revise the nature of Dalit politics' in India. Kanshiram was born in Khwaspur village in Ropar district of Punjab.[1] He originally belonged to the Ramdasia subcaste among the Chamars who had converted to Sikhism. After getting his Bachelor in Science (B.Sc.) degree, the 'young shaven Sikh' left Punjab, and in 1957, found employment through 'reserved quota' with the Survey of India, 'whereupon his appointment he refused to sign a bond binding him to his job for a certain number of years'. While refusing the offer of a job, Kanshiram had stated that 'he did not wish to be a bonded labourer'. In 1958, he found a job as a chemical assistant at the Explosive Research and Defence Laboratory (ERDL), in Pune, Maharashtra, where he became aware of intense caste discrimination suffered by SC employees. This was a new experience for Kanshiram, considering that his early years in Punjab was not as socially oppressive as the one he was exposed to in Maharashtra. He said: 'Because of the Sikh religion (and) also because most of the Chamars (had) adopted the Sikh religion, notably the Sikh Panth or the Khalsa Panth there was some upward mobility. The teaching of the Sikh gurus (was) more egalitarian'.[2] While employed in the Pune laboratory, Kanshiram took part in an agitation led by an SC employee. Dinabhana, a Dalit employee, was suspended for protesting and 'questioning the logic' of the cancellation of an official holiday commemorating the birthday of Dr. Ambedkar and Buddha even as a holiday was sanctioned for the birthday of Tilak, including an additional day added to the officially declared holiday for Diwali. Despite being told by 'upper caste' officers not to get involved with Dinabhana, a Class IV staff, with whom he as an officer had 'very little in common', Kanshiram entered into an altercation with an 'upper caste' officer over this incident and was suspended. Kanshiram contended that similarity indeed existed between Dinabhana, belonging to the Bhangi caste and he himself a Chamar since 'both had the same problems', and 'this struggle' was not for the Class IV worker alone. Despite intimidation from the EDRL management, Kanshiram filed a case in the district court against Dinabhana's suspension and for the restoration of the two official holidays. After two years, the court revoked Dinabhana's suspension and restored the two holidays. In yet another incident, he sought to mobilize SC colleagues to fight against the denial of promotion to a women colleague belonging to the SC. On this occasion, it is said that Kanshiram reportedly slapped his senior and did not even bother to attend the disciplinary proceedings.[3] By that time, in 1964, he had decided to quit his job. Kanshiram's early experience of discrimination of SC in Pune and the 'arrogance of upper caste authorities in the organization' and the means he adopted at personal cost to defend his SC colleagues made him determined to take the struggle to the level of organizational politics to fight for the 'identity, rights, problems and leadership' of the Dalit community. He began associating with various Dalit organizations in Maharashtra. Prominent among them were the Peoples Education Society and the Buddha Club. During the early 1960s, he was introduced to the political philosophy of Ambedkar's writings by D.K. Khaparde, a committed Ambedkarite and his colleague at the Pune laboratory. Kanshiram subsequently joined the Mahar caste-dominated self-styled Ambedkarite Republican Party of India (RPI) as an 'ordinary party worker', a party of the dalits and the poor in the midst of a political crisis for Dalit politics in Maharashtra. By 1971, Kanshiram had set his sights into organizing a new form of Dalit politics. He not only 'formally' resigned from his job in Pune but also left the RPI, which lay 'fragmented due to schisms and clashes between political personalities'. Thereafter, he wrote a '24-page letter' to his mother Bishan Kaur that he would 'never marry, never return to his village (and he would) abjure all family functions such as wedding parties, birthdays and funerals (and) that his personal commitment towards the building of a "bahujan samaj" would leave him with no time to fulfil other familial responsibilities'.[4] Over the decade of the 1970s and in the early 1980s, his political ideas centred around an uncritical acceptance of an authoritative Dalit leadership, an 'organized body of workers' and a pragmatic conceptualization of marginalized group identity ideologized to build a Dalit-Bahujan constituency in Uttar Pradesh.

To unravel the organizational work for a 'new' Dalit politics, it is necessary to explore Kanshiram's ideological critique of the 'state of Dalit struggle', which he considered as a 'political setback' for the 'oppressed majority' in post-1947 India.

Republican Party of India and Dalit Panthers in Maharashtra: A Setback for Dalit Movement

Shortly before his death in 1956, Ambedkar had stated:

> With great difficulty I have brought it (the welfare of the untouchables) to where it stands today. Whatever are the obstacles this mission should continue' (and if it cannot continue effectively) 'it must be left where it is (at the moment). Under no circumstances should it regress.'[5]

This statement served as a reminder to Ambedkar's supporters and especially the 'qualified and educated Dalits', who were to serve as the vanguard of their respective communities, not to shift allegiance, falter on ideological convictions and stated objectives, even as a steady number of his 'lieutenants' began to 'explore other avenues of political advancement'. In the immediate post-Ambedkar period in Maharashtra, his political legacies – Buddhism and RPI – became central to the construction of a 'Dalit identity'. The RPI, which had held out a promise for equality-based politics, created a 'convergence of politics' constantly being identified as a party of the 'ex-Mahars' turned neo-Buddhists, socially awakened, relatively progressive and politically organized close-knit community. For the other SCs who refused to follow Ambedkar in his journey into Buddhism, a 'political division' was effected between the ex-Mahar neo-Buddhist and other SC groups keen to retain their Hindu identity. The other political consideration of non-Mahar caste groups was the danger of losing special constitutional status and economic privileges in the event of adopting a new religion. The dominance of Mahar neo-Buddhists in matters of leadership and organizational politics of RPI reinforced the shift of the arena from the 'people' to the 'lobby' and diverted RPI's attention from the urgent task of political mobilization.[6] The political entente of the RPI with the Congress Party in Maharashtra in the late 1960s diverted the struggle of the untouchables into a 'vicious circle of votes, demands, reserved seats and concessions'. The RPI leaders co-opted by the 'establishment became a self-serving group impervious to the suffering of their own people'. Compulsions of electoral politics to retain their political presence and the Congress Party's desire to appropriate the Dalit movement in Maharashtra led to the fragmentation of the RPI into a number of splinter groups. The entire history of splits, reunions and renewed splits in the RPI that followed had no ideological basis but occurred due to clash of personalities and personal political ambitions.[7] By the 1967 elections the Maharashtra Congress leaders weakened the RPI and were consciously working to its end.

Cramped by the 'slumbering RPI' and dissatisfied with merely writing about continued degradation and atrocities against the untouchables, some of the writers, who were former RPI party activists, formed the Dalit

Panthers (DP). Dalit Panthers, set up in 1972, brought to its fold a band of militant and enlightened youth of the Dalit community with the aim to defend dalits from atrocities and revolt against the social structure which had caused them much of their sufferings. As young educated dalits, Dalit Panther advocates espoused a 'humanitarian Ambedkarism', perceiving the plight of the dalits as being a result of caste and 'Brahminical-capitalist oppression'. These committed activists of the DP felt that the escape from oppression lay in the dalits themselves, and that it was their obligation to awaken and motivate the downtrodden into a mass protest. The Panther leaders tried to avoid a communal approach by defining the term 'Dalit' to mean 'all downtrodden people – workers and landless labourers – SCs and other 'socially and economically exploited groups' – in the country in a bid to organize a truly 'republican front of the oppressed'. Political unity with 'like-minded groups and parties' was considered necessary to broaden the political struggle which could lead to an increased electoral presence in the state assembly and the parliament. For many of the young members of the DP, 'who lived in the slums of Bombay, caste discrimination was not a social or cultural issue but the framework within which they had always lived, often in close juxtaposition with middle class, "upper-class liberals" living nearby, and the contradictions of such an alliance did not escape them'. The adoption of non-institutional means and objectives, which received legitimacy with the joining of youths, gave Panther leaders 'a revolutionary ardour, often expressed in a vulgar and unsophisticated manner'. But this was, as evident in its actual portrayal, only 'skin-deep'. There was nothing militant about them except their 'political' stance. In the case of DP, when their normal life was disturbed consequent to their 'confrontationist posturing', their radical ideas receded. In the aftermath of the March 1976 riots in Worli, a locality in South Mumbai, alleged to have been orchestrated by the Shiv Sena between OBCs and the SC, DP leaders reviewed their political-ideological strategy.

> Factions within the party had already emerged as the founders of Dalit Panthers, Dhale and Dhasal, differed on methodological aspects of the movement. Such indecisiveness over the appropriate form that radical politics should take in matters regarding questions related to poor among SC and caste Hindu; conceptualizing the possibility of a revolution through an assertive Dalit culture and the resultant socio-economic transformation etc. defeated the political ideals that the Panthers had set out to achieve.

The political failure of the Panthers was a result of their inability to move 'beyond a clash with brahminical elite', its figureheads and symbols. As a consequence, the DP failed in the primary task of protecting dalits in the face of mounting atrocities by upper-caste and 'caste Hindu' rural elite.[8]

Kanshiram's 'Expose' on Dalit Parties in Maharashtra

In his book, *Chamcha Yug,* written in 1982, Kanshiram elaborates upon three critical aspects that have weakened and disunited Dalit struggles in India: the failure of Dalit political parties in Maharashtra; the Poona Pact and the pliant leadership of the subaltern class. He gives a narrative account that historicizes the 'failure of Dalit movement'. Kanshiram states:

> In 1956 Ambedkar ushered in a (Dalit) movement that emerged on all fronts; societal, economic, political as well as religious.[9] But the 'self-proclaimed followers' of Ambedkar were not able to 'hold on to the movement' ... resulting in the fragmentation of the movement. The 'regression ... was of a fundamental nature and multi-dimensional, that is, the social, religious and political movement lost its identity'. As a consequence of the failure of the Ambedkarite movement most of the organizations established by Ambedkar suffered 'fratricidal conflicts'.[10]

Kanshiram writes further:

> [I]n Pune (he) was first exposed to the miseries of the Mahars and Mangs ... and thereafter 'immersed (himself) in the (Dalit) political culture of Maharashtra' by reading Dr. Ambedkar's books "*Annihilation of Caste*" and "*What Gandhi and the Congress Have Done to the Untouchables*" which profoundly influenced him. Later (he) came to know about Mahatma Jyotirao Phule.[11]

Kanshiram recollects that in the period 1964–1971, when he represented the RPI as an 'ordinary party worker', 'the party was one that was stricken with famine'. He adds that 'after working for four years (he) found that intra-organizational fights' and 'the deep distrust that existed between rival RPI leaders rendered them incapable to focus on the basic (organizational) tasks.

In the meanwhile,

> the Party went to pieces though (he) tried (his) best to stall this decline but (his) stature was too low (in the Party) to force anybody to heed (his) advice and when (his) voice gained some credibility the RPI was already in ruins, split into twelve factions.

Further, the leaders pushed the larger concerns

> aside even as the self-interest of leaders became their primary objective. Dalit leaders were (divided) among themselves; and further, 'small-time worker' took great interest in the movement while the 'big officers' (leaders) were hardly interested. One who was capable did not contribute. One who was incapable of doing anything stuck on.[12]

During the period of turmoil, Kanshiram claims that he made an effort to talk to the leaders of various factions within the RPI, such as the 'Gawai group', the 'Khobragade group', 'Shantabai Dani group' but 'could not avert splits' within the party. The turning point came during the 1971 mid-term parliamentary polls when a 'bizarre' seat pact was effectively reached between the RPI leaders Dadasaheb Gaikwad and Mohan Dharia (the latter subsequently joined the Congress Party) and the Congress Party in Maharashtra in respect to 'seat allocation' for the approaching state assembly elections. For the Congress, the 'seat allocation pact' proved extremely beneficial to the detriment of the RPI. Kanshiram states, 'after that there was no hope of recovery of the party from political eclipse'. Thereafter, Kanshiram shifted his political activities from Pune to Mumbai, hoping for a better political environment in which Dalit politics could be successful. However, he found out in Mumbai that 'Dalit worker-officers were either pursuing research on Dalit-related issues or were criticizing RPI leadership'. Kanshiram argued that the 'incapacity' of the RPI must not deter those who criticize, to become leaders of the RPI. The RPI faced financial difficulties and was 'facing a shortage of funds (to organize activities); (the Party) did not have an office in Mumbai and lacked adequate (number of party activists) by which they could spread the movement'.[13] Under such circumstances, Kanshiram said, 'it was not possible to work in unison' with Dalit worker-officers in Mumbai in a 'new way' and to organize Dalit-oppressed society'. Critical of the RPI and its political leadership, Kanshiram said: '[T]aking responsibility of a special community (the Dalits) and then dividing them into small divisions (fractions), would in sum mean that nothing (else) could be done'. Evaluating the disappointing state of events of the RPI Kanshiram said:

> I have learnt a lot from the people of Maharashtra. I have learnt a half lesson for running the Ambedkar movement from Dr. Babasaheb Ambedkar. The other half lesson I have learnt from the Mahars (here it means Mahar-dominated RPI) in Maharashtra. I have learnt from Babasaheb how to run the movement (and) from Mahars of Maharashtra I have learnt how not to run a movement. If you do not know how not to run the movement then you will never be able to know how to run it.[14]

Commenting on the state of Dalit Panthers, Kanshiram said that the '(outfit) emerged and with even greater pace faded away from the political horizon as it lay divided into six groups'. He concluded that lack of a focused and committed leadership and a durable party organization significantly undermined Dalit movement in India. Logically, an inept Dalit political leadership could not boast of a credible organization or a political party that would challenge an upper caste ruling (Congress) Brahminic ideology which had cast its pervasive influence through caste inequality in the socio-economic and political spheres of life.[15]

A Political Critique of the Poona Pact

Deducing an argumentative exposition to the political oblivion of Dalit movement in India, it is pertinent to highlight Kanshiram's critique of the Poona Pact (1932), which is tersely written with a view to provide a larger political perspective to a 'notion of social justice' compiled in his book *Chamcha Yug*. In September 1982, Kanshiram started an 'agitation' to oppose the signing of the Poona Pact on its 50th anniversary[16] celebrations, which invited condemnation from all other Dalit organizations, and the Congress Party. The 'Poona Denunciation Programme' became a platform to criticize the

> 'general secretary of the RPI, designated party officials of Dalit Panthers and a few experienced party men' who belonged to the (Mahar) community including leaders such as R.R. Bhole who worked with Ambedkar but were planning to 'celebrate' '50 years of the Poona Pact' rather than (leading) political protests.[17]

Kanshiram inferred that the Poona Pact had institutionalized a mutually inclusive relationship between a 'social (caste) order', or what he termed as 'brahminical social order' (BSO), and the 'political practice of (democratic) politics'. The 'caste order' had to be 'inverted' to advance the legitimate rights of the Dalit-Bahujans. Viewed in this context, the defeat of the 'aspiring goals of the Dalits' since the Poona Pact was ideologized by Kanshiram as a 'historical setback'.[18] In this regard, Kanshiram outlined the consequences of the 'eventful deliberations' that took place at the Second Round Table Conference (1931) that led to the promulgation of the Communal Award and Gandhi and Congress Party's opposition to it through a political compromise effected by the Poona Pact (1932) concerning the political future of the untouchables. Kanshiram said: While Ambedkar showed 'great leadership qualities' to 'wrest concessions from the British' in the form of separate electorates which would provide separate and 'autonomous' political representation for the untouchables, 'the road from dark age'[19] – the perpetuation of the caste system by the 'sanatan-vad'[20] – to a 'bright age' (a samta-mulak samaj)[21] 'could not materialize'. '[Thus] the untouchables slipped into the era of stooges, and the "dark age" continued'.[22] Gandhi, representing the 'upper caste cliché' Congress Party appeared as the 'chief obstacle' to the realization of the goal of the Depressed Classes. Gandhi is considered as a 'great human being (though) of the 'manuvadi order'. To protect the social order as envisioned by Manu, (he) put his life at stake. Kanshiram writes further

> that [i]n a letter written to the British Prime Minister Ramsay McDonald in September 1932 Gandhi 'confessed' that Ambedkar's arguments were more incisive than his arguments, and that, he was left with no

> option but to go on a 'fast unto death' because (his) religion (was) in danger (of oblivion). ...

Gandhi is considered an advocate of 'modern-day brahminism',[23] (keeping) the shudras in their place'; (and) 'dividing the country'; while (he) is 'working for the unity of the country, pledging to remove all social disabilities that afflict a majority of the people in India'.[24] Thus, Gandhi and the Congress, through the Poona Pact, opposed any specific concession to the depressed classes and (took away) the 'independent voting rights' of the depressed classes. The 'system of joint electorates' and 'reserved seats' defeated the 'autonomous untouchable social movements'.[25] The Congress, on its part, in the 1930s, strengthened the iniquitous social order by realizing the need for chamcha's (agents and lackeys) to 'substitute genuine SC representatives' to counter the social and political aspirations of the dalits.[26] Kanshiram states that 'for 24 years' since the 1932 Poona Pact, Ambedkar struggled to find a practical solution to the legitimate social grievances of the SCs; but even for a 'person of his stature' it was 'an elusive goal' to circumvent the political ramifications of the Poona Pact and the consequences of the 'stooge era'.[27] Thus, the Poona Pact maintained and reinforced the status quo of the minority upper castes (and) a 'hegemony' was imposed through the 'ideology of brahminism' (by the) Indian state in every realm of society – in 'power, politics, bureaucracy, "hereditary" economic system, religion and culture' – through the educational system (that integrated and socialized) the younger generation and (ensured) the continuation of an unequal system'. All government policies based upon (such a caste-based social order) have failed to uplift the dalits after independence. The establishment of a (political) democracy and adult franchise has helped the 'savarnas' and 'upper caste' political parties to continue their dominance over the social and political system by means of 'vote banks, money power and false promises'. Hence, Kanshiram states: '(Whether) we attempt to establish capitalism, communism or socialism, it would make no difference so long as the power of the state is in the hands of the upper castes'. In this situation, poverty is seen as a result of 'social and political powerlessness rooted in the brahminical (social) system', and not in an economic condition to be dealt with through government policies. A critique of the Poona Pact was interpreted within the larger political question of resisting the 'exploitative' upper caste brahminical social order and the political stratagem to overcome it through a new-found Dalit assertiveness.[28]

The 'Stooge' Leadership of the Oppressed

Kanshiram observes with clarity and provides a personal political insight into the complex dynamics of the emergence of SC chamchas (stooges), what he considers a 'post-Poona Pact phenomenon', that proliferated in the post-independence period as a political requirement in the process of governance.

He affirms that in the immediate post-1947 period, the Congress Party was the only political party capable of 'specializing in creating and maintaining lower caste/Dalit 'chamchas'. Thereafter, 'newly constituted (political) parties (in the 1960s and 1970s) also learnt the 'talent of the Congress and nurtured their respective group of stooges'.[29] Kanshiram elaborates that a 'pliant Dalit (chamcha) leadership' which comes in 'bewildering variety and form' – 'caste', 'community', 'reluctant', 'initiated', 'aspiring', 'helpless', 'ignorant', 'Ambedkarite', 'foreign' and 'party' chamchas – cannot represent the poor. (Thus), the Dalit-Bahujan population is '85%' yet ... without political leaders.[30] (Even) 50% of the dalits are not familiar with Ambedkar's life and his mission; (and that) it is in such a situation that the bahujan populace is ruled by a 'minority' of upper-caste Hindus who have been able to successfully place 'stooges amongst the bahujan majority' and rendered 'Indian democracy meaningless'.[31]

Kanshiram graphs the emergence of 'political agents' – the educated Dalit leadership – responsible for manipulating bahujan aspirations to ostensibly serve the political interests of the dominant class. He opines that after being accorded the status of a 'primary identity', an epithet used by Kanshiram to mean provisions of legal protection and constitutional safeguards for SC/ST, 'SCs and STs in ever moderate numbers achieved education; and (were employed) in government service.' Kanshiram suggests that 'a section of educated (SC and ST personnel) were used by political parties to strengthen their vote banks' among the Dalit-bahujan groups. They became the 'exploited elite group', who were 'educated but powerless' amongst the poor. The exploited elite groups 'represent political parties and not their community, and that their 'market value' within a (political party) rose 'depending on their clout to create a 'circle of additional stooges', especially amongst the educated sections of Scheduled Castes and Scheduled Tribes', thereby turning potential resource into political capital for the ruling class.[32] Also, the exploited 'educated elite' group seeks to protect its vested interests in quota politics; and with the 'timely policy' of reserved jobs and 'political tokenism' through patronage politics, the struggle against the caste system has ended, even as the alienation of Dalit-bahujan masses from their 'leaders' is complete. The larger question of not addressing backwardness has become a 'vested interest'.[33]

In like manner, Kanshiram identifies an approach of 'economics to scale' with regard to the availability of such 'agents' to serve the interests of the governing elite. He suggests the inverse, but a proportionate relationship that exists between a 'significant increase in chamchas' to fragment a proliferation of autonomous Dalit movements when they appear in the public sphere, and consequently, a 'decrease' in the number of 'agents' coinciding with a phase of political inactivity among marginalized sections of society. Kanshiram suggests that for an 'array of stooges', the period till 1975 was a phase spent in comfort. The 'comfortable situation' of 'such' (stooge) Dalit leaders severely affected the autonomous movements of the poor as one after another 'proxy' leaders began to 'surface with such magnitude that the Ambedkarite movement almost became defunct'.[34] However, he states that by the mid-1970s, with the 'end of a broad-based autonomous movement among the exploited class (possibly a reference to the decline of the RPI and DP) the necessity for stooges decreased'. However, Kanshiram claims that despite the 'weakening of organized movements among the oppressed', a 'sizeable number of (Ambedkarite) stooges still proliferated the 'political marketplace'. With the emergence of 'independent movements' among the socially oppressed in the early 1980s, the 'inconsequential' or 'light-weight stooges' amongst them were overwhelmed by 'heavy-weight stooges'.[35]

In a broader sense, Kanshiram contends that there are further negative consequences of an inept Dalit leadership. He states that

> people living in rural India cannot fight for their identity and rights (as they) depend (on) the landholders for their existence. It is not possible to resist the 'exploiters' because of the fear for hunger; and (that) the 'slightest (organized) resistance' of the agricultural labourers [would lead] to the brutality of caste violence.[36]

No effort is forthcoming from the ruling 'castes' to change the 'exploitative village economy', and further ... even those among the oppressed elite group, who may be in a 'position to contribute', (would) fail (as) they have been alienated from the 'large mass' of (bahujan) people.[37] In the urban towns and cities, the number of 'bastis' (squatter settlements) are on the rise, people belonging to the lower and the backward (castes) are in great majority migrating to the cities, fleeing the oppression of the feudal landholders in their villages and getting trapped in the vices of the 'dadas' (local toughs) who manage and control life in 'bastis'. The urban poor are eking out a living under despicable conditions 'on footpaths (and) near railway lines (and) "falling victim to nefarious social activities" (yet) the "exploited elite group" remains unconcerned'.[38]

Kanshiram states that due to the 'underprivileged position of the religious minorities and backward classes', they are unable to enjoy their constitutionally mandated rights. He states:

> 'After independence religious minorities have been living off the "benevolence of the ruling castes" of India. The Muslims, the largest minority community in India, have been victims of communal riots (that) have made (them) wary; the Christians appear helpless, the Sikhs are struggling for a dignified identity'.[39]

These unfortunate developments in the Indian polity prove that the state of the 'religious minorities of India is a reflection on the state of their (fragmented) political leadership'.[40] Kanshiram writes in *Chamcha Yug* that one of the political casualties of the 'chamcha' era has been the fate of the Other Backward Classes (OBC), the social position of the backward classes remains static (devoid) of the twin principles of 'identity and equality' that Ambedkar guaranteed as political safeguards for the SC and STs.[41] Kanshiram opines that the majority of the OBC have got 'partnership in the form of a minority'.[42] (Thus) it becomes clear that the (upper castes) are trying to take away the rights of the 'backwards'.[43] Kanshiram does not clearly suggest which section of the OBC is being referred to, but the political agenda of an 'organic solidarity of bahujans' would suggest the poor, exploited landless 'most backward castes' who form the major 'bahujan' caste constituency in the OBC.[44]

BAMCEF: A 'Movement from Above'

Offering a political direction to the Dalit-Bahujan masses 'struggling for rights and ... recognition'[45] in the context of a continuous assessment of socio-political issues facing them, Kanshiram categorically states that the question of 'political leadership of the oppressed' cannot be a task left to the excluded sections of society 'because of their psycho-cultural orientations and deprived economic status'. He suggests that what is required is an '(union type) association for the oppressed majority' on a large scale (so as to) to provide root to a 'rootless society'.[46] Such an 'association' built on the principles of horizontal ethnic solidarity would emerge by way of 'organizing community leadership' from 'innumerable educated oppressed Indians, primarily those to whom all avenues of advancement are closed in the field of agriculture, trade and commerce and industry, except the government services.' The implications for building an associative institutional body was premised on the belief that there are some educated employees who feel deeply agitated about the 'miserable existence' of their fellowmen.[47]

A useful 'experimental mobilization' of the 'stigmatized and isolated' in the Explosive Defence Research Laboratory in Pune gave Kanshiram an opportunity to forge a 'different (kind of an) organization'. This new 'constituency' of attracting SC employees to the Dalit cause was supposedly 'plural and national in its character' than the narrow base of Mahars and neo-Buddhists of the 'republican'[48] variety.

Kanshiram, assisted by his colleague D.K. Khaparde, a Mahar Buddhist,[49] inaugurated 'The Scheduled Castes and Scheduled Tribes, Other Backward Classes and Minority Communities Employees Association' on October 14, 1971, at Pune. The objective of the association was to 'subject (Dalit-Bahujan) problems to close scrutiny and find out quick and equitable solutions to the problems of injustice and harassment of educated (SC government) employees in particular'. Within a year of its inception, there were more than 1,000 members, mostly Mahar Buddhists, from the defence and post and telegraph department, where 'Kanshiram and Khaparde made friends and influenced people'.[50] This association prefigured Kanshiram's future organizations since it had already endeavoured to 'federate employees' who were dalits, tribes, lower castes and those belonging to the religious minority. Among the five 'vice-presidents' who assisted Kanshiram were one Mahar, one SC, one member from an 'adivasi' (tribal), one 'mali' (gardener), a 'lower backward' OBC, one Muslim, one Christian. They were representatives of what he considered the bahujan samaj (society of the oppressed majority). The professed aim of this organization was based on the premise 'jati todo samaj jodo' (break the caste system to strengthen the society of the oppressed)[51] and to aggregate all castes and tribes that were victims of discrimination related to their social status and to transform them into a 'social coalition' intent on opposing the 'alpjan' (minority) political class. The association focused on the SC 'elite', amongst other constituent groups of the bahujan samaj, who were a 'salaried class of officers with 'intellectual qualifications', employed in government service' through affirmative action policies.[52]

In 1973, at Pune, the 'association' was christened a Backward and Minority Communities Employees Federation (BAMCEF), a 'powerful public sector trade union of the specific disadvantaged groups'. At a conference in Punchkuian Hall in Delhi on December 6, 1973, on the death anniversary of Dr. Ambedkar, a decision was taken to undertake a 'course of action' to identify the guiding principles of BAMCEF. Thereafter, a three-day conference gave an opportunity for a 'group of "Dalit friends" from different departments of government', who were members of the BAMCEF, to take a pledge to 'Pay Back to the Society', 'create awareness among the Dalits for 25 years and then launch a political party'. The objective of BAMCEF was to bypass 'government service rules' that barred state employees, holding government positions in various capacities, from participating in political activities. BAMCEF would be 'non-political, non-agitational and non-religious organization' yet provide a strong non-political foundation (to) succeed in the political sphere.[53] Kanshiram decided to give BAMCEF a 'national face'. Yet again he sought assistance from the employees of Indian Railways, the telephone offices and the post and telegraph offices across several cities. Over the next few years, he developed an intense rapport with salaried SC employees interested in his task of building an ever broadening 'Bahujan Samaj' of dalits and other disadvantaged groups. As BAMCEF activities expanded, it became a 'confederation' to mobilize educated employees of the 'oppressed classes' under the nomenclature 'bahujan', with the aim to establish an 'ethno cultural unity'.[54] Within the BAMCEF, SC employees held a privileged position due to the fact that according to the 'desired intentions of the organization (they were) in the best position to take advantage within the given situation'.[55] 'Dalit' government employees would take the lead in 'organizing the interests' of the bahujans expected to 'cut intermediaries out' to assume leadership positions and 'derive strength from the people'. Three years later, Kanshiram left Pune, a political decision that he took to mobilize Chamars of north India and opened a 'central office' of the BAMCEF in New Delhi on December 6, 1976. Two years later, on Ambedkar's 22nd death anniversary, BAMCEF 'launched with great fanfare' a 'formal office' with a 'permanent address' in Karol Bagh, New Delhi, that coincided on the same day with 'claims of 2,000 delegates' joining a successful procession to the Boat Club Lawns near India Gate in New Delhi. The destination of dissent displayed a 'broad, if not a dense, network of contacts' established by Kanshiram in Maharashtra, as well as 'sympathizers' recruited to the 'organization' from Punjab, Haryana, Uttar Pradesh and Madhya Pradesh.[56]

To the BAMCEF, Dalit politics appeared as an 'altruistic Ambedkarite mission', a 'sacred goal', a 'noble aim' and a 'glorious mission'. At a BAMCEF conference in Nagpur in 1978, Kanshiram stated that if the 'upper band of Dalits and lower castes that had managed to get into the government by taking advantage of the reserved quota' guide their community, then 'it must lead not be led'; and further that BAMCEF (could) 'not be deterred by the momentary displeasure of (its) own people' and 'lose political direction in society'.[57] In pursuit of the 'goal of a bahujan samaj', BAMCEF leadership would foster an 'organic relationship' between 'oppressed public sector employees' working in various government departments all over India and the bahujan masses.[58] The federation would act as a 'forum of political education' to raise the consciousness of the bahujan masses[59] and outline measures to 'develop BAMCEF as the "major support" organization for a later, if indefinite, political thrust'.[60]

Kanshiram observed that since educated SC employees could work in a disciplined manner due to 'their training in bureaucracy' and had 'time, money and talent' with itself to 'pay back' to (bahujan) society,[61] collection of funds for BAMCEF organizational activities was of 'primary importance', a responsibility to be entrusted to the SC government employees. Kanshiram figuratively quoted that '(organizational work would) be fulfilled with even Rs 1 crore'; or even that 'in lakhs (it could) commence the mission'.[62] SC employees were expected to contribute one-tenth of their salary 'to community and social work'.[63] Kanshiram felt that with 'no shortage of brain, talent and money' that was embodied in the educated SC employees, there would be no 'specific difficulties' in founding a political party.[64]

However, BAMCEF's organizational expansion coincided with the promulgation of 18 months of emergency (1975–1977) in the country. During that period, BAMCEF activists who were public functionaries became victims of routine harassment and were transferred across cities and towns. BAMCEF became a 'shadow organization'. 'It had no office. There were no records of thousands of office-bearers.' As Kanshiram reminisced later: '(O)nly [sic] we (knew) the workers'. The harassment by the central government intensified even as the Congress Party became wary of the widespread popularity of the non-political 'federation' among Dalit and lower-caste employees in north India and the possible impact it could have on Congress' electoral base among marginalized sections of society in the region. In the post-emergency period following the electoral victory of the Janata Party in March 1977, the victimization of BAMCEF 'officers' considerably lessened.

BAMCEF began to organize 'programmes' in the form of conventions, conferences, seminars, symposia, workshops and 'cadre camps'.[65] Conferences were held across the country – at Bhopal on April 29, 1979, at Chandigarh on April 21–22, 1979, at Ahmedabad on May 6, 1979, at Bombay on May 9, 1979, at Bangalore on May 20, 1979, at Hyderabad on May 27, 1979, at Nagpur on June 3, 1979, at Calcutta on June 6, 1979, at Delhi in November 1980 and Chandigarh in October 1981. In Delhi, a seminar was held from June 11–14, 1979, at the Constitution Club of India on the topic 'Will Ambedkarism Revive or Survive?' These conferences and seminars were intended to create 'public awareness' on the condition of dalits across India. In addition, BAMCEF's organizational programmes included 'camps' to train BAMCEF activists who themselves held 'propaganda classes' in 'Dalit neighbourhoods.' On a broader scale, BAMCEF raised the social consciousness among dalits through various forms of cultural events such as 'organized slide shows' that depicted the life and works of 'bahujan icons' such as ' Phule, Shahu Maharaj, Periyar and Ambedkar, as well as other Dalit saints'. BAMCEF felicitated Dalit poets on Ambedkar's birthday. A BAMCEF programme which became popular was the 'Ambedkar Mela on Wheels', shown at '34 destinations in 9 states' between April and June 1980, comprising of gigantic paintings and 'propaganda newsprint' depicting oppression, poverty and atrocities on the 'bahujan samaj'. A typical programme began with 'speeches by BAMCEF activists', followed by 'dance, music, drama, songs and poetry recitals which reinforced the content of the speeches'. Almost all the contents of this 'mela' were provided by Kanshiram, consisting of 'portraits, photographs and books of Ambedkar, including sketches of atrocities against Dalits'. Another feature of BAMCEF activity was the launching of 'cycle marches' across the major cities and towns in the country. In that context, Kanshiram said:

> '(The) bahujan samaj is short of means as it is kept poor by manuvadis (supporters of exploitative caste system). We do not have our fast (cars, scooters, buses, trucks) means of travelling; so why should we brood over that? We have the cheapest means of traveling (cycle) at our disposal'. To motivate his (supporters) Kanshiram illustrated the example of (Chairman) Mao Zedong (who) 'went on a Long March (between October 1934 to October 1935) on foot and brought revolution and (in this way Kanshiram) reminded his (supporters) 'to work in a given situation without complaining.[66]

The BAMCEF in Uttar Pradesh

By the late 1970s the expansion of BAMCEF activities was notable with the deep organizational presence of the 'association' in Uttar Pradesh. In UP, the 'successful membership drive of low-caste Class III employees was enhanced by the active contribution of a number of national-level politicians of a 'socialist variety' and 'Ambedkarite activists'. Kanshiram, as 'President' of the BAMCEF by now, commanded the services of almost all SC officers (primarily Chamars) in the state to help the 'federation' exploit the intense caste politics against the SC employees in the state bureaucracy. However, the 'organization' faced difficulty in recruiting officers from Ambedkarite 'political circles' associated with the existing Uttar Pradesh Republican Party of India (UPRPI). The state unit of the RPI advised Dalit officers that associating with Kanshiram would lead to official reprimand and disciplinary action that would affect their careers. In contrast, mobilizing 'supporters of Jagjivan Ram', a national-level untouchable leader, was relatively easier due to his political decline.[67] In 1978, BAMCEF opened its first office in Agra. A year later, another office was opened in Lucknow by Raj Bahadur, an employee of the state telephone department. The prominence of the 'educated' Chamar-Jatavs within the 'association' became evident by their sheer numbers as middle-level administrative functionaries or as 'subordinate officers', which was viewed with concern and animosity by the Brahmins and Kayasthas competing for state jobs and employment in administrative services. Chamar-Jatav state employees continued to face intense social discrimination in state services, often 'denied important posts in the district as well as the state capital'.[68] It is this literate section of 'clerks and subordinate officers' that became politically conscious and 'radicalized' finding political expression in the organizational activities of the BAMCEF. Assuming the political leadership of SC communities in UP, this 'class of administrative officers' were intent upon participating in the political system as 'office seekers rather than benefit seekers'.[69] The consolidation of BAMCEF presence in UP coincided with a spurt in membership across cities. Between 1978 and 1983, Uttar Pradesh, followed by Maharashtra, took the lead in increasing its membership to over 2,00,000, which included '500 PhD scholars, 3,000 doctors, 15,000 scientists and 70,000 office staff'.[70]

Kanshiram's exploration with a 'unique style' of Dalit politics in what he termed as the 'political laboratory' of UP, considered as the 'nucleus of brahmanvad', begins during this period. Kanshiram's focus for a more intense political activity in UP, dominated by Chamar BAMCEF members, led to 'differences with the neo-Buddhist Mahar "Maharashtra section" of the SC employees' led by his colleague D.K. Khaparde, who was unwilling to provide additional (organizational) funds on account of 'differences between the two groups'. Khaparde was keen to maintain the pre-eminence of the BAMCEF as a 'national organization', a sort of 'social and national consolidation' before any kind of politics could be conceived. On the other hand, Kanshiram took a definite political direction as he began to give increasing prominence to use BAMCEF activities to build a 'new political organization' with the aim to radicalize lower castes' in rural areas.[71] In UP, Kanshiram had realized that meeting Chamar government employees in urban slums had many advantages. They had their 'roots in villages', and it helped Kanshiram penetrate rural Dalit 'pattis' (settlements) and get a sense of their problems. Along with his 'loyal band of followers', Kanshiram met villagers in the fields, banks of ponds, 'chaupals' (community building or space) and engaged in 'conversational' politics to create a 'sense of camaraderie and a sense of a collective cause' especially for Chamar officers 'jointly sharing the expenses of hosting such meetings'. It was clear that Kanshiram was apparently trying to affect 'a directing and helping agency' role for the BAMCEF, well fitted to perform the role of 'organizing political activities in the rural regions of UP'.[72] The political stage was being set for a 'Chamar-dominated 'political organization' in the midst of UP undergoing a phase of 'urbanization and occupational mobility' that had begun to provide the rural poor other prospects of livelihood, thereby loosening the feudal hold over their traditional occupation of agricultural labourers. Evaluating a successful operative strategy of BAMCEF, Kanshiram was prophesizing a set of 'favourable political circumstances' which could propel the association towards a not-too-distant 'Dalit politics'. Kanshiram felt that Chamar 'leaders' could utilize the 'privileges of government control', howsoever modest, for sectional benefit which would create 'opportunities for political action' to challenge oppressive patterns of caste in society and politics[73].They had a context: a 'historical struggle' of a rich tradition of 'Chamar-dominated' Dalit mobilization for 'equality and political power' since the pre-independence period. Other factors that were of consequence was that UP possessed a sizeable Dalit population which could determine the electoral outcome in several constituencies in the state and a good number of salaried government employees conscious willing to contribute 'money and mind' to the task of organizing Dalit politics in the state. Finally, there were 'large numbers of unemployed Dalit youths committed to take the message of Dalit empowerment to the rural areas'.[74]

The Structural Alignment of Politics in Uttar Pradesh

Kanshiram's commentary and his consequent political effort to organize a new age Dalit activism coincides with a broad shift in the paradigm of social and political forces in Uttar Pradesh. Increasing prosperity of the landed non-Brahmin castes across the state highlighted the structural tensions that existed between the 'rich' farmers and lower classes. They utilized 'local structures of power, state machinery, police and village-level bureaucracy' to neutralize any pro-poor legislative and political initiatives of the state government. The 'new' land-owning castes shared the concerns of the upper castes, notably the political fermentation among lower castes and Dalit groups, the 'army of bonded labourers', seeking an alternative form of political mobilization in the state. The intermediate castes would, in due course, be successful in putting political pressure on the Janata Party government (1977–1979) to look into the question of 'backward class' reservation. Back at the Centre, after the 1980 Parliamentary elections, the Congress Party in UP was driven by changing socio-political dynamics in the state to reconfigure Dalit-lower caste support in the wake of continuing caste atrocities by upper and landed middle castes. However, the Congress Party, in power, deferred the recommendation of the 'Mandal Commission' set up during the Janata Party rule, to look into 'Backward class' reservation, that could benefit the landed middle castes and instead tabled the Chhedi Lal Saathi Commission formulated during the emergency years seeking Most Backward Caste (MBC) representation in jobs and education sector at the state and central level. Politically, the re-integration of SCs appeared in the form of a 'policy of tokenism' by ceding some key posts to 'SC elites' in the party and the state government.

To apprehend the Congress Party's political incomprehensibility to reconfigure the changing dimensions of politics in UP, one needs to look back to the decade of the 1970s, wherein lay the source of its declining political fortunes. Congress' reactive politics in that decade was symptomatic of the failure of the 'rural regeneration programmes' – post-1971 massive electoral victory for the party that had promised to promote with special care the educational, employment and economic interests of SC and backward classes. Yet the failure of the populist rural regeneration programme precipitated a crisis of legitimacy for the Congress Party as Jagjivan Ram, the most 'trusted Dalit leader' of Indira Gandhi, criticized Congress' 'non-performance and political excesses' during the emergency and left the government. Jagjivan Ram's political exit from the Congress Party symbolized a significant shift of subaltern and low-caste clientele support for the party. The Janata Party (JP), a national coalition of political parties with diverse and opposing ideologies, some of them prominently representative of backward caste interests from north India, came to power in March 1977 but failed on the political promise to elect Jagjivan Ram to the post of prime minister. It was a political assurance that had been given to Jagjivan Ram, 'chief mobilizer' of Dalit and low-caste voters for the Janata Party. It disappointed the dalits, especially the Chamars in north India, a caste to which Jagjivan Ram belonged, who had hoped that in his capacity to emerge as a national leader, dalits would be empowered.[75] In one of his political speeches, Kanshiram retained the choicest words for Jagjivan Ram, the 'Dalit mascot' of the Congress. He said that Jagjivan Ram 'was a 'sycophant' and dismissed his untouchable well-wishers as the 'chamchas of a chamcha'. Kanshiram said:

> He (Jagjivan Ram) was a stooge not a leader. Till such time he continued to be a stooge (of the Congress Party), he had a good time. Later the stooge wanted to be a PM (in the Janata Party headed coalition government at the centre), but nobody makes a stooge a PM. Then he made his own party, first Janata (J) and then Congress (J). He was finished. Babu Jagjivan Ram was a product of the existing powers and it was the existing powers that destroyed him.[76]

Concerned at a depleting electoral base of dalits, the political response of the Congress Party to a broad-based 'commercialization of agriculture' across the state, which post-dated western UP-centred impact of 'Green Revolution' (1966–1978) leading to the economic resurgence of the middle caste landowners, was complicated by the 'political flight of the Brahmins and Rajputs from the party' by the early 1980s. The Brahmins shifted political support to the Bharatiya Janata Party (BJP), formed in 1980 from the erstwhile Jan Sangh, a coalition partner in the Janata Party government, and the Rajputs eventually allied with the Rajput born 'Raja of Manda' V.P. Singh led Janata Dal by the late 1980s. In the light of an increased fragmentation of its vote base, the Congress Party was 'forced to respond to the demands of the middle castes that its policies enriched but who still positioned the Congress as their principal political enemy' even as atrocities against dalits took a form of severity in the state. By the mid-1980s, it was clear that in UP political power slowly would shift to the influential peasant-farmer lobby 'entrenched in state politics and districts (even as there appeared) precipitated rounds of fiscal transfers'.[77]

Dalit Shoshit Samaj Sangharsh Samiti: The 'Quasi-Political' Movement

Underlined by the ethos of the associational politics of BAMCEF and its 'Dalit conscious' leaders, and the propensity for a 'new age' Dalit movement in the midst of a realignment of social and political forces, in early 1980s, Kanshiram was ready to contemplate 'a rural political thrust' to expand a 'bahujan' movement in Uttar Pradesh. In this regard, Kanshiram's politico-historical project marked out other non-Congress Dalit political fronts, the 'rump elements' of the erstwhile 'Dalit' political parties which had lost their political appeal in Uttar Pradesh. The Congress Party had already factionalized the 'state unit' of the RPI in the 1967 general elections and the 1971 mid-term Parliamentary elections and in the process 'snatched away their (RPI) leaders' such as B.P. Maurya and 'their agenda'. By the early 1980s, the splintered UPRPI had become an insipid political group,[78] and there was no specific directive coming from the UP unit of RPI advising 'supporters' not to join BAMCEF. Kanshiram was indifferent to the activities of the 'UP branch' of Dalit Panthers, aware that even sporadic revolutionary or militant methods of political action could lead to repression by a 'brahminical' state government. Kanshiram was equally disinterested in the rise of the Bharatiya Dalit Panthers (BDP) in UP, formed in 1980, which adopted a non-party platform to mobilize the 'rural poor against atrocities'. Local units of the BDP were formed in former RPI strongholds, and 'young intellectuals' were nominated as 'conveners' by disbanded RPI leaders. On the BDP, Kanshiram wrote in the 'Oppressed Indian' that there was a 'difference' between 'sincere (Bharatiya) Dalit Panthers who (would) join the (BSP) movement and other (activists) who did not and (fell) back on criminal activities in partnership with corrupt police officers'.[79] In general, the BAMCEF and the Dalit Shoshit Samaj Sangharsh Samiti (DS-4) had already been or were on the verge of becoming focal points of Dalit-Bahujan activity in Uttar Pradesh, attracting an impressive number of supporters and effectively marginalizing the UPRPI and BDP and its smaller Dalit affiliates from state politics.

On the question of the founding of the Dalit Shoshit Samaj Sangharsh Samiti, Kanshiram was clear in his political intentions when he said:

> I started with the idea of social transformation and economic emancipation. I still want my people (Dalits) to advance socially and economically. But I have realized that unless we have political clout, we cannot advance much on those sides.[80]
>
> Kanshiram held no regret the way BAMCEF would eventually recede into the background, since he no longer regarded it as his priority to organize SC government employees.

The DS-4 was founded on December 6, 1981, on the 25th death anniversary of Ambedkar, much to the dislike of a few senior BAMCEF 'Dalit officers' who left the organization. DS-4 dispensed with the official euphemisms 'backward class, scheduled castes', preferring instead the words 'Dalit' and 'shoshit' (oppressed) that politicized the usage of the term 'untouchable' frequently to designate themselves. The DS-4 was supposed to be a radical political organization capable of mobilizing the 'larger body of Dalits' – a 'historical vulgate in which the shudras, ati-shudras and the OBCs were bracketed together that included the tribal population – to create a strong and socially secure bahujan samaj'.[81] The DS-4 was a 'quasi' rather than a full-fledged political party, partly because administrative functionaries belonging to the SC cadre who played an important role in connecting with the rural poor were not permitted to take part in electoral politics.[82] However, unlike the BAMCEF, the activities of the DS-4 were to be taken ahead by students, women and 'awakening squads', the politically conscious village activists, all falling outside the purview of civil service conduct rules that influenced the service conditions of government employees. The new organization served as a 'fastener', a bridge between Kanshiram's 'trade union style' BAMCEF activities and his emergence as a full-fledged politician.[83]

In his book *Chamcha Yug*, Kanshiram outlines the political strategy that the DS-4 was to undertake to challenge the 'caste system' in Uttar Pradesh. A closer examination of DS-4's method of political activity suggests a broad similarity of strategies with the BAMCEF of the post-emergency period. The book offers both 'a short-term and a long-term solution' that would involve 'intensive' social action with the formation of 'Jagruti Squads (awakening squads)' by a 'students wing' and a 'women's wing', which, it was believed, would inevitably spread out to all parts of the country. A 'social awakening campaign' would be part of the 'political agenda' that would include lectures, songs, music and street theatres and the mobilizing of the 'oppressed samaj' on 'general (social) and specific (political and electoral) issues'. The methods used by the 'awakening squads' had to be effective, otherwise the 'three-stage level of consciousness' of being 'politically awakened and electorally involved' could not emerge in the bahujan constituency. Curiously, Kanshiram explained that 'social action (involving the Dalit-oppressed community) should be mild but continuous, without a break, to make it meaningful and effective'. Occasionally '(it would) have to be wild, but non-violent. It (would) depend upon the type(s) of struggle(s)' that would be undertaken.[84] The long-term solution was 'political action' with the formation of a political party. As a precursor to the formation of a 'political party', Kanshiram said that 'some experiments were being conducted towards 'Limited Political Action' till (the DS-4 felt) sure of forming a political party'.[85]

DS-4s political 'awakening campaigns' began by organizing a 1-month 'Denunciation of the Poona Pact' programme held between September 24 and October 24, 1982, starting from Poona and ending in Jalandhar, Punjab. It was closely followed by the launching of the 'People's Parliament' agitation on December 25, 1982, to protest against the 'non-representation of the Dalit-oppressed community' in Parliament. The People's Parliament would move from Delhi to other parts of the country and mobilize public opinion so as to ensure that the Indian Parliament became a 'representative body'.[86]

In March 1983, the DS-4 'awakening squads' inaugurated a '3,000 km' bicycle ride and a '300 km walk', 'covering 35 "important places" in 7 states of northern India within 40 days'. Punjab, Haryana, UP and Bihar became the locale of DS-4s intensive 'political events'. Much like the BAMCEF, the 'cycle ride' was led by Kanshiram, who used the bicycle as a metaphor to show that it was the best weapon for (dalits) in their agitation; to show their strength; and further that 'if their two feet (were) all right (sic) they would reach any place ..., including (political) campaigns during elections'.[87] Another 'cycle march' was organized by the DS-4 between December 1983 and February 1984, known as the 'Equality and Respect Movement' to mobilize people in the countryside. The cycle march with 'fluttering blue flags' aimed to link 'five corners' of India – Kanyakumari (southern India, December 6, 1983), Kargil (northern India, December 18, 1983), Kohima (northeast India, January 19, 1984), Puri (eastern India, January 28, 1984) and Porbandar (western India, February 22, 1984). Nearly 3,00,000 DS-4 activists participated in the cycle march, raising a number of slogans on the way: 'Babasaheb (Ambedkar) amar rahein' (Long live Babasaheb), 'Kanshiram Zindabad' (Hail Kanshiram), 'Bharat ki majboori hai, Kanshiram zaroori hai' (It is India's requirement, Kanshiram is necessary), 'Ab bahujan ki bari hai – ikkeesvi sadi hamari hai' (It is now the turn of the bahujans; we will own the twenty-first century). 'In 100 days, the cyclists covered 1,00,000 km to reach Red Fort grounds enroute to Boat Club ground, where a 'highly impressive (political) rally' concluded the 'prachar yatra' (publicity journey). A vast rally of lower castes and dalits was addressed by Kanshiram even as it received extensive media coverage. 'Dalit officers and workers (working in state offices in close vicinity to the political rally) left their work to attend the rally'. Kanshiram wanted to prove that dalits could be 'mobilized in hordes and made politically visible'.[88]

The DS-4 would be remembered for launching 'highly provocative and occasionally propagandistic' campaign. Yet Kanshiram testified to the fact that DS-4's popularity in Uttar Pradesh depended upon avoiding any kind of mass agitation that would bring them into a political conflict with the state machinery. DS-4's 'rural', 'political' programme was marked by 'pithy slogans' to mobilize low-caste rural population – 'Brahmin, Bania, Thakur chor, baki saab hain DS-4', which pointed out that 'the upper castes were unscrupulous and the rest of the population were the poor and the exploited – the DS-4'; 'tilak, taraju aur talwar, inko maro joote char' (beat the upper castes with shoes); on the nature of representative politics – 'vote hamara, raj tumara, nahi chalega, nahi chalega' (our votes your power, this cannot go on, this cannot go on); on the notion of a 'revitalized' democratic politics – 'jiski jitni sankhya bhari, uski utni bhagidari' (those with the largest numbers should be best represented); and the need to capture political power and state administration – 'vote se lenge PM/CM, aarakshan se lenge SP/DM' (through votes/elections we will take the posts of prime minister and chief minister and through reservations the posts of superintendent of police and district magistrate).

DS4's active phase of political activity lasted less than three years. During the short active phase of the DS-4, Kanshiram had increasingly begun to trust Mayawati, the 'president' of the mahila wing of the 'association'. He had known Mayawati for a few years and was impressed by her steady rise as a 'leader of repute' from Uttar Pradesh. However, what became a bone of contention for many senior BAMCEF leaders was the political coronation of Mayawati, to be vested with a political responsibility, to mobilize the critical Dalit constituency in UP. Bypassing the political criticism, Kanshiram spoke with admiration of his protégé having acquired all those attributes a 'Dalit leader' could possess. To Kanshiram, Mayawati was impeccably suited to lead bahujan politics in the state. She was

> 'value-based' (yet) driven by interest (was) popular (who)possessed far-sightedness (and) patien(t) [sic] and determin(ed) [sic] and (one who had) the 'required sensitivity of the people'. He further surmised: Mayawati had an understanding of the 'configuration of social and political forces'; (was) 'sensitive to time and priority (and could) undertake difficult tasks Thus, Mayawati was flawless and an 'ideal' 'authoritative' leader that Kanshiram had 'discovered', who would fulfil the 'service to the bahujan samaj'.

Seeking to capture the political imagination of the Dalit-bahujan masses in rural UP, Kanshiram was already contemplating the formation of a full-fledged political party. Apparently apprehensive of the difficulties that might be posed to his acceptance as a 'Punjabi origin leader', in UP, Kanshiram promptly began to 'organize bahujan politics' by offering 'posts' to 'leaders' of DS-4 branches in UP. Jang Bahadur Patel, a backward Kurmi leader, who became the 'president' of the UP unit of the BSP; Dr. Masood Ahmad, a lecturer from Aligarh Muslim University, and Mayawati, a Chamar-Jatav leader representing the Dalits, were entrusted with the task of mobilizing diverse sections of the bahujan samaj.[89]

Notes

1 Kanshiram was the eldest among Hari Singh's seven children. Kanshiram had three brothers and three sisters. His Hindu name has a story behind it. Apparently, 'a saint named Kanshiram had been visiting the village when Bishan Kaur was expecting the child'. People in the village had great faith in him. They found his discourses pleasing and elevating. Bishan Kaur would regularly go to listen to them. The saint had predicted that Bishan Kaur would give birth to a son who would be a great leader, and whose name would resonate across India, bringing glory to his family. So, when her son was born, the elders in the family suggested she name him after the saint.

Badri Narayan, *Kanshiram; Leader of the Dalits*, New Delhi: Penguin Viking, 2014, pp. 12, 13.

2 As a young boy, Kanshiram studied till Standard 4 at Government Primary School in Malakpur, which was about 2 km from his own village. Kanshiram along with other Dalit children were seated separately and had a different pot for drinking water. 'Sikh religion despite being egalitarian offered no hope of equality for the Dalit community as there was underlying social discrimination among Sikhs despite allowed to perform all the religious rituals, regardless of socioeconomic status and caste, unlike the Hindus'. Kanshiram's family belonged to the Ramdasia community, a Sikh subgroup and was a victim of social inequality, and so the entire family converted to the Khalsa Panth. Following Guru Nanak, the Khalsa Panth gave due respect to the laboring castes by negating birth-based caste identities. This position was affirmed by the Adi Granth, considered the sacred book of the Sikhs, which includes the verses of Kabir and Ravidas, popular saints of marginal communities and Dalits. Kanshiram's father Hari Singh, stung by the caste discrimination his son faced in school, shifted him to Islamiya School, Ropar, where he studied till Standard 8. Kanshiram moved to DAV Public School, Ropar, for Classes 9 and 10. Due to the presence of Arya Samaj and the Khalsa Panth, caste discrimination in these two schools were not so obvious. Kanshiram finally graduated in 1956, with a B.Sc. from Government College, Ropar.

Badri Narayan, *Kanshiram: Leader of the Dalits*, pp. 13, 14, 20.

3 Kanshiram's mother recounts that her son would fly into a rage when someone was wrongly insulted or humiliated. Once, when he went to a restaurant in Ropar, he overheard some landlords, who were also eating there, bragging about how they had beaten up some Chamars working in their fields, to teach them a lesson. Hearing this, Kanshiram got so angry that he picked up his chair and started beating those men with it, smashing all the dishes and plates laid out on the table in the process.

Badri Narayan, *Kanshiram; Leader of the Dalits*, pp. 14, 15.

4 Ajoy Bose, *Behenji: A Political Biography of Mayawati*, New Delhi: Penguin Viking, 2008, p. 29; Kanchan Chandra, *Why Ethnic Parties Succeed: Patronage*

and Ethnic Head Counts in India, United Kingdom: Cambridge University Press, pp. 143–5; Christophe Jaffrelot, *India's Silent Revolution: The Rise of Lower Castes in North India,* New Delhi: Permanent Black, 200, pp. 389–90; K. Chandra, *Why Ethnic Parties Succeed*,. pp. 144, 145; Sambaiah Gundimeda, *Dalit Politics in Contemporary India*, New Delhi: Routledge, 2016, pp. 85–7; Badri Narayan, *Kanshiram: Leader of the Dalits*, pp. 14, 15, 20, 21.

5 Satnam Singh, Bahujan *Nayak Kanshiram* [Bahujan Hero Kanshiram], New Delhi: Samyak Prakashan, 2005, p. 65.

6 The overwhelming political astuteness of the Mahar neo-Buddhists served to isolate them further from other Dalits as they, for instance, received almost 83% of scholarships available to Dalits in Maharashtra.

Elizabeth LoGuidice, "The diversity of revolt: Dalit movements in India", *Comparative Studies of South Asia, Africa and Middle East*, 1989, 9, 1, p. 60.

Jayashree Gokhale, *From Concessions to Confrontation: The Politics of an Indian Untouchable Community*, Bombay: Popular Prakashan, 1993, p. 212; Lata Murugkar, *Dalit Panther Movement in Maharashtra: A Sociological Appraisal*, Bombay: Popular Prakashan, 1991, pp. 42, 114, 115.

In Maharashtra, in the post-independence period, the 'Brahmin-non-Brahmin conflict was fought within the Congress and with the formation of the Maratha-speaking state in 1960, the non-brahmin caste of Marathas acquired control of the Congress organization'. The Marathas emerged as a dominant caste in Maharashtra by 'coopting and domesticating' other backward and Dalit castes. Y.B. Chavan, the chief architect of this strategy of integration employed the term 'bahujan' to give a call to all non-brahmins and backwards to support his regime. In reality, the Maharashtra Congress came to be controlled by a few 'high-caste' Maratha clans and not bahujans.

Vora and Palshikar, *Indian Democracy*, pp. 275, 276.

7 Murugkar, *Dalit Panther*, pp. 114, 115; Prahlad Gangaram Jogdand, *Dalit Movement in Maharashtra,* New Delhi, Kanak Publications, 1991, p. 70; Vivek Kumar, *India's Roaring Revolution: Dalit Assertions and New Horizons,* Delhi, Gagandeep Publications, 2006, p. 37; Gokhale, *Concessions to Confrontation,* p. 37.

8 Murugkar, *Dalit Panther*, pp. 44, 45, 63, 68, 83, 84, 102; Satyamurthy, *Region, Religion, Gender*, p. 368.

9 Kanshiram, *Chamcha Yug* [An Era of Stooges], Hindi edition, Bombay: Samta Prakashan, 1998, p. 94.

10 Satnam Singh, *Bahujan Nayak Kanshiram* [Bahujan Hero Kanshiram], New Delhi: Samyak Prakashan, 2005, p. 65.

11 Jaffrelot, Christophe, The Bahujan Samaj Party in north India: no longer just a dalit party? *Comparative Studies in South Asia, Africa and the Middle East,* Vol. XVIII, No. 1 (1998), p. 35; Christophe Jaffrelot, *Dr Ambedkar and Untouchability: Fighting the Indian Caste System,* New York: Columbia University Press, 2005, p. 153.

12 Satnam Singh, *Bahujan Nayak*, pp. 30–2.

13 Satnam Singh, *Bahujan Nayak*, pp. 30–2.

On the question of seat allocation pact reached between the Congress and the RPI in 1971, Kanshiram recollects a conversation between two prominent members of the RPI, Dadasaheb Gaikwad and Mohan Dharia, 'that till 1971 no compromise had been struck between "Gandhi's party and Ambedkar's party," yet, subsequently a seat sharing arrangement arose in which Gandhi's party, the Congress Party (Indira), got 520 seats to contest in Parliament while the Ambedkar party, the RPI, got 1 seat'.

Badri Narayan, *Kanshiram; Leader of the Dalits*, p. 30.

14 Akela, *Sakshatkar*, p. 13; Kanshiram, *Chamcha Yug*, p. 94; Abhay Madhukar Dongre (15.03.15) "What BSP and Kanshiram have done to the untouchables" URL: https://www.drambedkarbooks.com (accessed on 13.3.18)
15 K.C. Das *Indian Dalits: Voices, Visions and Politics*, New Delhi: Global Vision Publishing House, 2004, pp. 212, 250; Zoya Hasan, *Parties and Party Politics in India*, New Delhi: Oxford University Press, 2002, pp. 379, 383, Ian Duncan, Dalits and politics in rural north India: the Bahujan Samaj Party in Uttar Pradesh, *The Journal of Peasant Studies*, 27, 1, October 1999, p. 36; Ghanshyam Shah, *Caste and Democratic Politics in India,* New Delhi: Permanent Black, 2002, p. 271; K. Chandra, *Why Ethnic Parties Succeed,* pp. 217, 259–60.
16 Satnam Singh, *Bahujan Nayak*, p. 49.
17 Ashok Kumar Jha, *Dalitisation of Dalits*, Delhi: Adhyayan Publishers, 2004, p. 107.
18 Kanshiram, *Chamcha Yug*, p. 76.
19 Satnam Singh, *Bahujan Nayak*, p. 53.
20 Kanshiram, *Chamcha Yug,* p. 81.
21 Satnam Singh, *Bahujan Nayak*., p. 54
22 Satnam Singh, *Bahujan Nayak*, p. 53.
23 A.R. Akela, *Kanshiram ke Sakshatkar* [Kanshiram's interviews], Delhi: Manak Publications, 2007, p. 162.
24 Satnam Singh, *Bahujan Nayak*, p. 82; R.K. Singh, *Kanshiram aur BSP: Dalit Andolan ke Vaicharik Adhar Brahmanvad Virodh* [Kanshiram and BSP: Dalit movement's ideological viewpoint of anti-brahmanism], Allahabad: Kushwaha Book Publishers, 1994, p. 31.
25 Satnam Singh, *Bahujan Nayak*, p.55; Kanshiram, *Chamcha Yug,* p. 85.
26 Satnam Singh, *Bahujan Nayak*, p.56; Kanshiram, *Chamcha Yug*, pp. 80, 81.
27 Kanshiram, *Chamcha Yug*, pp. 93, 85.
28 Kanchan Chandra and Sangha Mittra, *Dalit Identity in the New Millennium: Dalit Leader*, Vol. 8, New Delhi: Commonwealth Publishers, 2003, pp. 167–70; Vinita Damodaran and Maya Unnithan-Kumar (Eds.), *Post-Colonial India History, Politics and Culture,* New Delhi: Manohar Publishers, 2000, p.136; R.K. Singh, *Dalit Andolan*, p. 29; Vivek Kumar, *India's Roaring Revolution: Dalit Assertions and New Horizons*, Delhi: Kalpaz Publications, 2006, p. 130; K.C. Das, *Indian Dalits*, p. 226.
29 Kanshiram, *Chamcha Yug*, p. 104; for an elaboration of 'types of stooges', see Kanshiram, *Chamcha Yug*, pp. 85–92.
30 Satnam Singh, *Bahujan Nayak*, p. 58.
31 Kanshiram, *Chamcha Yug*, p. 101; Vivek Kumar and Uday Sinha, *Dalit Assertion and Bahujan Samaj Party: A Perspective from Below,* Lucknow: Bahujan Sahitya Sansthan, 2001, p. 70.
32 Kanshiram, *Chamcha Yug*, pp. 96, 91, 92.
33 Kanshiram, *Chamcha Yug*, pp. 96, 97.
34 Satnam Singh, *Bahujan Nayak*, p. 72.
35 Kanshiram, *Chamcha Yug*, pp. 104, 105.
36 Kanshiram, *Chamcha Yug*, p. 97.
37 Ibid.
38 Ibid.
39 Kanshiram, *Chamcha Yug*, p. 87.
40 Ibid.
41 Kanshiram, *Chamcha Yug*, p. 100.
42 R.K. Singh, *Dalit Andolan*, p. 64.
43 Ibid
44 Kanshiram, *Chamcha Yug*, pp. 101, 104.

45 Jaffrelot, *India's Silent Revolution: The Rise of Lower Castes in North India,* New Delhi: Permanent Black, 2003, pp. 389, 390.
46 Kumari Mayawati, *Mere Sangharshmay Jeevan Evam Bahujan Movement ka Safarnama,* Part 1 [My Struggle in Life and the Travelogue of the Bahujan Movement], New Delhi: Bahujan Samaj Party, 2006, p. 278.
47 Duncan, *Dalit and Politics*, p. 40.
48 Kumari Mayawati, *Safarnama,* Part 1, p. 260; Shah, *Dalit Identity and Politics*, p. 293; K.C. Das, *Indian Dalits*, p. 148.
49 Bose, *Behenji*, p. 31; Vivek Kumar, *Roaring Revolution*, p. 116; Jaffrelot, *Silent Revolution*, pp. 389, 390; Corbridge,UK: Hariss, *Reinventing India,* p. 214.
50 Bose, *Behenji*, p. 33; Duncan, *Dalit and Politics*, p. 40.
51 Bose, *Behenji,* p. 33; Jaffrelot, *Silent Revolution,* p. 391; Hasan, *Party Politics in India,* pp. 379, 383; Duncan, *Bahujan Samaj Party,* p. 36; K.C. Das, *Indian Dalits,* p. 50; Ghanshyam Shah (Ed.), *Caste and Democratic Politics in India,* New Delhi: Permanent Black, 2002, p. 271; K. Chandra, *Why Ethnic Parties Succeed?,* pp. 217, 259, 260.
52 Jaffrelot, *Bahujan Samaj Party*, p. 36; Jaffrelot, *Ambedkar and Untouchability*, p. 155.
53 Niraja Gopal Jayal, Affirmative action in India: before and after the neo-liberal turn, *Cultural Dynamics*, 2015, 27, 1, p. 126; Kumari Mayawati, *Mere Sangharshmay Jeevan Evam Bahujan Movement ka Safar Nama* [My Struggle in Life and the Travelogue of the Bahujan Movement], Part I, New Delhi: Bahujan Samaj Party, 2006, pp. 278, 260.
54 Bose, *Behenji,* p. 33; Vivek Kumar, *Roaring Revolution,* p. 116; Sudha Pai, *Political Process in Uttar Pradesh: Identity, Economic Reforms and Governance,* New Delhi: Pearson Longmans, 2007, pp. 195, 196; Badri Narayan, 'Demarginalisation and history: dalit re-invention of the past', *South Asia Research*, 28, 2, July 2008, p. 172; Mohandass Namishray, *Bahujan Samaj*, Delhi: Neelkanth Prakashan, 2005, p. 23; Duncan, *Dalits and Politics,* p. 40; Badri Narayan, *Kanshiram: Leader of Dalits,* p. 39; Jayal, *Affirmative Action in India*, p. 126.
55 Namishray, *Bahujan Samaj,* pp. 22, 23.
56 Jaffrelot, *Bahujan Samaj Party*, p. 36; Duncan, *Dalit and Politics*, p. 40; Kalyani Shankar, *Gods of Power: Personality Cult and Indian Democracy*, New Delhi: Macmillan, 2002, p. 7, 8.

The popularity of the BAMCEF in north India among the salaried SC employees in the government sector can be gauged by the fact that between 1977 and 1980 the organization distributed 250,000 calendars in north India.

Gundimeda, *Dalit Politics in Contemporary India*, p. 88.

57 Bose, *Behenji,* p. 34; 'The changing scene in UP', *Frontline,* 11, 2, January 15–28, 1994, pp. 4–5; Sudha Pai, *Political Process in Uttar Pradesh*, p. 195; Gail Omvedt, *Reinventing Revolution*, Armonk, New York: M.E. Sharpe Incorporated, 1993, p. 67; Mayawati, Safarnama, Part I, pp. 261, 278.
58 Shah, *Caste and Democratic Politics*, p. 297.
59 Akela, *Sakshatkar*, p. 49.
60 A.K. Jha, *Dalitisation*, p. 106.
61 Kanshiram once stated: Industrialists like Tata and Birla are not amongst us; our society does not possess land and property; neither do our people have their own business. If we are to question as to who are the well-to-do class of an oppressed society, then it is (the) employees. It is this 'class' that can help in a more direct manner 'pay back' to our society; this class has the 'time, money, and talent' with itself.

Satnam Singh, *Bahujan Nayak,* pp. 32, 33; Vivek Kumar, *Roaring Revolution*, p. 118.

62 Namishray, *Bahujan Samaj*, p. 17.
63 Satnam Singh, *Bahujan Nayak*, p. 33.
64 Akela, *Sakshatkar*, p. 13.
65 V.D. Chandanshive, *Kanshiram The Crusader: A Golden Phase in Post-Ambedkarite Movement*, Nanded, Maharashtra: Blue Dawn Books, 2005, p. 27.
66 Kanshiram recalled that boys (in the village) would follow (him) saying *'paagal aaya hai'* (a mad person has come). During this period, Kanshiram started two periodicals 'Bahujan Sangathak' (*lit.* organization of the majority) in Hindi and Oppressed India, in English, simultaneously published from Punjab, Nagpur (Maharashtra) and Gujarat. In the cities, the BAMCEF offices formed of 'brotherhood' centres for city slum dwellers included medical and legal advice centres, and cooperative stores. In Uttar Pradesh, BAMCEF activities began to acquire a deep organizational presence. The Bhratri Sangh focused on the migrant population in the cities to 'escape hunger, poverty, and exploitation', while the Dastak Sangh targeted the rural population and looked into issues of education, job quota etc. for the Dalit-bahujan community. In addition, BAMCEF 'employees' were expected to educate the poor SC, ST, OBC, and religious minorities on laws, plans, programmes, rules, regulations and the state budget that apportioned programmes meant for the poor. Further, BAMCEF set up activity-centred bodies, such as, 'Historical Section', 'Volunteer Force', 'Awakening Squads', 'Parliamentary Contact Branch' etc.

   Chandanshive, *The Crusader*, pp. 27–28, Mayawati, *Safarnama,* Part 1, p. 274;

   Gundimeda, *Dalit Politics in Contemporary India*, pp. 87, 88.
67 Bose, *Behenji*, pp. 36, 37, 35; Sudha Pai, *Political Process in Uttar Pradesh: Identity, Economic Reforms and Governance*, New Delhi: Pearson Longmans, 2003, pp. 195, 196; Prahlad Gangaram Jogdand, *Dalit Movement in Maharashtra,* New Delhi: Kanak Publications, 1991, p. 238; Chandanshive. *The Crusader,* p. 27, Vivek Kumar, *Roaring Revolution,* p. 118.
68 Duncan, *Dalit and Politics*, p. 40; Vivek Kumar, *Roaring Revolution*, p. 118; Corbridge, Hariss, *Reinventing India*, p. 218.
69 Due to a stagnant economy, and consequently the lack of avenues for employment, state sector government jobs remained the most attractive career option for the upper castes, and quota-based reservation of jobs became the principal channel of upward mobility among the SCs.

   Chandra and Mittra, *Dalit Identity*, p. 163; Hasan, *Party Politics in India*, p. 391; Vivek Kumar, *Roaring Revolution*, p. 118; Corbridge, Hariss, *Reinventing India*, p. 218, Sudha Pai, *Political Process in Uttar Pradesh*, p. 192; Zoya Hasan, *Parties and Party Politics in India,* New Delhi: Oxford University Press, 2002; pp. 173, 174.
70 V.D. Chandanshive, *Kanshiram the Crusader: A Golden Phase in Post-Ambedkarite Movement*, Nanded, Maharashtra: Blue Dawn Books, 2005, p. 27.
71 The mainstream discourse on the Chamar caste in UP was apparently based on the flawed assumption about their occupation. The colonial official prepared a forceful case of Chamar 'criminality' based on their imagined caste occupation as 'leather workers' and their criminal proclivity for poisoning cattle to claim hides of dead cattle. Yet facts suggest that Chamars were primarily agricultural labourers (40%) and cultivators (40%), and only 4% were identified as leather workers, according to the 1911 census.

   By 1961, the number of Chamars identifies as cultivators (50%) had increased. In fact, it was the Muslims who dominated the leather industry in UP in the 20th century. The increase in the number of Chamars in the leather industry, especially since the latter half of the 1960s, was not because of tradition but it was one of the few employment opportunities available to them.

Javed Sheikh, Who needs identity? Dalit studies and the politics of recognition, *India Review*, 11, 2, 2012, pp. 202, 204.

Kanshiram's priority to actively engage the Chamars was not only based upon their demographic majority among SC groups in Uttar Pradesh or the fact that they had embraced 'bhakti resurgence' and Adi-Hindu as a means to fight 'segregation and exclusion' and social inequality in cantonments, civil lines, municipalities despite relaxation of caste subordination. It was based on numerous Chamar-Jatav associations (1917–1938) that were founded, which led to the crystallization of community 'notables' taking over the mantle of leadership of the Dalits in UP. Representing the 'cause of the Dalits' in municipal boards and legislative council following the general elections held in 1937 gave a clear indication that the Chamar-Jatavs were the vanguard of Dalit aspirations in UP, but in reality it demonstrated the vested interest of the Chamars to monopolize benefits that accrued from political concessions from the colonial government. Chamar 'politics' set in motion the institutionalization of political reformism, which played into the hands of the Congress Party.

Chandra and Mittra, *Dalit Identity*, pp. 177, 178; Sudha Pai, *Dalit Assertion*, pp. 77, 78; Jaffrelot, *Silent Revolution,* p. 90; Gundimeda, *Dalit Politics in Contemporary India*, p. 93.

72 Sudha Pai, *Dalit Assertion*, pp. 105, 106; Badri Narayan, *Kanshiram: Leader of the Dalits,* p. 46.

73 Sudha Pai, *Dalit Assertion,* pp. 83, 77, 78.

Despite being a numerical majority among SC population in UP, a majority of Chamars are at the receiving end in a semi-feudal land relation facing the Jats as the traditional landholding community in western UP, and in central-eastern UP face the brunt of non-cultivating landlords such as the Rajputs and intermediary tenant castes like Kurmis and Yadavs.

Chandra and Mittra, *Dalit Identity*, p. 163; Hasan, *Party Politics in India,* p. 391.

74 It is doubtful whether Kanshiram had a deeper understanding of colonial United Provinces (Uttar Pradesh), and specifically the land tenure system or the nature and origin of social activism among the subaltern poor or even the subsequent crystallization of non-elite movements centred on the intensification of caste identities. Kanshiram was ideologically clear about the political objectives to build a 'Bahujan State', that is a focus on using the tools of government institutions to affect a 'social transformation from above' by a subaltern elite rather than leading a movement pressuring for change through grassroots agitation. This subaltern elite was to be the Chamar leadership who were politically conscious and resourceful and had led a social movement cum institutional reform agenda through numerous caste-based associations since the colonial period till the second decade after independence, by which time it fell prey to the political machinations of the Congress Party. In a significant way, Kanshiram was traversing and reiterating the historical tradition of social elite-based political mobilization of the poor in UP, a state in which fundamental redistributive change had not occurred that could have forged a collective mobilization of the poor. To Kanshiram, Chamar social elites had a pivotal role to play to prepare the ground for 'organizing' bahujans; there was no other alternative course of politics to explore, emulate and pursue.

Gundimeda, *Dalit Politics in Contemporary India*, pp. 93, 94.

75 Chandra and Mittra, *Dalit Identity*, pp. 163, 168; Hasan, *Party Politics in India*, p. 391; Hasan, *Quest for Power,* pp. 72–76; Jaffrelot and Kumar, *Rise of Plebeians?*, p. 33, 40; Rajendra Vora and Suhas Palshikhar (Eds), *Indian Democracy: Meaning and Practices*, New Delhi: Sage Publications, 2004, pp.

273, 274; Vivek Kumar, *Roaring Revolution*, pp. 89, 90, 107; Chandra and Mittra, *Dalit Identity*, p. 168; Ghanshyam Shah, *Caste and Democratic Politics*, p. 405; Zoya Hasan, *Quest for Power*, pp. 31, 38. Jaffrelot and Kumar, *Rise of the Plebeians?*, p. 31; Sudha Pai, *Dalit Assertion*, pp. 82, 83, 77, 78; K. Chandra, *Why Ethnic Parties Succeed?*, p. 180; Sudha Pai, *Political Process in Uttar Pradesh*, pp. 192, 194, 195; Abhay Kumar Dubey, *Aaj ka Neta, Aalochnatmak Adhyayanmala: Kanshiram* [Today's Leader Kanshiram: A Critical Study], New Delhi: Rajkamal Prakashan, 1997, p. 58.

76 Badri Narayan, *Kanshiram: Leader of the Dalits*, New Delhi: Penguin Viking, 2014, p. 68; K.C. Das, *Indian Dalits: Voices, Visions and Politics*, Delhi: Global Vision Publishing House, 2004, p. 217.

77 Chandra and Mittra, *Dalit Identity*, pp. 163, 168; Hasan, *Party Politics in India*, p. 391; Hasan, *Quest for Power*, pp. 72–76; Jaffrelot and Kumar, *Rise of Plebeians?*, p. 33, 40; Rajendra Vora and Suhas Palshikhar (Eds), New Delhi: Sage Publications, 2004, pp. 273, 274; Vivek Kumar, Roaring Revolution, *Indian Democracy: Meaning and Practices* pp. 89, 90, 107; Chandra and Mittra, *Dalit Identity*, p. 168; Ghanshyam Shah, *Caste and Democratic Politics*, p. 405; Zoya Hasan, *Quest for Power*, pp. 31, 38. Jaffrelot and Kumar, *Rise of the Plebeians?*, p. 31; Sudha Pai, *Dalit Assertion*, pp. 82, 83, 77, 78; K. Chandra, *Why Ethnic Parties Succeed?*, p. 180; Sudha Pai, *Political Process in Uttar Pradesh*, pp. 192, 194, 195; Abhay Kumar Dubey, *Aaj ka Neta, Aalochnatmak Adhyayanmala: Kanshiram* [Today's Leader Kanshiram: A Critical Study], New Delhi: Rajkamal Prakashan, 1997, p. 58.

78 Like its predecessor, the UPRPI did maintain a tradition of organizational protests. In the 1940s, organizational politics featured a 'massive parade' in the district of Agra against the Poona Pact; the branding of Gandhi and Jagjivan Ram as 'traitors'; equating Ambedkar with Ram, who was to be addressed as 'Bhim' by supporters, and even bargaining with the colonial government for 17% reservation for Dalits in state legislative bodies and government jobs. The UPRPI had influential leaders such as T.C. Kureel, Chedi Lal Saathi and B.P. Maurya. In 1957, a year before the inception of the party in Agra, Maurya organized a 'conversion meeting' where 100 000 Jatavs converted to Buddhism. In the 1962 state assembly election, the party entered into a coalition with the Muslims in the background of the rioting that took place, killing 36 Muslims, and won 8 assembly seats in western UP. In 1964, the party organized a political struggle to occupy fallow lands which led to the arrest of 30,000 activists. Such means to demand a radical redistribution of land and agricultural reform to improve the economic position of the lower castes continued. By the late 1960s, a political schism appeared within the party as a section of UPRPI leaders left the party on grounds that the party was abdicating 'class interests' even as an increasing number of leaders began to sway towards identitarian mobilization of Buddhists, SC, ST and OBCs. Further, a section of middle class Chamar-dominated UPRPI leaders began to show the desire for participation in the 'new constitutional order' supporting laws such as untouchability and reservation of seats in state legislature to enter the power structure in state politics. In this endeavour, they began to support the Congress Party. Sensing a political opportunity, the Congress began to '[promote] or co-opt' UPRPI untouchable leaders. Like the UPSCF, the RPI confined to the same districts of Agra, Meerut, Kanpur, Lucknow and Allahabad besieged by organizational weakness that failed to mobilize a 'trapped' [Dalit] community submerged in a larger Hindu identity. By the 1967 assembly elections, the UPRPI's vote share in its area of influence had shrunk substantially. A political crisis gripped the UPRPI as it lay marginalized, suffering 'ideological opaqueness'.

Sudha Pai, *Dalit Assertion*, pp. 77, 78.

Jaffrelot, *Silent Revolution*, p. 90; Vivek Kumar, *Roaring Revolution*, p. 107, 84; Gundimeda, *Dalit Politics in Contemporary India*, pp. 58–64.

79 Sudha Pai, *Political Process in Uttar Pradesh*, pp. 192, 194, 195; Vivek Kumar, *Roaring Revolution*, p. 107; Sudha Pai, *Dalit Assertion*, pp. 82, 83; Abhay Kumar Dubey, *Aaj ka Neta, Aalochnatmak Adhyayanmala: Kanshiram* [Today's Leader Kanshiram: A Critical Study], New Delhi: Rajkamal Prakashan, 1997, p. 58.

80 Jaffrelot, *Silent Revolution*, p. 393

81 Sudha Pai, *Political Process in Uttar Pradesh*, p. 196; Jaffrelot, *Bahujan Samaj Party*, p. 37; Shah, *Caste and Democratic Politics*, p. 269; Sudha Pai, *Dalit Assertion*, p. 101; Jaffrelot, *Bahujan Samaj Party*, p. 37;

82 Duncan, *Dalit and Politics*, p. 40.

83 Satnam Singh, *Bahujan Nayak*, p. 35; Bose, *Behenji*, p. 57.

84 Satnam Singh, *Bahujan Nayak*, p. 35; Kanshiram, *Chamcha Yug*, pp. 114–18.

85 Bose, *Behenji*, pp. 58, 59

86 Akela, *Sakshatkar*, p. 14; Shah, *Caste and Democratic Politics*, p. 299; Kanshiram, *Chamcha Yug*, pp. 114–18

87 Satnam Singh, *Bahujan Nayak*, pp. 34–35; Jayashree Gokhale, *From Concessions to Confrontation: The Politics of an Indian Untouchable Community*, Bombay: Popular Prakashan, 1993, p. 238; Kanshiram, *Chamcha Yug*, pp. 114–18.

> On the question of a bicycle being the cheapest and most effective means of transport for the marginalized Dalits, Manohar Ate, a close friend and associate of Kanshiram in his Pune days recounts that a small Irani hotel in Pune was the meeting place for Kanshiram, where late till night he would discuss his political vision for a Bahujan Samaj. On one occasion his cycle was stolen. Exasperated Kanshiram vented his spleen that if the cycle was not found he would report it to the police. Finally, the cycle was found; it had been stolen by a waiter who had returned it upon the threat of a police complaint. Ate had asked him as to why was he so angry over the loss of a cycle. Kanshiram replied that 'the cycle was not just "an iron vehicle". It [was] the most important instrument for enhancing the movement. [W]hen the cycle was stolen, I felt as if I had lost my life'.
>
> Badri Narayan, *Kanshiram: Leader of the Dalits,* pp. 35, 36.

88 This fact was confirmed by Mr. Ambeth Rajan in an interview, New Delhi, January 21, 2009. Mr. Ambeth Rajan, a former LIC officer and an ex-BSP MP joined the BSP in 1984. He is often considered as a 'joint founding member' of the party with Kanshiram. Subsequently he became the personal secretary of Kanshiram. He was treasurer of BSP from 1984 to 2006. In July 2020, he joined the BJP. At present he heads the state BJP unit in Tamil Nadu. Interview with Ram Achal Rajbhar, Hardwar, UP, April 14, 2009. He also said that in 1983 Kanshiram and his supporters led a cycle march from Kanyakumari to Jammu, traveling 4,500 km.

Ghanshyam Shah, *Dalit Identity and Politics: Cultural Subordination and Dalit Challenge,* Vol. 2, New Delhi: Sage Publications, 2001, p. 298; Badri Narayan, *Kanshiram: Leader of the Dalits*, pp. 54, 55.

89 Mayawati, a resident of Badalpur, Ghaziabad, was a young Dalit school teacher belonging to the Chamar-Jatav community, having graduated from a Delhi University college. After completing her B.Ed. from a Ghaziabad college, which was affiliated to Meerut University, she 'took up a job of a government school teacher, and consequently enrolled herself in first year of LLB course in Delhi University'. Attending functions with her entire family to celebrate Ambedkar Jayanti on April 14 was not uncommon to her, but it is clear that before she

grasped Ambedkar's politics and social philosophy, the awe and respect accorded to the Dalit icon mesmerized her. After school hours she was already involved in activities of the BAMCEF. But what caught Kanshiram's attention was the 'courage shown by Mayawati at a three-day conference organized by the Janata Party at Delhi's Constitution Club in September 1977 to discuss ways and means of fighting caste prejudices'. The 'irrepressible Raj Narain, at the height of his political fame having defeated Indira Gandhi from Rai Bareilly in the just concluded general elections, and one of the chief speakers unmindful of the furore he might create, continued to refer to the untouchables as 'Harijans'. Mayawati got up when her turn came to speak and lashed out at Raj Narain, his party and government, as well as the entire political mainstream for what she considered insulting to the SC community by the usage of the term 'Harijan'. Mayawati pointed out that Ambedkar had used the term Scheduled Castes and not Harijans in the Constitution to designate Dalits. She also did not miss an opportunity to condemn Gandhi's followers. She ended her speech with slogans 'Down with Raj Narain', 'Down with the Janata Party', hailing the memory of Babasaheb Ambedkar. Leaders and activists from various organizations representing the Scheduled Castes crowded around Mayawati and congratulated her for showing such courage. The defining political moment between Kanshiram and Mayawati came shortly thereafter. On one wintry December night in 1977, as Mayawati sat after dinner with her pile of books to study for the Indian Administrative Services (IAS) entrance examinations, the 'holy grail' that all aspiring educated SC's must achieve to advance socially and economically in life, Kanshiram came to the house to meet her. Kanshiram, by now a known SC leader-activist tutored Mayawati on the futility of becoming a collector. He said: 'I think you are making a big mistake' and further 'by being a collector you would not be able to serve [your] community', much to her father's surprise and disappointment. Then Kanshiram emphatically stated: 'Your courage, dedication to the Dalit cause and many other sterling qualities has come to my notice. I can make you such a big leader one day that not one but a row of collectors will line up with files in front of you waiting for orders. You can then truly serve the community and get things done'. Kanshiram's vision had indeed influenced Mayawati. To Mayawati 'the irresistible tug of the brave new world of political adventure could not be matched by the safe enclosure of government service bound by rules and regulations.' The conflict between Kanshiram, Mayawati and her father continued for quite a few years. Mayawati gave up her aspirations to be an IAS officer as she became increasingly involved in the activities of BAMCEF. Finally, matters came to a head between father and daughter one day. Prabhu Das served his daughter an ultimatum: 'Either you stop meeting Kanshiram, give up this silly politics and start preparing for the IAS examinations or leave my house immediately'. 'Mayawati took out the money that she had saved from her schoolteacher's salary, packed a few clothes and belongings in a suitcase and simply walked out of the house that she had grown up in. She took shelter in the BAMCEF office at Karol Bagh. Later she moved in with her brother Siddharth into a rented one-room accommodation facilitated by Kanshiram'.

Bose, *Behenji*, pp. 21, 22, 23, 26, 42, 43, 45, 46, 57, 65; Kanshiram, *Chamcha Yug*, pp. 101, 104; Satnam Singh, *Bahujan Nayak*, p. 35.

3 The Enterprise of Social Justice

BSP: Institutionalizing a 'Unique' Dalit Politics

The DS-4s 'push into politics' began with limited political activity as an 'unrecognized registered political party' in the 1982 Haryana assembly elections. The 'quasi-political outfit' put up 46 candidates and expectedly none of its candidates won. But the real intention of DS-4 was to measure the low-caste support base,[1] which according to its estimate suggested an 'increasing vote share'. A year later, in 1983, the DS-4 selected 'several dozen candidates' for elections to the legislative assembly in Delhi and Jammu and Kashmir.[2]

The initial political experience gathered by the DS-4 among the Dalit masses and the 'organizational overreach' of the BAMCEF convinced Kanshiram to form the Bahujan Samaj Party (BSP) on 'Ambedkar's birthday' (April 14) in 1984. The formation of a 'full-fledged political party did not imply much more than a change of name, but by rechristening his organization that way Kanshiram consummated his shift 'towards party politics'.[3] Even before the founding of the BSP, Kanshiram had begun to streamline political responsibilities for a future 'political task' between the two complementary 'halves' for a new age Dalit movement in Uttar Pradesh. One, the 'educated' (BAMCEF) members of the party would control the 'election office' and 'election accounts'; two, 'party workers' and 'party cadres', many of whom were DS-4 activists handpicked as 'coordinators' by Kanshiram, would 'fulfil BAMCEF objectives' of 'fanning out' into villages, small towns and cities to provide 'accurate information' of the 'ground realities' of UP.[4] After the formation of the BSP, Kanshiram's 'endless ventures' into politics of caste to build a bahujan samaj'[5] began with an electoral strategy in 'pockets of influence' in particular localities in eastern UP. It was to be the initial electoral base whose specific 'Dalit' socio-political profile made them receptive to the ideology of the party.[6]

Positioning Ideological Politics beyond a Philosophical Complexity of Caste

To understand Bahujan Samaj Party's organizational effort to resurrect a failed 'Dalit project' in Uttar Pradesh in the early 1980s, one does not need to

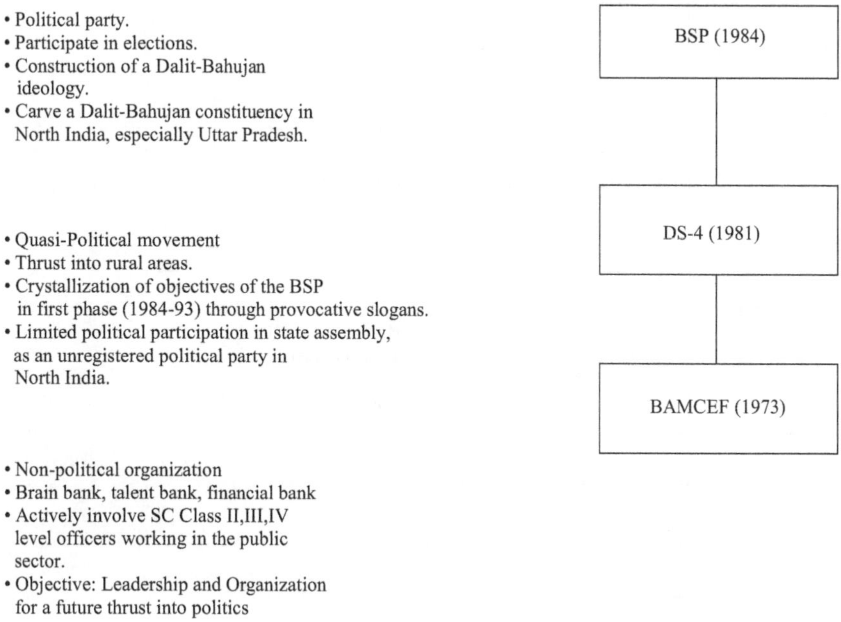

Figure 3.1 Formation of the BSP. *Source*: Author.

enter into a debate on the multiverse of bahujan struggle. Understandably, based upon his perception of an 'appropriate' Dalit-Bahujan politics, Kanshiram, was, at the onset, disinclined to engage with the central question that bahujan thinkers and philosophers have grappled over a century – humiliation and deprivation of self-respect that are characteristically marked out by social institutions that Dalit and lower castes confront and which leave a long-term impact on the constitution of their selves. Certainly, for the same reason, Kanshiram, while symbolizing Phule's 'anti-Brahminical ideology', did not explore Phule's ideas within objective historical and social conditions that defined the sufferance of the poor and the oppressed. Neither did the BSP leader introspect the legitimate grounds for a specific form of political struggle, for instance, nurturing 'bahujan culture', not necessarily the 'valorization', as Phule stated, but on an insistence of political form to egalitarian aspects of customs and traditions of caste groups against brahminical hegemonic social and political systems of thought, social order and political governance. Kanshiram does not mention the need to elevate Phule's universalistic dimension of human rights that would have formed the context not only of the 'reconstitution of the self, an endorsement of equality based rights', but also provide space for the 'realization of rights, claims and responsibilities that are equal with shared public and community experience when

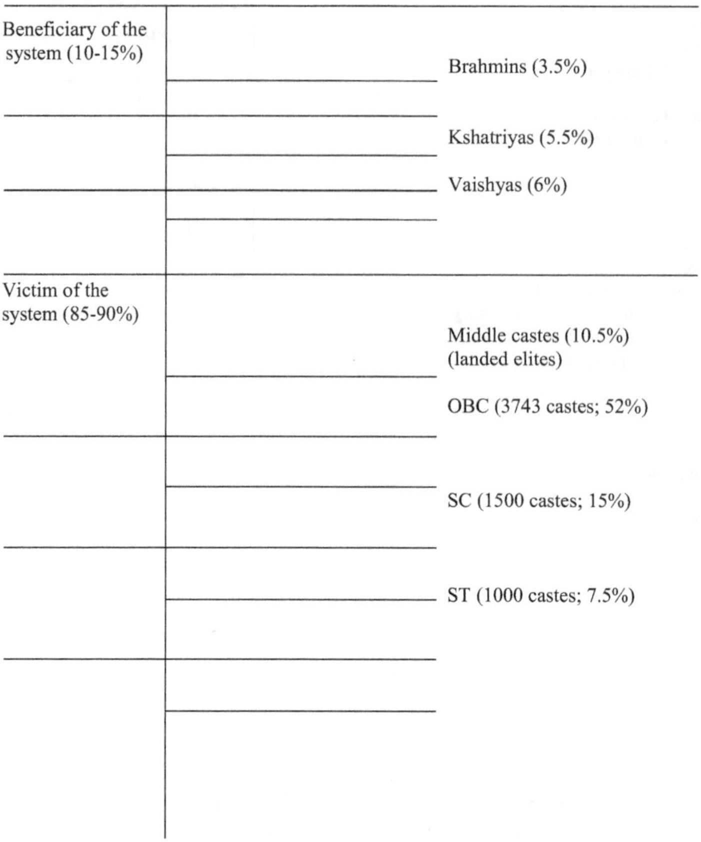

Figure 3.2 An Ideological Expose on Brahminism. *Source*: Kanshiram, *Chamcha Yug* (An Era of Stooges), Nagpur, Samta Prakashan, 1998, p. 124.

values deeply inimical to rights rule the roost in the domain of society'.[7] If the discursive traditions of humiliation, self-respect and a substantive conceptualization of equality did not find mention, it is unlikely that Kanshiram reflected upon the deep and complex relational engagement between a 'modernized caste identity and a range of acts that produce caste stigma – spatial segregation, sexual violation, the use of insults and epithets, demeaning caste labour and the caste body; caste massacres; technologies of the body from rules governing physical proximity to the comportment of the physical body and its appearance – in essence caste violence'.[8]

Instead, the political ideology of the BSP was exclusively oriented to turn the party into an 'institution to retrieve authentic democracy' – by upturning a discriminatory 'Brahmanical (social) order', using caste as a tool of political mobilization by working from within the caste structure to win political power and establish a 'Dalit-Bahujan' state. In a broader sense, it meant that the BSP premised that

> if individuals (were) part of castes and castes (were) part of the hierarchically organized social order then the first step towards the realization of an "individual-based society" (equal treatment of individuals) would (have to) be equalization of castes rather than annihilation of castes.

This ideological position was logically justified since 'a Dalit (was) discriminated against and humiliated not because of his personality or behaviour but his caste. Thus, caste would be used against caste to weaken caste-mindset'.[9] Apparently, viewed in this perspective, Ambedkar's vision of a casteless society was theoretically sound but was practically unrealizable. Kanshiram's abrasive ideology 'mobilized caste against caste-based hegemony' by castigating 'the Aryan ruler, the modern-day avatar (the) the savarna (who would) never work for the (bahujans) betterment'.[10] It became evident that BSP was seeking to demarcate a constituency of the socially oppressed shaped by 'Dalit assertiveness' posited as an 'oppositional caste ideology', the 'irreconcilable opposite' that would contest the pervasive hegemony of the 'manuvadi order'. Fighting upper caste dominance would require a politically organized Dalit-led Bahujans caste groups deemed as numerically strong to 'subvert the existing political structure' and capture political power not by 'piggy-backing' on the upper castes.[11] It would not be a substitution of power holders solely by a Dalit-Bahujan class, leaving undisturbed a predisposition of a prejudicial mentalite′ of a 'Brahminical Social Order' which would entail a static subordinate position of the subaltern majority controlled by a 'minority' upper caste section of society. What the BSP advocated was a thesis of 'social transformation' centred on the desired indication of the position of power, that is the superordinate position dalit-bahujans would occupy, and who would condescend 'minority upper caste rule'. In sum, BSP's conceptualization of social justice was 'not (to be) a moral and ethical position, but a plan of action and a tool for mobilization' to be 'constructed and modified by the bahujan leadership, based upon the exigencies of the situation'. The declared objective of the party was to gain 'access and exclusive control over state structures to accomplish the administrative and political potential within the state necessary towards the emancipation of the bahujans' by 'altering and effecting the implementation of existing government policies rather than the enactment of new legislations' in favour of the poor.[12]

However, Kanshiram's premise on the possibility of a successful Dalit-Bahujan politics was based upon a specific observation that outlined a changed political perception: the primacy of elected institutions and its ability to influence state structures over non-elected institutions such as the police and the bureaucracy which '(did) not trump the elected institutions'.

This 'new axis of empowerment politics was crucial to the prospect of improving the (social life) of the marginalized sections in society'. In such a way, political power would be directed towards an increase in share of a wide array of state benefits and activation of laws that would seek protection 'from entrenched (social) prejudices' to address the dual inequalities of status (dignity) and income (material welfare).[13]

A Political Language to Local Caste Histories

An ideological critique of the 'Brahminical Social Order' (BSO), the social axis upon which the politics of caste was to be based, required an anti-hegemonic narrative of bahujan culture. Kanshiram took a lead role in endorsing a political language representative of the actual symbols of the people by providing a critique of the 'Brahminical cultural dominance'. He said (that) 'epics, scriptures and ancient religious texts such as the Vedas, Puranas, Ramayana and Mahabharata were full of falsehood and fiction (that) have been used to maintain the intellectual, economic and cultural superiority of upper castes (elites)'.[14] To reverse the dominant narrative, the Dalit-Bahujan narrative had to be contextualized in a 'political (cultural) education programme' by 'collating local caste histories to reconstruct bahujan and Dalit literature. It was meant to create "an alternative grand Dalit history" for the "bahujan class", reminding them of their ancestors ruling the country when India was known worldwide for its prosperity'. Historically, Uttar Pradesh had 'mapped socio-cultural resistance through religious reform movements', such as the Bhakti movements led by saints like Kabir, Ravidas, Shiv Narayan, Daria Sahib and Jagjivan Das popular among the Dalits. The point was to identify and provide the emerging 'recognizable centres of heterogeneous anti-Brahminical social forces', the cultural means for political empowerment in the state.[15]

To the BSP, caste as a 'shared experience' consisted not only of experience of oppression but also 'internal life of the community, such as history, myths, beliefs, community practices', along with the biographical histories of specific caste leaders, and it could 'construct political identities for determining access to resources and entitlement to rights in a modern democracy'. Since the mid-1980s, Kanshiram directed party activists to organize 'symbols of identity' by way of popularizing local heroes of various castes and communities to mobilize illiterate and semi-literate Dalits at the grassroots level. The BSP was seeking to construct a Dalit public sphere – an alternative space where stories of historical oppression, stigma and humiliation, and a sense of dignity and self-respect, were to be inculcated among the Dalit public. A Dalit public sphere was expected to be fashioned as a 'social forum to create a Dalit identity which would be articulated and reconstructed to acquire political power'. Further, it was widely believed that the 'attainment of political power would concomitantly usurp the hegemonic public space'. On face value, 'the social space of the Dalits hitherto restricted to segregated pockets of villages and cities would be transformed by the BSP'. The BSP believed that in such a way, large segments of Dalit castes would be aligned with the party under the rubric of 'bahujanwad'. Local cadres and 'intellectuals', mainly 'school teachers', at the block level, who were 'interested in folklore and history, were instructed to collect information from various castes about their caste history, caste heroes and panthis (sects)'. 'Kanshiram appealed to such Dalit "writers" or intellectuals to write booklets – about fifty to sixty pages long – highlighting the "problems" and "achievements" of the Dalits, Adivasis and OBC groups', but, more importantly, through their writing engage in the task of 'resurrecting' the life stories of Dalit caste heroes, saints and such other 'important political figures'. A 'political face' to these "heroes" sometimes included the narrative itself, which had a description of the 'hero', but 'often they needed to create an image that would fit into the general narrative when no other visual source was available'. 'Sketches were developed and statues of local Dalit heroes came up across UP'. Local caste heroes were concentrated in their 'regions of popularity',[16] for instance, Jhalkaribai, belonging to the Kori caste in Hamirpur, Lalitpur, Banda; Bijli Maharaj, a Pasi, in Lucknow, Bahraich, Barabanki, Jaunpur, Allahabad; Veer Pasi of Awadh in Pratapgarh, Sultanpur, Allahabad; Buddhists of Poorvanchal region such as Mahamaya in Varanasi, Ghazipur, Ballia, Basti, Deoria; Sant Ravidas of Chamars in Varanasi, Jaunpur, Allahabad and Azamgarh among others.

Organizational efforts were also made to revivify narratives claiming a 'respectable and valiant position' for the Dalits in Hindu mythology and the 1857 rebellion against the British East India Company. The heroism of Shambhuk in 'Shambhuk Vada' (The Killing of Shambhuk), who endured all difficulties imposed on him by Brahmins; the 'treacherous role' played by Brahmins and Kshatriyas to dispossess lower castes; the story of 'Ekalavya's Tyaag' (The Sacrifice of Ekalavya); the 'sacrifice' of the Dalits in the 1857 rebellion eulogized in 'Veer Naari Jhalkaribai' (The Valiant Lady Jhalkaribai) and 'Dalit ki beti Udadevi' (The Daughter of a Dalit Udadevi) along with the other unsung heroes of the 'rebellion' such as Ballu Mehtar, Udariya Pasi, Chetram Jatav, Banki Chamar, Ganga Baksh, Malka Pasi, Matadin Bhangi, Avantibai Pannadhai, Mahaviridevi etc. became prominent representative symbols of Dalit consciousness.[17]

The folk cultural productive form of 'mela' (fairs) that was quite popular in the late 1970s under BAMCEF's 'awakening programmes' was now put to use by the BSP in Uttar Pradesh. 'Melas' vividly portraying political messages through 'folk' drama, such as 'Shahuji Maharaj mela' advocating reservation; 'Periyar' and 'Ambedkar mela' that critiqued the caste order; 'Buddha Jayanti mela' or 'Phule's mela' focusing on solidarity of the majority and education for the poor'; melas were also organized concerning Sant Ravidas, Kabir, Swami Achutyananda, Chokamela, Satnam Guru, Ghasidas and others. There were other entrants to BSP's folk 'political' melas such as 'Jhalkaribai Leela' and the 'Shambhuk Leela'. Both the folk dramas idealized previously 'demonized characters' such as Ravana and Kansa and critiqued the 'moral nature' of traditional heroes like Ram and Krishna.

Kanshiram clearly believed that 'political fairs' could operate beyond structures of cultural dominance and become a medium to 'tell and retell' the stories of heroes, both 'mythological and local, become a purveyor for building memorials, statues', organize celebrations around stories of struggle and autonomy in order to 'create a collective memory in the minds of the Dalits'.[18]

Despite initial potential in the possibility of creating a dalit public sphere — resist dominant caste order through multiple counter-narratives and protest — it became apparent that Kanshiram was aiming to build a legitimate political front of oppressed classes in their ethnic denominations suitable for the party to pursue political power in Uttar Pradesh. The more sustained and difficult task of institutionalizing an autonomous sphere of protest was never intended to be the primary goal. This would become evident over years as material iconography as the living manifestation of dalit history and culture became inextricably linked to BSP's ethnic politics.

Constructing a Politics of 'Caste': Ideology and Exhortative 'Truth-Telling'

Even as a political effort to create an anti-Brahmanical autonomous 'collective memory of the exploited and oppressed' began, Kanshiram engaged in an ideological diatribe against an oppressive 'anti-Dalit BSO'. In his informal interactions with BSP activists, Kanshiram would highlight the '(political) struggles undertaken by such (Dalit) leaders' and the way (they resisted) the manuvadi samaj. He added:

> the pain that our forefathers (Dalit heroes and saints) (had) endured (was) something (the Dalit-bahujans of today) (had) not seen and (that) (the bahujan samaj) (had) made a big mistake of tolerating injustice (because) the (community) (was) unaware of (social) inequality. (They) (had) become a community used to living in poverty.

Kanshiram urged party activists to analyze that 'if (they) did not have the source of information (of their subjugated selves) then how could (they) be able to end (their) present "state of hurt" as well as be prepared to face obstacles that would (emerge) [*sic*] in the future?' Kanshiram cautioned that

> the manuvadi samaj (would) ensure that the contributions of (Dalit) leaders (were) stopped from reaching the poor. Thus, (BSP) must (appreciate) the contributions made by (Dalit leaders) at different places, at different times; and then 'work on them',[19] that is analyze their thoughts for possible modes of social and political action by the poor.

Kanshiram focuses on another crucial aspect of Brahminical dominance that is legitimized through electoral politics. The 'plight of the oppressed' under 'brahman ki boli, Thakur ki goli and bania ki jholi' (the sermon of the Brahmin, the bullet of the Thakur and the purse of the Bania), that signifies a culture of denial, violence and exploitation endorsed by 'Savarna' political parties, such as the Congress Party, Bharatiya Janata Party (BJP), the two communist political parties and a number of regional political parties across different regions in India (to legitimize) the iniquitous and exploitative caste-based social structure. Further, these political parties are 'no changers' and 'uphold consciously the degrading character of the social and political system'. Thus, 'Brahmins and other upper castes' and the political elite (have managed) to control society by means of 'mean (political) tactics', such as vote banks, money power, false promise, and the policy of divide and rule.[20] Kanshiram contends that a conceptual understanding of the political hegemony of the 'savarna class' must emphasize the predicament of electoral practice and caste votes, the operation of 'Brahminical political parties' catering to the 'exclusive alpjan (minority) caste' fellowmen in a 'democratic system' and the consequent emergence of the 'exclusive governing elite'. In contradistinction, exploitation of subaltern groups, in sufferance of atrocities, economic insecurity, social exclusion and powerlessness under an 'unrepresentative' government must acquire the broad political frames for a bahujan struggle.

To shape BSP's 'project' of social justice, Kanshiram asserts:

> 'Do not expect anyone's support; we do not oppress anyone; but we would not tolerate injustice perpetuated on us; once we stand on our legs, we would provide an answer to those who oppress us'. Political activity is (required) to construct an 'authentic' Dalit which is contrasted (to) the negated persona of the marginalized identified with a life (of) 'perpetual bondage' (that) is manifested in a timid character and an effaced personality. (With) the aim to inspire the Dalit-Bahujan community towards greater unity Kanshiram states that 'we must use (our) small resources in big numbers' (and) counsels that 'slaves die not a martyrs death' (but prefer) 'kutte ki maut marna' (a dogs death); that 'enslaved people move on in life with "dande aur joote" (sticks and shoes)'. On an optimistic note, Kanshiram alludes to the fact that the Dalit-Bahujan community through 'caste-unity' '(must) proceed (ahead) without (any) support and '(take) responsibility (to protect their) rights'. They must bring '(political) change' through a more "vote-based government" and democracy'. They must stop voting for the upper caste political parties '(who) buy and loot votes of the exploited Dalit-OBC community. Further, (the majority oppressed community) must not give (their) vote to anyone except (themselves) and build strength to protect (their) votes. In this way (bahujan) 'caste votes' would be used as political resource to deny the upper caste the space to manipulate (elections).[21]

The 'Dalit' 'Bahujan' Mobilization: Problematic Politics

The BSP became a 'lightening rod' for educated Chamar who financed the party and became its early political leaders. The search for Chamar 'Dalit' community leaders appeared never to be in scarcity since there were overwhelming responses to enlist as 'cadres' to set up local party units. As one BSP local leader described it:

> If there was a community leader in the village, someone educated, we caught hold of them. If he was not useful, we found another, preferably his rival. Then we added on others. We found ready-made community leaders wherever we went.[22]

The biographies of some of the early BSP members in UP reveal them all to be 'college-educated, in the age group of 20s and 30s, and engaged in some form of political or associational activity before joining the BSP'.[23] The emergence of Chamar SC leaders coincided with their newly acquired status of becoming a 'modernizing elite' for the party.[24] However, the dominant Chamar caste prevented the incorporation of other castes such as the Balmikis and Pasis within the party.[25] This became evident with the total overlap between the 'legislative' and 'organizational' wing of the party, which ensured that those who headed local party units were mostly Chamars and were also the BSP's election candidates.[26] In eastern and western UP, 80% of 'party' posts were occupied by members of the Chamar caste. It is only at the lowest level of the party organization that a broadening of the caste profile of the BSP could be seen.[27]

An exclusive 'political constituency' of Chamars/Jatavs, who constitute nearly 60% of SC population and marginal political support among other SC communities would not turn the 'electoral arithmetic' in BSP's favour.[28] It was worth a political scrutiny since the emphasis was to be on 'bahujan politics' (inclusive of non-Dalit poor), a long-term electoral strategy of Kanshiram interwoven in the political agenda of the BSP. The significance of the nomenclature 'bahujan' was evident. In fact, the name 'bahujan' adopted at the founding of the BSP was not only a conscious decision but also a strategic political move to suggest that the new party was a 'party that (could) win, with a majority'.[29] Two premises underlined the party's political decision to strategize a wider social constituency. Firstly, 'Dalit political parties were constantly vulnerable to the accusation that they were casteist' and were aware that 'if they are successful in consolidating particular caste groups, they may appear to be uninterested in the welfare of others'. Secondly, Dalit groups, despite prospects of economic mobility due to modernization, continue to be excluded from resource and opportunity structures of the state's economy due to the perpetuation of caste discrimination. Primarily, Dalits appear in the rank of agricultural labourers. As is peculiar to the demography of the state, like other caste groups,

Dalits do not form a dominant preponderant caste group across a set of assembly and Parliamentary constituencies in Uttar Pradesh. Simply put, if in a region(s) in or across the state other non-Dalit caste groups are united against Dalits, the latter stand to lose in elections. Addressing an Ambedkar rally in 1991 one BSP leader outlined this political dilemma and contended in unequivocal terms:

> It is possible to consolidate the (SC) vote, but that will not suit my purpose. If (they) vote overwhelmingly for the BSP it might alienate other components of the bahujans like 'backwards' and Muslims. I am trying to unite all these groups.[30]

Therefore, built in within the 'project of bahujanwad' has always been the political priority of forging an 'electoral pact' with non-Dalit exploited groups that would centrepiece the interests of the Dalits.[31]

BSP and the 'Political Partnership' of Backward Caste Blocs

Posing a neo-Ambedkarite electoral strategy – Phule's notion of war between Aryans and the backwards – based upon the ideal of fraternization, the BSP began to mobilize the exploited bahujans, the '50% landless', and the marginal farming community who were 'identified as supporters of the BSP'.[32]

In an election campaign speech in Haryana in 1987 Kanshiram said:

> The other limb of the bahujan samaj which we call OBC needs this party badly. Thirty-nine years after independence, these people have neither been recognized nor have they obtained any rights; (and) the government of this country is 'not ready to recognize them'; under Article 340[33] of the Indian Constitution, (and) the Kaka Kalelkar (Commission) (while the) Mandal Commission Report was not considered on the pretext that there are more than 3,000 castes that (could be listed) as OBC. Thus among 85% of the population, 52% are 'without recognizable identity and rights'. When these castes are not even recognized, where is the question of obtaining their rights?[34]

Continuing further Kanshiram contended:

> (That) in India there are very few District Magistrates (DM) from the (poorer backward castes) much less than even SCs.[35] If in the republic (Republic of India) 52% of the people cannot participate, then where (is) the system in which they (could) participate? Brahmin and Kshatriyas (have taken) away the rights of the backward classes. They are 'grossly over-represented' in public services, in Parliament and in (State) Legislative Assemblies[36] due to the (support) of the bahujan-majority (who) have 'got partnership in the form of a minority'.[37]

Addressing another public rally to the backward castes in Haryana in April 1987, Kanshiram outlined the political solution: the electoral voting strength of bahujan unity that would affect electoral losses to 'savarna governments'. He said:

> The 'Congress government is existing because of the votes of the backward classes; the day the backward classes "open their eyes and start understanding what is good or bad for them", that day they would ensure that the chances of Congress (and it possibly means other non-Congress "savarna" political parties) capturing political power is finished. That government which continues to exploit the votes of the backward classes but does not do anything to reduce their backwardness (cannot) stay in power' (forever).[38]

Addressing the problem of 'under-representation' of this majority section of the 'backwards', who endured discrimination and exploitation by a combination of upper castes-OBC landlords, Kanshiram admitted that SCs were comparatively better than 'this component of the bahujan samaj' at least as far as state services were concerned. The SCs and STs had a presence in administration and government because of the 'quota system', and hence, a special (political) effort had to be undertaken in favour of 'non-recognized' OBCs. Kanshiram's political rallies were intending to effect a community-invoked notion of a monolithic Dalit low-caste poor that would expectedly materialize into a broader social solidarity, outlining a vast electoral potential for the party.

On July 18, 1989, a public protest march from Lal Qila (Red Fort) to the Boat Club, Delhi, was undertaken by BSP leaders to implement the 'satyagrahi' Mandal Commission Report. With the slogan 'vote hamara raj tumhara nahi chalega, nahi chalega' (our votes, your rule, it cannot go on, it cannot go on), Mayawati addressed the public gathering as it reached Boat Club, asserting that 'since the self-serving OBC leaders could not carry on the "struggle", the BSP had decided to take responsibility to lead the backward communities';[39] and further, that 'rights were (being) snatched and to snatch rights (from the upper castes) strength needed to be built'.[40] At another BSP rally on December 29, 1989, held at Patel Chowk near the Indian Parliament, the BSP 'exposed' the National Front (1989–1990) government by criticizing Prime Minister V.P. Singh for the gap between 'kathan aur karni' (promise and performance) and raised political slogans for the implementation of the Mandal Commission'. On that day another BSP political rally marched from Ferozshah Kotla to the Indian Parliament with a slogan 'Mandal ayog lagu karo ya kursi khali karo' (implement the Mandal Commission or step down from the office/government).[41]

In Uttar Pradesh, the focal point of BSP's experiment with Dalit-Bahujan politics coincided with Mayawati's rising political stature as a Jatav Dalit leader. In a series of political meetings held between 1986 and 1988,

Mayawati, 'urged caution and struggle' as crucial to the unity of the Dalit-Bahujans. On a 'padyatra' (journey by foot) to Nainital in September 1986, Mayawati, in an interactive 'question and answer' political rally, attacked the (manipulative and exploitative) Congress government that had 'fooled' the masses (since independence). In the rally, she posed a political question: 'why, despite 95% Dalits voting for the Congress party, only 5% Dalit ministers/leaders were found in the Congress as against 55% Brahmins in Congress-ruled states.' She further stated that out of '22 chief ministers (in Congress-ruled states in 1986) not even one (was) a Dalit'. 'It (was) hopeless to even think that there (would) be a change of heart '(among) upper caste ministers and leaders (for the better)'. In successive political speeches, Mayawati emphasized the broader implications of political fraternization of the subaltern majority. At Mathura, on January 1, 1987, addressing a political rally Mayawati said that the 'principles of fraternity' (among the Dalits and bahujans) and the emergence of the BSP as a political force (was) a mutually enduring inclusive relationship that would ultimately lay the foundation of a 'legitimate majority government'.[42] At another political rally at Mainpuri in August 1987, Mayawati emphasized that fraternization was viewed as a political threat (by) a manuvadi government that did not want a 'ekattha aur ekjut' (to come together and be united) (bahujan) since a united bahujan samaj would bring progress to a 'upekshit aur nirdhan' (neglected and poor) community. On October 20, 1987, at Agra, Mayawati's political speech reiterated the need to 'fraternize as a means to liberate (bahujans) from oppression (and only then) come to power' (so that it) would then become possible to 'throttle the neck of our (manuvadi) enemy'. On the same day at Mathura, Mayawati affirmed that the principle of fraternization would identify two kinds of (political) enemies: first from 'our community', who are 'swarthy aur bikey huye' (self-interested and sold out), and second, the manuvadis'.[43] At Sitapur, in March 1988, Mayawati declared that 'fraternization' was 'bhaichara' (brotherhood), to be interpreted as an agency of equality through political (union). A close associate of Kanshiram emphasized that there would not be any further (degradation) of (low) caste groups but an 'upgradation in a representative political community'; fraternization would seek to imbue '(precepts) of equality' in an oppressive (casteist/ brahminical) political order.[44]

For a period of one year, between August 15, 1988, and August 15, 1989, Kanshiram launched 'five' 'social transformation movements' at an all-India level to highlight five interrelated themes on social justice: 'struggle for self-respect', 'struggle for liberation', 'struggle for equality', 'struggle to uproot caste' and 'struggle to unite a fragmented society' 'to liberate 85% Indians from injustice, oppression and terror'. These 'transformational movements' were patterned much in the same manner as the BAMCEF and DS-4 mobilization programmes. The BSP leader inaugurated a series of 'cycle rallies' that would begin from 'five different locations' in the country. The rallies began on September 17, 1988, from Kanyakumari, Tamil Nadu, on the occasion of the birthday of the 'Periyar'; the second rally began from Kohima, Nagaland; the third from Kargil, Jammu and Kashmir; the fourth from Puri, Odisha; and the fifth from Porbandar, Gujarat. On March 27, 1989, the 'five cycle marches' converged in Delhi. In the latter half of 1989, Kanshiram held a 'series of conferences' to once again highlight the BSP's political concern for the 'constituent parts of the bahujan samaj'. On September 10, 1989, at Moradabad, Uttar Pradesh, a conference was held to 'uphold the concern' for Muslims. On September 13, a conference for the Scheduled Castes was held in Delhi. On October 1, at Kanpur, Uttar Pradesh, a conference was held to 'attend to the cause' of the backward class.[45] On October 8, at Ludhiana, Punjab, a conference was addressed to the Sikh community. On October 15, two conferences were held: one at Bilaspur, Chhattisgarh, which focused on the 'interests of the Scheduled Tribes', and the other at Bangalore, Karnataka, which addressed the 'concerns of the Christian community' in India. Between December 6, 1990, and March 15, 1991, a '130-day rally' was organized by the BSP. Kanshiram atop a 'vehicle of social transformation' travelled through 13 states of Tamil Nadu, Kerala, Karnataka, Andhra Pradesh, Maharashtra, Gujarat, Madhya Pradesh, Uttar Pradesh, Haryana, Punjab, Himachal Pradesh, Jammu and Kashmir and Chandigarh to Ambedkar's birthplace at Mhow, in Maharashtra.[46]

'Bhagidari' as Representative Politics: Muslims and Bahujanwad

In the mid-1980s, Uttar Pradesh witnessed incidents of communal violence against Muslims following a Hindu backlash in the aftermath of the 'Ram Janmabhoomi' movement (1986), orchestrated by right-wing Hindu nationalist organizations. The ineptitude of the Congress Party pertaining to the 'temple movement' was exposed as it swung away from what BJP considered as 'appeasement of Muslims' to desperately playing the 'Hindu vote card' to build a new 'majority' social constituency. The 'Ayodhya movement', and the communal violence that followed, forced the Muslim populace and its orthodox clergy-driven conservative political leadership, a product of the Congress' post-1969 split as 'protector of minorities (Muslim) interests', to search for other alternative political formations which could 'secure' the socio-political interests of the Muslims in Uttar Pradesh.

The BSP critiqued the Congress 'policy of co-option' of Muslim 'religious figures' and leaders in an attempt to hold onto the 'Muslim vote'. The BSP suggested that the Congress Party engaged in petty politics of helping a candidate register a win or vote against a candidate to affect a loss.[47] The BSP targeted the Muslim electorate by underlining two political criteria: firstly, the notion of 'bhagidari' or 'partnership' in administration and government, which was based on the notion of 'under-representation' of the Muslims in state administration and politics in comparison to the strength of their population; secondly, as a consequence of a deeper crisis of political legitimacy of the Indian state, there was the 'inexorable march of the Muslims towards backwardness.[48]

Kanshiram offered a 'historical' perspective to the 'conditions of backwardness', which afflicted the Muslims in India. The BSP leader claimed:

> (That) in 1935 (here the probable reference is to the Government of India Act 1935), when India was under colonial rule, 'Muslims received 35*% representation in the highest (paid) jobs'. '(After) independence, this "percentage was halved", and (as a result) their children were denied education. [T]his (was) the reason why they (have) moved towards bondage'. 'The "Brahmanvadi" ruling class (further) reduced the Muslims to poverty to the extent that (there is) less than 1% are in the fray' for employment in state-level administrative service and the public sector. Kanshiram states: '(In this way) Muslims have become "helpless and dependent"; the restrictions on (access to) education (that is concomitant to social and economic advancement) (is) a conspiracy to bind them to bondage'. The BSP leader further stated: (since) 'lower class' (Muslim) artisan communities of weavers, dyers, butchers etc. apparently 'belonged to the Dalit constituency', originally low-caste 'exploited' Hindus before their religious conversion to Islam, Muslims are inseparable from the Dalits. (Thus) to 'participate in government', they need to (unite) with the shudra (lower backwards) and ati-shudras (Dalits).[49]

Kanshiram attempted to provide an interpolated political discourse of the 'history of the subjugated' so that it appeared inclusive and dialogical.

'Socio-religious security for Muslims' and 'bahujan representation' were the core themes that Mayawati addressed in a series of political rallies held in the aftermath of the 'temple movement' in Ayodhya. Addressing BSP supporters in July 1987, at Bijnore, western UP, in the background of the communal riot in Meerut, Mayawati said that the manipulation of the two 'victim communities' – Dalits and Muslims – against one another further emboldened a 'planned massacre of "Muslim brothers" by the police, Provincial Armed Constabulary (PAC)' and the politicians complicit in fuelling communal violence. The Meerut communal riot was contextualized amongst a spate of riots that took place in numerous UP towns such as Aligarh, Moradabad, Allahabad, Barabanki, Faizabad and other towns throughout the decade of the 1980s, causing 'irreparable harm to their (Muslims) daily livelihood and business'. A month later, speaking at a 'bhaichara jalsa' (informal meeting of 'brothers') at Jama Masjid,[50] Delhi, on August 15, 1987, Mayawati forewarned that even as Muslims turn towards (small-scale trade and craft) vocations and (sought to improve) their quality of life, 'manuvadis (upper castes) through (organized) conspiracy' created communal polarization among the Muslims and Dalits, leading to communal riots. Mayawati noted that such 'oppression would continue till the (bahujans demonstrated) unity'. At a 'bhaichara banao' (create brotherhood) cycle rally in Moradabad, on October 8, 1987, Mayawati chose to 'lampoon' UP Chief Minister H.N. Bahuguna, 'who (had spoken) of the importance of Muslim representation in police administration as a cure to communal hostilities but did little when in office'.[51]

Outlining the political objectives that required immediate political consideration to address the 'insecurity' of the Muslims, the BSP suggested that 'proportional' representation of the Muslims in state police force and the Provincial Armed Constabulary (PAC) needed to be assured as a 'pre-requisite counter-guarantee measure'. It would act as a check on a 'section of UP police', which had become 'defenders of Hindu interests' during communal riots. Mayawati said that such a 'policy of (Muslim) community representation would liberate them from a 'day.niy' (pitiable condition). In the context of the Ram Janmabhoomi movement and the extreme religious fanaticism displayed by Hindu religious and political organizations, Mayawati indicted the Congress government for violating the 'policy of religious neutrality' by its political interference in the Muslim Personal Law Board, and (thereby) 'undermining and weakening' Islam.[52] The BSP continued to plan a series of 'Bahujan-Muslim' rallies to mobilize the Muslims in UP. One such rally was held on October 9, 1987, at Aligarh, in which 'Dalits, Muslims, Sikhs and Christians – the "looted and beaten brothers" – from Aligarh, Atrauli and Bareilly, which also included backward groups such as Lodh, Kol and Baghel caste associations from Hathras, were gathered and "weighed in silver coins", and the money was given to Mayawati'. Ramesh Chandra Ratan, a Jatav, Shamim Ahmad Siddiqui, a Muslim, Saheb Singh, a Baghel, P.L. Verma, a Lodh on behalf of their respective 'samaj' gave Rs. 6,000 each[53] as token of political support to the BSP leader. In another 'bhaichara banao sammmelan' (brotherhood conference) organized on January 9, 1988, at Bijnore, Mayawati reiterated that the 'only way to secure the life and property of the Muslims (was for the community) to be fraternized with the SC, ST and backward social groups'.[54]

BSP's extensive 'bahujan awareness' campaigns to seek legitimacy for 'rights of backwards' appeared to be a populist broad-basing of its political-cum-ideological vision underpinned by the vast electoral potential of the mega bloc constituency in the period before the Mandal Commission Report was implemented. As an alternative political voice of the 'dominated and oppressed', the difficult political process of electoral mobilization of bahujan castes for votes had begun for the BSP. On the other hand, political discourses of 'solidarity with Muslim bahujans' suffering 'historical injustices' reflected in their present socio-political predicament was based upon analysing the category of 'insecurity of a religious minority' through 'bahujanwad', since the former connoted the oppressed existence of marginalized groups. 'Bahujanwad' and not a variant restrictive ethno-religious category appeared as a reliable interpretive category that comprehended similar socio-economic conditions and the identification of Muslims with poor backward classes.

'Prestigious' Electoral Contests (1984–1989): Dalit to Bahujan

Possibly, the utility of BSP's 'bahujan' ideology can be observed from three vantage points: firstly, 'bahujanism' appeared to the party as an electorally reliable political formula to prop up and secure 'priority-based' Dalit interests; secondly, to appear as an interpolation of 'Dalit' and 'bahujan' political categories, reinforcing the interpretive context for a legitimate 'empowerment politics'; thirdly, Dalit identity becomes an 'inclusive' constituent element of bahujan solidarity under certain and/or different political contexts. Bahujan ideology beckoned the political mobilization of social groups belonging to the oppressed social class while at the same time it could negotiate between Dalit and mega-cultural 'bahujan' constructs to formulate an electoral strategy in a caste-driven Uttar Pradesh politics.

BSP's schema for empowered 'bahujan' politics in Uttar Pradesh could be conceptualized as the 'territorialization of power as politics', a 'rooting of power to a particular place', wherein the 'site of (political) representation' was the politics of bahujanwad and the 'stability of the location' the state of Uttar Pradesh. Clear about the electoral strategy that the party would pursue to win political power in Uttar Pradesh, Kanshiram summed up the 'politically important state' as the 'neck (if) India (was to be seen as a) 'purush' (man); and further that if the 'neck was strangled, the rest of the limbs in the body (meaning other regions or states and 'Brahminical' political parties) would become useless and (then the BSP) would be able to control'. He added that the party '(wanted) "nothing short of control" over the Government of India'.[55]

During the period between 1984 and 1989, Kanshiram's strategic mobilization of the 'bahujan samaj ke teen kamaan: Dalit, OBC aur Mussalman' (the three constituent parts of bahujan samaj are Dalits, OBCs and Muslims) began with numerous 'single constituency contests' in UP, which was hedged upon the pivotal role of Chamar 'Dalit' votes. Assured of a rise in the party's vote share, Kanshiram declared the BSP as a 'national morcha' (national front) which had the potential to be a 'jeetnewala party'[56] (a party that can win). The BSP outlined 'three crucial stages' to capture political power. Political participation in elections was critical to 'train people to win elections' so that BSP candidates would be 'in a position to decide who (had) to win and who (had) to lose'. In the first stage, participants in the elections would 'lose' – the objective being to evaluate the party's popularity among 'target' electoral constituencies. In the second stage, participate in elections to 'make' others (rival political candidates preferably from national political parties) lose – the objective being to defeat "certain political parties" (such as the INC and the BJP) to enable other (regional) political parties to win. In the third stage, participate in elections to win – the objective being political consolidation through 'leverage' in administration and politics to pursue the social justice agenda of the party.[57]

BSP's electoral debut began with the eighth general elections in 1984, with the party contesting from the Kairana Parliamentary constituency in western UP. The constituency with a sizeable Muslim population (30%) and Chamar-dominated SC population (18%) offered the party a political incentive to increase its vote share[58] in the wake of a fragmented Muslim-Dalit vote bank of the INC.[59] However, failure of the Charan Singh-led Dalit Mazdoor Krishak Party (DMKP), the successor of Bharatiya Lok Dal, to compete with the Congress Party, which was riding a nationwide 'sympathy wave following the assassination of Prime Minister Indira Gandhi', turned BSP's maiden entry in electoral politics a relatively unsuccessful venture.

The Kairana seat was won by the INC candidate, polling 52.98% votes. Mayawati came 'third among eight other contestants' (see Table 3.1), securing 44,445 votes with a 9.94% vote share.

Kanshiram began his electoral career in 1984 (see Table 3.2) by contesting as an independent for the Janjgir Lok Sabha constituency in erstwhile Madhya Pradesh, now a district in Chhattisgarh. With lower backward caste support, Kanshiram polled an impressive 32,817 votes with a vote share of 9%.[60]

Yet, BSP's political ascent in Uttar Pradesh can be traced to the Bijnor (Reserved constituency) by-elections to the Lok Sabha, held in December 1985. It became an important political milestone for the BSP to measure the extent of the popularity of the party among the poor. The election was held due to the death of veteran Congress leader Girdhar Lal, who had won the seat in 1984 Lok Sabha elections, defeating Lok Kranti Dal (LKD) candidate Mangal Ram Premi.[61] The BSP's electoral strategy was clearly to unnerve and 'spoil' the chances of Congress SC candidate for the Bijnor 'seat', Mrs. Meira Kumar, in favour of LKD candidate Ram Vilas Paswan. BSP leader Mayawati, who had been nurturing the 'Dalit constituency' for 'six months', leading to the by-elections and 'spitting fire', had made the Congress Party wary, whose entire poll campaign appeared chaotic [and] disorganized.[62] Yet, the ruling party poll managers spared no effort 'to retain the seat' with leaders and ministers, 'regularly camping and campaigning' in this reserved constituency. The electoral contest was special in another sense that Meira Kumar's (president of Congress (J) and Jagjivan Ram's daughter) victory would perhaps be a forerunner to her father's re-entry into the Congress Party.[63] The Bijnor reserved Lok Sabha constituency had a 39% Muslim population and 23% SC population, of which 20% belonged to the Chamar caste.[64] While Mayawati was able to mobilize a significant section of the Scheduled Castes, the politicization of the Shah Bano controversy heightened the Congress' insecurity in the midst of an overall decreasing Muslim vote share for the party. Thus, the by-elections became a matter of political prestige for the Congress Party.[65] The result of the Bijnor

Table 3.1 Political Graph of Mayawati: Lok Sabha Elections (1984–1992)

Year	*1984*	*1985*	*1987*	*1989*	*1991*	*1991 (Nov) Re-election*	*1992 Re-election*
Constituency	Kairana (UP)	Bijnore (SC) By-election (UP)	Hardwar (SC) By-election (UP)	Bijnore (SC) (UP) Hardwar (SC) (UP)	Hardwar (SC) (UP) Bijnore (SC) (UP)	Bulandshahar (UP)	Hoshiarpur (Punjab)
Votes	44,445	61,504	1,25,399	1,83,189 1,11,194	22,384 1,59,731	67,531	90,461
Percentage of votes	09.94	18.00	32.70	37.96 22.63	04.28 30.47	15.26	26.54
Result	Lost	Lost	Lost	**Elected** Lost	Lost Lost	Lost	Lost

Source: URL : http//www. eci.gov.in [accessed on Sept. 15, 2008]; URL: http//www.ceopunjab.nic.in (accessed on Sept. 15, 2008).

Table 3.2 Political Graph of Kanshiram: Lok Sabha Elections (1984–1992)

Year	*1984*	*1988*	*1989*	*1991*
Constituency	Janjgir* (now in Chhatisgarh)	Allahabad (UP) By-election	Amethi (UP) East Delhi (Delhi)	Etawah (UP)
Votes	32,817	69, 517	25,400 81,095	1,44,290
Percentage of votes	09.00	19.00	06.31 11.23	31.31
Result	Lost	Lost	Lost Lost	Elected

Source: URL : http//www. eci.gov.in (accessed on Sept. 15, 2008)
* Contested the election as an independent.

by-elections need to be contextualized within the 'not too impressive performance' of the Congress (I) in the UP assembly elections held in March 1985. In the assembly elections, the Congress won 269 out of 425 seats, registering a sharp drop in its mean vote share of 39.25%, on an average through all the assembly constituencies. The LKD won 84 out of 385 seats, with 21.43% vote share and the BJP 16 out of 347 seats, with a 9.83% vote share. The BSP did not win any seat but polled 4% of the total votes.[66] In the Bijnor by-elections, the INC candidate Meira Kumar won with 1,28,986 votes, by a 'wafer thin margin' over LKD candidate Ram Vilas Paswan, who polled 1,22,747 votes. Mayawati won 61,504 votes and secured 18% of SC and Muslim votes.[67] After the election, Mayawati said that the 'close electoral contest indicated the growing support of the Dalit base' of the BSP in the state. Mayawati testified to the fact that '(she) was born of a Chamar mother', underlining the 'difference between her "open allegiance" to the SC and Meira Kumar's reticence' towards the SC community. Mayawati declared that '(she had) not forgotten (her) Dalit and oppressed brothers the way that others (had) (and) with an obvious reference to Meira Kumar clarified that '(those) who (lived) as slaves in brahminical (political) parties (had) forgotten them'. The Bijnor election was contested amidst the rapidly growing political reputation of the BSP as a 'party with the strength to make other (political parties) lose'. In two successive assembly elections in UP and Punjab in 1985, the BSP was able to dent the electoral prospects of the Congress Party. In UP, though none of the BSP candidate won, the party took away 2.44% of the total votes polled, which was enough to ensure the loss of the Congress Party in the districts of western UP. In all, the BSP ensured the defeat of Congress candidates in 51 seats, resulting in the victory of 45 Lok Dal and 6 Janata Party candidates. In Punjab, because of the support of the BSP among the Dalit-Sikh community, the Congress lost as many as 30 assembly seats. The BSP, which polled 2,64,630 votes and 2.2% of the vote share, helped the Akali Dal gain several seats as it split Congress

Party's vote base among the 'mazhabi' Dalit-Sikhs. Yet Kanshiram was realistic about the party's electoral prospects. In a political rally addressed to BSP supporters and ticket-holders, Kanshiram pointed out that in 'the March 1985 assembly elections (in UP) (the party) had given tickets to 237 candidates'. (He) (had) told the candidates that (the party) ticket (was) only a platform ticket, and with (that) ticket (one) (could not) (even) reach Lucknow.' The popularity of the BSP confirmed the fact that the party had begun to '(appropriate) the politics of Ambedkarite parties' in the state and was emerging as the new 'Dalit phenomenon' in UP. One of the slogans that were commonly heard during that period of the political expansion of the 'Dalit Party' was 'Baba (Dr. Ambedkar) tera mission adhura, Kanshiram karega pura' (Babasaheb/Dr. Ambedkar your mission remains unfulfilled, Kanshiram will complete it).[68]

In a significant way, the Hardwar (Reserved) Lok Sabha by-election held in March 1987 underlined the political failure of the Congress Party's Scheduled Caste-Muslim 'vote bank' politics. The Hardwar Lok Sabha constituency with 25% SC, with Chamars accounting for 90% of the population, and 27% Muslim population,[69] became 'another electoral battleground' for the BSP. In this election, the political propaganda of the BSP highlighted the failure of the INC as a 'ruling party (which) raised slogans but practically (did) nothing (for the welfare of the poor)'. With 'homespun' logic, BSP argued that 'the number of poor in the country would not have increased or remained the same after 40 years of independence had the government been sincere in its protestations'.[70] Among the poorer castes in the constituency there was increasing acceptance of BSP's 'social justice' politics that the 'Brahmin (political parties)' could never do any good for the vast majority of weaker castes'. As elections to the Hardwar Lok Sabha by-elections approached,[71] the BSP addressed Muslims with political speeches that made reference to the prospect of 'Islam (that was) in danger because of the (state and the central government's) mishandling of the Babri Masjid imbroglio in Ayodhya'.[72] The BSP organized a political campaign for this Parliamentary constituency, with Mayawati leading an electoral campaign with 'hundreds of volunteers belonging to the (lower) backward castes campaigning to make political inroads into villages'.[73] The Congress political campaign to counter the 'BSP threat' 'dwelled on the sacrifices of party leaders from Gokhale to Indira Gandhi, urging the people not to be swayed by caste considerations and vote for the "casteless party", the Congress'.[74] In the Hardwar Lok Sabha elections, Mayawati came second with 1,25,399 votes, losing by 23,000 votes to the winning Congress candidate Ram Singh, polling 1,49,335 votes. Ram Vilas Paswan of the Janawadi Morcha (JM) who had hoped to corner the SC votes stood fourth with 34,225 votes. The vote share of the BSP increased to 26.30%, behind the Congress with 33%, while opposition parties such as the JM, BJP, Lok Dal (LD), Communist Party of India (CPI) etc. in all registered a mere 2% of the votes polled.[75] Kanshiram summed up the party's electoral performance at Hardwar by stating 'that the SC, backward castes and (religious) minorities (had) been awakened to fight for their rights (and) that the poor (could) no longer remain in a passive state giving in to the upper castes; and finally, (the) party (had) been able to deliver this (political) message'.[76]

The three 'electoral battles' enabled Mayawati to gain political stature as a Dalit leader of repute in Uttar Pradesh. Kanshiram's admiration for his protégé's was confirmed. He said:

> In (each election) '(Mayawati) went from village to village (and her presence continued) to increase the (Dalit-bahujan) vote bank. In Hardwar she improved the "vote bank of BSP 14 times". But her seniors became furious. They put pressure on me for giving opportunity to Mayawati (so) much so that most of them left the movement'.[77]

It was certainly not a misplaced notion as Kanshiram and Mayawati were seeking to imbue a 'cult personality' – as 'audacious and dynamic' leaders of the 'oppressed people' by projecting themselves as 'symbols and agents of massive social change' and 'establishing a kind of a (political intimacy) with the (bahujan) public'. A unique method of fostering 'close' relationship with the (bahujan) 'voting population' was the manner in which Kanshiram collected funds for the party. The BSP leader said: '(We must) change the habit(s) of the people; (they must) "pay for the movement" that he was leading. Moreover, the followers (must) become conscious (of) their struggle and gain confidence in their leaders as the movement (grew) day by day'. Kanshiram claimed that 'followers obliged (him with) donations', and that '(it) injected lots of enthusiasm' in the BSP.[78]

The Allahabad Lok Sabha by-elections held in June 1988 became a much-publicized event that centred on the Congress and opposition political parties vying to take a 'high' moral ground in national politics. The sitting MP, the well-known cine actor Amitabh Bachchan, had resigned in July 1987 following charges of involvement in a Rs. 640 million 'Bofors gun scandal'. Though nothing was found against him, the stage was set for a bitter electoral contest. Vishwanath Pratap Singh, Minister of Finance, a prominent member of the Rajiv Gandhi cabinet, had also resigned with the revelation of the 'scandal' and was consequently selected as the candidate of all non-Congress 'opposition (political) parties'. After his resignation, V.P. Singh had raised the question of 'credibility' and 'moral high ground' in an approaching electoral contest with Amitabh Bachchan. Since Bachchan resigned, V.P. Singh[79] eventually decided to contest against Congress nominee Sunil Shastri, son of Lal Bahadur Shastri, 'by not (betraying) the trust reposed on him by the entire non-Congress opposition'.[80] What significantly influenced the outcome of the by-election was: firstly, a high proportion of Brahmins (14%) and Thakurs (8%) – a BJP support base that would comply to support V.P. Singh – and secondly, the 'Kanshiram factor', which sought to disturb the political equation against the Congress Party by mobilizing SC (25%), primarily the Pasis and Chamars. The Muslims (12%) voting preference would, it was believed expectedly, shift away from the Congress due to the massive political implications of the 'Ayodhya temple movement'.[81] What was evident in this election was the presence of a growing organizational network of the BSP that corresponded to a unique campaigning style. Kanshiram asserted that (his) 'workers were churning out elephants (the party symbol) at the rate of Rs. 150 per minute, suggesting (that) (the BSP had arrived) in a big way'. The 'workers were divided into six squads: printing, painting, awakening squads, cycling and begging (for subscription money and votes) and speaking squads'. Kanshiram was portrayed as a 'saviour of the poor', reminiscent of the campaign slogan 'Gham ke badal hat gaye, khushi ke badal chha gaye, bhim ke roop mein Kanshiram aagaye' (the clouds of sorrow have moved away, the cloud of happiness have arrived, Kanshiram, manifesting as 'bhim' – in this case Bhimrao Ambedkar – has arrived).[82] The BSP leader categorically stated:

> 'The elephant does not know its strength. The day it does it will trample others. Similarly, the bahujan samaj does not know its strength. The day it does (one would) see that for oneself', and further added that (he was) 'organizing these people to establish a society which will be structured horizontally and not vertically as it is at present'.[83]

V.P. Singh with 2,02,996 votes won by a huge margin over Sunil Shastri of the Congress Party. Shastri secured 92,245 votes with Kanshiram of the BSP coming third with 69,517 votes, gaining 19% of the votes and securing his 'Dalit' political constituency.[84] The Allahabad by-election was yet another successful attempt by the BSP to play a 'subversive (electoral) role' to weaken the Congress in UP. A steady increase in Dalit 'vote share' that required an adept use of 'vote politics' to defeat Congress candidates was not an isolated pyrrhic political victory for the 'Dalit Party'. BSP's electoral tactics paid political dividends in the 1988–1989 Municipal and Gram Panchayat elections, in which it captured 188 municipalities as against 54 by the BJP, 45 by the Congress, 14 by the Janata Dal and 3 by the Left coalition. The BSP also won 24,000 Gram Panchayats as against 24,700 of the Congress.

The BJP, which had begun consolidating its political presence in UP post 'Ram Janmabhoomi movement', had begun to note with political concern the increasing popularity of the BSP. Kanshiram had pointed to the receptivity of the BSP in an editorial written in 'Oppressed Indian' in April 1985, in which he stated that the Rashtriya Swayamsevak Sangh (RSS) in its annual report released on March 15, 1985, had devoted a full paragraph to the success of the BSP in 'uniting the oppressed and exploited caste groups and securing brotherhood against the BJP and the Sangh Parivar (an umbrella term used to mean a collection of Hindu nationalist organizations created by the RSS). It was a perception confirmed by the then RSS chief Balasaheb Deoras, who was quoted in the *Illustrated Weekly of India* in 1988, describing the BSP as 'one of the real problems for the RSS in north India'.[85]

The Congress' defeat in the ninth Lok Sabha elections in 1989 reduced the 'Grand Old Party' to 192 seats, a sharp drop of more than 200 seats from 414 seats it had won in the 1984 Lok Sabha elections. The biggest 'political gainers' were the BJP and the Janata Dal (JD), the latter, the new political avatar of BLD and BKMP. The JD won 142 seats, and despite intra-factional disputes, the party was poised to herald a non-Congress National Front (NF) government supported by a disparate spectrum of regional parties such as the Telugu Desam Party, the Dravida Munnetra Kazhagam and the Asom Gana Parishad. The BJP won 85 seats compared to its miniscule tally of 2 seats won in the 1984 elections Parliamentary elections,[86] and it became the biggest coalition partner, lending 'outside' support to the NF government.

Indicative of its reduced number of seats post-1989 Lok Sabha elections, the Congress Party in Uttar Pradesh faced the reality of a steady erosion of SC-Muslim-upper caste voters. The 'upper caste' Rajput community moved out of the Congress with V.P. Singh, to his newly formed Janata Dal. The influential agricultural landowning OBC privy to the factional tussle among backward caste leaders of north India lent support to the Janata Dal. The Brahmins supported the BJP, while the Muslims showed their preference for JD candidates, and only when there was no 'winnable' JD 'national' candidate did they support the BSP, while a section of the Most Backward Class (MBC) supported the BSP.[87] As major caste groups searched for new political alignments, the BSP finally registered an electoral victory.

In the 1989 Bijnor (SC) Lok Sabha elections, the BSP made political inroads into the Congress vote bank of SC and Muslims. With a focus on the Muslim vote in political rallies leading up to the day of the election, Mayawati made it a point to underscore that the 'BSP alone (was) the true friend of Muslims and alleged that the Congress (had) started 'using the PAC and the army to attack Muslims'.[88] What turned into a 'political victory' for Mayawati from Bijnor reserved Lok Sabha constituency were the 'Badaun riots' and the palpable tense atmosphere post-Ayodhya temple movement. It helped the BSP 'siphon (off) crucial Muslim votes' away from the Congress Party. It was exactly the same combination of 'riots and high-handed state machinery' against the Muslims in Aligarh, Meerut and Moradabad in 1961 which had left 36 dead. Back in 1961, the communal disturbances in the affected cities gave a fillip to RPI's electoral prospects as it had then won eight seats in the 1962 UP assembly elections. In the 1989 Lok Sabha and assembly elections (see Tables 3.3 and 3.4), the BSP won two parliamentary seats in UP and one seat from Phillour in Punjab. Mayawati won the Bijnor reserved Parliamentary seat with 1,83,189 votes. The overall voting percentage for the BSP in UP and Punjab in the Lok Sabha elections were 9.7% and 8.81%, respectively. In the UP assembly elections

Table 3.3 Uttar Pradesh Assembly Election Results 1989

Party	*Seats*
INC	94
BJP	57
JD	208
BSP	13

Table 3.4 Uttar Pradesh Lok Sabha Results 1989

Party	*Seats*
INC	12
BJP	8
JD	54
BSP	2

Source: Compiled by author.

that were held simultaneously, the BSP won 13 seats in Afzalgarh, Nagina, Nazibabad, Thakurdwara, Jalalpur, Mau, Phulpur, Saraimir, Mohammad Gohna, Nawabganj, Konch, Orai and Kalpi. It was an evenly distributed though scattered political victories in assembly constituencies across western, central and eastern UP. In each case, the winning combination of SC and Muslim votes worked to the benefit of the BSP. Out of 13 victorious candidates, 6 were Muslims, 5 SC and 2 OBC. The BSP with an overall 9.46% vote share in the state assembly elections had 4 'second place finishes' and 46 'third place finishes'.[89] In assembly constituencies where the BSP won with the support of Muslims and Dalits, votes polled for the 'Dalit Party' ranged between 37% in Mau and 61% in Afzalgarh, Nagina and Nazibabad. The BSP would probably have won more assembly seats had it not been for the strategic voting of the Muslim electorate for 'JD-backed candidates'. Muslims voted for the BSP and to a significantly lesser extent the Congress where JD candidates were not in the fray. The fragmentation of the Muslim vote worked to the advantage of the BJP, as upper caste voters shifted to the 'parent' party.[90] Clearly, the BJP had consolidated a core vote base.

'Mandal – Kamandal' Politics

The V.P. Singh-led National Front government at the Centre, formed with outside support of the BJP, faced an imminent political crisis of keeping a faction-ridden JD united. In a political masterstroke to undermine the 'status quoist' Congress Party and check BJP's drive to consolidate the 'Hindu vote' across the country, V.P. Singh announced in August 1990 the decision of the government to implement the recommendations of the Mandal Commission. The Mandal Commission[91] recommended reservations of 27% employment for backward castes in central government-aided public sector jobs. In hindsight, the implementation of the Mandal Commission recommendations was critical for the JD to hold on to the backward caste vote in UP and other north Indian states.

The consequent impact of the Mandal Commission proved to be a political cataclysm for the broad aggregative (Congress) party system heralding the beginning of coalition-based governments at the Centre. The emergence of 'Mandal politics' presented the BJP as it did to other 'national' political parties a political dilemma that required a readjustment of its ideological and political objectives across north India. 'Mandalization' of polity endorsed a 'cleavage-based politics', which became a characteristic norm of political survival, as political parties, both 'established and new political entrants, began to represent not broader and more inclusive aggregation of social groups but narrower identities and interests'. It opened the possibility of the polity growing accustomed to several leading 'ideological discourses in Indian politics' shifting the arena of contestation for power towards state politics. One of the significant aspects of the Mandal politics was that it exposed the irredeemably upper caste and upper class political leadership of the Indian state to the 'distinct prospect of losing power to politically assertive economically powerful backward and marginalized social groups'. Mandal politics confronted the Indian electorate with the prospect of transforming an upper caste brahminical base of power, which could fundamentally alter the process of democratic politics and society. It was evident that the biggest political impact of Mandal Commission, in its initial phase, would centre on the states of UP and Bihar that led to a fervent political mobilization of numerous caste groups.[92] It was obviously with these political considerations in mind that BJP leader Lal Krishna Advani, announced his decision to launch a 'rath yatra' (chariot journey) from Somnath temple in Gujarat on September 25, 1990. The 'yatra' would take a circuitous route across north India and reach Ayodhya on October 30, 1990. As the 'yatra' came closer to the destination, winding its way through Bihar and UP, it set in a frenzied political atmosphere among thousands of 'kar sevaks' (voluntary workers offering services for free) heading towards Ayodhya to 'remove the Babri mosque' and in its place 'construct a Ram temple'. Mulayam Singh Yadav, the prominent 'Yadav' OBC leader and the JD chief minister of UP, denounced the BJP through a series of political speeches defending 'secularism' and rights of the Muslim minorities in India, and ordering the police to arrest kar sevaks on their way to Ayodhya. Activists of numerous Hindu cultural-nationalist organizations left a trail of religious antagonisms, riots and deaths in the wake of the rath yatra.

Mulayam Singh Yadav's action against the kar sevaks created an atmosphere of resentment among upper caste sections of the Hindu population in UP. On the other hand, Laloo Prasad Yadav, another emerging backward caste leader and the CM of Bihar, stopped the rath yatra cavalcade on October 23, 1990, at Samastipur and arrested Advani. The BJP promptly withdrew support from the V.P. Singh-led National Front government, which thereby lost its majority in Parliament. A new political alliance broke away from the JD – a JD 'socialist' faction led by Chandrasekhar Singh – christened as Janata Dal (Socialist) Party (SJP). Mulayam Singh Yadav, who supported Chandrasekhar, joined the party and struck a 'political deal' with Congress Party, which anointed Chandra Shekhar Singh as Prime Minister. The 'deal' preserved Mulayam Singh Yadav, an erstwhile winner on a JD ticket, in office as chief minister of UP. The 'Chandrasekhar government' at the Centre lasted for seven months (November 1990–June 1991), an 'interlude' to the next Parliamentary elections. In the interregnum, Rajiv Gandhi and central leaders procrastinated even as UP Congress leaders urged the Congress 'High Command' to 'dump Mulayam Singh Yadav' and go to the polls immediately. Justified mutual suspicions of each other's political intentions, the Congress on one side and Devi Lal and Chandrasekhar on the other, culminated in a farce in the first week of March 1991 when Rajiv Gandhi apparently discovered that his house was under the surveillance of the Haryana police. In the midst of all these recriminations, shortly thereafter, Chandra Shekhar resigned. The Congress, in turn, withdrew its support to Mulayam Singh Yadav in UP.[93]

The May–June 1991 mid-term Lok Sabha elections were held in the midst of the tragic assassination of former PM Rajiv Gandhi. Despite a sympathy wave riding the Indian voters, a number of factors contributed to BJP's electoral success in the tenth Lok Sabha elections and assembly polls held simultaneously in Uttar Pradesh: first, a flawed political belief of the JD that the support of the Muslims and backward castes could be retained without a corresponding consolidation of upper caste vote[94]; second, the question of 'Hindu resentment' against alleged 'pampering' of Muslims, a political campaign successfully fashioned by the BJP; third, the impact of the Mandal decision that polarized the upper caste elite and the backward castes – UP election results confirmed that the 'anti-Mandal' sentiments were high among upper caste Brahmins, Thakurs, Bhumihars and the 'urban' Bania class; fourth, the perceived discriminatory exclusion of certain landholding castes, such as the Jats of western UP, from the purview of the Mandal Commission led to political resentment; fifth, the fragmentation of backward castes' political support noticeable with the departure of Mulayam Singh Yadav[95] from the JD faction coinciding with the fall of the National Front government in October 1990 gave political leverage to Mulayam Singh Yadav to consolidate his political future in Uttar Pradesh. Lastly, the strong measures adopted by the Mulayam Singh Yadav government against the 'kar sevaks' created a state-wide swelling of political support for the BJP. Seizing the opportune political moment and the potential to expand his electoral base of Yadavs and 'plus votes' notably of the Muslims in the state, Mulayam Singh Yadav shortly thereafter formed the Samajwadi Party (SP). On the other hand, reacting to the intense politicization of Yadavs across 'Awadh Pradesh' (central UP), Kurmis, included in the MC report, in conflict with Brahmins, Rajputs and Yadavs for 'control of local resources, political power and land' voted for the BJP. Underlined by a distinctive 'Hindutva' ideology emerging, Kalyan Singh, of the Lodh caste and the OBC political leader of the BJP in the state, played a significant role in mobilizing this populous backward caste to expand the 'OBC social constituency' for the party. The Muslims voted for the SP in the assembly elections and not JD as 'community sentiments' were divided between V.P. Singh and Mulayam Singh Yadav. In the state Lok Sabha elections, Muslims voted for JD candidates. Both the leaders were seen to have 'protected Muslims and saved the mosque at Ayodhya'.[96]

In UP Parliamentary elections, the BJP won 51 seats, the JD 22, the Congress 5 and the SJP 4 seats, respectively. In the assembly elections, the BJP secured 221 out of 415 seats, with a vote share of 31.76% in seats contested. In two years, it was a remarkable turnaround by the BJP (see Table 3.3 and Table 3.4). The Congress could register wins only in 46 out of 413 seats, with a sharp fall in its vote share that almost halved to 21.05%. The SJP won 34 out of 399 seats, with a vote share of 13.13%. Had the JD and the SJP been united, a combined political strength would have amounted to 37 Lok Sabha seats in UP.[97]

In UP, electoral battles across assembly constituencies saw intense 'triangular-quadrangular' political contests between the JD, SJP, BJP and the BSP, with low winning percentage of votes. The nature of the 'political contests' ensured that the BSP captured new assembly segments in eastern and central UP, winning reserved seats in Jalalpur and Sagri with 25.76%, Nizamabad and Lalganj with 27.06%, Lalganj and Kalpi with 28.61% and Majhwa with 25.61% vote shares. In the 'general' constituencies, the BSP won from Nawabganj, Bara, Tindwari, Baberu, Banda and Khutahan. The 1991 elections demonstrated the capacity of the BSP to mobilize Chamars and geographically scattered lower backward caste support to fashion electoral victories even as a sizeable section of the Muslim vote went to the SP.

However, the BSP was not able to replicate its performance in the Lok Sabha elections in UP. Mayawati, who contested from two constituencies – Bijnor and Hardwar – could not hold on to the Bijnor Lok Sabha seat in 1991 as she lost by a substantial margin to Mangal Ram Premi, polling 1,59,731 votes to 2,47,485 votes. In the Hardwar SC constituency, Mayawati could secure only 22,384 votes, much less than her performance in the 1989 Lok Sabha elections when she secured 1,11,194 votes, and significantly lesser than the Congress candidate who polled 77,832 votes. The Hardwar SC seat was won by BJP candidate Ram Singh, winning a close contest over JD candidate Dharam Singh by 2,05,182 votes to 1,97,985 votes. The SP proved to be a 'spanner in JD's political prospects', carving out 5,503 votes enough to ensure the victory of the BJP candidate.[98] The success of the BJP in winning the 'Bijnor seat' was an interesting case of capturing 'sections of caste groups' on either end of the social continuum. The BJP benefitted from a 'split' in SC votes, especially the non-Chamar votes, accounting for 3–4% out of the total 23% of SC votes. It cornered a sizeable section of the Jats (8%) and MBCs such as Malis and Sainis (5%) along with the Vaishyas and Brahmins. Post-poll analysis suggested that a section of the Muslims belonging to this Parliamentary constituency split their votes between the CPI (M) and the BSP.[99]

The 1991 Etawah 'Seat Pact': The making of a 'Plebian' Political Alliance

The 'mandal' (effect of OBC reservation on state and national politics) and the 'kamandal'[100] (rhetorically, Hindutva politics of the BJP) at a broader level did impact the electoral prospects of the BSP. The BSP's vote percentage in UP Parliamentary elections fell to 8.4%. Mayawati faced 'comprehensive defeats' in both her constituencies and decided to contest the Bulandshahr Lok Sabha by-elections in November 1991[101] but lost. It is in the context of a lacklustre BSP performance in the state that the Etawah Lok Sabha seat 'pact' between the SP and the BSP acquires political significance. The Etawah Lok Sabha seat, a political stronghold of the 'Yadav strongman' Mulayam Singh Yadav offered a new and a decisive turn to BSP's 'bahujan politics'. The BSP allied with Mulayam Singh Yadav as a 'co-plebian partner' to defeat the BJP. Mulayam Singh Yadav entered into an 'electoral agreement' with Kanshiram, allowing him to contest from Etawah. Kanshiram won a close electoral contest over his BJP rival Lal Singh Verma by polling 1,44,290 votes to 1,21,824 votes. While Kanshiram was able to mobilize a sizeable Chamars (16%) support, a majority of the Muslim vote (8%), the MBC denoted Kushwaha and the Gadariya castes (7%), the OBC Lodhs (6%), the prominent landowning caste in the region, the Yadavs, significantly enlarged the vote share of Kanshiram.[102] After winning the Etawah elections, Kanshiram said: '(The elections showed) that Yadav votes (could) be transferred to Dalit candidates and vice versa (and that) clearly a future alliance (could) be seen in the making'.[103] Was the Etawah Lok Sabha victory a possible forging of political ties between 'anti-upper caste landholding gentry and the poor Dalit 'agricultural and landless community' to maximize the potential of bahujan politics? It seemed difficult to perceive it as a long-term election plan except to seize an opportune political context to limit the vote base of the BJP. The biggest political challenge was whether, if at all, future coalition pacts between the SP and the BSP would critically address the prevalence of an oppressive feudal social order and an economic structure of appropriation which had turned the landholding Yadav community into exploiters of the impoverished Dalit population in the villages.

Notes

1 Namishray, *Bahujan Samaj*, p. 40.

2 In the Delhi Legislative Assembly elections in January 1983, independents contested 243 seats, won none, vote share was 1,32,397, which was 7.35% of total votes polled. URL: http://www.eci.gov.in/SR_key Highlights/ SE_1983/ Statistical Report Delhi_ 83.pdf (accessed on June 20, 2007).

In Jammu and Kashmir assembly elections held in June 1983, independents contested 254 seats, won 2, vote share was 2,20,204, which is 10.05% of total votes polled. URL: http://www.eci.gov.in/ SR_KeyHighlights/SE_1983/Statistical Report_JK_1983.pdf (accessed on June 20, 2007); Bose, *Behenji*, p. 63.

In the short duration, the DS-4 remained active, particularly in UP, the organization acted as a facilitating agency operating in 'close coordinated association' with BAMCEF. In Punjab, the DS-4 became popular among the Dalit-Mazhabi Sikhs, who had remained a 'loyal vote bank' of the Congress. The DS-4 was active in the Doaba region, which included the Congress bastions of Jalandar, Hoshiarpur, Kapurthala and Nawashahar. With nearly 29% of a Dalit-Sikh vote bank being significantly influenced by the DS-4, the Congress by early 1980s had begun to 'worry at what appeared to be a dangerous subversion of the party's electoral prospects. However, the emergence of Sikh extremist violence harmed the campaign to mobilize the Dalit-Sikh community in Punjab. Kanshiram, and his 'political invention', the DS-4, never fully recovered from the spate of extremist violence in Punjab, and could not retrieve their lost 'social constituency' in Punjab even after terrorism ended.

Out of the 28.3% of Dalit-Sikh population in Punjab, 31% are Mazhabis, 27% Chamar-Ramdassia Sikhs, 15% Adharmis and 12% Balmikis. There is uneven literacy among the four major divisions of the SC population in Punjab. Adharmis with 40% are ahead of Ramdassias with 29%, Balmikis with 22% and Mazhabis with 13%. The Adharmis and Ramdassias were well mobilized by the BAMCEF and the DS-4.

K. Chandra, *Why Ethnic Parties Succeed?*, p. 192; Bose, *Behenji*, pp. 59–63.

3 Jaffrelot, *Bahujan Samaj Party*, p. 37.

4 Party cadres who were ideologically committed, educated, employed, a part of the mobile community in urban slums and party workers, semi-literate, illiterate, part-time workers, unemployed youths, field labourers and street vendors in small towns and cities complained of the condescending attitude of 'educated' BAMCEF members. They felt that either the BAMCEF members were incapable or purposely provided wrong information of the rural areas to misguide Kanshiram.

Badri Narayan, *Kanshiram: Leader of the Dalits*, pp. 134, 135.

5 Jaffrelot, *Bahujan Samaj Party*, p. 39.

6 Role of Casteism in Indian Politics, Symposium held on March 27, 2004 at India International Centre, New Delhi, organized by Lala Diwan Chand Trust. The proceedings of the symposium were published as 'extracts' in January, 2005; Jaffrelot, *Bahujan Samaj Party*, p. 39.

7 Shivmurti Pathak, *Rashtra Nayak Kanshiram*, Allahabad: Shekhar Prakashan, 1995, pp. 17, 18, 19, 27, 53; Vivek Kumar, *India's Roaring Revolution: Dalit Assertions and New Horizons,* Delhi: Kalpaz Publications, 2006, pp. 129, 130; Valerian Rodrigues, *Dalit-Bahujan Discourse*, New Delhi: Critical Quest, 2008, pp.17, 27, 29, 30.

8 Anupama Rao, *The Caste Question: Dalits and Politics of Modern India*, Ranikhet: Permanent Black, 2010, p. 27.

9 Sudha Pai, 'Dalit question and political response, comparative study of Uttar Pradesh and Madhya Pradesh', *Economic and Political Weekly*, 39, 11, March

11, 2004, pp. 1141–1150; Gundimeda; *Dalit Politics in Contemporary India*, p. 116.

10 Radhika Ramaseshan, 'Dalit politics in UP', *Seminar*, No. 425 (Annual), January, 1995, p. 73

11 Ibid.

12 Sudha Pai, *Dalit Question and Political Response,* pp. 1141–1150.

13 Sudha Pai, *Dalit Question and Political Response*, pp. 1141–1150; Arvind Sivaramakrishnan (Ed.), *Short on Democracy: Issues Facing Indian Political Parties,* Haryana: Imprint One, 2007, pp. 109,110; Hasan, *Party Politics*, p. 379; K.C. Das, *Indian Dalits,* p. 179; *The Hindu*, New Delhi edition, June 5, 2009 Banerjee-Dube, *Themes*, p. 226 Arun Jana and Bhupen Sarmah (Eds.), *Class, Ideology and Political Parties in India,* New Delhi: South Asian Publishers, 2002, pp. 244,245; Craig Jeffrey et al. Dalit revolution? New politicians in Uttar Pradesh. *The Journal of Asian Studies,* 67, 4, November 2008, p. 1370.

14 Pathak, *Rashtra Nayak*, p. 53; Jaffrelot, *Silent Revolution*, pp. 389, 390; K.C. Das, *Indian Dalits*, p. 225; Badri Narayan, 'National past and political present', *Economic and Political Weekly*, 39, 31, July 31, 2004, p. 3539.

15 Gundimeda, *Dalit Politics in Contemporary India,* pp. 95, 96, 99; Badri Narayan, *Kanshiram: Leader of the Dalits,* p. 112.

16 Gundimeda, *Dalit Politics in Contemporary India*, pp. 95, 96, 99; Badri Narayan, *Kanshiram: Leader of the Dalits,* pp. 120–122.

17 Gundimeda, *Dalit Politics in Contemporary India*, pp. 95,96,99; Badri Narayan, *Kanshiram: Leader of the Dalits,* pp. 11, 112, 132, 120, 121, 122; K. Satyanarayana, Dalit reconfiguration of caste: representation, identity and politics, *Critical Quarterly*, 2014, 56, 3, p. 54; Shaikh, *Who Needs Identity?*, p. 205.

18 Gundimeda, *Dalit Politics in Contemporary India*, pp. 95,96,99; Badri Narayan, *Kanshiram: Leader of the Dalits*, pp. 11, 112, 132, 120, 121, 122; K. Satyanarayana, *Dalit Reconfiguration of Caste*, p. 54; Shaikh, *Who Needs Identity?* p. 205.

19 K.C. Das, *Indian Dalits*, p. 225; Badri Narayan, *National Past and Political Present,* p. 3539; *Interview* with Ram Achal Rajbhar, BSP MLA, Hardwar, UP, 14.04.09; R.K. Singh, *Kanshiram aur BSP*, pp. 53, 54, 59, 61, 62 Pathak, *Rashtra Nayak*, p. 82; Mayawati, *Safarnama,* Part 1, p. 197; Anuj Kumar, Bahujan Nayak *Kanshiram ke Avismaraniya Bhashan* [Leader of the Oppressed Kanshiram's Unforgettable Speeches], Delhi: Gautam Book Centre, 2000, pp. 71, 72, 82, 83, 84.

20 Jaffrelot, *Silent Revolution*, pp. 389-90; Interview with Ambeth Rajan, New Delhi, January 21, 2009; *The Hindu*, New Delhi edition, June 5, 2009; Pai, *Dalit Assertion*, p. 118.

21 Kanshiram would often use the metaphor of a ballpoint to symbolize the unequal access to power and education between upper castes and the Dalit majority. The top of the pen represented the 15% upper castes ruling the country, while the remaining 85%, 'the body of the pen', have become aware of their fate and of their numerical strength. The point was to 'reverse' the political order in favour of the bahujans.

Anne Waldrop, 'Dalit politics in India and new meaning of caste', *Forum for Development Studies,* 31, 2, pp. 275, 276.

'Kanshiram: my fight is against Brahminism', *Sunday*, 21, 7, 13–19 February 1994, p. 27; R.K. Singh, *Kanshiram aur BSP*, pp. 53,54, 59, 61, 62; Interview with Ambeth Rajan, New Delhi, January 21, 2009; Shivmurti Pathak, *Rashtra Nayak Kanshiram* [National Hero Kanshiram], Allahabad: Shekhar Prakashan, 1995, pp. 28,29; Mayawati, *Safarnama*, Part 1, p. 191; Sudha Pai, *Dalit Assertion and the Unfinished Democratic Revolution: The*

Bahujan Samaj Party in Uttar Pradesh, New Delhi: Sage Publications, 2002, p. 118; Anuj Kumar, *Bahujan Nayak Kanshiram ke Avismaraniya Bhashan* [Leader of the Oppressed Kanshiram's Unforgettable Speeches], Delhi: Gautam Book Centre, 2000, pp. 14,15, 71,72.

22 Sudha Pai, State *Politics: New Dimensions (Party System Liberalisation and Politics of Identity)*, Delhi: Shipra Publications, 2000, pp. 119-121; Banerjee-Dube, *Themes*, p. 226; Kanchan Chandra, Why *Ethnic Parties Succeed?*, p. 186.

23 Kanchan Chandra, Why *Ethnic Parties Succeed?*, p. 186.

24 Kanchan Chandra, Why *Ethnic Parties Succeed?*, pp. 257, 258.

25 Kanchan Chandra, Why *Ethnic Parties Succeed?*, pp. 187, 188.

26 Kanchan Chandra, *Why Ethnic Parties Succeed?*, pp. 187, 188.

27 Kanchan Chandra, *Why Ethnic Parties Succeed?*, pp. 188, 189.

28 Pradeep Kumar, *Dalits and the BSP*, p. 824.

29 Kanchan Chandra, *Why Ethnic Parties Succeed?*, p. 149.

30 Duncan, *The Bahujan Samaj Party in Uttar Pradesh*, pp. 39, 38

31 Duncan, *The Bahujan Samaj Party in Uttar Pradesh*, pp. 39, 38; Abhay Kumar Dubey, *Aaj ka Neta*, p. 22.

32 Shah, *Caste and Democratic Politics*, p. 289; K.C. Das, *Indian Dalits*, p.169, 151.

33 Kanshiram's perspective on a political strategy to mobilize the OBC is set prior to the implementation of the Mandal Commission. Kanshiram argued that unlike SC, OBC, which constitutes 52% of the population, did not have adequate legal protection and safeguards and thus their condition (especially MBC) were worse than Dalits. While framing his argument, Kanshiram ideologically conceived the parameters of 'representation and reservation' from the vantage point of Ambedkar's position on SC in the Simon Commission (1927), in which he demanded among other safeguards political protection and special treatment (that is, reservation) for SC. This political position was to be interpreted within the 'spirit' of Article 340, which made it obligatory for government to promote welfare of OBC by removing difficulties and improving their conditions.

The BSP was politically ignorant of the possible impact of the MC on the nature of democratic politics in the post-1990 period, especially in north India, where numerous cleavage-based parties representing narrow social constituencies would challenge national parties and play a significant role in state and national government formation.

Interview with Ram Achal Rajbhar, BSP, MLA, Hardwar, UP, April 14, 2009.

34 Kanshiram, *Chamcha Yug*, pp. 100, 101.

35 Jaffrelot, *Bahujan Samaj Party*, pp. 38, 39; Kanshiram, *Chamcha Yug*, pp. 100, 101; Sudha Pai, *Dalit Assertion*, p.122; R.K. Singh, *Kanshiram aur BSP*, pp. 64, 29.

36 Jaffrelot, *Bahujan Samaj Party*, pp. 38, 39; Kanshiram, *Chamcha Yug*, pp. 100, 101; Sudha Pai, *Dalit Assertion*, p.122; R.K. Singh, *Kanshiram aur BSP*, pp. 64, 29.

37 Kanshiram, *Chamcha Yug*, pp. 100, 101; R.K. Singh, Kanshiram aur BSP, pp.64, 29.

In the neighbouring state of Haryana, years of BAMCEF activity had created a network of Dalit castes (19%) consisting of Adharmi, Balmiki, Chamar subcastes, Dhanak, Kabirpanthi, Khatik, Pasi etc. On the other hand, the state's OBC population stood at 24% with a high proportion of them being lower backwards such as Dhimar, Mallah, Dhobi, Khewat, Bhishti etc. The Dalit-Bahujan castes were apparently ready-made political capital and their negligible social position made them conducive to the BSP if the BSP leader was to be believed.

38 Jaffrelot, *Bahujan Samaj Party*, pp. 38, 39; Kanshiram, *Chamcha Yug*, pp. 100, 101; Sudha Pai, *Dalit Assertion*, p.122; R.K. Singh, *Kanshiram aur BSP*, pp. 64, 29.

39 Mayawati, *Safarnama*, Part 1, pp. 167, 202.

40 Mayawati, *Safarnama*, Part 1, pp. 167.

41 Mayawati, *Safarnama*, Part 1, pp. 174.

42 Mayawati, *Safarnama*, Part 1, pp. 139, 140, 142; Bose, *Behenji*, pp. 68, 69.

43 Mayawati, *Safarnama*, Part 1, pp. 148, 149.

44 Mayawati, *Safarnama*, Part 1, p. 155; R.K. Singh, *Kanshiram aur BSP*, p. 61; Interview with Ambeth Rajan, New Delhi, January 21, 2009.

45 Namishray, *Bahujan Samaj*, pp. 50, 51.

46 Namishray, *Bahujan Samaj*, pp. 50, 51, 52.

47 S.T. Devkar, *BSP Supremo Mananiya Kanshiram: Bhashan evam Sakshatkar* (In Gratitude of Mr. Kanshiram: Speeches and Interviews), Aurangabad, Maharashtra: Daulat Prakashan, 2005. (The slogan has been taken from the backcover.); Mayawati, *Safarnama*, Part 1, pp. 458, 459; A.G. Noorani, 'Indira Gandhi and Indian Muslims', *Economic and Political Weekly*, Vol. 25, No. 44, 3 November 1990, p. 2417.

48 K. Chandra, *Why Ethnic Parties Succeed?* p. 259, 260, 217; Mohammad Mujtaba Khan, 'Muslim and electoral politics', *Seminar*, 571, March 2007, pp. 37–42.

The Muslims received one-third (about 33%) 'representation' in the Central Legislature under the Government of India Act 1935. The Muslim League continued to rigidly enforce the 'communal ratio' in public offices, particularly in regions where Muslims had a better population ratio in comparison to Hindus.

49 R.K. Singh, *Kanshiram aur BSP*, pp. 64, 65; Narayan, *National Past*, p. 3539.

50 Platts, *Dictionary*, p. 372; Mayawati, *Safarnama*, Part 1, pp. 142,151, 152, 458,459.

51 Mayawati, Safarnama, Part 1, pp. 142,151, 152, 458, 459.

52 The term day.niy (pitiable) condition of the Muslims is an expression Mayawati used in a speech addressed to the Lok Sabha in June 1990 as MP from Bijnore, UP.

Mayawati, *Safarnama*, Part 1, pp. 203, 204, 196, 197, 147; K.C. Gupta and S.K. Mittal, Covering and Reacting to a Tragedy: Some Reflections on the Meerut Communal Holocaust, *PUCL Bulletin*, October 1988, p. 12; Also see URL: http//www. pucl.org/from-archives/Religious-communalism/meerut.htm (accessed December 19, 2007)

Almost five years later, addressing the Muslim community in Agra, in June 1992, Mayawati discussed the fate of the Muslims in the aftermath of the 'state-wide communal riots' (Kanpur in April-May 1990, Lucknow in October 1990, Agra in November 1990 etc.) due to L.K. Advani's rath yatra (lit. journey by chariot) on the issue of Ram mandir. She said that in the name of curbing, riots the Mulayam Singh government during that critical period had 'oppressed the Muslim community' and alleged that Prime Minister V.P. Singh and the police, 'an institution of the manuvadi system', were 'complicit in the perpetuation of communal violence in the state'.

Mayawati,*Safarnama*,part1,pp. 203,204, 458, 459.

53 Mayawati, *Safarnama*, Part 1, pp. 148, 149.

54 Mayawati, *Safarnama*, Part 1, pp. 152, 151.

55 Duncan, *The Bahujan Samaj Party in Uttar Pradesh*, pp. 39, 38; Abhay Kumar Dubey, *Aaj ka Neta*, p. 22;

It is to be noted that BSP's territorialization of power as politics is not a 'politics of locality', as Derrida means as he voices concern over the intense technologization of sociopolitical decision-making processes that is transforming traditional spaces and sites of representation of democracy in western societies. He emphasizes a return to the 'politics of locality' that would retrieve the dearth of 'democratic' political spaces.

For further details, see Michael Peters, 'Education, post-structuralism and the difference', *Policy Futures in Education*, 3, 4, 2005, pp. 439,440.

56 Mayawati, *Safarnama,* Part 1, p. 174; Kanchan Chandra, *Why Ethnic Parties Succeed?*, p. 149; Interview with Ram Achal Rajbhar, BSP. MLA, Hardwar, UP, 14.04.09.

57 Interview with Ambeth Rajan, New Delhi, January 21, 2009.

58 H.D. Singh, *543 Faces of India*, New Delhi: Newsmen Publishers, 1996, p. 276; J.C. Aggarwal and N.K. Chowdhury, *Elections in India*: 1952-96, Delhi: Shipra Publications, 1996, p. 235.

59 'Prestigious contests in UP', *Frontline,* 1, 2, December 15, 1984, pp. 22-23.

60 Bose, *Behenji,* p. 64.

In the 1984 Lok Sabha elections in UP, the INC won 83 out of 85 seats barring Etah and Baghpat. In most Lok Sabha constituencies, the INC won between 40% and 60% vote shares in each constituency.

URL: http//www. eci.gov.in statistical Reports/LS 1984/vol_I_84 pdf (accessed on June 8, 2007)

61 URL: http//www. eci.gov.in Statistical Reports/LS 1984/ Vol_I LS_84 pdf (accessed June 8, 2007)

62 *Indian Express*, New Delhi edition, December 15, 1985.

63 *The Hindu*, Madras edition, December 15, 1985, Nehru Memorial Museum and Library (NMML), Microfilm, Acc. No. 362, R.8707.

64 Aggarwal and Chowdhury, *Elections in India*, p. 233; Arun Kumar, *Elections in India: Nehru to Vajpayee*, New Delhi: Gyan Publishing House, 2001, p. 311; H.D. Singh, *Faces of India*, p. 266

65 *The Hindu*, Madras edition, December 15, 1985, NMML, Microfilm, Acc. No. 362, R.8707.

66 URL: http//www. eci.gov.in/SR_ Key Highlights/ SE_ 1985/Statistical_Report_ Uttar Pradesh_1985. pdf (accessed June 10, 2007) ; Pai, *Dalit Assertion*, p. 156.

67 URL: http//www. eci.gov.in/Bye Election/bye_election.asp (accessed on June 10, 2007); Pai, *Dalit Assertion*, p. 156.

68 'The changing scene in UP', *Frontline,* 11, 2, January 15–28, 1994, p.5; K.Chandra, *Why Ethnic Parties Succeed?*, p. 236; URL: http//www.drsureshmanebsp.com (accessed on Sept. 15, 2008); Anuj Kumar, *Avismaraniya Bhasan,* p. 73; Jaffrelot, *Dr. Ambedkar and Untouchability*, pp. 154, 155.

69 K.Chandra, *Why Ethnic Parties Succeed?*, p. 155; Arun Kumar, *Nehru to Vajpayee*, p. 316; Aggarwal and Choudhury, *Elections in India*, p. 235; H.D. Singh, *Faces in India*, p. 273.

70 *The Times of India,* Bombay edition, March 19, 1987, NMML, Acc. No. 418, R.6779.

71 *The Times of India*, Bombay edition, March 28, 1987. NMML, Acc. No. 418, R.6779.

72 *The Times of India*, Bombay edition, March 18, 1987. NMML, Acc. No. 418, R.6779.

73 *Indian Express*, Bombay edition, March 20, 1987. NMML, Acc. No. 418, R.6779.

74 *The Times of India,* Bombay edition, March 19, 1987. NMML, Acc. No. 418, R.6779.

75 Pai, *Dalit Assertion*, p. 156; *Indian Express*, New Delhi edition, March 29, 1987.

76 At the time when Kanshiram and Mayawati were consolidating their position within the BSP, another 'split' took place in 1986 within the BAMCEF on the issue of the 'future role of the organization and Mayawati's position of authority' within the party. T.S. Jhalli, Jitendra Kumar and B.J. Patel broke off from the BAMCEF members loyal to Kanshiram. Jhalli, head of the Punjab unit of the BAMCEF (1988) with limited influence in Punjab, said that 'Kanshiram was leading Dalits up the garden path and diluting the intensity of the struggles of the downtrodden'. In 1987, Kanshiram 'dissolved' UP faction of the BAMCEF. By that time BAMCEF volunteers were financing, organizing and supervising the party at the local level and introducing candidates to Kanshiram and supervising their campaigns.

Sudha Pai, *Dalit Assertion*, pp. 105, 106, 196; 'The changing scene in UP', *Frontline*, 11, 2, January 15–28, 1994, p. 5; *Indian Express*, New Delhi edition, March 29, 1987.

77 Bose, *Behenji*, p. 66.

78 It was reminiscent of a catchy political phrase 'one vote, one note,' coined during this period, that weighed Kanshiram on a 'tola' of Rs. 12,000 'one-rupee coins' equal to his bodyweight. On his 52nd birthday in 1986, he was presented with a purse of Rs. 52,000. That amount became the benchmark for all political meetings involving the dalit leader. At one time he claimed to have conducted '40 meetings at the rate of Rs. 52,000 for each meeting'; and he held 7 'out-of-turn meetings at the rate of Rs. 1 lakh per meeting'.

Bose, *Behenji*, p. 66 ; Kalyani Shankar, *Gods of Power*, p. 4; Vivek Kumar, *Roaring Revolution*, p. 127.

79 The Allahabad Lok Sabha bye-elections captured nationwide attention. Mr. V.P. Singh, the Jan Morcha candidate, was backed by 23 political parties, including the CPI and CPI(M). The chief ministers from Kerala, Karnataka, Andhra Pradesh, West Bengal and Haryana canvassed and extended full support to Mr. V.P. Singh. The 'press barons' put their services at the disposal of Mr. V.P. Singh.

URL: http//www.drsureshmanebsp.com (accessed on September 15, 2008)

For details on this issue, please see 'We trapped V.P: Congress leaders', *Patriot*, New Delhi edition, May 25, 1988; 'V.P. upstaged by Congress', *The Times of India*, Bombay edition, May 24, 1988, NMML, Microfilm, Acc. No. 436, R.6797; 'Odd controversies in Allahabad', *Statesman*, New Delhi edition, May 30, 1988, NMML, Microfilm, Acc. No. 291, R.6965.

80 *Patriot*, New Delhi edition, May 25, 1988.

81 Aggarwal and Choudhury, *Elections in India*, p. 233; H.D. Singh, *Faces in India*, p. 259; *Hindustan Times*, New Delhi edition, May 28, 1988, NMML, Microfilm, Acc. No. 454, R.6197; *The Times of India*, Bombay edition, May 25, 1988, NMML, Microfilm, Acc. No. 436, R.6797.

82 *Indian Express*, New Delhi edition, August 3, 1988; *Hindustan Times*, New Delhi edition, June 10, 1988, NMML, Microfilm, Acc. No. 456, R.6199.

83 *Indian Express*, New Delhi edition, August 3, 1988; *Hindustan Times*, New Delhi edition, June 10, 1988, NMML, Microfilm, Acc. No. 456, R.6199.

84 URL: http//www. eci.gov.in/Bye Elections/bye-elections. Asp (accessed July 21, 2007); Pai, *Dalit Assertion*, p. 156.

85 URL: http//www.drsureshmanebsp.com (accessed on Sept. 15, 2008); Bose, *Behenji*, p. 67.

86 Bose, *Behenji*, p. 66; Harold Gould and Sumit Ganguly (Eds.), *India Votes: Alliance Politics and Minority Governments in the Ninth and Tenth General Elections*, Boulders, USA: Westview Press, 1993, pp. 15, 16.

87 'On the road with Rajiv', *Sunday*, 16, 20, November 19, 1989, p. 31; 'Mauled mercilessly', *India Today*, December 15, 1989, p. 43.

88 *The Times of India*, Bombay edition, November 18, 1989, NMML, Microfilm, Acc. No. 461, R.7029.

89 Mayawati, *Safarnama*, Part 1, p.52; URL: http//www. eci.gov.in/SR_KeyHighlights/ SE_ 1989/ Statistical_Report_% 20 UP_1989. pdf (accessed August 2, 2007); H.D. Singh, *Faces in India*, pp. 266, 284, 259, 271, 261, 278, 282, 274, 275; Pai, *Dalit Assertions*, p. 157; *The Times of India*, Bombay edition, 29.11.89; URL: http//www.drsureshmanebsp.com (accessed September 15, 2008).

Within a year after the 1989 Lok Sabha elections, assembly elections were held in Madhya Pradesh. The BSP won two seats. The party had put up 187 candidates though it achieved an overall vote share of only 3.55%. The weak presence of the BSP, in Madhya Pradesh, indicative of a low vote share, could not transform organizational presence into electoral support for the party among sections of the poor and the backward in the region. Post-1989 Lok Sabha and assembly elections, the BSP got state recognition in UP and Punjab and was registered as a political party in Madhya Pradesh.

90 Gould and Ganguly, *India Votes*, p. 22; URL: http//www.drsureshmanebsp .com (accessed September 15, 2008).

The decline of the Congress was evident in the sharp fall of its popularity in terms of votes, between 1984 and 1989, viz, down from 51% to 31%; BJP up from 6.4% to 20%; and JD, or rather its former 'avatar', the Bharatiya Lok Dal and Bharatiya Krishak Mazdoor Party that registered an impressive vote share of 25.2% to 40% for the JD. In the 1989 Lok Sabha elections in UP, the BJP secured 8 seats, the Congress 15 seats and the JD 54 seats. In the UP assembly elections, the Congress secured 94 out of 410 seats, competing with a winning vote share of 27.90%; BJP secured 57 out of 275 seats with a 11.61% vote share and JD won 208 out of 356 seats with a 29.71% vote share.

'Mauled mercilessly', *India Today*, December 15, 1989, p. 43; URL: http// www. eci.gov.in/SR_KeyHighlights/SE_1989/Statistical_Report_% 20 UP_ 1989.pdf (accessed August 21, 2007).

91 The Mandal Commission formed in 1978 under former Bihar CM Bindeshwar Prasad Mandal by Morarji Desai submitted its report in 1980 to the next Prime Minister Indira Gandhi. The report was 'tabled indefinitely' by Mrs. Gandhi. Rajiv Gandhi when asked about the Mandal Report told his aides: 'It's a can of worms. I won't touch it'. L.R. Naik, the only Dalit member of the Commission, refused to sign the report saying only a new elite of educated Dalits, Adivasis and OBCs would benefit from reservations.

'1979 – The Mandal Commission: Stirring the Caste Cauldron', *India Today*, December 24, 2009.

URL:http//www.m.indiatoday.in/story/1979-The Mandal Commission: Stirring the Caste Cauldron/1/76365.html (accessed June 8, 2014).

92 Yogendra Yadav, 'Open contests, closed options', *Seminar*, 534, February, 2004, pp. 62, 63; Rob Jenkins, 'International Development Institutions and National Economic Contests: neoliberalism encounters India's indigenous political traditions', *Economy and Society*, 32, 4, (2003), p. 590;; URL: http//www.ceri-sciencespo.com/archive/Sept04/arty.pdf (accessed on May 24, 2007) ; D.L. Sheth, 'Secularisation of caste and the making of new middle class', *Economic and Political Weekly*, 34, 34–35, August 21, 1999, pp. 2502–2510; Neerja Gopal Jayal, *Democracy and the State*, New Delhi: Oxford University Press, 1999, p. 190.

93 Gould and Ganguly, *India Votes*, pp. 255, 256, 257.

94 Former prime minister Rajiv Gandhi on an election tour to Tamil Nadu was assassinated in Sriperumbudur on May 20, 1991, by a 'human bomb' belonging to the separatist Liberation of Tamil Tigers (LTTE), a group based in Sri Lanka fighting for a separate Tamil 'eelam', or nation, in Sri Lanka.

'Going Places', *Sunday*, 18, 24, June 1991, pp. 37, 38.

95 Gould and Ganguly, *India Votes*, p. 258.

96 Gould and Ganguly, *India Votes*, pp.266-9; Peter Ronald de Souza and S. Sridharan (Eds.), *India's Political Parties,* New Delhi: Sage, 2006, p. 110.

97 URL: http//www. eci.gov.in/SR_KeyHighlights/SE_1991/Stat_Rep_UP_91. pdf (accessed August 21, 2007); Gould and Ganguly, *India Votes*, p. 280.

98 Mayawati, *Safarnama,* Part 1, pp. 52, 53; URL: http//www. archive. eci. gov. in/GE 2004 /pollup/pc/states/partycomp 01. htm; http//www.eci.gov.in/ Statistical Reports/ LS_1991/vol_II_91. pdf (accessed August 24, 2007)

99 H.D. Singh, *Faces of India*, p. 266.

100 John. T. Platts, *Dictionary*, p. 849.

101 Mayawati contested and lost from Hoshiarpur Lok Sabha constituency in Punjab in 1992, the only time she contested outside Uttar Pradesh. However, the party performed well in the November 1992 assembly elections in Punjab, winning nine seats at Banga (SC), Shapur (SC), Bhadaur (SC), Dharamkot (SC), Mahilpur (SC), Balchair, Garhshankar, Adampur and Sham Chaurasi. In Punjab, despite the perpetual threat of Sikh terrorism, the electoral performance of the BSP demonstrated the possibility of further consolidation of the 29% Dalit-Mazhabi Sikh community, which also included Balmikis, Mahashas and other dalit subcastes. From the perspective of the BSP, the political situation in Punjab assumes importance since a year later Kanshiram's Party emerged from a stupendous electoral performance in the UP assembly elections held in November 1993, and entered into a coalition government with the Samajwadi Party. It was, perhaps, at this juncture that a stable solid BSP constituency in Punjab failed to be activated, as the party began to solely concentrate on capturing political power in UP. In 1996, in alliance with the Akali Dal, the BSP secured three seats in the Lok Sabha elections.

In Madhya Pradesh, the BSP had created bases of political support among the 'poor' backward castes in Vindhya, Chambal (Gwalior, Guna, Bhind district) and in some regions, now part of Chhatisgarh. Yet, UP-centric politics did also affect the party's prospects in the coming Lok Sabha and assembly elections in the state. In 1996, the BSP did manage to win one seat with an 'increased vote share of 8.18%, a proof of party's weak organizational presence in the state. In subsequent Lok Sabha elections in 1998 and 1999, and assembly elections in 2001–2002, in Madhya Pradesh the poor performance of the BSP came as no surprise.

Bose, *Behenji*, p. 74; H.D. Singh, *Faces of India*, p. 269; URL: http//www.eci .gov.in/Statistical Report/LS_1991/Vol_II_91.pdf (accessed on Aug. 28, 2007); URL: http//www.ceopunjab.nic.in (accessed September 15, 2008); Namishray, *Bahujan Samaj*, pp. 59, 60.

102 Bose, *Behenji*, p. 74; H.D. Singh, *Faces of India*, p. 269; URL: http//www.eci .gov.in/Statistical Report/LS_1991/Vol_II_91.pdf (accessed August 28, 2007); URL: http//www.ceopunjab.nic.in (accessed September 15, 2008); Namishray, *Bahujan Samaj*, pp. 59, 60.

103 Shah, *Dalits and Democratic Politics*, p. 301.

4 In the Forecourt of Political Power

On December 6, 1992, right-wing Hindu 'nationalist' organizations destroyed the Babri Masjid in Ayodhya. It was the culmination of an aggressive and overtly militant and religious 'Ram Janmabhoomi movement' to construct a temple for 'Lord Ram' at his 'birthplace'. Leaving a trail of communal violence before and after the unfolding of the ghastly incident, it led to the immediate dismissal of the BJP government in Uttar Pradesh by the central government led by Narasimha Rao of the Congress Party which was in a coalition arrangement with the BJP. The Centre imposed President's Rule in the state that lasted from December 1992 to November 1993. Post-Babri Masjid demolition, the BJP was 'squarely attacked' for the 'barbaric' act by the press, media, and opposition political parties in the country. There was widespread condemnation across the world with reports of hostility towards Hindus in Pakistan and Bangladesh. Unlike the withdrawal of political support to the JD-led National Front government in 1990, the reason for the BJP to continue to support the Congress Party at the Centre (1991–1996), post-Babri Masjid demolition, was that in three years (1989–1992) the perception in the BJP was that it had crafted an electoral strategy of 'Hindutva and social engineering'[1]; that the BJP was a 'national political party' which had adjusted to the changed political parameters of 'coalition politics' and begun to make political inroads into non-traditional bases of support critical for the party to increase its electoral presence in other states and win political power at the Centre.

Quite contrary to the communal frenzy that gripped the state in the wake of the Babri Masjid demolition, the political undercurrents of the Mandal effect were being felt in Uttar Pradesh. Irrespective of the new caste alignments that were reconfiguring state politics with their political consequences, in a general sense, 'mandalization of caste' posed a political challenge to BJP's newly crafted majoritarian politics. Post-Mandal Uttar Pradesh witnessed an assortment of non-Brahmin landowning castes and politically conscious low-caste social groups that began to leverage for political power. With the founding of the Samajwadi Party (SP) in October 1992, Mulayam Singh Yadav's political ambition grew as his party built a successful Yadav-Muslim electoral coalition. Muslims were juxtaposed in the midst of a 'caste equation' to negate the political threat emanating from the BJP. Mulayam Singh Yadav followed a two-pronged strategy: one, to build a solid bloc of Muslim votes, and two, divide Hindu votes into two sections — of the 'forward' and the 'backward' castes — to project the SP as the sole 'representative' and protector of the backward communities in the state. On the other hand, in eastern UP, a favourable condition for the rise of lower castes emerged with the 'ensuing tension between former (Thakur) landlords and smaller landowning castes', which led to a more 'fluid political context providing space for Dalits', accounting for approximately 47% of the total landless labour force in the region, to politically assert, against Thakur landlords. This base of Dalits translated their newly found organized protest into political support for the Bahujan Samaj Party.[2]

SP-BSP Coalition Government: A Tenuous Secular Pact

Apprehending state polls at the end of a year of Presidents Rule, the two socially incomprehensible political parties forged a 'secular' front to defeat the BJP. In that context Kanshiram said:

> '(The) Congress and the BJP were (Brahmanwadi parties) and that while he had been trying to destroy the Congress (he) has felt that (in this endeavor) Narasimha Rao (the PM belonging to the INC) (was) better than (him)'; and that he had 'laid down (his) arms (to let) Narasimha Rao deal with the Congress'; (BSP) would (focus) attention to the BJP'.[3]

A few months before the 'pact' was sealed, Kanshiram had attempted to forge political ties with individual political leaders of the JD and SP but failed due to the threat of a revolt by the UP unit of the BSP. In the context of his ineffective political efforts, Kanshiram had remarked: '(BSP) may improve; (with their support) but the (other political parties) would be strengthened'.[4] Yet in the post-November 1993 assembly elections in UP, Kanshiram changed his political strategy, declaring, despite opposition within the party, that 'collaboration with other political parties was politically worthy and that alliances (could be) valuable and (could produce) tangible (political) results'.[5] Whether BSP's prospective political alliance with SP would heighten social tensions was discussed in detail by the respective party leaderships of the SP and the BSP for the larger political interest that it held for them. The prospect of 'attaining political power collectively' and thereby defeat the 'dominant' Brahmins and Thakurs castes eventually brought SP to break the 'mental barrier' and agree to a political arrangement with the BSP. The SP and the BSP, which appealed to voters as 'embodiments of two mutually irreconcilable sections of the population', in the competitive politics of 'Mandalism', were to appear to be in apparent (political) harmony successfully bringing down the BJP 'Mandirites'.[6] The pre-poll alliance was evidently clear from the beginning when Kanshiram stated:

> '(N)either [sic] Mulayam Singh Yadav' (who was a bit apprehensive joining forces with Kanshiram) nor (he could) stand alone in UP'. 'That is why we got together. Our purpose was to get the BJP defeated'. Kanshiram further asserted: '(Ab) hum dono (BSP and SP) BJP ko Lucknow mein gherenge' (lit. the BSP and SP would corner the BJP in Lucknow). We have to 'snatch the 'kursi' (lit. chair, here meaning power) from BJP and give it to Mulayam Singh Yadav; and further, 'we will have to move step by step'. The potency of a 'secular plebeian alliance would be a 'representative government (and not) merely an efficient government (which) would ensure justice for all sections of the society'.[7] Kanshiram further remarked that 'We (BSP) have started from zero (and after) forming the government in UP (he) was confident that the BSP would expand to 'Madhya Pradesh, Bihar, West Bengal, Maharashtra, Andhra Pradesh, Karnataka, and (that it would) be through these states that (the BSP would) march to Delhi'.[8]

The success of the 'political agreement' was evident in Mulayam Singh Yadav's cryptic statement that while 'the Congress and the JD wanted an alliance (with the SP) (he) chose the BSP'.[9] On the other hand, Kanshiram's pretentious comment in public suggested that it was the BSP that was instrumental in forming the 'secular front', by claiming that 'Mulayam Singh Yadav had been dependent on JD leaders like Chandra Shekhar, V.P. Singh (and) Devilal'; and that (it was) (Kanshiram) who had 'made him (Mulayam Singh Yadav) an independent leader'.[10] The coalition agreement between the SP and BSP (was) 'not sthayi (not permanent) but tikau' (durable)[11] and in the event of an SP-BSP government coming to power in UP, the 'Dalit Party' would review 'Mulayam Singh Yadav's performance for six months'. Kanshiram emphasized: If '(the) government promise(d) to deliver on our principles and expectations then we (could) experiment with "the coalition" in other parts of the country, otherwise it would be limited to UP'.[12] The BSP preferred a 'majboor sarkar (dependent government) to a mazboot sarkar' (stable government); a government that would be dependent on BSP and would be forced to 'listen to the voice of the Dalits'.[13] Kanshiram stated: 'We are looking for an unstable polity. That helps us consolidate our (political) position' in the government; and '(be in a position to) feed on (its) carcass'.[14] In a '(political) coalition', the (BSP) was quite willing to 'antagonize even sections that (would) support its partners in alliance'. 'The rationale seems to have been that the 'BSP's need is less than the partners need to keep the coalition going'. The BSP 'advocated the need to pursue its (Dalit) agenda and if the (coalition) partner (did) not like some elements of the (social) "agenda" so (it) be'. In unequivocal terms Kanshiram affirmed that the SP-BSP coalition was a 'no compromise with brahmanvad forces, whether it was the Congress brahmanvads A team, (or) BJP B team (or) JD C team (or even) Communists D team'.[15] The BSP was keen that 'neither of the (national) political parties — the Congress, BJP and JD — be "finished", though the Party hoped to "defeat" them, and by virtue of it ensure that one amongst the brahminical (political) parties (competing for votes among themselves) would (survive)'.[16] In expectation of an SP-BSP coalition government in Uttar Pradesh, the BSP's principle of 'control' of SP, its coalition partner, was laid clear by Kanshiram's 'agenda' politics. It would become the underlying motive for a political policy for a decade and a half for the BSP.

In the November 1993 assembly elections, a strong Dalit presence at the polling stations was attributed to the 'magic of Kanshiram' and the strict security arrangements against booth capturing that 'allowed Dalits to vote without fear'.[17] The large Muslim presence in the state elections was seen as an endorsement to vote strategically for the SP-BSP alliance.[18] In the assembly elections, 'Ayodhya' and the 'Hindutva ideology' did not transform into political capital for the BJP.[19] Neither did the elections mark an intense 'polarization of the bahujans' under the SP-BSP coalition. The SP-BSP secured 36% of the Dalit and 33% of the OBC votes higher than 22% Dalits for the Congress, 28% OBC vote (Kurmis, Lodhs) for the BJP and 13% OBC support for the JD. The upper castes voted in significant numbers for the BJP.[20] A majority of Muslim vote of 18% in the state shifted in favour of the SP-BSP alliance even as a much weakened Congress Party was able to poll more than 15% and the JD about 16% among the Muslims.[21] The SP-BSP made impressive political gains in eastern and central UP. In eastern UP, where the BJP won 83 out of 159 seats, the SP-BSP combine made a major dent to BJP's electoral prospects costing the party 31 seats. The JD lost 28 seats in the region, while the 'coalition' gained 54 seats. In western UP, Rohilkhand and 'Uttarakhand region', the SP-BSP coalition captured 13, 15 and 2 seats, respectively. In western UP, the BJP and the SP-BSP (see Table 4.1) made political gains at the cost of the JD.[22] The success of the political coalition can be gauged by the fact that in Faizabad district in which Ayodhya was located, the 'combine' won seven seats. On the other hand, in western UP, where the BJP did well, Muslims followed Shahi Imam Syed Abdullah Bukhari's political advice to vote for the JD. There was a division of vote between SP-BSP and JD benefiting the BJP.[23] The SP-BSP combine could not get a sizeable section of the backwards' vote, but the political coalition clearly appealed to the Dalits and the Muslims. The SP-BSP combination won 42 out of 88 reserved seats, the BJP won 34 and the Congress was reduced to 6 seats.

In 99 assembly constituencies with more than 25% SC population, the 'coalition' secured 33.9% votes and won 59 seats.[24]

The assembly election results conclusively proved that majoritarian politics could take a 'commanding position intermittently only to be pushed aside by caste'.[25] The SP won 107 seats which was a significant improvement from 53 seats it held in the 1991 assembly election. The BSP increased its tally to 69 seats — which included 16 B.A., 7 M.A., 15 LL.B. and 1 Ph.D MLA — from 12 seats (see Table 4.2) it won two years earlier. In comparison

Table 4.1 Region-wise Party Performances in 1993 UP Assembly Elections

Regions in UP	*BJP*		*SP*		*BSP*		*Cong(I)*		*JD*	
	Seats Won	*Vote %*	*Seats Won*	*Vote %*	*Seats Won*	*Vote %*	*Seats Won*	*Vote %*	*Seats Won*	*Vote %*
Hill districts	10	1.34	1	0.23	0	0.10	6	1.19	0	0.28
Uttar Pradesh (west)	56	8.81	24	4.09	1	1.36	7	4.06	12	4.45
Bundelkhand	7	1.46	1	0.18	9	1.20	2	0.97	2	0.50
Uttar Pradesh (central)	31	6.00	31	5.05	6	0.99	3	2.93	4	1.46
Uttar Pradesh (east)	49	11.52	36	5.72	51	7.13	7	4.39	5	3.65
Rohilkhand	24	4.22	16	2.83	0	0.32	3	1.44	4	2.03

Source: The Battle for UP, *India Today*, November 1995, p. 52.

Table 4.2 UP Assembly Elections (1991 and 1993)

Assembly Elections	*BJP*	*SP*	*BSP*	*Cong(I)*	*JD*
1991	221	53	12	46	92
1993	177	107	69	28	28

to the JD government in UP in 1990 where upper caste representation was 50% and in the 1991 BJP government where it stood at 51.61%, the SP-BSP coalition government of 1993 registered an alarming decrease in the upper-caste representation in the UP state legislature. Upper caste representations stood at a mere 6.66%, while the share of the OBC and SC increased to 40% and 33.33%, respectively, in government.[26]

As the political alliance began to take effect post-election, Kanshiram coined a catchy phrase: 'miley Mulayam Kanshiram/hawa mein ur gaya jai shri ram' (with Mulayam and Kanshiram coming together "victory to Lord Ram" — BJP's poll agenda for consolidation of 'majority (Hindu) votes' — has gone up in thin air); and further that the SP-BSP 'political pact' had been founded to fight the 'dadagiri' (intimidating and coercive behaviour) of BJP's 'jai shri ram' (glory/victory to Lord Ram).[27] The state assembly election results made it near impossible for the BJP, Congress and JD to come together to form a coalition government in UP. It was in that context Kanshiram said: (It was) 'now our votes, our goal, our share and representation. (We would) try to give (the poor) justice'.[28] The SP-BSP government would be, as Kanshiram declared, 'supported by the Congress unconditionally'; that 'Mulayam (could) run the government with the JD and BJP's political support since the 'BJP (was) afraid of elections (as another state election would) be a big setback for (BJP)'.[29] Mulayam Singh Yadav identified the SP-BSP government as the 'first ministry in the state of the poor and the downtrodden'. The SP leader said:

> The SP-BSP combine that had a greater representation of the poor in its support base, (had) come to power; (that) the 'pro-poor' elements in these (political) parties would be able to assert their views. Development of the poor, that is, the farmers and the workers, uplift of villages and agriculture, on which depend not only the rural economy but also the country's economy would be the most challenging task ahead for the SP-BSP coalition in UP. Special attention (would) be given to liberate Dalits from exploitation.[30]

The elevation of Mulayam Singh Yadav to the post of Chief Minister of Uttar Pradesh was a grand occasion for his huge mass of 'Yadav' supporters. A song written by a Mulayam Singh supporter to mark the 'victory of the SP-BSP alliance' in UP in December 1993 went as follows: Pragati disha, nav nidhiki dhor/Vir Mulayam chahun dish oar/Kanshiram ka lag gaya zor/ Vir Mulayam chahun dish oar. (The beacon of progress is lit by the first rays of the sun/Brave Mulayam you are hailed from all directions/The strength of Kanshiram is with you/Brave Mulayam you are hailed from all directions.)[31] It was Mulayam Singh Yadav who insisted that the songwriter put in at least one line about Kanshiram as a 'political sop' to his 'bahujan' ally. Mulayam Singh Yadav's 'political coronation' as CM of UP was marked by the 'several hundred thousand who came to the victory rally, rowdy and full of swagger'. The 'other group' came for 'saheb' (Kanshiram) 'barefoot and not equipped for the Lucknow winter'.[32] Kanshiram asserted that '(Mulayam Singh Yadav) must deliver'; and to 'achieve (the social agenda) he could use (BSP) party men to run his government'. Mayawati said that the government must 'crush reactionary forces to bring about land reforms, empower Dalits at the grassroots level, and end atrocities; and that (the) force of state power (must) be used to bring peace (which meant security for Dalits) to Uttar Pradesh'. Reacting to the 'SP-BSP victory', one Rajput 'pradhan' (headman of a village) from Hathras said: 'I never used to have to do this (guard his land from supposed Dalit attackers) but now somehow everything is different. We Rajputs feel under attack. Among certain sections of the upper castes in western UP there were fears of the coming OBC-Dalit raj (rule)'.[33]

BSP: A UP-Based Political Party

Kanshiram was aware that an organizational imbalance had stuck to the Party since the early years of its inception due to a concentration of political activities in north India. The party units in the four south Indian states were formed in 1989, five years after the BSP formally set up party units in the north Indian states. Yet, for a party that had little to claim in terms of durable grassroots party machinery in other states, Kanshiram was keen to effect a broad, though certainly not a dense, political network of a mélange of struggling and exploited castes across states. In clear political terms, such 'castes and communities' were or could possibly be core social constituencies of certain non-savarna/regional political parties or those in the making. This political observation appeared as a latent ideological position for an electoral strategy of low-caste (bahujan) politics which could be achieved through an inter-party consultation, an arrangement of 'pacts' or an extension of political network to 'win certain seats in certain states'.[34] With a presumed credibility of a rising political party, the BSP leader in typical political bombast laid out an optimal mathematical calculation and 'winning percentage' that had been reached to usher in a 'Bahujan State' in India:

> '600 jatis, which is 10 per cent of the total (number of) jatis (had) directly impacted the political fortunes of the Party; (and that the Party

> had) achieved fourth position in the country behind Congress, BJP and the CPI(M). If (the Party) (was) able to add "400 castes" (it) would touch 1,000 "jatis" which would translate into increased number of elected representatives in the Indian Parliament and State Assemblies' (and) 'then BSP would be the "number one" political party; a party in a position to govern at the Centre; (with) "50 per cent (half) of 85 per cent" of the total population (which) was adequate to win political power'. Kanshiram pegged the 'winning caste coalition' percentage down "realistically" to "40 per cent"; (and if not even that then it was certainly) 35 per cent at all costs.'[35]

After the formation of the SP-BSP government in Uttar Pradesh, Kanshiram went on a 'political tour' of the country to expand the BSP's 'nationwide presence'. It began in south India, where the Party believed that 'rules of electoral politics' could change with the emergence of the BSP as a 'coalition party' with regional political parties. In Andhra Pradesh, Kanshiram declared 'he would have no truck with the Congress or the Telugu Desam Party' but was seeking to forge a 'unity of Kapus and OBC' concentrated in nine coastal districts of the state. In Karnataka, Kanshiram held political meetings with Deve Gowda, the state president of JD, who represented the powerful Vokkaliga caste in the state and expelled Congressman and influential 'Kunha politician', former Chief Minister of Karnataka S. Bangarappa. In Kerala, Kanshiram met political activists of the Sree Narayan Guru Dharma Paripalan Yogam (Sree Narayan Guru Forum for Maintaining Ethical Way of Life) belonging to the backward Ezhava caste. The BSP leader was keen to forge a political alliance with Muslim and backward classes in the state and met K.R. Gowri, an expelled leader of the Communist Party of India (Marxist) – CPI(M). Despite the possibility of forging a common front, political differences arose as Kanshiram advocated 'Dalit' rule, while Gowri advocated 'welfare of the "deprived classes" in all communities'. Kanshiram's parleys with regional leaders of south India met with no political success. Having completed an unsuccessful tour of south India, Kanshiram began to selectively tour other states in the rest of the country. In the third week of January 1994, Kanshiram addressed a public meeting attended by a small crowd of 5,000 people at Shivaji Park, Mumbai. Kanshiram claimed in his speech that 'he would (become the Chief Minister) of Maharashtra by the end of 1995'.[36]

What is significant is the political importance given to the 'Kanshiram phenomenon' by political parties in states the BSP leader toured. In Andhra Pradesh, remedial measures for the poor, such as the setting up of a backward class commission to consider the case of the Kapus and 'hiking reservations' for backward classes in local body polls from 25% to 33% were announced. In Maharashtra, the Marathwada University was renamed after Dr. Ambedkar. In West Bengal, Kanshiram's political presence in December 1993 compelled the ruling CPI(M) to direct each ministry to submit a report specifying measures taken to uplift backward sections, including the process by which additional benefits could be specified for SC candidates appearing for the Medical and Joint Entrance Examinations. In Gujarat, the 'Kanshiram effect' influenced the Chimanbhai Patel government to grant a higher percentage of jobs and admission in educational institutions for socially and economically backward classes in the state. In Bihar, Laloo Prasad Yadav planned to expand his 'Yadav-Muslim' electoral equation to forge a new 'Adivasi, Harijan, Muslim, Yadav political axis to pre-empt Kanshiram from influencing the 1.04 crore Dalits who constituted over 18 per cent of the state's population'. Laloo Prasad Yadav's populist programme 'Kaya Palat Abhiyan' (mission for a change of form) witnessed the CM 'personally bathe and wash the hair of Dalit youths'.[37] In the third week of January 1994, Kanshiram addressed a rally at Sambhalpur, Orissa. Addressing the rally, Kanshiram said that '95 per cent out of 100 per cent are poor SC and ST and if they (demonstrated) their strength then both the "Patnaiks", that is "Biju and J.B." would be defeated'. Kanshiram remarked that in Orissa 'no government could be formed without the bahujan samaj'. (It) was so due to the fact that in the state there were 'facilities for reservation for one-third of its people'. '(What) was required was for the candidates to prepare and publicize the issues in an organized way'. He added that people should 'not look at notes (money) but look at votes because they (had) no shortage of votes'. On October 8, 1994, prior to the assembly elections in Andhra Pradesh, Kanshiram addressed a public rally at Kurnool, a drought-prone Rayalseema region of Andhra Pradesh. Kanshiram stated that there was a need to awaken the 'slumbering shame' of the poor people in the region. In his speech, Kanshiram urged the 20,000 (strong) crowd not to fear the dominant Reddy caste and suggested that in Andhra Pradesh, if '(the bahujan) are strong and united then the Reddys would be (politically) checkmated'. The BSP leader even went on to the extent to suggest that out of '294 Vidhan Sabha seats the BSP (could) win 100 seats, 50 seats from coastal Andhra Pradesh and 50 seats from Telengana and Rayalseema regions' of the state.[38] With no organizational presence and political support among the 'excluded sections of society', the BSP's electoral participation in the assembly elections in Andhra Pradesh in 1994 was a political failure. The Party competed in 235 seats and won none and came up with a measly 1.65% vote share in seats contested. In 1994, the BSP also competed in the assembly elections in Karnataka and managed to win 1 out of 77 seats with a vote share of 2.23% in seats contested. In 1996, in the assembly elections in Tamil Nadu, the BSP contested only nine seats and did not win a single seat and ended up with a vote share of 1.38% in the seats that it contested. In the 1996 Kerala assembly elections, the BSP contested 12 seats and did not win a single seat, and ended with a miniscule 1.57% vote share for the contested. In Maharashtra, the BSP contested 145 seats in the 1995 assembly elections and did not win a single seat and had a meagre 2.82% vote share in the seats competed. In the 1996 assembly elections, in West Bengal out of

48 seats the party contested the BSP won none registering a miniscule 1% vote share for the seats competed.[39] The abject election results pointed to the fact that the BSP was a 'UP political party' and the political programme initiated by Kanshiram to popularize the 'ideology of the bahujan samaj', in the context of an absence of grassroots mobilization and unworkable political alliances magnified the almost complete 'non-presence' of the BSP in other states. Till 2009 the larger national 'political project' of the BSP was effectively set aside.

Before embarking on a political tour of several states across the country, Kanshiram had clearly suggested that he wanted a 'Mulayam-installed' government to run on the perpetual influence of the BSP. The BSP gave a 'policy priority' to the SP to prevent the physical intimidation and violence against the Dalits as it was a more sensitive issue than the static age-old problem of landlessness suffered by the poor and land illegally occupied by the landowning OBCs. It was felt that acquiring legal propriety over land rights required a more complicated manoeuvring by the two coalition partners at the level of government.[40] Even as the coalition government began to govern the state, the 'political ascent' of the BSP in UP and a noticeable increased SC assertiveness' became a source of political concern for upper-caste Brahmins and Thakurs and the OBCs, particularly the Kurmis and Yadavs.[41]

Conflicting Agendas and the 'Politics of Negativity'

During Kanshiram's absence from the state, fissures had developed in the SP-BSP government. The new assertiveness of the 'agricultural farm labourer' and the 'propertied' backwards led to an increased confrontation in the first five months of the SP-BSP government. The clashes occurred at Dauna, Fatehpur, Badaun, Barabanki, Hardwar, Azamgarh, Basti and Varanasi which indicated that Dalit-OBC violence was spreading throughout the state. The ensuing political tension brought a political response from BSP. The national secretary of the BSP, Mayawati, 'In charge' of UP, assumed the role of a 'caretaker' of Dalit interests. She publicly stated that 'she would make it a point to visit Lucknow "every 10 days" to keep a watch on the functioning of the coalition government'. She was prepared to give the alliance only 'pass marks' (urging Mulayam) 'to protect the people who have voted for (the alliance)', but, she claimed, that Mulayam's attention '(was) never drawn to atrocities against dalits until (she) pointed them out to him'. Pre-empting any questions on her role as the 'custodian of the poor', Mayawati clarified that if she did not interfere, 'nothing (would) be done to set right the wrongs that (were) taking place in the state'.[42] Mayawati cautioned the government that '(the BSP would) be forced to do "some re-thinking" and go to the people and ask them to vote (the BSP) to power independently'.[43]

Mulayam Singh Yadav's tenure as Chief Minister of UP was characterized by political patronage of the Yadavs. District-level recruitment and promotions across the state favoured the 'Yadav caste': recruitment to the state police, the Provincial Armed Constabulary (PAC), accounting for '2,500 out of 3,000 posts went to the Yadavs'. Kurmis, Koeris, Lodhs and other lower backwards caste groups were left out of the 'recruitment drive' leading to 'anti-Yadav sentiments'.[44] On its part, the BSP began interfering with senior bureaucratic postings by directing the Mulayam's government to transfer upper-caste government officials and that 'their (BSP) favourites' be given plum posts in the state administration. The case of the UP Chief Secretary T.S.R. Subramanium being referred to as the 'Brahmin Chief Secretary' is a case to the point. Such was the unabated interference of Mayawati in senior bureaucratic appointments that it led the UP Indian Administrative Service (IAS) Association to resort to the unprecedented step of making a formal representation to the Governor. The petition expressed the 'officers' are against caste and other extraneous considerations in the postings and transfers of bureaucrats'. Unperturbed, the BSP confronted the SP-headed government with the demand that at least '25 per cent of the key posts in the police force and civil administration' be reserved for 'Dalit' officers. Subsequently, 'two SC officers' began to decide the bulk of the postings of officers within the state.[45] SP-BSP government continued to falter even as Kanshiram stated that 'all government land in the state belonged to his (P)arty' [sic]. Kanshiram's statement gave a fillip to local BSP leaders to go on 'installing statues of B.R. Ambedkar on any plot of land that was lying vacant'. Such incidents were witnessed at Allahabad University, Barabanki, Badaun and Meerut. To the BSP activists, the installing of Dr. Ambedkar's statues was an act of 'new age Dalitism'. BSP's 'statue-installing spree' was actively resisted by SP activists and upper-caste-OBC community, who in an act of organized violence displayed their dominance over the Dalit community in the state.[46] SP cadres took 'possession of (Dalit) houses by force'. Such incidents were reported in Ghaziabad, Barabanki, Meerut, Sitapur and Hardoi.[47]

As political tensions arose between the two coalition partners, Mulayam Singh Yadav outlined two political strategies to contain the BSP: one, it began a lateral expansion of the SP presence in the UP assembly to enlist political support independent of the BSP. By April 1994, the SP had successfully garnered the support of sections of non-Yadav OBC, particularly the Lodhs and the Kurmis and certain non-Chamar Dalit groups such as the Balmikis, Pasis and Kumhars negligibly represented in BSP. Caste leaders of these groups were 'allowed to wield power at various levels of the administration' even as the government introduced 'special schemes' to benefit some of these communities. The expansion of the Party's base outside the coalition arrangement was not evident in the June 1994 assembly by-elections in the state where the 'SP-BSP combine' won four out of six seats, with Ghazipur and Manjhapur won by the BSP and SP winning the Bhagwant Nagar and Nidhauli Kalan seats.[48] But in April 1995 Panchayat and Zila Parishad elections, the SP revelled in (its) spate of electoral victories as the 'Yadav Party' gained control over 45% of the 52,111 gram (village) panchayats. The

BSP could gain only 10% in the panchayat elections. Kanshiram accused Mulayam Singh Yadav of 'rigging the panchayat elections' and stated that his BSP would 'have nothing to do with the SP in the state assembly by-elections that followed the panchayat polls'. In the four assembly by-elections held in May 1995, the BSP failed to win a single seat.[49] Faced with a reversal of its electoral fortunes, the BSP attempted to restrict the 'popularity of the SP' by holding political 'rallies to mobilize Pasis, Khatris, Kewats, Kushwahas to "dilute" its image as a "Chamar-Jatav Party".[50] Two, a political ruse that Mulayam Singh Yadav used effectively to weaken Mayawati's growing political intervention[51] in SP-led government was to engineer defections within the BSP. Masood Ahmed, a senior Muslim leader of the party, suddenly decided to quit the party in June 1994 after raising a 'series of charges' against Kanshiram and 'general secretary' Mayawati. Masood Ahmed's resignation was followed by Mohammad Islam, state general secretary, and Syed Mujibur Hassan, Delhi unit convener of the party. Ahmed stated that a significant number of BSP MLAs were critical of Mayawati's interference in government, a move he described as an 'anti-leadership' campaign.[52] The dissident leader was critical of the 'anti-Muslim bias of the leadership (that had) claimed that as the party got stronger the representation of the community which had 12 MLAs in the assembly would be reversed. He felt there was an obvious attempt to "block and throttle" the emergence of a Muslim leadership' within the BSP. Masood claimed that '40 out of 69 "rebellious" BSP MLAs were supporting him who could ensure that the SP-BSP government could function effectively'. In response, Kanshiram announced at a press conference that the date for 'withdrawal of support' had been set from the SP-BSP government.[53] The SP instigated another factional struggle, known as the 'Raj Bahadur episode' in the BSP, further exposing the opposition of a section of BSP MLAs, cadres and activists to Mayawati's 'superior control over organizational structure' within the Party. It became apparent that a section of the BSP MLAs had decided to create a 'political faction' within the Party. Raj Bahadur, a prominent local Chamar leader and chief organizer of the BSP in eastern UP, alleged that Mayawati 'had planned to finish (him) politically'. Some of the dissidents made no secret of their 'admiration for Mulayam Singh Yadav'. In the ensuing political crisis within the BSP, it became apparent that the SP leader began to treat with greater consideration (BSP) legislators who had 'problems with the BSP leadership so as to obtain their personal loyalty'. Apart from victories achieved in the by-elections, SP tally grew to 131 seats in the state assembly owing to defections from JD and the CPI.[54] The SP eventually 'assisted' a split in the BSP as '25 BSP MLAs under Raj Bahadur broke away from the BSP' and was given official recognition as BSP (Raj Bahadur), a new political party.[55]

By the time the Panchayat and Zila Parishad poll results became public, the BSP had entered into an undisclosed agreement with the BJP which would extend the support of 177 MLA's to form the next 'minority' government with Mayawati as the Chief Minister of UP. However, on June

2, 1995, SP activists belonging to the Lohia Bahini (Lohia Brigade) and Samajwadi Yuvjan Sabha (Socialist Youth Council Assembly) locked in 7 BSP MLAs and Mayawati in a guest house where the BSP leader had gone to address a meeting of party workers. The SP activists began 'shouting slogans against Mayawati and pelted stones at the suite' occupied by Mayawati. 'Gun-toting Special Protection (SP) men' surrounded the guest house. Mayawati and her party workers 'without water supply, telephone and power supply' spent a night inside the guest house. Eventually, the Central Industrial Security Force requisitioned by Governor Motilal Vora rescued the BSP leader and her group of MLAs.[56]

Politics on Social Justice: The 'Convenient' BSP-BJP Pact

The BJP's decision to support a BSP-led 'minority' government in Uttar Pradesh led by Mayawati was indicative of a political acceptance of a 'meta-language of electoral discourse in which (non-upper) castes had become major political contenders in the state'. The 'marginal (electoral) defeat' in November 1993 state polls had compelled the BJP to recast the ideology of Hindutva in favour of 'percentage politics'. The BJP's political objectives were directed to consolidate a range of non-upper-caste groups and construct a 'new' social base by addressing 'Dalit' interests and benefit from BSP's bahujan 'vote-bank'.[57]

BJP's political position was put in perspective by the RSS:

> '(Dominant) upper caste base could be made to accept this alliance because of the overriding need to capture power at the Centre. If any electoral alliance (with the BSP) materialise(d), (the BJP could) make significant gains not only in UP, but in Gujarat, Madhya Pradesh and Maharashtra where Dalit votes (were) decisive.[58]

Tactically, till such time the BJP mobilized OBC votes under Kalyan Singh, the 'OBC mascot' of the party in the state, it was necessary to ensure that the SP had to be kept out of power. The BJP viewed the opportunity for a political coalition with the BSP to 'strike at Mulayam'. The BJP planned to support the BSP government till the 1996 Lok Sabha polls to ensure that 'when voters lined up in front of the ballot boxes, a "friendly government", that is, BJP propping up a "Dalit" government, in UP is in "power" in the state'.[59] As the political parleys continued towards a coalition arrangement, BJP national and state-level leaders voiced their support to a 'novel' political experiment soon to be realized to take charge of administering India's most populous and electorally influential state. BJP leader Advani declared that 'no party was untouchable'. Kalyan Singh added that 'the BJP had appointed a Dalit woman as the CM', while another perception was put in context by a BJP legislator who said: '(That) the party never believed in caste system nor (did) its leaders (practice) untouchability'.[60]

In the coalition government led by the BSP, Kanshiram and Mayawati positioned themselves as 'kingmakers' engaging in a process of 'using the upper caste party (BJP) to achieve political power'. Kanshiram defended the 'unlikely' 'political agreement' suggesting that 'all parties approached (him) to change Mulayam Singh Yadav'. Under those circumstances, he 'got the opportunity to make Mayawati the Chief Minister of Uttar Pradesh'. He further added that '(to rid the state of) Mulayam Singh Yadav's "goonda raj" (rule of goons),[61] the support (of the BJP) on (this) central issue (was necessary)'. Kanshiram clarified: 'We (BSP and BJP) have only joined hands as co-sufferers of Mulayam Singh Yadav'. 'We have come together for a "short time" to fight criminals'. Kanshiram asserted: 'Our people were being intimidated. They began asking whether it was our (bahujan) government or an "enemy government".[62] Advani commented that '(while) the Mulayam Singh government was a "criminal government", Mayawati (was) a "rising (political) star".[63]

Mayawati and the 'Dalit' Agenda

Mayawati's cabinet resembled BSP's new political formula for representing multi-caste groups in government. The cabinet had 10 SC, 7 OBC, 3 Yadavs, 5 Kurmis, 4 Muslims and 1 each from the Brahmin, Bania and Gujjar communities. Thakurs and Kayasthas went unrepresented. It would be a 'Dalit government' where 'bahujan interests (would) be protected' providing 'an administration (free from) from corruption, injustice and crime'. Yet it (would also) cater to the interests of the 'sarva samaj' (entire society)' who will get justice without discrimination and not on the basis of religion and caste'. In one of her first efforts to engage the upper castes, Mayawati mentioned that the '(BSP) was not opposed to Manu but manuvadi (forces), not against Brahmins but Brahminical cult'. Kalyan Singh, the state BJP leader, was circumspect and felt it was 'necessary to discuss the "points of disagreement" with the BSP in the running of the government, (but) the national leadership of the BJP which had fashioned the (coalition) pact (did) not wish to interfere in the day-to-day functioning of the government'.[64]

Mayawati's four and a half months tenure as UP Chief Minister was symptomatic of BSP's 'Dalit agenda'. The short tenure of the Mayawati government ensured that state structures and local administration acted in the interest of the Dalit population. Mayawati took significant steps to ensure complete political control over state-level bureaucracy. Fifty-seven Indian Administrative Service (IAS) officers and 108 Indian Police Service (IPS) officers were transferred in 18 days and 60% of them replaced by SC officers.[65] To 'ensure that there (was) an SC District Magistrate in each district', the BSP government went on the 'overdrive to fulfil the required representation of the SC' in the state administration. Among 14 Deputy Inspector General (DIG) officers, as many as 'nine were SC and not one of them (was) a Brahmin or a Bania'.[66] The end of July witnessed more than '400 orders of transfers and re-transfers' issued by the Mayawati government. Some officials had been 'transferred five times within a month'. More than 1,500 IAS, IPS and Public Service Commission (PSC) officers were transferred in three months.[67] One of the reasons that the BSP government cited for such a 'massive transfer' of state officials was the critical 'pace of development' in certain constituencies and districts — Deoria, Siddharthnagar, Basti, Padrauna — even as the Chief Secretary was directed to 'make entries into the character files of District Magistrates (DM)'. A top priority of the Mayawati government was to provide security against 'physical violence' of the Dalit population. To ensure effectual law enforcement in the state, the BSP revived the Gangster and Goonda Act to check crime and fix responsibility on each district magistrate for maintaining law and order'.[68] It is in this regard that senior UP IAS officers Bhagwati Prasad Verma, DM of Gorakhpur, and Arun Singhal, DM of Maharajganj, were suspended for their inability to monitor law and order and development in their respective districts.[69] Though no official record is available, it is estimated that in four and a half months as the CM of UP, Mayawati ordered the arrest of approximately '1,45,000 anti-socials and criminals'. This 'policy' coincided with the 'September 2 to September 19 tour' that Mayawati undertook in all the 68 districts of the state to review law and order.[70]

Mayawati introduced a number of rural and urban developmental measures for Dalits. The Ambedkar Village Programme (AVP) adopted by the BSP proclaimed that in every block in the state, villages with 50% Dalit population, the state administration would direct 'allocated funds under the AVP' to benefit the poor. Subsequently, the BSP lowered the required Dalit population to 22–30% to cover more villages under the scheme. 'Thirty-seven developmental programmes' were authorized to be implemented in denoted villages of which 11 programmes were to be specially monitored and funded, such as the construction of link roads covering 3,260 km, 5,000 primary schools, construction of drainage facilities, hand pumps, drinking water and rural electrification. With the launch of the AVP, all social welfare programmes in the state ended so that funds could be diverted to the selected 'Ambedkar villages'. State functionaries were directed to give priority to such villages. A 'Special Component Plan' was also initiated by the BSP designed to include Dalit children and women in the AVP. A number of state-level 'education scholarships' were introduced for Dalit children studying up to secondary school. Funds were earmarked to build 'hostels for Dalit students', especially girl students in urban areas, and numerous 'coaching centres' were planned to assist Dalit students in their education. Dalit women were to be provided adequate days of labour under employment schemes and the housing scheme sanctioned under Indira Awaas Yojana (Indira Gandhi Housing Scheme) was increased. The 'Ambedkar Rozgar Yojana' (Ambedkar Employment Programme) for Dalit women, which cost the state exchequer Rs. 60 crores, was initiated, the outlay on health and family planning was raised, and 50% of the outlay was reserved for Dalits.

Employment-generating policies for the Dalits were initiated through the allocation of 'work contracts' in labour-intensive jobs such as stone quarries and cane crushing. Under a special drive, 81,500 Dalits were granted ownership of 52,379 acres of land and 1,58,000 Dalits were given actual possession of land. Additionally, 20,000 Dalits were given about 15,000 acres of Gaon (village) Sabha land and all cases of illegal occupation of such lands against them were withdrawn. 'Bhumidari (landholder) rights' were given to tenants in possession of the land for ten years. Special 'fast-track' courts for Dalits in all the districts of the state were set up to try 'atrocity cases' against Dalits through the enacted law of Prevention of Atrocities Act 1995. State officials were directed to lodge FIRs made by SC based on complaints against any injustice and exploitation that arose as a consequence to the implementation of the AVP. Officials not lodging complaints made by SC could face government tribunal of inquiry. All 'SC cases' had to be solved within 60 days from the date the complaint was registered. A Dalit from Hapur in western UP said:

> After 'behen' (sister) Mayawati came things have changed. The police will now register a case and even if nothing much happens thereafter; we are at least treated with respect. The policeman knows that if word reaches Mayawati that he has ill-treated Dalits or refused to register their complaints, there will be hell to pay.[71]

The Mayawati government initiated schemes and programmes for Muslims and 'backward groups'. In Muslim-majority constituencies, '577 primary schools and 144 senior basic schools were given permission to open' so that Muslim school teachers could be provided employment to overcome backwardness and achieve 'equal partnership' (in society). The BSP government earmarked 27% of the state budget and allocated '25 per cent of state-level administrative posts' to benefit the OBC. A 'Bhagidari Bhawan' (lit. a citizen-government partnership building) was inaugurated at Gomti Nagar, Lucknow, to coach backward caste students appearing in state-level competitive examinations. Government 'patta' (a title deed to a property) lands were to be given to low-caste OBCs such as Nishad, Kewat and Mallah. If there were no claimants, then such 'ownership rights' would be given to the Scheduled Castes.

To contest the hegemony of abstract 'elitist-upper caste-Brahminical standards' of public-national symbols, BSP provided an alternative representation of iconography to endorse an 'egalitarian' cultural narrative of the disempowered in the public sphere.[72] Dalit symbolism appeared in the form of memorials, institutes, roads, universities and districts renamed after 'revered' Dalit icons and social reformers. The Agra University was named Dr. Bhimrao Ambedkar University; the Agra Stadium after Ekalavya, the 'sufferer and victim of oppression by manuvadis'; the Kanpur University was renamed Shahuji Maharaj University; land was allocated for the construction of a 'Parivartan Chowk' (square of transformation) in Lucknow which would also include a 'Parivartan Sthal' (place of transformation) in the 'chowk'; land was acquired to construct a Dr. Ambedkar Park in honour of the 'architect of the Indian Constitution' among several significant 'iconic landmarks' to be built by the BSP government. A number of 'awards' were named after 'lower caste reformers' such as Mahakavi Valmiki Sahitya Memorial Award (Great Poet Valmiki Literature Memorial Award), Dr Ambedkar Gaurav Award (Dr. Ambedkar Pride Award) and the Sant Ravidas Memorial Award (Saint Ravidas Memorial Award). Sixteen new districts were carved out and subsequently named after '(Dalit) saints' and 'gurus' (spiritual leader or teacher in Hindu religion).[73]

Whether it was a question of guaranteeing 'physical protection' to Dalits against caste atrocities or seeking a change in the dominant clientelist pattern of state structures through a policy of transfer and postings of upper-caste officials or outlining the objectives of AVP and imposing a Dalit iconography in public spaces, BSP's brand of Dalit politics was emblematic of the Party's aspirations towards a 'Dalit empowering politics'. However, during the brief tenure of its rule in UP, political crisis gripped the party. Ramdeo Patel and Sonelal Patel from the influential Kurmi community rose in revolt against the Mayawati government and held a 'Kurmi mahasammelan (big convention)' in Lucknow. The Sammelan 'accused the Mayawati government of a political injustice' to the 'backward' Kurmi castes that was borne out by the skewed pattern of selections of certain preferred caste groups behind transfers and postings. Subsequently, the Kurmi caste leaders formed the 'Kurmi mahasabha (big assembly)' and founded Apna Dal. The formation of the Apna Dal symbolized Ram Lakhan Verma, a Kurmi leader's protest at being denied the post of secretary in the BSP. The BSP's preoccupation with Chamars, noted in their selection to 'plum' government posts and as a major beneficiary of the AVP, further alienated the Pasi, Balmiki and Kumhars caste groups from the Party.[74]

Mayawati and Kanshiram: Between 'Practicality' and the 'Ideological'

The BSP-BJP alliance brought to the fore an intra-party politics between Mayawati and Kanshiram. A part of the reason for ending the coalition government was based on the BSP chief Kanshiram's scepticism of the increasingly 'close personal equation' that Mayawati had developed with state BJP leaders. Mayawati had apparently started taking 'independent decisions and creating her own faction' within the BSP. Kanshiram proceeded to ensure that Mayawati engaged on a '(political) course correction' by attending a 'Periyar mela' (fair), which would also include the installation of the Periyar statue near the historic Begum Hazrat Mahal Park in Lucknow. The Periyar mela was expressively directed towards Mayawati to 'secure the Dalit-Bahujan constituency, not as 'Chief Minister' but as

'General Secretary' of the BSP to emphasize that core political values of 'anti-Brahminism' remained the central theme of BSP politics. The Periyar mela was opposed by the BJP which considered him as a political pariah who had 'all his life abused Lord Rama'. Facing political opposition from the BJP, the statue of Periyar was erected at the UP Bhawan in Delhi. Mayawati reciprocated by withdrawing the permission that had previously been granted to the Vishwa Hindu Parishad (VHP) to offer 'mahayagna (big religious offering)' at a spot close to the Krishna Janmasthan-Shahi Idgah mosque complex in Mathura. Upon the refusal of permission, the BJP took a decision to withdraw support to the four-month-old BSP government.[75] Following the end of the short-lived BSP government, Mayawati said: '(That her party) practiced the politics of principles (by) stopping communal elements (from) spreading hatred; and that (she) did not submit to the BJP's selfish and conspiratorial intent'.[76]

1996 Lok Sabha Elections: Advantage BJP

A 'divisive electoral preference' enabled the BJP to win 52 parliamentary seats (see Table 4.3) in the 1996 Lok Sabha elections in Uttar Pradesh with a 33.43% of votes. The 'electoral performance' was attributed not to ideology of Hindutva but was moulded by a schema of 'technocratic rationality' to increase non-core support by 'vote arithmetic'. This political stratagem was noted by other political parties in UP which experimented with lesser degree of political success in mobilizing 'plus votes' in an increasingly fragmented electoral landscape. The BJP benefited by registering political support from an ensemble of non-Yadav OBC caste groups to consolidate the Party's 'core' upper-caste constituency. The SP gained 16 seats and the BSP 6 seats with a 20.60% vote share displacing the Congress in both seat won and vote share. The BJP wanted to emerge as a 'responsible national party', a fact that could be alluded to the party's inability to extend its '13-day tenure' at government formation at the Centre post-1996 Lok Sabha elections, when it was treated as (politically) 'untouchable' and not given support by any political party at the time of the 'floor test' in Parliament.[77]

Table 4.3 Seats and Percentage of Votes Polled by Major Political Parties in 1996 UP Lok Sabha Elections

1996 Lok Sabha Elections	*BJP*		*SP*		*Cong(I)*		*JD*		*BSP*	
	Seats Won	*Vote %*	*Seats Won*	*Vote %*	*Seats Won*	*Vote %*	*Seats Won*	*Vote %*	*Seats Won*	*Vote %*
	52	33.4	16	20.8	05	8.1	02	4.3	6	20.6

Source: Sudha Pai (Ed.), *Political Process in Uttar Pradesh*, Delhi: Pearson Longman, 2007, p. 182.

1996 Assembly Elections: The Pre-Poll BSP-Congress and SP-Dominated United Front Alliance

With a stratagem to peripheralize the JD and the SP in the state assembly elections, the BSP entered into a pre-poll alliance with the Congress Party, the latter posing no political threat to the BSP in UP. Kanshiram remarked that 'Dalits were his blind (political) supporters and that he could shift their votes to the party of his choice' if the exigencies of politics across assembly constituencies so required. In a 'dictated' political pact with the Congress, Kanshiram stated that the Bahujan Samaj Party would contest 299 seats, while the Congress would compete in 126 assembly seats.[78] As the assembly elections approached, the BSP began a calibrated exercise to gain the support of the Muslims and 'backwards' without identifying the upper castes as their common enemy. The BSP (see Table 4.4) kept its core constituency intact by giving 29.84% of its 'tickets' to Dalits which was lesser in proportion to the 37.30% among backward caste candidates. It was an expedient political measure to downplay core caste identity by highlighting the common identity of 'downtrodden groups' to corner a vote share of non-Yadav OBCs to check the political expansion of the BJP. Upper-caste candidates represented 14.92% of the total number of seats in which the BSP contested. Under the agenda of 'minority protection' and an 'anti-communal' political platform, 52 Muslim candidates appeared in the BSP list for the state polls. In the October 1996 state polls, the BJP polled 41.70% of the non-Yadav OBC votes[79] and overall, 32.50% vote share winning 177 seats. The SP won 109 seats and 19.70% vote share while the BSP secured 67 seats with 11.20% vote share. BSP's winning candidates included 24 B.A., 2 M.A. 19 LL.B. and 1 Ph.D. The 1996 Vidhan Sabha election (see Table 4.5) results were almost identical to the 1993 assembly elections. It was as if no elections had been held.[80]

The Congress-BSP political alliance failed to outstrip the Janata Dal-sponsored United Front (UF) in seat count in the state assembly elections. The UF, a motley group of political parties consisting of SP (109 seats), BKKP (8 seats), JD (7 seats), Congress(Tiwari) (4 seats), CPI(M) (4 seats) and CPI (1 seat), won 133 seats to Congress-BSP's 100 seats. The vote share of the BJP

Table 4.4 Caste-wise Ticket Distribution in the 1996 UP Assembly Elections

Party	*UC*	*IC*	*OBC*	*SC*
Congress	63.3%	0	15.15%	9.09%
BJP	48.60%	5.52%	21.51%	22.08%
BSP	14.92%	1.49%	37.30%	29.84%
SP	15.60%	0.92%	31.19%	16.52%

Source: Christophe Jaffrelot and Sanjay Kumar, *Rise of the Plebeians? The Changing Face of Indian Legislative Assemblies*, New Delhi: Routledge, 2009, p. 57.

Table 4.5 UP Assembly Elections 1996

1996 Assembly Elections	*BJP*		*Cong(I)*		*SP*		*BSP*	
	Seats Won	*Vote %*	*Seats Won*	*Vote %*	*Seats Won*	*Vote %*	*Seats Won*	*Vote %*
	177	32.5	33	8.4	109	19.7	67	11.2

Source: Vivek Kumar, Behind the BSP Victory, *Economic and Political Weekly,* 42 (24), June 16, 2007, p. 2237.

in alliance with the Samata Party, a political party with minimal presence in the state, was 33.77%; the UF 30.25% and that of the Congress-BSP coalition at 28.7%.[81] The major loser in the assembly elections was the BJP. The BJP, contrary to its performance in the Lok Sabha elections in April-May 1996, 'lost sufficiently in all parts of the state' barring the hill districts. The party won 22 fewer constituencies in western UP and 40 fewer in eastern UP. In central region of the state, the BJP won 15 seats, down from 22 seats in 1993 assembly elections. The assembly election results show that the BJP lost the 'winning edge' in 66 constituencies in four months.[82] In turn, the UF won in 34 more assembly seats and the Congress-BSP alliance won 22 more assembly seats and performed well in regions which were not their political strongholds.[83] Mayawati was circumspect about the 'pact with Congress' and calculated that the Party lost about 100 seats by a small margin where bahujan candidates were given assembly 'tickets'. This was due to the fact that while BSP's Dalit-Bahujan vote was transferred to Congress candidate, upper-caste Congress votes did not transfer to BSP's candidates. Instead, it went to other political parties in the state. What Mayawati was suggesting was that if BSP's candidates received even 1–2% of upper-caste votes, the party would have won 100 more seats. A positive development for the BSP was a revival of non-Chamar Dalit support. Despite an erosion in the support of non-Chamar Dalits due to unfulfilled promises and 'political misgivings' and BJP's efforts to garner votes by allocating tickets to SCs in the assembly elections, a sizeable section (45.7%) of the Pasi community votes polled voted in favour of BSP next only to 73.80% among the Chamar caste.[84]

Advantage BSP: Orchestrating a 'Beneficial' Social Compact

The 1996 assembly elections in Uttar Pradesh produced an uncertain political verdict despite national and state political parties orchestrating coalition alliances and manipulating political defections.[85] Coalition negotiations among the BJP, SP and BSP towards government formation initially took the form of a 'grand' secular combination of political forces between the UF and the BSP-Congress alliance to ensure that the BSP did not enter into another opportunistic 'political deal' with the BJP. Kanshiram remarked that the BSP was, indeed, a project of 'social transformation' and that it would associate with 'any political party that accepted its goals (of social transformation) even in part'. The BSP leader wished to elicit a response from the UF that the 'front' would support Mayawati as Chief Minister of the state. With the SP as the major political partner of the UF coalition, the 'bargain offer' was at the onset (politically) unworkable.[86] Thereafter, the political objective of the BSP was to prevent the UF and the Congress from coming to power betraying its own political desperation.[87] On the other hand, the BJP central leadership advocated that the party had to 'work towards a (political) coalition' with the BSP irrespective of political opposition from prominent state-level BJP leaders such as Kalyan Singh, Lalji Tandon and Kalraj Mishra. The central party leadership concluded that the BSP was agreeable to a political coalition as long as Mayawati was accepted as Chief Minister of the state. Kanshiram said that the BSP was willing to work towards a 'different coalition pact' with the BJP. The BJP bargained for a 'Deputy Chief Minister' and 60% of the membership of the cabinet posts to which the BSP opposed. Ultimately, the BJP agreed to 50% of the cabinet posts and gave up the 'idea of a Deputy Chief Minister'. Kanshiram said that the BSP was in political agreement to establish a 'steering committee' consisting of BJP and BSP leaders to 'guide the government but not to intervene in the functioning of the government'. Yet the unpredictable nature of the BSP political leadership came to the fore at a BSP rally on December 29, 1996, in Ludhiana, Punjab, where Kanshiram indicated that the party would accept nothing short of outside support and ruled out a coalition with the BJP.[88] On February 13, 1997, BJP leader Atal Bihari Vajpayee said: 'All doors (had) been closed for the BJP'. Yet the BJP, the 'political untouchable', and Kanshiram's BSP, the 'social untouchable', pulled off another political coalition. The political coalition was a product of 'compulsions and force of (political) circumstances'. Vajpayee, the senior BJP leader, on the occasion said: 'Big issues kept us apart but bigger issues brought us together'.[89] A 'six monthly Chief Ministership' based on rotation was formulated, whereby Mayawati as CM of UP would rule the state for a period of six months 'from March 21, 1997 and, consequently, at the completion of her tenure pass the Chief Minister's post to Kalyan Singh on September 22, 1997'.[90]

BSP-BJP in an inverse relationship of 'Consolidation' and 'Dependency'

As Chief Minister of Uttar Pradesh, Mayawati hinted at reviewing certain policy decisions taken during Governor Romesh Bhandari's[91] rule in the state which the ruling coalition alleged proved beneficial for Mulayam Singh Yadav 'who (virtually) ruled the state by proxy'.[92] Mayawati's tenure as 'CM of the state in 1995' was revisited with the objective of enforcing 'Dalit' development programmes. In the two-party coalition government, the BSP had a substantial representation of SC members which stood at 30.43%. It was marginally higher than 29.91% share of lower backward OBCs, a significant portion of which was represented by the BJP. SC lawmakers leveraged Mayawati in running the administration of the state. On the other hand, BJP's low-caste OBC representation in government in comparison to the upper castes (17.39%) and intermediate landholding backward castes (8.69%) was a clear indication that the prominence of the 'low-caste backwards', by their sheer numerical strength in the legislative assembly, could form a significant political equation to the emerging power dynamics underlining UP caste politics.[93]

Mayawati's agenda for 'Dalit-based development' was evident in her remark: '(She would) do in three months what others had not been able to do in three years'.[94] In the first two months, Mayawati 'inaugurated five new districts'. The creation of each new district entailed a heavy expenditure on the state exchequer which meant diverting funds allocated for public health and other development projects.[95] The carving out of new districts was not only intended to symbolize 'Dalit-specific districts' but appeared to be a 'gerrymandered' electoral strategy to undermine Kalyan Singh's political influence. Carving Mahamayanagar out of Aligarh district was a case to the point'.[96]

The AVP 're-convened in 1997' by the BSP brought on a new set of 'Dalit' upliftment programmes. It was overshadowed by Mayawati's 'Ambedkarization project', the Ambedkar 'Udhyan' *(*rising sun) Project, to be built at a cost of Rs. 80 crores over 28 acres of prime land in the city of Lucknow. Domes and statues within the 'park' would signify Ambedkar as the 'tallest statesman of India' and eight huge elephant statues that would symbolize the strength of the bahujan samaj. Besides, Mayawati's agenda of Dalit symbolism to reconstruct a subjugated history continued. A majority of Dalit heroes of UP from the past became statues of obeisance and respect, in addition, to their names being used to rename colleges, universities, hospitals, guest houses, roads and districts.[97] The BSP planned to build a Jyotiba Phule Swachkar Ashram Paddhati Vidyalaya[98] (Jyotiba Phule Sweepers Residential Guide School) on the outskirts of Lucknow which would cater to '1,000 school-going children of sweepers'. The government earmarked funds to set up B.R. Ambedkar IAS and Provincial Civil Service (PCS) coaching centres at Aligarh, Agra and Varanasi. The BSP renewed its plan to ensure the disbursement of 'pattas' allotted to the Dalits. The Mayawati government allocated about 1,58,000 landless Dalits with legal possession of 1,20,000 acres of government land. Besides, a special campaign was started to give new 'pattas' to the Dalits. In this case, the numbers of 'new beneficiaries were 81,500 and 52,879 acres of land' were allotted. Eviction of Dalits from land given to gram sabha which they had occupied was stopped. Such a measure benefited 20,000 Dalits owning 15,000 acres of land. According to the State Information Directorate, by May 31, 1997,

5,503 Dalits had been returned the land they 'owned' and another 7,249 land disputes involving Dalits had been identified. The Party's efforts to marshal government intervention to settle disputes over land rights concerning Dalits was taken seriously when it was renegotiated with state officials through a SC officer or the village 'pradhan'. The government took an initiative to regularize those Dalit 'pattedars' (those having land on lease) with more than ten years ownership of land.[99]

The 'development work conducted in rural areas under the AVP scheme was claimed as an economic success' by the BSP. AVP target-oriented goals claimed that '1,500 link roads (had been) constructed in Ambedkar villages (and) thousands of hand pumps (installed) while electricity had begun to reach 11,524 Ambedkar villages'. The 'Ambedkar Villages' programme (see Table 4.6) to benefit 22% of the population cost the state's rural development budget Rs. 700 crores. Evaluating the performance of the AVP, a senior bureaucrat said, '(It was) an answer to the Green Revolution that had empowered the middle castes in UP; and further, (as long) as Mayawati (was) there, Dalits believed it (was) their turn' (to be empowered)'. The Mayawati government identified a further 11,000 'villages', which could be covered under the AVP scheme, costing Rs. 350 crores in public revenue. Villages with 30% SC population would be earmarked as 'beneficiary of AVP' and funds for it were to be taken out from the state government's 'Special Component Plan'.[100]

Mayawati continued the earlier policy of issuing 'prompt transfer order' to state-level officers. Transferring upper-caste bureaucrats and substituting them with 'favourable' Dalit officers in key ministries was a policy-driven

Table 4.6 Ambedkarization Programmes (status till 1997)

Project	*Cost (Rs.)*	*Status*
Ambedkar Villages (11,000)	350 cr.	Under implementation
Ambedkar Udhyan, Lucknow	120 cr.	Under construction *
Sant Ravidas Park, Varanasi	50 cr.	Foundation stone laid
Shahuji Maharaj Centre, Lucknow	12 cr.	Completed
Parivartan Chowk, Lucknow	10 cr.	Near completion
Jyotiba Phule Ashram, Lucknow	6 cr.	Near completion
Ambedkar Stadium, Lucknow	5 cr.	Completed
Ambedkar VIP Guest House, Lucknow	5 cr.	Completed
Ambedkar Hostels (12 Districts)	3 cr.	Budget sanctioned
Ambedkar IAS Coaching Centre (3)	1 cr.	Under construction
Ambedkar Statue, Lucknow	25 lakhs	To be installed
Annual Ambedkar Gaurav Samman	1.25 lakhs	Instituted

Source: Statue Symbols, *India Today*, July 28, 1997, p. 39.
*Many projects remained incomplete as the Mayawati government remained out of power till it entered into a coalition with the BJP to form a government in UP in May 2002. The coalition lasted till August 2003. Many older projects were either scrapped or renewed under new 'names' when the BSP came to power in UP in May 2007.

measure adopted to enhance the party's governmental presence in the state. In all, during Mayawati's six-month tenure, 1,350 civil and police officials were transferred. 'Yadav and Muslim state-level officers' recruited during Governor's rule, seen as 'Mulayam's men', were transferred out of key posts in the state bureaucracy. Mayawati ensured that not one out of the state's 74 districts had a Yadav DM or a police chief. On her course of action to transfer state officials, Mayawati said '(Officers had) to be set right (and that she was) here to cater to the public not the officers'. Under Mayawati, daily review of law and order became a top priority and punitive action was initiated against erring state functionaries. Mayawati outlined a directive to deter non-performing or errant officers through 'punishment transfers' of senior police and administrative officers, which on one occasion included an Inspector General of Police (IGP), a Deputy Inspector General of Police (DIGP), a District Magistrate (DM) and three Senior Superintendent of Police (SSP). Mayawati lifted the ban on recruitments to fill the SC quota 'for lower rung government employees'. Secretaries across government departments and public corporations were directed to 'recruit peons, "lekhpals" (village policemen) and other Class III and Class IV employees. About 250 constable-clerks were recruited from among Scheduled Castes and Scheduled Tribes. State secretaries who did not comply were shunted out'.[101]

The BSP's objective to reform the administrative machinery of the state was aligned to forcibly instil probity towards Dalits and other excluded caste groups through a political practice of creating an insecurity of tenure among apparent 'casteist' state-level functionaries and bureaucrats. In significant ways, Mayawati's assertive Dalit politics also represented a precursor to 'crime-fighting' against SP. The BSP government held the SP responsible for the proliferation of 'mafia groups in various districts' and for the 'criminalization of the police force' even as the government prepared a 'data of 1,385 police officers from constables to Superintendents of Police with suspect credentials'. The SP contended that BSP's effort to curb lawlessness in the state was tantamount to a 'witch hunt against SP workers'. The SP testified that (at least) '100 activists (had) been killed and another "10,000 arrested and 98,000 cases registered" in two and a half months under the National Security Act (NSA) and Goonda Act.[102]

Political tensions surfaced between the BJP and BSP from the third week of June due to the BSP-led government's decision to implement the SC Act. The SC Act would enable 'authorities to book anyone who (oppressed) or (used) derogatory language against a person belonging to a Scheduled caste'. The Act stated that any officer, who (was) not a Dalit, and (neglected) duties towards Dalits, (was) liable for punishment.[103] In defence of the SC Act, the BSP government indicated that atrocities against SC which stood at 2,767 in 1995 and 1,757 in 1996 came down to 1,611 in 1997. However, the State Crime Records Bureau noted that 'women and Dalits' had become 'victims of crime' as official figures for April 1997 recorded that 116 Dalits were murdered and 474 women raped out of which 126 belonged to the Dalit community. It marked a significant increase over 1996 figures. Notwithstanding the intense level of physical violence directed against Dalits and women, the state BJP unit demanded a 'thorough review of the implementation of the Act so that it (was) not used to harass members of the upper caste'.[104] Realistically, the SC Act was being seen by state BJP leaders as a 'political weapon' that symbolized the way in which Mayawati attempted to project herself as a 'super' CM and the 'sole protector' of Dalits.[105]

After taking over as Chief Minister of UP on September 22, 1997, Kalyan Singh issued a Government Order (GO) designed to 'preventing the misapplication' of the SC Act. It was a decision that brought the Kalyan Singh government into direct conflict not only with Mayawati but also BJP national party leaders who had given a political assurance to the BSP that no decision of the outgoing government would be reversed.[106] The GO stated that 'some of the cases registered under the SC Act were found to be false, (and there was a possibility that) the Act (was disrupting) social harmony'. With the quashing of the SC Act, riots against Dalits occurred in several parts of the state that began with the desecration of Ambedkar statues. Rohana, Ghaziabad, Muzaffarnagar and Faizabad districts were declared 'disturbed areas'. What prompted the Kalyan Singh government to issue a GO was twofold, that is, to limit Mulayam Singh Yadav's anti-Dalit campaign that 'had won him many sympathizers among the upper castes, as well as to send the right political signals to the upper castes, including those in administration, that under (BJP) administration they (would) be secure.[107]

On October 19, 1997, the 67-member BSP withdrew political support to the Kalyan Singh-led BJP government. Commenting on the end of the coalition with the BJP, Kanshiram said: '(When) we felt that we were not benefitting any longer we (ended) it and added further that (he) was looking for a "suitable ladder" to forge another political alliance with another political party if it was going to strengthen the BSP'.[108] However, on October 20, Kalyan Singh successfully 'engineered a split' in the BSP. Twelve BSP legislators defected to BJP. Thereafter, Kalyan Singh cobbled together a 'majority' by subsequently splitting the Congress Party and the Janata Dal. 'Party defectors' swelled the BJP-led government in the state assembly to a 'loosely knit 222-member' coalition that consisted of a newly formed 22-member Loktantrik Congress and a 3-member JD (Raja Ram Pandey) faction apart from Samata Party MLAs and a number of independent legislators.[109]

Notes

1 In the 1991 parliamentary and assembly elections in UP, the BJP, riding the 'crest of the Ram Janmabhoomi movement' successfully breached the Congress' traditional upper-caste, particularly the Brahmin, base, even as it expanded the backward caste base of the Party in the state. As a result, the BJP won 52 Lok Sabha seats and 221 assembly seats, the latter with a vote percentage of 31.45%.

Sudha Pai (Ed.), *Political Process in Uttar Pradesh*, pp. 114–16.

2 Sudha Pai, *Political Process in Uttar Pradesh*, p. 175; A.K. Verma, 'The Elusive Samajwad', *Seminar*, No. 571, March 2007, p. 44.

The dynamic-capitalist development in western UP maintained the monopoly of the numerically stronger Jats on landownership providing less space for the OBCs and the Dalits to organize themselves electorally and to resist the domination by the former. Thus, differing patterns of mobilization and agricultural development explained the strong base of the BSP in eastern and central UP.

Duncan, *The Bahujan Samaj Party in Uttar Pradesh*, p. 47.

Sudha Pai, *Dalit Assertion*, p. 161; Duncan, *The Bahujan Samaj Party in Uttar Pradesh*, pp. 37, 47; please see D. Gupta, 'Peasant "Unionism" in Uttar Pradesh: against the rural mentality thesis', *Journal of Contemporary Asia*, 61.22, 2, 1992, p. 165; Jens Lerche, 'New Wine in Old Bottle: Caste, Local Action, Social Movements and General Elections: Scheduled Caste Agricultural Workers in Uttar Pradesh, India', CDR Working Paper 94:12, Copenhagen: Centre for Development Research, 1994.

3 Abhay Kumar Dubey, *Aaj ke Neta*, p. 23.

4 In 1991, Kanshiram had attempted to forge political ties with individual political leaders of the JD and SP but failed due to the threat of a revolt by the UP unit of the BSP.

Abhay Kumar Dubey, *Aaj ke Neta*, p. 23.

5 Sudha Pai, *Dalit Assertion,* p. 162; Vinita Damodaran and Maya Unnithan-Kumar, *Postcolonial India*, p. 138.

The BSP opposed the JD for a set of different reasons. First, that the benefits of Mandal Commission would find favour with the backward landowning caste as part of JD's calibrated exercise in dispensing patronage and benefits to the social base of the party. Second, a fragmenting JD post-1991 Lok Sabha and assembly elections would increase the political presence of the BJP in UP politics. Third, to further check the JD's 'rump' factions from revisiting the constituencies of the backward castes, especially MBCs, in an electoral alignment with the Muslim vote and its partial support among non-Chamar SCs in UP.

Sudha Pai, *Dalit Assertion*, p. 162; Vinita Damodaran and Maya Unnithan-Kumar, *Postcolonial India,* p. 138; Gould and Ganguly, *India Votes*, pp. 26, 256.

6 'The winning duo, Mulayam Singh Yadav and Kanshiram', *Frontline,* 10, 25, December 17, 1993, p. 11; Susan Bayly, *Caste, Society and Politics in India from the Eighteenth Century to the Modern Age,* UK: Cambridge University Press, 1999, pp. 302, 303.

7 Praful Bidwai, 'The backward bandwagon: a regressive social agenda would not fit the bill', *Frontline,* 11, 3, February 11, 1994, p. 98; Kalyani Shankar, *Gods of Power,* p. 72; Kanchan Chandra, *Elite Incorporation in Multi-Ethnic Societies,* Working Paper in Department of Political Science, Massachusetts Institute of Technology, 2000, p. 25 (the paper was subsequently published in the *Asian Survey* in September/October 2000); Akela, *Sakshatkar,* p. 106.

8 'Kanshiram: my ultimate goal is Delhi', *Sunday,* 20, 48, December 5–11, 1993, p. 38.

9 'Man of the year', *Sunday*, 20, 51, December 26–January 1, 1994, p. 29.

10 'Caste conscious', *Sunday*, 21, 7, February 13–19, 1994, pp. 26, 27.

11 'Mulayam se samjhauta mahaj UP mein, woh bhi sthayi nahin' [*lit.* 'Pact with Mulayam in UP and that too not permanent'], *Amar Ujala,* Lucknow edition, October 19, 1993.

12 Vinod Agnihotri, 'Mulayam ko che mahiney tak parkhenge' [*lit.* 'We would review performance of Mulayam for six months'], *Navbharat Times,* New Delhi

edition, November 12, 1993; 'Man of the year', *Sunday,* 20, 51, December 26–January 1, 1994, p. 31.
13 Thakurta and Raghuraman, *A Time of Coalitions,* p. 185.
14 Shah, *Dalit Identity and Politics,* p. 289.
15 Thakurta and Raghuraman, *A Time of Coalitions,* p. 186; 'Against all odds', *Sunday,* 22, 7, February 12–18, 1995, p. 37; Agnihotri, 'Mulayam ko che mahiney tak parkhenge' (*lit.* 'We will observe Mulayam for six months')', *Navbharat Times,* New Delhi edition, November 12, 1993.
16 Dilip Awasthy and Javed Ansari [Interview with Kanshiram], 'I do not want a stable government', *India Today* (Hindi edition), December 31, 1993, p. 65; Akela, *Sakshatkar,* p. 143.
17 Sudha Pai, *Dalit Assertion,* p. 163.
18 'Enter Kanshiram', *Sunday,* 21, 4, January 23–29, 1994, p. 37.
19 'Ram was not enough', *Sunday,* 20, 48, December 5–11, 1993, p. 31.
20 Sudha Pai, *Dalit Assertion,* p. 163.
21 'Caste conscious', *Sunday,* 21, 7, February 13–19, 1994, p. 32.
22 'A secular victory in UP: big blow to Hindutva', *Frontline,* 10, 25, December 17, 1993, p. 9.
23 'A secular victory in UP: big blow to Hindutva', *Frontline*, 10, 25, December 17, 1993, p. 9; 'Ram was not enough', *Sunday,* 20, 48, December 5–11, 1993, p. 31.
24 Sudha Pai, *Dalit Assertion,* p. 165.
25 'A secular victory in UP: big blow to Hindutva', *Frontline*, 10, 25, December 17, 1993, p. 9.
26 The Congress, which had registered a decline since the early 1990s, fell from 46 to 28 seats. The rapid downward swing of the JD from 92 to 27 seats was largely attributed to the success of the SP-BSP political coalition in eastern and central UP, and the BJP, with a strong presence in western UP, among Jats vary of lower caste consolidation, underlined by a notable electoral presence across UP.

'Enter Kanshiram', *Sunday*, 21, 4, January 23–29, 1994, p. 37; Jaffrelot and Kumar, *Rise of the Plebeians?*, p. 59; Jaffrelot, *Religion, Caste and Politics in India*, p. 563; 'A secular victory in UP: big blow to Hindutva', *Frontline*, 10, 25, December 17, 1993, p. 10.
27 *Recorded Speeches of Kumari Mayawati and Kanshiram,* C and P 2001 [All Rights Reserved with Panchshil Cassettes], Abdullahpur, Nagar Nigam, Meerut, UP.
28 Ibid.
29 'Kanshiram: my fight is against Brahminism', *Sunday,* February 13–19, 1994, p. 27.
30 'With a new mandate', *Frontline,* 10, 26, December 31, 1993, pp. 18–19.
31 Bose, *Behenji,* p. 78
32 Bose, *Behenji,* pp. 78, 79.
33 'Kanshiram: my fight is against brahminism', *Sunday,* 21, 7, February 13–19, 1994, p. 26; 'Kanshiram: my ultimate goal is Delhi', *Sunday,* 20, 48, December 5–11, 1993, p. 38; 'Kanshiram: we'll bring peace', *Frontline,* 11, 5, March 11, 1994, p. 11; Bose, *Behenji*, p. 78; Susan Bayle, *Caste, Society and Politics*, p. 358.
34 Interview with Ambeth Rajan, New Delhi, January 21, 2009; Kanchan Chandra, *Why Ethnic Parties Succeed?* pp. 164–65.

It did not convey much in terms of politics considering that BSP's assessment not to invest in the 'south' was based on an evaluation of BAMCEF activities after 'several years of fruitless efforts among government employees in the region'. In the northeast region, while BAMCEF and DS-4 activities took root among the ST population', BSP's presence made less sense pragmatically in the region where 'few seats were available'. From the point of electoral strategy to proceed ahead to capture political power, 'north east' was not a 'priority region' for the BSP.

R.K. Singh, *Kanshiram aur BSP*, p. 56; Anuj Kumar, *Avismaraniya Bhashan*, pp. 76, 82, 85; Abhay Kumar Dubey, *Aaj ke Neta*, p. 23.

35 R.K. Singh, *Kanshiram aur BSP*, p. 56; Anuj Kumar, *Avismaraniya Bhashan*, pp. 76, 82, 85; Abhay Kumar Dubey, *Aaj ke Neta*, p. 23

36 'States of play', *Sunday*, 21, 7, February 13–19, 1994, pp. 34–37; 'Enter Kanshiram', *Sunday*, 21, 4, January 23–29, 1994, pp. 34, 37.

37 'States of play', *Sunday*, 21, 7, February 13–19, 1994, pp. 34–37; 'Enter Kanshiram', *Sunday*, 21, 4, January 23–29, 1994, pp. 34, 37.

38 Devkar, *Mananiya Kanshiram*, pp. 3–4, 13–15.

39 URL: http://www.eci.gov.in/KeyHighlights/SE_1994/StatisticalReport_AP94.pdf; http://www.eci.gov.in/KeyHighlights/SE_1994/StatisticalReport_KT94.pdf; http://www.eci.gov.in/KeyHighlights/SE_1996/StatisticalReport_TN96.pdf; http://www.eci.gov.in/KeyHighlights/SE_1996/StatisticalReport_KA96.pdf; http://www.eci.gov.in/KeyHighlights/SE_1995/StatisticalReport_MAH95.pdf; http://www.eci.gov.in/KeyHighlights/SE_1996/Statistical Report_WB95.pdf (accessed August 10, 2008).

40 'Man of the year', *Sunday*, 20, 51, December 26, 1993–January 1, 1994, p. 31.

41 'Dalits vs the OBCs', *Sunday*, 21, 9, February 27–March 5, 1994, p. 13; 'States of play', *Sunday*, 21, 7, February 13–19, 1994, pp. 34–37; 'Enter Kanshiram', *Sunday*, 21, 4, January 23–29, 1994, pp. 34, 37.

42 'Maya memsahib' *Sunday*, 21, 28, July 10–16, 1994, p. 25.

43 Sudha Pai, *Dalit Assertion*, p. 167; 'The atrocities against dalits continue, despite Kanshiram', *Sunday*, 21, 7, February 13–19, 1994, p. 28, 32; 'Dalit vs the OBCs', *Sunday*, 21, 9, February 27–March 5, 1994, pp. 10–12.

44 Sudha Pai, *Dalit Assertion*, p. 166; 'Against all odds'', *Sunday*, 22, 7, February 12–18, 1995, p. 37.

45 'Soft target', *Sunday*, 21, 31, July 31–August 6, 1994, p. 47.

46 'Maya memsahib', *Sunday*, 21, 28, July 10–16, 1994, p. 26.

47 'Where might is right', *Sunday*, 22, 2, January 8–14, 1995, p. 27.

48 'Toppling to conquer', *Frontline*, 12, 13, June 30, 1995, p. 12; Sudha Pai, *Dalit Assertion*, p. 167; 'Gaining ground', *Frontline*, 11, 13, July 1, 1994, p. 33.

49 Sudha Pai, *Dalit Assertion*, p. 167; 'Enough is enough', *Sunday*, 22, 23, June 4–10, 1995, p. 41; 'The great fall', *Sunday*, 22, 24, June 11–17, 1995, p. 37.

50 Sudha Pai, *Dalit Assertion*, p. 168.

51 'Masood Ahmad: I have fought wordy wars', *Frontline*, 11, 15, July 29, 1994, p. 14.

52 'Reprieve in UP', *Frontline*, 11, 15, July 29, 1994, pp. 4, 9; 'A topsy-turvy tenure', *Sunday*, 22, 1, January 1–7, 1995, p. 44.

53 'Masood Ahmad: I have fought wordy wars', *Frontline*, 11, 15, July 29, 1994, p. 13; 'Maya memsahib', *Sunday*, 21, 28, July 10–16, 1994, p. 24; 'Toppling to conquer', *Frontline*, 12, 13, June 30, 1995, p. 9.

54 'Allies of convenience', *India Today*, June 30, 1995, p. 51.

55 'Toppling to conquer', *Frontline*, 12, 13, June 30, 1995, p. 12.

56 The intimidatory tactics of the SP heading the coalition government was evident. 'Mulayam wanted to be boss of everything and (continuously) humiliated BSP party leaders.'

Interview with Ambeth Rajan, New Delhi, January 21, 2009; 'The Great Fall', *Sunday*, 22, 24, June 11–17, 1995, pp. 37, 38, 39, 40; 'Reprieve in UP', *Frontline*, 11, 15, July 29, 1994, pp. 4, 10, 11.

The events of June 2–3, 1995, are unclear. Another version suggests that SP workers led by half a dozen MLAs and their followers stormed the guest house with knives and guns and attacked BSP MLAs. After a two-hour battle, the SP mob dragged away '12 BSP MLAs'.

'The decline and fall', *Frontline,* 12, 13, June 30, 1995, p. 6.

57 Sudha Pai, *Dalit Assertion,* pp. 84, 85, 99, 127, 137.

58 'Allies of convenience', *India Today*, June 30, 1995, pp. 47, 52, 54, 55.

59 'Allies of convenience', *India Today,* June 30, 1995, pp. 47, 52, 54, 55; 'Lucknow theatrics', *Frontline,* 12, 14, July 14, 1995, p. 114; 'The great fall', *Sunday,* 22, 24, 11–17 June, 1995, p. 41; 'Allies of convenience', *India Today,* June 30 1995, p. 54.

60 *The Pioneer,* Lucknow edition, June 11, 1995, NMML, Microfilm, Acc. No. 600, R.8767; 'Kalyan Singh: the BJP has installed a dalit women as the CM of the country's most populous state', *Outlook,* 22, 25, June 18–24, 1995, pp. 30–31.

61 Of the 25 MLAs led by Raj Bahadur that broke away from the BSP that was given official recognition by Speaker Dhaniram Verma, 13 returned to the BSP increasing the tally of the BSP to 57 MLAs.

'Allies of Convenience', *India Today,* June 30, 1995, p. 47.

Akela, *Sakshatkar,* p. 244; Sushri Mayawati, *Bahujan Samaj Party ki sarkar ke sadey char mah ki safaltayein aur uplabdhiyan* [*lit.* Four and a half months of the success and achievements of the Government of Bahujan Samaj Party], published by the BSP, Lucknow, Uttar Pradesh, 1995, pp. 12, 13.

Governor Motilal Vora announced the decision of BSP forming a government with the support of the BJP, Congress and the Communist Party of India (CPI).

'The decline and fall: power games come to a head in UP', *Frontline,* 12, 13, June 30, 1995, p. 5.

62 *The Pioneer,* Lucknow edition, June 4, 1995, NMML, Microfilm, Acc. No. 600, R.8767; *The Pioneer,* Lucknow edition, June 2, 1995, NMML, Microfilm, Acc. No. 600, R.8767.

63 'It's no alliance', *India Today,* June 30, 1995, p. 52; 'Living on the edge', *India Today,* July 15, 1995, p. 50; *The Pioneer,* Lucknow edition, June 21, 1995, NMML, Microfilm, Acc. No. 600, R.8767.

64 'Mayawati: I am not merely the leader of the bahujan samaj', *Sunday,* 22, 25, June 18–24, 1995, pp. 22, 23; Mayawati, *Uplabdhiyan,* pp. 12, 28; *The Pioneer,* Lucknow edition, June 4, 1995, NMML, Microfilm, Acc. No. 600, R.8767; *The Pioneer,* Lucknow edition, June 26, 1995, NMML, Microfilm, Acc. No. 600, R.8767; *The Pioneer,* Lucknow edition, June 29, 1995, NMML, Microfilm, Acc. No. 600, R.8767; *The Pioneer,* Lucknow edition, June 7, 1995, NMML, Microfilm, Acc. No. 600, R.8767; *The Pioneer,* Lucknow edition, June 12, 1995, NMML, Microfilm, Acc. No. 600, R.8767.

65 'Cracks to the fore', *Frontline,* 12, 15, July 28, 1995, p. 25; Sudha Pai, Dalit *Question and Political Response*, p. 1143.

66 'Living on the edge', *India Today,* July 15, 1995, pp. 49, 50; Jaffrelot, *Religion, Caste and Politics in India,* p. 503.

67 'State of limbo', *Frontline,* 12, 17, August 25, 1995, p. 88, 'Convenience to confrontation', *India Today,* September 30, 1995, p. 88; Jaffrelot, *Religion, Caste and Politics in India*, p. 503.

68 *The Pioneer*, Lucknow edition, June 10, 1995, NMML, Microfilm, Acc. No. 600, R.8767.

69 *The Hindustan Times,* New Delhi edition, September 10, 1995, NMML, Microfilm, Acc. No. 459, R.6202.

70 Vivek Kumar, 'Uttar Pradesh: politics of change', *Economic and Political Weekly,* 38, 37, September 13, 2003, p. 3870; Mayawati, *Uplabdhiyan,* pp. 13, 21.

71 Mulayam Singh Yadav had allotted special funds for the socio-economic development for two years to villages where population comprised at least 50% Dalits.

Christophe Jaffrelot, *Religion, Caste and Politics in India*, London: Hurst and Company, 2011, p. 503;

Sudha Pai, *Dalit Question,* pp. 1145, 1146; Sudha Pai, *Dalit Assertion,* p. 172; Mayawati, *Uplabdhiyan,* pp. 7, 9, 13, 14, 16, 18, 19, 20, 21; Thakurta and Raghuraman, *A Time of Coalition*, p. 186.

72 "Harsh Wankhede, Dalit symbolism and the democratization of secular spaces", *Mainstream,* vol. XLVIII, No. 12, March 13, 2010, pp. 29–32.

73 There is nothing known as government 'patta' land. Land in India is either 'patta' or 'peremboke'. Patta land is privately owned and can be sold and purchased freely. Peremboke land is government-owned property given to poor farmers to grow crops and live in. Farmers can pass peremboke land to their children to continue farm from generation to generation but they cannot sell it. It is a crime to do so and a crime to purchase it. There are numerous ways in which fraud is perpetrated. A lot of fraud involves Peremboke land mixed in with Patta land. There is also government land which is offered for sale by purported owners, but this is of course complete fraud. Government patta land in the text refers to the transfer of illegal possession of land to the poor people.

Sudha Pai, *Dalit Question,* pp. 1145, 1146; Sudha Pai, *Dalit Assertion,* p. 172; Mayawati, *Uplabdhiyan,* pp. 7, 9, 13, 14, 16, 18, 19, 20, 21. 'State of limbo', *Frontline,* 12, 17, August 25, 1995, pp. 38, 39; 'Falling apart', *Frontline,* 12, 21, October 20, 1995, p. 26.

74 'The rot within', *Frontline,* 11, 23, November 17, 1995, p. 128.

75 'Mayawati: wait and see how our market goes up', *India Today,* November 15, 1995, p. 62; 'Going their own ways', *India Today,* November 15, 1995, p. 61.

The BJP was troubled by Mayawati's nomination of nine members to the UP Legislative Council that included no upper-caste candidate. Mayawati was also nominated to the Legislative Council as she needed to be either nominated or elected to either House in the state before the expiry of six months since her party came to power.

Hindustan Times, New Delhi edition, October 16 and 18, 1995, NMML, Microfilm, Acc. No. 567, R.7556.

76 'Falling apart, *Frontline*, 12, 21, October 20, 1995, p. 26; *Hindustan Times*, New Delhi edition, October 18, 1995, NMML, Microfilm, Acc. No. 567, R.7556.

77 'Kanshiram: Congress is reduced to a C-team now', *Outlook*, 2, 28, July 10, 1996, pp. 4–5; 'Kanshi's one-point plan', *Outlook*, 2, 33, August 14, 1996, pp. 20, 21; 'Kanshiram: a helpless Congress will toe our line', *Outlook*, 2, 37, September 11, 1996, pp. 10–12.

78 'Kanshiram: Congress is reduced to a C-team now', *Outlook,* 2, 28, July 10, 1996, pp. 4–5; 'Kanshi's one-point plan', *Outlook,* 2, 33, August 14, 1996, pp. 20–21; 'Kanshiram: a helpless Congress will toe our line', *Outlook,* 2, 37, September 11, 1996, pp. 10–12.

79 The assembly elections in Uttar Pradesh were held in the month of October 1996 after a year of President's Rule recommended by Governor Motilal Vora after the BSP-BJP coalition government collapsed in October 1995. The end of President's Rule summed up the state of politics in Uttar Pradesh over the next five years. The five-year term of the state assembly (1996–2001) was interspersed by three political regimes hedged by two rounds of President's Rule.

In early May 1996, Motilal Vora was removed from the post of Governor and it was only in the third week of July that Romesh Bhandari was appointed the next Governor of Uttar Pradesh.

(See reference note 108 for further details.)

In the 1996 state polls, 'chunks of OBC votes' became the context for political competition amongst the political parties. The 'strategy to expand a party's base outside ethnic blocks that traditionally belonged to it to (separate) caste polarization, characteristic of UP politics, did not succeed as the Vidhan Sabha elections led to a hung assembly in the state'.

Sudha Pai, *Political Process in Uttar Pradesh,* pp. 114, 115; Sudha Pai, *Dalit Assertion,* pp. 172–76; Sudha Pai, 'Electoral identity politics in Uttar Pradesh: hung assembly again', *Economic and Political Weekly,* 37, 14, April 6, 2002, pp. 1334–45; Jaffrelot, *Ambedkar and Untouchability*, p. 158; Waldrop, *Dalit Politics in India,* pp. 275, 276.

80 Vidya Subramanium, 'From heady hindutva to voter disenchantment', *Seminar,* 571, March 2007, pp. 52–56; A.K. Verma, 'Reverse osmosis in Uttar Pradesh', *Economic and Political Weekly,* 42, 10, March 10, 2007, p. 818; Jaffrelot, *Religion, Caste and Politics in India*, p. 563.

81 'A broader vote-base', *Frontline,* 13, 22, November 15, 1996, p. 21.

82 'UP eludes the BJP', *Frontline,* 13, 21, November 1, 1996, pp. 4, 5, 7.

The break-up of seats of UF partners – SP 110. BKKP 8, JD 7 Congress (Tiwari) 4, CPI(M) 4 and CPI 1.

83 Sudha Pai, *Dalit Assertion,* p. 177.

84 *'Bahujan Samaj Party dwara Bahujan Samaj Prerna Kendra sthapana diwas par behen Mayawati Ji ka bhasan'* [Under the auspices of the Bahujan Samaj Party a speech by Ms. Mayawati on the occasion of the founding of the Bahujan Samaj Center for Inspiration], June 3, 2005, *CD-ROM*, Vols. I and II, Lucknow, Uttar Pradesh, 2005.

85 During the period of uncertainty, the threat of defections of its MLAs to other parties was so high that the BSP locked up its MLAs and placed them under armed guard for the entire duration of coalition negotiations.

Kanchan Chandra, *Elite Incorporation in Multi Ethnic Societies,* p. 25.

86 'Exploring coalition possibilities', *Frontline,* 13, 21, November 1, 1996, pp. 11, 14.

87 'Shifting alignments', *Frontline,* 13, 22, November 15, 1996, p. 16.

Party sources say that the BJP high command sought to placate him by promising an effort to 'break' the BSP in the coming six months, thus giving BJP an absolute majority.

'Together again', *Outlook,* 3, 14, April 2, 1997, pp. 6–12.

88 'BJP's predicament', *Frontline,* 14, 1, January 24, 1997, p. 28; *The Tribune,* Chandigarh edition, March 29, 1997, NMML, Microfilm, Acc. No. 521, R.11170.

89 'Together again', *Outlook,* 3, 14, April 2, 1997, pp. 6–12; 'Opportunism Inc.', *Frontline*, 14, 6, April 18, 1997, pp. 13, 17, 18; 'Mayawati: we have no reason to disbelieve the BJP', *Frontline*, 14, 6, April 18, 1997, pp. 14, 15; *The Tribune*, Chandigarh edition, March 20, 1997, NMML, Microfilm, Acc. No. 521, R.11170; *The Tribune,* Chandigarh edition, March 26, 1997, NMML, Microfilm, Acc. No. 521, R.11170; Vidya Subramanium, 'Voters disenchantment', p. 52–56; *The Tribune*, Chandigarh edition, March 28, 1997, NMML, Microfilm, Acc. No. 521, R.11170.

90 *The Tribune*, Chandigarh edition, March 20, 1997, NMML, Microfilm, Acc. No. 521, R.11170.

91 'As President's Rule came into force, Governor Bhandari "administered" the state on personal fiat as government formation failed to make headway. His

code of conduct came up for scrutiny by the Allahabad High Court, including the neglect of more than 60 government departments waiting for him to take speedy decisions and endorse policies to run the state. Even as his conduct as Governor went to the Supreme Court which eventually struck down the High Court decision, Bhandari effected more than 200 transfers of IAS officers at the 'behest of Mulayam Singh Yadav', for whom, apparently, he had 'ditched Congress friends'. BJP, on its part, took the opportunity to 'demand his recall' in UP. Bhandari maintained a low profile, while Mayawati was on a six-month rotational Chief Ministership from March 21, 1997, as she dismantled 'Mulayam raj' in the state'.

Bhavdeep Kang (05.01.98): "Villain No. 7 Romesh Bhandari". URL: https://www.outlookindia.com (accessed July 5, 2017).

92 *The Tribune,* Chandigarh edition, March 21, 1997, NMML, Microfilm, Acc. No. 521, R.11170; *The Tribune,* Chandigarh edition, March 22, 1997, NMML, Microfilm, Acc. No. 521, R.11170.

93 Subhash Gatade, 'Subverting the Shudra-Ati-Shudra revolution: a close look at the complex interplay of hindutva and bahujanwad in UP', *Mainstream,* XLI, I, December 27, 2003, p. 70; Jaffrelot and Kumar, *Rise of the Plebeians?*, p. 59.

94 'Fractured legacy', *Outlook,* 3, 31, July 30, 1997, p. 27.

95 Buddha Nagar, earlier a part of the district of Ghaziabad, came into existence on April 1, 1997. Three days later, Mayawati announced that Kaushambi would be separated from Allahabad district. Moradabad gave birth to Jyotiba Phule Nagar on April 15; on May 2, Mahamayanagar was created out of Aligarh district; Banda was split into Banda and Shahuji Maharaj Nagar on May 6, 1997.

The Tribune, Chandigarh edition, May 15, 1997, NMML, Microfilm, Acc. No. 523, R.11172.

96 *The Tribune,* Chandigarh edition, May 15, 1997, NMML, Microfilm, Acc. No. 523, R.11172; 'Divide and rule', *India Today*, May 31, 1997, pp. 74, 75; 'Pressures on UP alliance', *Frontline,* 14, 11, June 13, 1997, p. 36; *The Tribune,* Chandigarh edition, March 20, 1997, NMML, Microfilm, Acc. No. 521, R.11171.

97 'Statue symbols', *India Today*, July 28, 1997, pp. 38, 39; 'Mayawati: I'll definitely hand over charge to the BJP', *India Today*, August 11, 1997, p. 55; Zoya Hasan, 'Transfer of power: politics of mass mobilization in UP', *Economic and Political Weekly*, 36, 46 and 47, 24 November, 2001, p. 4404; 'A captive legacy', *India Today*, September 1, 1997, p. 47;

98 Gatade, *Shudra Ati-Shudra*, p. 70; 'Fractured legacy', *Outlook*, 3, 31, July 30, 1997, pp. 24–31. Platts, *Digital Dictionary*, p. 232.

99 Gatade, *Shudra Ati-Shudra*, p. 70; 'Fractured legacy', *Outlook*, 3, 31, July 30, 1997, pp. 24–31.

100 'A captive legacy', *India Today,* September 1, 1997, p. 47; 'Double speak duo', *India Today,* September 22, 1997, pp. 24, 25; 'Fractured legacy', *Outlook,* 3, 31, July 30, 1997, p. 28.

101 Until April 22, 1997, 442 orders of transfers and postings were issued, an average of about 15 orders every day. Symptomatic of her Chief Ministership in 1995, the Mayawati government became synonymous with 'transfer raj' leading to the transfer of around 1,500 officials among whom were 470 IAS and 380 IPS officers.

'Uneasy partners', *India Today,* April 15, 1997, p. 42; 'Opportunism Inc.', *Frontline,* 14, 6, April 18, 1997, p. 18; 'Déjà vu in Uttar Pradesh', *Frontline,* 14, 9, May 16, 1997, p. 45; 'Pressure on UP alliance', *Frontline,* 14, 11, June 13, 1997, p. 37; 'Rallying forces', *Frontline,* 14, 13, July 11, 1997, p. 33; 'The reign of pawnbrokers', *Outlook,* 3, 40, September 29, 1997, pp. 8–9; *Times of India*, Bombay edition, July 2, 1997, NMML, Microfilm, Acc. No. 600, R.9130; *The Tribune*, Chandigarh edition, May 30, 1997, NMML, Microfilm, Acc. No. 524, R.11173; Jaffrelot, *Religion, Caste and Politics in India,* pp. 503–04.

102 Another source puts it at 68 killed on one pretext or the other.

The Tribune, Chandigarh edition, May 10, 1997, NMML, Microfilm, Acc. No. 523, R.11172.

'Déjà vu in Uttar Pradesh', *Frontline,* 14, 9, May 16, 1997, p. 45; 'A confrontation in Uttar Pradesh', *Frontline*, 14, 12, June 27, 1997, p. 38; 'Collision course, *India Today*, June 16, 1997, p. 32; 'Rally versus rally', *India Today*, June 30, 1997, p. 33.

103 'The mandir spillover', *Outlook,* 3, 41, October 6, 1997, p. 8; *The Pioneer,* Lucknow edition, August 3, 1997, NMML, Microfilm, Acc. No. 525, R.11174.

104 *The Pioneer,* Lucknow edition, July 28, 1997, NMML, Microfilm, Acc. No. 526, R.11174; 'Rallying forces', *Frontline,* 14, 13, July 11, 1997, pp. 31, 32.

The State Crime Records Bureau asserted that according to their findings, 'women and dalits' have been victim of crime in the recent past. Figures for April 1997, for instance, recorded that 116 dalits were murdered and 474 women raped, out of which 126 belonged to the dalit community. These figures marked an increase over last year's figures.

'A confrontation in Uttar Pradesh', *Frontline,* 14, 12, June 27, 1997, p. 39.

105 'The mandir spillover', *Outlook,* 3, 41, October 6, 1997, p. 8.

106 'Lonely at the top', *India Today,* October 6, 1997, p. 44.

107 'The mandir spillover', *Outlook,* 3, 41, October 6, 1997, pp. 8–9; Sudha Pai, *State, Politics: New Dimensions (Party System, Liberalisation and Politics of Identity)*, Delhi: Shipra Publications, 2000, p. 125.

108 Jaffrelot, *Religion, Caste and Politics*, p. 554.

On October 19, 1997, as the BSP withdrew support to the Kalyan Singh government, the incumbent Chief Minister, in touch with disgruntled Congress MLA Naresh Agarwal, rushed in to his support with 21 MLAs, after hurriedly forming a new party – Loktantrik Congress. On February 21, 1998, his government was dismissed by Romesh Bhandari. The Governor invited Jagdambika Pal to form a new government as the 'same Naresh Agarwal' withdrew support to the Kalyan Singh government. Agarwal became the Deputy CM in a '48 hour short-lived' Jagdambika Pal government. The Allahabad High Court stayed the order directing that status quo be maintained and reinstated the Kalyan Singh government. Naresh Agarwal, 'The "party hopper" returned to support the BJP with his "rebel" new party.

109 'Uttar Pradesh: shame or sham', *India Today,* November 3, 1997, pp. 28, 30; 'Advantage Kalyan', *India Today,* November 3, 1997, p. 18; 'Stooping to conquer', *India Today,* November 10, 1997, p. 34; *The Pioneer,* Lucknow edition, September 3, 1997, NMML, Microfilm, Acc. No. 526, R.11175.

5 Remaking the Caste Calculus

BJP: National Consolidation versus Organizational Weakness in Uttar Pradesh

The BJP-led coalition government that took oath of office in September 1997 and completed the remainder of the five-year term was a 'jumbo-sized' ministry with 'little interest in formulating policies for economic development'.[1] However, during this period, the BJP state unit was riven by factionalism among two influential caste groups — 'Brahmin' and 'Thakur' castes — that had so far been a politically reassuring factor for the Party even as it expeditiously utilized the 'Mandal sentiment' to mobilize large sections of the OBC groups. Left without a unified upper-caste base, Kalyan Singh-led 'OBC bloc' potentially challenged the predominant upper-caste factions and their leaders — Rajnath Singh belonging to the Thakur community, and Lalji Tandon and Kalraj Mishra representing the Brahmin lobby in the party.[2]

The political fortunes of the BJP government in Uttar Pradesh needs to be observed in the context of the 1998 and 1999 Lok Sabha elections. While BJP's electoral performance in Uttar Pradesh (see Table 5.1) fell away within a year, that of its all-India popularity rose. After the non-Congress non-BJP United Front produced two prime ministers — I.K. Gujral and Deve Gowda — in as many years (1996–1998) till it collapsed, the 12th Lok Sabha elections were held in 1998 in which BJP secured 182 seats in Parliament and along with its allies counted for 254 seats. Falling short of absolute majority, Atal Bihari Vajpayee continued as the 'caretaker' PM from March 10, 1998, to April 26, 1999, before President K.R. Narayanan dissolved the House and called for general elections to be held in the month of September—October 1999. In Uttar Pradesh, despite winning 57 seats in the 1998 Lok Sabha elections, the BJP rule in UP 'produced three chief ministers in three years' — Kalyan Singh (OBC), Ram Prakash Gupta (Bania) and Rajnath Singh (Thakur).[3] In the intra-party factional leadership struggle, the 'Brahmin lobby' was marginalized, but their ability to engage in divisive politics could not be underestimated.

Political compulsions of projecting Vajpayee yet again as the 'Prime Ministerial' candidate in the 1999 Lok Sabha elections forced the BJP to

Table 5.1 UP Lok Sabha Elections (1998–1999)

1998 Lok Sabha Elections	*BJP*	*% of Votes*	*Cong(I)*	*% of Votes*	*SP*	*% of Votes*	*BSP*	*% of Votes*
	57	*36.5*	*0*	*6.0*	*20*	*28.7*	*4*	*20.9*
1999 Lok Sabha Elections	29	27.6	10	14.8	26	24.0	14	22.1

Source: Sudha Pai (Ed.), *Political Process in Uttar Pradesh*, Delhi: Pearsons Longman, 2007, p. 182.

'think nationally' in terms of a wider coalition arrangement with regional political parties. It was a political lesson the party had admittedly learned due to its failure to muster a sufficient number of seats to form a government at the Centre following the 12th Lok Sabha elections in 1998. The BJP yet again adopted party guidelines to portray itself as 'nationally' acceptable to Dalits and other bahujan low-caste groups in society. On the other hand, a new 'strategic' party directive apparently was schemed exploring an electoral equation between the upper caste and Dalit combine in Uttar Pradesh. Yet, the new caste equation led to an ensuing intra-factional struggle among the dominant castes even as they separately directed their attack against Kalyan Singh-led OBC which led to his exit from the BJP. However, Kalyan Singh's exit was preceded by his success in sabotaging the party's electoral appeal by engaging in an anti-BJP backward caste 'motivational campaign' that resulted in huge loss of voters and seats for the party in 1999 Lok Sabha elections in UP.[4]

In the 1999 Lok Sabha elections held in the months of September–October, the BJP yet again was the largest single party in Parliament winning 182 seats. Yet, this time leading a National Democratic Alliance (NDA) of 24 political parties, the BJP-affiliated NDA won 270 seats and later expanded it to 279 seats and formed the first full-term national government since 1996. However, BJP's tally in the 1999 Lok Sabha elections in UP was 'halved to 29 seats' with a vote share of 27.64% and the winning margin of BJP candidates fell from 10% to 7%. The SP increased its tally to 26 seats gaining 6 seats, while the BSP registered a more significant rise from 4 to 14 Lok Sabha seats. The political failure of the BJP in the 1999 Lok Sabha elections in UP was indicative not of a convergence of 'secular forces' but 'greater tactical voting at the constituency level' as votes polarized against the BJP due to a reworked strategy of 'inclusionary politics' pursued separately by the BSP and the SP.[5] Kalyan Singh's decision to float a new 'backward' class political party, the Rashtriya Kranti Dal (RKD), to mobilize Lodh Rajput votes set off a chain reaction as Bhinds, Kashyaps,

Nishads, Majhis, Khagis, Kewars, Nais, Kumhars and other minor MBC caste groups moved away from the BJP depleting its low-caste 'backward' OBC base. The BJP also had to contend with two other OBC political formations — the Kurmi-dominated Apna Dal and Ajit Singh's Rashtriya Lok Dal, the latter a party primarily catering to the constituency of western UP Jat OBC peasantry.[6] BJP's decade-long strategic alliance with the influential Rajput community of western UP also came to an end as electoral results exposed a significant decrease in their support for the party. In eastern UP, the powerful Thakur community began to be successfully mobilized by the SP.[7] As a natural corollary to the emergence of Dalit politics in the state, upper-caste Brahmins, Tyagis and Thakurs started perceiving the SP as a major political force that could check the rise of the BSP.[8] To wrest back the 'fleeting Thakur votes' from the SP, the 'Bania' CM Ram Prakash Gupta, a RSS 'pracharak' (propagandist) and successor to Kalyan Singh following his exit, was replaced by 'Thakur' Rajnath Singh. With a political crisis affecting the state BJP unit, Mulayam Singh Yadav directed close associate and party's 'Thakur leader' Amar Singh to mobilize the Thakur caste and 'seize' 'upper-caste' votes that were deserting the BJP. In an effort to arrest the Party's political decline in the state, Rajnath Singh implemented the Hukum Singh Committee Report 2001 to provide 'overt representation' to Muslims, backward castes, non-Yadav OBCs and the non-Chamar Dalits ostensibly to isolate the two prominent Yadav and Chamar bases of support of the SP and the BSP. The Report stated that in state public services, non-Chamar Dalits were to be given 11% reservation; 'low-caste' backwards 14% which included 22 backward castes in the Muslim community; while Jats, Kurmis, Lodhs and Gujjars were to be offered 9% reservation.[9] Rajnath Singh's political ambition to revive the electoral fortunes of the BJP and to simultaneously enforce the dominance of the 'Thakur caste' in state politics was forestalled by an internecine Thakur-Brahmin factional struggle. Political supporters of Kalraj Mishra, leader of the Brahmin clique in the BJP, claimed that 'they could (have finished) off' the 'upstart' Rajnath Singh (politically) in no time if it had not been for the (assembly elections 2002) in the state.[10]

BSP: 'Broad Basing' Electoral Strategy

The altered parameter of the politics of 'Hindutva', which would have political consequences for the BJP, in actuality, became the context for the reconfiguration of BSP's 'Dalit politics' in UP. Out of power, the party began to make a conscious political effort to yet again shed the 'Chamar image' of the Party while intensifying the focus on the core ideology of 'social brotherhood' of the bahujan class. However, there were definite political indications that an evolving electoral formula of a 'sarvajan samaj' began during this period. The BSP began to endorse a 'strategy of political appeal' to diverse castes and groups for an 'exchange of votes' in its favour which was premised on following a non-patronage-based fair representation within the party and a political promise of an equitable distribution of state assets and resources.[11] The Party began to give greater attention to those caste groups — Brahmins, Thakurs, Banias and OBCs — whose 'concentration within the party was very low but high in society'. The BSP was endorsing the need to 'enter into a social coalition with these upper-caste OBC groups' so as to pre-empt post-election 'compulsive' political equations with other political parties. In this way, the BSP hoped to significantly expand its electoral concord to capture political power in Uttar Pradesh.[12]

In 1998 Lok Sabha elections,[13] the BSP had adopted a policy of withholding prior 'electoral arrangement' with any political party. It adopted a policy of selectively nurturing political constituencies with the intention to realize specific electoral results. For the first time, 'Dalit share of candidates' fell to 25% as the party targeted the backward castes offering 41% for the seats in the Parliamentary elections. However, in the distribution of election 'tickets', 66% of OBC candidates were allocated to the Most Backward Castes. To allay possible misconception that may arise between Chamars and non-Chamar BSP candidates, Mayawati stated:

> '(The Party had) given 21 seats to the SC (to contest the Lok Sabha elections in UP). Among (those) 21 seats 5 were given to the Pasi community, 1 to the dhobi community, 1 to the Koeri community, 1 to the Khatik community and 13 seats to the Chamar community'.[14]

The BSP approved an organized method of representing non-Chamar SCs as party candidates based upon their degree of political influence across certain constituencies in the state. In the context of the Lok Sabha elections in 1998, Mayawati remarked:

> I want to tell my Muslim brothers also that this time the BSP has given the single largest number of seats in UP to Muslim candidates. We allotted these seats where the Muslim samaj had at least 2 lakh votes. If in all these constituencies the 2 lakh Muslim votes come to us then I can assure you that all of the 14 candidates from the Muslim community will become MPs. I want to tell my backward caste brothers that your population in UP is also very large. (Therefore) [K]eeping this in mind we have given 35 seats to the (OBCs). In addition, we have given (political) opportunities to other communities (such as) the Sainis, the Mauryas, Shakya, Kashyap and the Kushwaha (castes)'.[15]

The BSP competed in the 1998 Lok Sabha elections on a 'single-point' agenda of 'anti-BJP-ism'. Kanshiram's statement exploring the distinct possibility of checking the rise of the BJP in various states was evident in a speech he gave while addressing a public rally in Saharanpur, western UP. The BSP leader contended:

> (So) why are we fighting the elections from all 85 seats in UP? (This is due to the fact that) our goal in UP (will be to) reduce the BJP by 25 (seats). In Madhya Pradesh we can reduce (the BJP) by 15 (seats). In Bihar, we have left the field open for Laloo Prasad Yadav because he can reduce the 20–25 seats the BJP has (in the state). In Punjab, we have allied with the Congress to get BJP's seats reduced, and not permit it to form the government. In Karnataka we have joined hands with Bangarappa in order to ruin the BJP. In Gujarat we are giving unconditional support (to) defeat the BJP. We have made arrangements that the BJP should not be in a position to win more than 100 seats (in Parliament) so that after the elections when they have less than 100 MPs, they will not be in a position to form government by buying MPs.[16]

The exaggerated prediction of BJP being electorally outmanoeuvred by the BSP and other political parties did not alter the poor performance of the party in the 1998 UP Lok Sabha election. Irrespective of the fact that BJP, SP and BSP distributed tickets to 'carefully selected candidates', belonging to 'non-core constituency', according to their ability to 'wield political influence', a polarized voting pattern emerged due to a lack of a cohesive 'non-BJP/secular' political alternative to the BJP. The BSP registered 20.90% of the vote share, but it could only manage to win four seats in Akbarpur, Misrikh, Bahraich and Azamgarh. Mayawati won the Akbarpur seat with 34% vote share, while the other three constituencies went to Muslim BSP candidates. Kanshiram was defeated at Saharanpur, a prominent Dalit constituency, by a wide margin of 59,000 votes.[17] The BSP was pushed back to its 'original' social base in the eastern districts of UP, gaining no seat in any other region of the state.[18]

In June 1999, BSP leader Kanshiram stated that there was a need for a 'political revival' of the BSP-SP political alliance with support from Muslims, OBCs and an expanding political constituency of Thakurs supporting the SP. It was felt that such a 'community-based alliance' would poll 45% of the total votes and win more than 70% of the 85 Parliamentary seats in UP. Mulayam Singh Yadav alluded to the idea that at the national level, political parties needed to break the 'bipolar' politics of the Congress and the BJP. However, Mayawati perceived the 'ensuing fermentation in UP politics' as a political opportunity for the BSP to commit Lok Sabha 'tickets' to backwards, Muslims and upper-caste candidates which would enable the BSP to broaden the 'social profile' of the Party. The 'multi-ethnic constituency' experiment was not a novel electoral schema. It had already been configured for the 1996 Lok Sabha and assembly elections. In the 1998 Lok Sabha elections in the state, this electoral tactic was used by the BSP in certain specific constituencies. Mayawati concluded that the BSP party activists needed to comprehend the changed perception and ensure that the party endorsed this electoral experiment comprehensively and must properly appeal to diverse castes and ethnic groups. Thus, the 1998 Lok Sabha 'electoral fiasco' could be conjured as a failure to appreciate the changed caste-community dynamics in the state rather than a failed electoral model of the party. It could be quickly redressed if the correct strategy of electoral mobilization was adopted. In the late 1990s, SP's support among Muslims had registered a sharp decline, from 79% in 1996 to 37% in 1999. Similarly, the OBC non-Yadav votes had also decreased substantially, from 38% in 1996 to 18% in 1999. The upper castes affected by divisive politics in the BJP state unit could no longer be deemed a secure vote bank of the BJP. The BSP was entering a phase of politics where 'free-floating' political resources decoupled from their traditional bases of political parties were available as electoral capital to be politically exploited by the most 'judicious' political party. Hence, rather than forming electoral alliances that would, to a significant degree, make the BSP dependent on the fortunes of its coalition partner, it made political sense to adopt a strategy that would enable the party to embrace an 'offensive battle' strategy[19] fuelled by a political realization that the Party must 'raid' the vote banks of other political parties to register an increased number of seats.[20]

In the 1999 Lok Sabha elections in UP, the BSP allotted 20 seats to the Dalits, 38 to the backward castes and 10 to the upper castes, 5 each to Brahmin and Thakurs. The electoral strategy to increase the tally of votes, and hence seats, was based on 'the selective distribution of tickets to candidates according to their strength in the population in a constituency or district'. The BSP wished to evolve a 'constituency-specific' winning combination of castes. Seats were allotted to Dalit candidates who could win, such as in Bundelkhand and eastern and central UP. 'Muslim candidates were selected in 17 constituencies, such as Amroha, Bareilly, Pilibhit, Unnao, Agra, Saharanpur and Nainital, Hapur, Meerut where it was felt that the Muslims were moving away from SP'. On this principle 'the BSP fielded a Gujjar in Baghpat, a Kashyap in Kairana, a Saini in Muzzafarnagar, a Burman in Hardwar'. The party nominated Brahmin candidates in Sitapur where they had expressed their opposition to the BJP prior to the elections. The BSP began to mobilize 'caste leaders' among the Pal, Shakya, Maurya, Baghel, Pushkar and Saini among 'backwards' and Sankhawar, Pasi, Dhobi, Balmiki and Khatiks among Dalits.[21] The BSP leadership addressed 'Muslims public rallies' stating that it was a 'secular party', not the Congress, and (they should) not divide votes by voting either for the SP or the Congress. The BSP contended that Muslims were now co-sufferers with Dalits due to a pronounced 'Yadavisation' political campaign and could be successfully weaned away from the SP.[22] A decreased level of support of the Muslims for SP, based upon an assessment of a drop in percentage from 72% in 1998 to 54% in 1999, did not mean a consolidation of 'Muslim vote' for the BSP. In reality, the 'BSP (was) "down in the rating" because the Muslim voters found Mayawati to be untrustworthy'. 'She had, (after all), joined hands with the BJP "twice" (in 1995 and 1997), (the latter) to form a government on a six-monthly basis', said Aizaz Ahmad, a resident of the Ayodhya assembly constituency. Another resident I.M. Khan of Faizabad added:

> '(W)hen [sic] (Muslims) voted for her in the last two elections it was to oppose the BJP, but she (had) insulted (Muslim) sentiments. We (would) never support her again. Mulayam Singh Yadav (could) decisively stop the VHP and (he was) the only person who (had) proved on that count'. 'We (would) vote either for the SP, or the Congress, whosoever (would be) in a better position' to defeat the BJP.[23]

The BSP won 14 seats in the 1999 Lok Sabha elections and increased the percentage of vote share of the party to approximately 22%. Two upper castes, two Muslims, two backward and eight Dalit candidates were the winning BSP candidates. The political influence of the party was apparent across all regions barring the newly-formed state of Uttarakhand carved out of UP. The BSP won three each in Bundelkhand and western UP and four each in central and eastern UP.[24] In the reserved constituencies of Ghatampur, Jalaun, Chail, Lalganj and Akbarpur, the BSP was able to maintain a vote share between 28–35% in a very competitive electoral contest due to a high proportion of Chamar-Jatav votes. At Amroha, Shahabad and Saharanpur, the electoral alignment of the bahujan samaj's 'oppressed Dalit-Muslims' was evident in the victory of BSP's Muslim candidates. At Sitapur, Salempur, Banda, Ghosi, Hamirpur and Sultanpur 'upper-caste-backward caste' candidates were chosen primarily to observe the political success of 'vote-transfer' of Chamar votes to 'non-Chamar, non-SC, non-Muslim BSP' candidates. The success of this 'social engineering' strategy was evident in a number of second positions the BSP achieved in this election. At Bilhaur, Bahraich, Basti and Fatehpur, the BSP lost narrowly. At Bilhaur, it was 30.37% to 29.86% vote share in favour of the eventual winner from BJP. A similar pattern to BSP's '(electoral) gains in the 1999 Lok Sabha elections was (also perceptible) in the Party's losses that were spread across the state', in constituencies of Pilibhit, Unnao, Faizabad, Khalilabad, Azamgarh, Saidpur (SC), Aligarh, Hathras (SC), Etawah, Misrikh and Hardwar (SC).[25] The 1999 UP Lok Sabha elections results (see Table 5.2) showed that the percentage of 'upper-caste votes' had marginally increased for the BSP from 3% seen in the 1996 Parliamentary elections in UP.[26] This election marked the beginning of a political transformation in intra-elite linkages, represented by competing caste groups seeking 'access to patronage, privileges and representation' within the BSP. While 'programmatic benefits would continue for the bahujan constituency "patronage benefits", which was vested with the Chamar BSP legislators began to decrease'.[27]

Table 5.2 Changing Support Base of BSP and SP and Total Votes Polled (in Percentage)

Lok Sabha/Assembly Elections	*Upper Caste*		*OBC*			*Dalit*		*Muslim*		*Vote Share %*	
	BSP	SP	BSP	*SP/JD 1991*	*Non-Yadav*	BSP	SP	BSP	SP	BSP	SP
1991 Lok Sabha	2	11	7		24 (includes Yadav)	30	13	4	49	9.06	21.82
1996 Lok Sabha	4	14	10	58	13	41	10	6	54	20.98	21.29
1996 Assembly Elections	4	4	10	61	20	62	9	12	48	20.12	22.41
1998 Lok Sabha	3	5	14	76	20	66	10	6	72	21.34	29.66
1999 Lok Sabha	4	6	13	83	30	70	6	5	54	22.61	25.04

Source: Sanjay Kumar, *The Prospects*, *Seminar*, March 2007, No. 571, pp. 67–68.

2002 Assembly Elections in Uttar Pradesh: Rudiments of BSP's 'Sarva Samaj'

An improved electoral performance in the 1999 Lok Sabha elections was comprehended by the BSP as a validation of its growing popularity in Uttar Pradesh. The party interpreted the electoral result in the foreground of the approaching 2002 assembly elections. The 2002 assembly elections would indicate whether the BSP could continue a lateral expansion of its popular appeal and create newer 'constituency-specific' bastions of political support to proportionately replicate its Lok Sabha seats to an increased number of seats in the state assembly.

Post-1999 Lok Sabha elections in UP, the BSP also began to make a conscious political effort to address the 'vote against the BSP' approach of the Muslim community. The Party adopted a policy of allocating more seats to 'backward' Muslims such as the Ansaris, Qureshis, Lalbegs and Chikwas leading to a 'record number of 86 Muslim BSP candidates' named to contest the 2002 UP assembly elections out of which one-third of the Muslim candidates were to contest from the Rohilkhand region in the north-western part of the state. With a sizeable electoral presence of Dalits in western UP, it was believed that BSP would be able to forge a Dalit-Muslim electoral equation.[28] Explaining the political potential of a Dalit-Muslim alliance for the 2002 state polls, Rashid Alvi, a BSP MP said:

> Mulayam Singh Yadav (used) emotive issues like 'Ayodhya demolition' to fool illiterate Muslims. (He knew) the Muslim pulse. What about the real issues? Muslims are beginning to see through Mulayam Singh Yadav's game so it is no surprise that our vote share and number of seats (were) going up.[29]

However, a 'decade-old' electoral record since the demolition of the Babri Masjid in 1992 suggested that in each Lok Sabha and assembly elections, the Muslims had resorted to a strategic political option, of supporting the SP, to defeat the BJP. This political option emerged in the aftermath of the political decline of the Janata Dal in Uttar Pradesh. With no other political alternative, UP Muslims in increasing numbers began to identify the SP with being a 'defender' of Muslim community. The BSP stratagem of broad basing socially and economically discriminated Muslims with their fellow non-Muslim brethren was intended to dilute the ethno-religious loyalties of religion and caste. Yet, much of the BSP's election strategy would depend upon the party's dynamics of ethnic linkage between 'bahujan mobilization' and 'government formation', to ostensibly advance the 'interests of the downtrodden'. In 2002 assembly elections, a large section of the low-caste backwards, who have no political benefactor in the state, appeared as a large 'bloc of voters' seeking to ally with a political party(s) with the capacity to mobilize and represent their socio-political interests.[30] The political contest to secure the Brahmin, Kayastha, Bania and Thakur votes of the BJP intensified between the SP and the BSP. The assembly elections emerged as a political battleground to test two relevant electoral strategies — SP's 'social coalition' as a counter to BSP's policy of forming no political alliance and allotting tickets to multi-caste candidates inclusive of the upper castes who were 'under-represented' in the party. The BSP gave election tickets to '37 Brahmin and 36 Thakur' candidates.[31] The overt representation of Brahmin and Thakur as 'BSP candidates' coincided with the party's political rhetoric of 'melting down' of caste polarization which was indicative of 'bhaichara banao' committees in numerous assembly constituencies to entice upper-caste votes. The new BSP slogan for the 2002 assembly elections was symptomatic of the party's changing perceptions on bahujan politics —'tilak, tarazu aur talwar, saab ho haathi par sawar' ('Tilak' symbolizing Brahmins; 'tarazu', the Bania or Vaishya class; and 'talwar', the Kshatriya/Kayastha must ride the elephant, the election mascot of the BSP).[32] Another political slogan 'haathi nahi Ganesh hai, Brahma, Vishnu, Mahesh hai' (the BSP mascot elephant is Ganesh, the Hindu god, as well as Brahma, Vishnu and Mahesh, the three supreme Hindu gods)'.[33] The BSP's political move from bahujan samaj to sarvajan samaj had begun. In the 2002 assembly election, the SP won 143 seats. The SP maintained the 1999 Lok Sabha percentage of 53% Muslim support. Further, upper-caste 'Thakur support' for the party showed an increase from 3% to 8%. The SP also gained 7% more upper-caste votes, 5.32% more OBC votes and 3.4% more SC votes in the 2002 UP assembly elections. The BJP won 88 seats registering a sharp drop of 12.36% in its vote share from 32.52% achieved in the 1996 assembly elections. The electoral debacle was due to a substantial decrease in Brahmin and upper-caste vote for the Party: a steep decline to 49% from 74% since the 1999 Lok Sabha elections.[34]

The BSP improved its electoral performance considerably in the 2002 assembly elections. It secured 98 seats of which 32 were upper castes, 16 Muslims, 27 Dalits and 23 OBC which was a net gain of 32 seats (see Table 5.3) since the 1996 assembly elections. The party performed well in

Table 5.3 UP Assembly Elections 2002

Parties	*Seats Won*	*Vote %*
Cong(I)	25	9.00
BJP	88	20.12
SP	143	25.43
BSP	98	23.20

Source: Vivek Kumar, 'Behind the BSP Victory', *Economic and Political Weekly*, 42, 24, June 16, 2007, p. 2237; A.K. Verma, 'Reverse Social Osmosis in Uttar Pradesh', *Economic and Political Weekly*, 42, 10, March 10, 2007, p. 818.

Table 5.4 Caste-wise/Community Support in UP Assembly Elections 2002

Parties	*Upper Caste*	*OBC*	*Dalit*	*Muslim*
Cong(I)	27	6	7	16
BJP	48 *Brh.50 n.Brh 47	21	7	2
SP	3	25 ** Yadav75 n.Yad 15	7	51
BSP	6	15	68 Chamar 79 Non-Chamar 55	10

*Brahmin/non-Brahmin
** Yadav/non-Yadav
Source: A.K. Verma, 'BSP's strategy in UP', *Economic and Political Weekly*, 40, 26, June 25, 2005, p. 2647; Sanjay Kumar, 'The Prospects', *Seminar*, March 2007, No. 571, pp. 66–68; Sudha Pai (Ed.), *Political Process in UP*, Delhi: Pearson Longman, 2007, p. 177.

western UP that vindicated the policy of increased representation of Muslim candidates and made a significant impact in central and eastern districts of the state where an increased number of low-caste backwards and Dalit candidates won.[35] The BSP gained 69% of its vote share from Dalits, 10% of Muslim votes, 7% of lower backwards vote, but only 5% of the Brahmin and upper-caste votes.[36] Despite negligible numbers of voting percentages for Muslims, lower backwards and upper castes, Mayawati's schematic electoral design involving a transfer of Dalit votes (see Table 5.4) to non-Dalit candidates ensured close political victories in 'triangular contests' for the BSP.

'Electoral Votes' and 'Dictated Alliance': Courting Political Confrontation

Post-2002 assembly elections, the process of forming a new government was stalled, since the SP, the single largest political party in the UP assembly, failed to solicit coalition support from the Congress Party[37] even as it attempted to entice 'a section of the BSP Muslim MLAs' to support an SP-induced initiative to form a coalition government in the state. In the ensuing constitutional crisis that gripped the state, ulterior political motives of the BJP and the BSP converged. At the Centre, the BJP-led NDA government received political support from the BSP to sail through the 'vote on Gujarat' in the Parliament in the wake of the communal violence in Godhra in 2001. The BSP ensured the support of its 13 MPs, which became critical, since one of the NDA alliance partners, the Telugu Desam Party, had distanced from the NDA's stated position on the Gujarat imbroglio. The BJP returned the 'political favour' by acceding to BSP's definite political inclinations to form a coalition government in UP. The political coalition was actively resisted by the BJP state unit that was evident in a political slogan: 'UP ki majboori hai, Mayawati zaroori hai (Uttar Pradesh has a compelling need for Mayawati)'. The coalition pact was 'a hastily patched up arrangement' initiated by the BJP's central leadership led by Prime Minister Atal Bihari Vajpayee and Home Minister Lal Krishna Advani who intervened to '(urge) party's state leaders to fall in line'. Vajpayee remarked that 'both parties (must) abide by the "coalition dharma"[38] and learn from past experience to ensure mistakes (were) not repeated'.[39] BJP's political maxim: keep the SP 'out' and the BSP 'in power', was defined in terms of the loss of upper-caste Thakur votes to the SP. The political analogy was based on the premise that if the SP came to power, backed by the influential Thakur lobby; 'other' upper-caste votes would continue to slip away from the BJP.[40] Another significant aspect to the 'political agreement' was the presumption that the BSP would act as a 'counterbalance' to constitutive partners of the NDA at the Centre.

The process of BSP's government formation included 'equal number of ministers, from both the (political) parties'. (Since) 'there were constraints in the (political) alliance, it was necessary for the MLAs to take every section of the society into confidence'.[41] A 'Dalit women' as CM, 'went down well with the sangh parivar', keen to transcend a 'Brahmin-Thakur-Bania' identity of the BJP. In the context of the 2004 national elections, the support for a BSP-led coalition government was an endorsement of an established electoral 'plan' that would potentially expand BJP's political presence among low-caste voters across states to win a high percentage of Lok Sabha seats.[42]

Chief Minister Mayawati made clear that 'it was the BSP and not the BJP that was "dictating" the nature of the coalition government'. Mayawati was categorical that the government would 'review all new schemes and only those that were absolutely in the public interest would be (realized)'; though political priority would be given to '(those) schemes that (were) in the interests of Dalits and other downtrodden sections of the (society)'.[43] Mayawati's tenure as CM of Uttar Pradesh from May 2002 to August 2003 was, markedly different from her earlier stints in political office. To Mayawati, a significant feature of her leadership abilities was to engage the SP in a political vendetta, to contest a 'vicious' political space that in the post-2002 assembly elections increasingly began to resemble a heightened 'egoistic' political clash with Mulayam Singh Yadav. Mayawati exemplified a political defiance towards the SP that was expected to represent a struggle between a 'conscientious victim' resisting the 'social oppressor' section of society, which, apparently, Mulayam Singh Yadav and the SP represented. Through the entirety of her political term in office, SP-BSP tensions heightened significantly as allegations and counter-allegations conspired to vitiate the political atmosphere.

The SP observed the day '(Mayawati) was administered the (CM) oath' as 'dhikkar diwas' (condemnation day).[44] In response, Mayawati highlighted the 'contentious' Muslim base of the SP. She said:

> My Muslim MLAs (said) that if Mulayam Singh Yadav was really secular, he would have extended support to the BSP-led government. But he is not; he only pretends to be a 'messiah of the Muslims' while doing nothing for their development.[45]

The BSP government's political clarification on 'Muslim interests' came even as the leader of the Shia Muslim Front Maulana Kalbe Jawaad urged 'Muslims (to) put pressure on their (Muslim) MLAs in BSP (to) split from the Party since in its quest for power the (party) had joined hands with the BJP'. However, political perceptions differed as the influential Muslim Samaj Sammelan said:

> Muslims must demand 10 per cent reservation, up from 8.44 per cent out of 27 per cent reservation for the OBC. (If) the (government) was interested in the progress and welfare of the Muslim community and undertook concrete steps towards that objective then Muslims would never leave BSP'.[46]

As a step towards engaging with the variant quasi-religious Muslim subaltern elite and the 'backward' Muslim voters, Mayawati announced a 'development package' for 'Muslim-dominated villages' under the Ambedkar Gram Yojana scheme meant to disburse benefit to (religious) minorities and backwards. The BSP allocated plans to open '577 new primary and 144 senior basic schools' across regions where Muslims had a sizeable population. The party earmarked a policy prerogative for the 'professionalization of education' among the Muslims in the form of 'new mini–Indian Technical Institute (ITI)' in 'madrasas' (a college of Islamic instruction), in the rural areas and coaching institutes for 'Pre-medical Tests, ITI and State-level engineering examinations'.[47]

The intensification of political bitterness between the SP and BSP increased its tempo as Mulayam Singh Yadav publicly aired Mayawati's 'money-spinning' construction plans that had turned the 'pet Ambedkar Park' project into a 'aiyyashi ka adda' (a den of vices). Countering the allegation, the BSP launched a political attack on the SP with a September 28, 2002, 'dhikkar rally'.[48] At a public rally in Lucknow, Kanshiram addressing BSP supporters declared:

> '(Mulayam) has gone (abroad for a period of) 10 days. Once he comes back, make him run so much that he runs away from the state for ever'.

> Mayawati remarked that '(Mulayam) has all along been practicing the "politics of Muslims and backwards". If Muslims and backwards desert him, he (would go) back to his traditional calling of grazing buffaloes'.[49]

The SP party workers organized the 'thoo-thoo' (symbolically 'spitting abuses') rallies at the BSP in a series of political rallies held across UP. The rallies were organized by the SP activists to remind people that BSP leaders were 'opportunists', and would 'stoop to any level for the sake of power'.[50] In contrast, BSP party workers observed Mayawati's birthday on January 15, 2003, as 'swabhimaan diwas' (self-respect day), an occasion to highlight the welfare services implemented by the state government for Dalits, backwards and minorities. Her 'birthday' was expected to 'represent Dalit pride', which legitimized 'free and equal' participation.[51] SP activists continued to target Mayawati alleging that the BSP leader had accumulated 'Rs. 300 crores' during her birthday celebrations.[52] Mayawati made a counter-allegation accusing Mulayam Singh Yadav of possessing illegal assets worth several crores of rupees. While the SP held an all-party meeting in the second week of January 2003 on the 'state of the Mayawati government', Mayawati focused her 'record on administration' by commending police officers involved in the arrest of Raghuraj Pratap Singh, known as 'Raja bhaiyya' and dacoit mafia Atiq Ahmad from Allahabad.[53] Mayawati's decision to arrest Raju bhaiyya, an independent MLA and a 'mafia-dacoit' from Pratapgarh in eastern UP, under Prevention of Terrorist Act (POTA) for 'murder and rape' was a political ultimatum to the SP. As a postlude to the 'arrest' of the Pratapgarh 'don', the SP began to entice 'sections of BJP MLAs and independents', known to have political sympathies with Raja bhaiyya, to join in a no-confidence motion against the Mayawati government'.[54] Mulayam Singh Yadav was also allegedly instigating an internal rebellion in the BSP. On the matter of a 'political divide in the BSP', the SP leader commented: 'aisa hi swar BSP mein bhi uth rahen hein lekin khulke nahi' [the voice (of rebellion) is brewing in the BSP, though not openly]'.[55] The SP yet again implicated Mayawati for using the 'position of Chief Minister' to 'make money (though) pacts with political parties, engineering political splits (and) distributing elections tickets (to political factions) and politicizing decisions regarding development programmes'. Mayawati retaliated by launching a 'pardafaash' (here it means 'to expose') rally on Ambedkar's birthday. Addressing a public gathering, Mayawati said that the SP was entrapped in a chakravyuh (maze).[56] The 'rally' also included an 'anti- Hindu dharma public denigration of Hindu gods and goddesses' and a 'recipe to embrace Buddhism'. The 'critique of Hindu dharma' was directed at the BJP state unit to remain politically committed to the ruling coalition. Despite political provocations, the BJP state unit complied with the party directive of national leaders not to upturn the 'coalition dharma' but felt that it had become the 'savarna prakosth' (upper-caste cell) of the BSP.[57]

Mayawati's 15-month tenure as UP chief minister was marked by 'populist programmatic goals' to implement the 'social justice' programmes of the Party. One of the critical aspects of the Party's social justice goals had been the 'transfer order' of senior administrative officials. As Chief Minister of Uttar Pradesh, Mayawati began relocating 'senior' administrative officers by transferring 47 IAS and Indian Revenue Services (IRS) and 17 IPS officers, which included a 'select number of senior DIGs, SPs and Sub-Superintendent of Police (SSP)'. The 'transfer raj' continued despite a Supreme Court decision ordering the Uttar Pradesh government to follow a transparent administrative procedure in cases of transfer of public officials. By August 2003, 95% of IAS officers in the state had been transferred.[58] In a government report, the BSP outlined that 'crime had been reduced by 69 per cent'; and 'crime against Dalits reduced by 62 per cent'. The BSP government initiated a new legislation to check the rise of land mafias and 'thekedar' (contractor) mafia. The BSP government extended 'the principle of reservations in the selection of police-officer-in-charge of a 'thana' (police station) to 20% for SC and ST, 25% for OBC and 5% for religious minorities. The government highlighted 'a communal riot-free year' at the end of the first year in office and stated that the (Ayodhya) 'temple issue' was on BJP's political agenda and 'warned that the government could (take punitive action) against those trying to disrupt communal harmony in Ayodhya'.[59] The BSP government was successful in completing the development programmes associated with 12,000 'Ambedkar villages' that were notified in its previous stint in government. As the ruling coalition partner in the state in 2002, the BSP government approved a decision to add 25 'new' Ambedkar villages each year. To increase the pace of 'development work', the Swarna Jayanti project (golden jubilee project) was inaugurated that would ensure that electricity, roads, education, health and employment reached 'target' villages. In 2002–03, 3,047 Ambedkar villages were 'enrolled in eleven development programmes' and the target of 'electrification of 1,829 Ambedkar villages' was completed.[60] Landless farmers numbering 89,000 were given ownership rights of land of variable productivity value, however, without any viable subsidy measure to increase crop yield. Predictably, most of the farmers in possession of land complained that low fertility inhibited sowing of seasonal crops. It appeared that propriety over land was a central issue with the BSP geared to instil Dalit pride and dignity for electoral mileage rather than it being a source of sustained livelihood. Occupancy rights were also given to '1.8 lakh SC populated areas' under a special 'Gram Samaj Policy Initiative'. The outlay for social programmes included medical institutions named after Chhatrapati (title of king) Shahuji Maharaj in Lucknow; a Gautam Budh Vidyalaya (school) was opened in Greater Noida in Uttar Pradesh; a Balika Shiksha (girls education) programme was inaugurated to educate young girls; a 'Swarnima Plan' for woman belonging to the backward classes was announced; a 'Sarvshiksha Abhiyaan' — a 'mega-campaign' to ensure education for all and a 'Students Development Programme' that would target students belonging to SC and other poorer sections of society. The BSP government also initiated the 'Annapurna and Antodaya Plans' to cater to 'the welfare of the weakest' living below the poverty line. The BSP government undertook measures to improve the erratic power supply in the state by ensuring an uninterrupted '8-hour electricity' schedule 'to provide relief to farmers engaged in agriculture'. To ensure that farmers got competitive prices for their crops, notably wheat and rice, the BSP government successfully claimed a procurement policy whereby the state government would become the largest buyer of crops from farmers. The BSP government outlined a policy to ensure 20% reservation for women in engineering and medical schools and a 'special entry for SC and members of the backward castes' in engineering colleges. The state government took possession of the '10 hectare' Indira Gandhi Prastisthan (foundation) land in Lucknow to build a Rs. 40-crore 'Ambedkar Library and Museum' on that land, adjacent to a Rs. 100-crores Ambedkar memorial. It further recommended to the Planning Commission to provide '50 per cent of the expenses' for the construction of the building.[61]

In August 2003, the Mayawati government collapsed as the BJP withdrew support in the wake of evidence of an illegal construction of a '175 crore Taj Corridor Highway' within 500 meters of Taj Mahal, in Agra. Apparently, the project had been cleared with Chief Minister's consent by the Ministry of Forests and Environment, Government of India.[62] Mayawati alleged that the BJP had initiated a Central Bureau of Investigation (CBI) enquiry into the layout plans of the Taj Corridor in a bid to weaken the credentials of the BSP government. With the impending collapse of the coalition government, the SP managed to split the BSP as 37 BSP MLAs left to ally with the SP. A majority of the rebel BSP MLAs were Muslims and upper caste who had always constituted a 'risk zone' for the BSP and been a target by the SP to entice defections. Out of the 37 BSP MLAs, 15 were Thakurs, 9 Muslims, 4 Brahmins and 3 each Yadavs, SC and others. On September 9, 2003, in the 'floor test', in the UP state assembly, the SP proved its majority. Out of the 398 votes polled, 244 were in favour of the 'motion'. The strength of the SP coalition government in the state assembly was 241 that consisted of SP 181, Congress 16, RLD 14, RKD 4 MLAs, besides 26 others as against 160 of the BSP, BJP and the Akhil Bharat Hindu Mahasabha.[63] An SP-INC-led coalition government was formed which completed the remainder of the term.

BSP: 'Bahujan-Savarna' Experiment of 'Transferable' Votes

With a political strategy to defeat the BJP in 2004 Parliamentary elections, Mayawati strategized an anti-manuvadi bahujan politics by pairing the Congress and the BJP as 'chacha-bhateeja', (here it specifically means one related to the other) who had conspired in differing political contexts to defeat the 'bahujan government' of the BSP.[64] The 2004 Parliamentary polls in UP was a 'multi-cornered electoral contest'.[65] BSP candidates with a 'higher percentage of winning' were selected for Lok Sabha seats in Bundelkhand region in south UP and western UP from a 'rainbow coalition of caste' consisting of non-Dalit, Muslim, Jat, Shakya, Thakur and Brahmin candidates. The 'vote share' of these specifically selected Parliamentary candidates was expected to increase 'transferable' Dalit votes by 30–40% in the region.[66] The BSP also included 'defector MLAs' in the list of Lok Sabha candidates such as Akbar Ahmad Dumpy, Rizwan Zaheer, Illyas Azmi, Talat Aziz, Mitrasen Yadav, Afroz Ali, Chaudhary Dalvi Singh, Chaudhary Lakshmi Narayan and Ravi Gautam. The Party perceived that each 'defector' had an autonomous social base, howsoever caste-specific or marginal, that would expand with tactical and strategic voting by Dalit-Bahujan groups.

The SP intensified its political campaign to ensure that a majority of the Muslim vote went to the party. Mulayam Singh Yadav was 'highlighted as a leader' who tried to save 'Allah's ghar a.k.a the Babri masjid' as the SP sought to politically sensitize the insecurity of the Muslims to 'majoritarian (BJP) and unreliable (BSP)' political forces in the state.[67] The 2004 poll result indicated yet again that the Muslim vote was tactical, in favour of the SP, the party most likely to defeat the BJP. This was best illustrated in Rampur, a Muslim-dominated constituency, where Muslims supported the SP's non-Muslim candidate film actor Jayaprada enabling her to win with a margin of over 85,475 votes over Begum Noor Bano of the INC. Another example of the minority community's voting preference was seen in Kaiserganj where Arif Mohammad Khan, a 'convert to BJP', was defeated by the SP candidate Beni Prasad Verma by over one lakh votes.[68] In Gonda, Pratapgarh, Rae Baraeli and Sultanpur, Brahmins, Thakurs and Rajput voted for SP. With an enhanced Yadav-Rajput-Muslim-Thakur base, the SP increased its tally from 26 to 35 seats in the UP Parliamentary elections. The BJP's tally fell to an all-time low of 10 seats as it became clear that at least in half of the 80 seats in the state, the Thakurs and Brahmins voted for non-BJP political parties.[69] The BSP with a select group of 'defector' candidates and a multi-ethnic constituency electoral formula increased its share of seats from 14 to 19 seats. The Party's vote share increased to 24.67% (see Table 5.5) that included the upper-caste votes, notably of Brahmins at 4%, OBC 14%, Dalits 65% and Muslims 10%.[70] Two 'rebel candidates' Illyas Azmi and Mitrasen Yadav won from the Shahbad and Faizabad constituencies in central UP. At Faizabad, Mitrasen Yadav received a vote share of 30.19%, largely due to the political support he received from SC (26%) and Muslims (11%). Bhalchandra Yadav won from Khalilabad (eastern UP) with 33.5% vote share, Ramakant Yadav won from Azamgarh (eastern UP) with 36. 30%, Umakant Yadav won from Machhlishahr (central UP) with 35.10% and Kailash Nath Singh Yadav won from Chandrauli (eastern UP) with 29.05%, winning a close race over Anand Katra Maurya of SP. Three BSP Muslim candidates Mohammad Tahir from Sultanpur (central UP),

Table 5.5 Seats Won, Percentage of Votes and Changing Support Base of BJP, Cong(I), SP and BSP in the 2004 UP Lok Sabha Elections

Parties	*Seats Won*	*Vote %*	*Upper Caste*	*OBC*	*Dalit*	*Muslim*
BJP	10	22.2	59 *Brh 60 n.Brh 59	22	7	3
Cong(I)	9	12.0	18	13	10	14
SP	35	26.7	11	32 **Yad. 71 n.Yad. 18	12	62
BSP	19	24.7	5	14	65	10

*Brahmin/non-Brahmin
** Yadav/non-Yadav
Source: A.K. Verma, 'BSP's strategy in UP', *Economic and Political Weekly*, 40, 26, June 25, 2005, p. 2647; Sudha Pai (Ed.), 'Political process in Uttar Pradesh', Delhi: Pearson Longman, 2007, p. 182; Sanjay Kumar, 'The prospects', *Seminar*, March 2007, No. 571, pp. 66–69.

Mohammad Muqeem from Domariaganj (eastern UP) and Mohammad Shahid from Meerut (western UP) won. The winning caste-community electoral arithmetic was based on SC and Muslim support, though one Muslim candidate Mohammad Muqeem did receive the 'Brahmin vote'. At Fatehpur (central UP), the winning BSP candidate Mahendra Kumar Nishad, a lower backward, won with SC and Muslim support. Mayawati's calibrated exercise to woo the upper caste – 'Brahmin samaj' – was evident in this election. Rajesh Verma, a Brahmin BSP candidate, won with 28.79% vote share with SC-Brahmin political support over Mukhtar Anees of SP in Sitapur. At Unnao, another winning Brahmin BSP candidate Brajesh Pathak won with a 32.57% vote share. Pathak received significant political support from the transferable votes of SC communities in the constituency.[71]

The 2004 Lok Sabha elections in UP, much like the assembly elections in 2002, demonstrated that the 'political anti-thesis' to the Yadav-dominated SP — the Brahmin vote — did not transfer to the BSP. The sharp ideological and political differences that existed between the SP and the BSP had still not created a politically congenial atmosphere for the 'Dalit Party' to reap upper-caste Brahmin 'plus vote'. In a general sense, the SP had a far better proportion of upper-caste and Brahmin vote share in the 2004 Lok Sabha elections in UP. Post-2004 elections, the BSP deliberated an 'ethnically segmented' model — a practical attachment of political capital to the differential economic and social resources of various social groups inclusive of their strengths and needs — that would direct an innovative method of grassroot organization for electoral mobilization under the nomenclature of 'sarvajan politics', reducing the 2007 state assembly elections to 'a two-way political fight' with the SP.

The Sarvajan Ideology: Perfecting the Caste Arithmetic

The political decline of the Brahmins as a dominant ruling caste in Uttar Pradesh in the era of coalition politics coincided with the community's perceived disenchantment with the BJP. Rajendra Bajpai, a one-time BJP party worker and a 'sanghi' (affiliated to the RSS), and a 'convert' to the BSP said: 'The BJP is no longer a party that works for the benefit of upper caste Hindus. It only works for its own benefit'.[72] The initial impetus of the BSP towards an expeditious mobilization of the Brahmins began with the 'encashment' of the political loyalty of a majority of Brahmin MLAs who had not left the party in 'SP engineered defections' in the aftermath of the fall of the BSP-led coalition government.[73]

Mayawati's illogical pursuit to embrace dominant caste groups at the centre of a new ideological-cum-electoral strategy militated against the political narrative of bahujan politics. To Mayawati a far more important consideration was to garner upper-caste votes to design a 'triumphant caste arithmetic' which would be based upon mobilizing a political combine of Brahmin and Dalit castes and founded upon the transferable vote strategy of Dalit groups.[74] On the other hand, the voting preference of the Muslims in the 2004 Lok Sabha elections gave Mayawati and senior party leaders a reason for formulating a winning political formula that could at least enable the Party to win 33–34% of bahujan and upper-caste votes to form a majority government in the 2007 assembly elections. A new political maxim outside the bahujan frames of party-directed mobilization factorized, outlining a greater compatibility based upon 'interests' between Dalits and Brahmins, two communities at the opposite end of the social hierarchy, to initiate a 'sarvajan' (here it means for all castes and social groups) mobilization strategy.[75] The BSP began the process to create a 'multi-caste social compact' to translate the 'mission of a sarva samaj' into a political reality. To construct a sarvajan electoral strategy, Mayawati inducted the former Advocate-General of Uttar Pradesh, Satish Chandra Mishra, a 'Brahmin lawyer' within the BSP who could take along the state's powerful bureaucracy. Mishra was entrusted with the task of mobilizing Brahmin support for the party, as well as forging a 'fraternal alliance between Brahmins and Dalits'. Mobilizing previously adversarial caste groups owing political allegiance to different political parties was to be achieved through 'Brahmin jodo abhiyan' (unite Brahmin campaign/mission). With Satish Mishra, Mayawati began to groom an upper-caste leadership in the BSP. She changed the party's defining slogan from 'jiski jitni sankhya bhari, uski utni bhagidari' (representation of each caste according to their population) to 'jiski jitni taiyyari, uski utni bhagidari' [representation of each caste according to their (ideological) preparedness].[76]

The political mobilization of Brahmins and other upper castes was formulated in two interrelated parts by the BSP. It was a coalition of the 'top and bottom' of the society, 'seemingly trapping all other social denominations' within it. Externally, it was a mix of 'apex social engineering' through Brahmin jodo sammelans (conferences) and 'bottom social engineering' through bhaichara committees. The former was reflected in the 'coming together of Mayawati-Satish Chandra Mishra at the top, while the increased political contact among Brahmins and Dalits at the local level indicated social engineering from below'.[77] The Brahmin jodo sammelans were a political success. Since 2005, such conferences to 'entice' Brahmins to the BSP began to be held in Lucknow, Allahabad, Maharajganj, Bahraich, Mirzapur, Sultanpur, Gonda, Gorakhpur and Kannauj. The political success of numerous Brahmin jodo sammelans was witnessed on June 9, 2005, in Ambedkar Maidan (*lit.* open space), Lucknow, where an impressive 'Brahmin mahasammelan' (grand conferences) rally was 'attended by close to 5 lakh BSP supporters belonging to the (Brahmin) community'. In the political rally, Mayawati 'sought to dispel all doubts about BSP's attitude towards the Brahmin community. The most significant 'event' of the political rally was the 'elegant manner in which the BSP president Mayawati was greeted and received' at the venue.

> As Mayawati arrived at the venue, 'she was greeted with brahminical rituals. A group of priests chanted Vedic hymns and blew conches. A silver axe was presented to her, the weapon of Parashurama*, the warrior saint who vowed to kill all Kshatriyas, professedly to protect the Brahmin community'.[78]

The 'symbolic' 'killing of Kshatriyas' was a political diatribe on the SP — a party of intermediate landholding castes dominated by Yadavs — who claimed to trace their genealogy to the 'Kshatriya-Kayastha' clan of pastoral warriors. The crowd chanted not only BSP's traditional slogan 'jai Bhim' (victory to Bhim, that is Bhimrao Ambedkar) but also 'jai Parashurama' (victory to Parashurama). Regardless of it, Mayawati was 'not suffering from any illusion about the political commitment of the upper castes (joining or supporting) BSP'. In this regard, her political speech on June 3, 2005, in Lucknow assumes relevance. Inaugurating the Bahujan Samaj Prerna Kendra (Bahujan Society Inspiration Centre) — a monument — dedicated to advocating a 'new cultural politics', articulating a 'new vision of the moral, political and spatial order' against the symbolic exclusion of Dalit from public space,[79] Mayawati said:

> Bahujan samaj should not trust the upper castes (who) are joining the party (since) it will take some time to change their hearts. Hence, they (bahujan samaj) should not rely or trust upper castes in the constituencies where the candidates are from (the) bahujan caste. The upper caste will not cast their votes in the favour of (the) bahujan caste candidate. But bahujan caste voters should prop up their natural alliance and transfer their votes totally in favour of (the) upper caste candidates in every constituency where they are contesting on (the) BSP ticket, though

> in such constituencies also the upper castes will not vote en masse for the upper caste candidate contesting on the BSP ticket. (In) this process if (the BSP) upper caste candidate gets 2 to 3 (additional) per cent of the upper caste votes, the BSP as a party will enhance its tally from the present by 50 to 60 seats. This will give the BSP a chance to form a majority government for a full five-year term in the state.[80]

In each Brahmin jodo (unite) conference that were held over a period of two years (2005–2007), Mishra clarified that 'Brahmins would be given their rightful share in power if they joined the BSP'. The BSP's political philosophy, Mishra said, '(was) a just society with no disparity, (which could) be achieved with the help of all sections of society'. Mishra affirmed that the BSP was in fact 'pro-Brahmin' pointing to the fact that in 1995, as Chief Minister Mayawati made 'Brahmin' R.N. Trivedi her advocate general and (he) was made the attorney general in 2002–2003 when the BSP headed a coalition government. Mishra stated that the 'number of Brahmins in Lok Sabha was on the decline and the BSP alone could ensure victory to Brahmin candidates with the support of the Party'. Mishra said the awareness of 'terror-stricken Brahmins "helpless before Thakur and Yadav dons" motivated the BSP to take up the cause of the Brahmins'.[81] In political terms, the BSP exploited the 'physical and economic insecurity' of the Brahmins to emerge as a 'political saviour resisting SP's gangsterism'.[82]

The other innovative electoral strategy used by the BSP to crystallize the 'Brahmin-Dalit bloc' of political support was the 'social engineering strategy from below' through Dalit-Brahmin bhaichara (brotherhood) committees spread across the state. The BSP's 'bhaichara committees' were based on the slogan 'vote dena aur lena' *(*give and take votes). Simply put, 'where there was a Brahmin candidate this slogan would be sold to the Dalits and where there was a Dalit candidate this slogan would be sold to Brahmins'.[83] The Brahmin-Dalit political alliance was centred on treating the Brahmin almost like a 'separate political party' within the BSP. A 'Brahmin conclave' within the BSP offered legitimate political protection and a new political identity which was expected to translate into electoral support for the BSP. The impress of the Brahmins within the BSP was evident in the political slogan — 'Brahmin shaankh bajayega/haathi dilli jayega or haathi badta jayega' (The Brahmin will blow the conch; the elephant will go to Delhi or the elephant will continue to advance). The 'Bhaichara Banao Samiti, Brahmin Samaj BSP' was formed in all the 403 assembly constituencies of the state. Every 'samiti' had 400 members, 300 Brahmins and 100 Dalits, with a 'Brahmin chairman' and Dalit 'General Secretary'. These 'bhaichara' committees 'visited villages and strategized the feeling of "brotherhood" between the Dalits and the Brahmins'. The composition of the 'samitis' did give the impression that it was the Brahmins who were extending their support to the Dalits.[84]

The stage was set for a political revival of the Dalit-Brahmins alliance in UP of the pre-1990 era. However, there would be a crucial difference to the 'social alliance' that the Congress sustained in which 'the Brahmins and other sections of the upper castes controlled the levers of (political) power, while there was a token presence (select political leaders) of Scheduled Castes and Muslims as poster boys'. The BSP's new electoral formula (was) a 'reversal of that (socio-political) order'. The upper castes would now receive patronage and not the Dalits who would control the dynamics of state power. It would appear to be a political combination that was potentially non-sectarian and inclusive.[85]

Preceding the 2007 assembly elections in UP, the BSP expanded the schema of 'sarvajanism' by entrusting a 'network of party commanders' (a Dalit 'Secretary' and 'President' from the designated caste group) on a mission to politically integrate a 'particular lower caste non-Dalit group' at the state, district and constituency levels for the Party. For this purpose, the BSP initiated steps towards the political mobilization of caste-based 'political conventions' among the Pal, Rajbhar, Nishad, Maurya, Kushwaha, Bindhi, Saini, Noniya, Kewat, Mallah and Kumhar. The BSP proved that if the 'less well-off and the more backward communities' were effectively mobilized through caste representation in the Party, then the possibility of their political alliance, under Dalit leadership existed. The BSP considered it as a 'bhai-bhai' (brother-brother) 'caste experiment'[86]

The BSP took a major political initiative to increase the quantum of Muslim support in a grand coalition of alliance with Dalits and Brahmins. Naseemuddin Siddiqui, 'the popular youth leader from Banda district', was entrusted by Mayawati to become the 'minority face' of the BSP. For the 2007 assembly elections, Siddiqui prevailed on the BSP leadership to 'distribute (election) tickets to candidates of his own personal choice'. Siddiqui's election campaigns focused on the 'poorer and backward sections' of Muslims such as the Ansari, Chikwa, Kasai, Ghosi, Gaddi, Churahar and Lalbeg. Siddiqui broadened the Party's political appeal to coalesce the marginal condition of 'Muslim samaj' with Dalits, highlighting that 'decades of political loyalty' to the Congress Party since independence and SP had given them neither security nor development and employment. Siddiqui addressing local Muslim leaders and Muslim voters stated that the 'critical value of progress that the BSP offered for the community' was underlined by a prior declaration of the Party not to enter into any political coalition with the BJP. In the past, such an alliance had in all likelihood 'negatively' transferred Muslim votes to SP. Along these lines, the BSP offered the prognosis of a political model of a 'samta-mulak samaj' (equality-based society) to the Muslims of Uttar Pradesh.[87]

Political Stratagem: The 'Informal' Practice of the Sarvajan Scheme

In October and November 2006, elections were held for 12 Municipal Corporations, 189 Municipal Councils and 417 Nagar Panchayats in Uttar

Pradesh. At stake were 618 elective posts of mayor/chairman and 11,141 posts in different civic bodies. The political significance of the municipal corporation's elections can be judged by the fact that they were held on the eve of the 2007 assembly elections. The BSP chose not to participate in the municipal corporation elections. To the BSP, the '(assembly) elections (were) the single most important item on the BSP's agenda and the party (had) worked towards a "fool proof election plan" over (a period of two years)'. On that point, Mayawati remarked: '(A plan) developed so painstakingly (could not) go waste: it (had) to work, and it (would)'.[88] In the municipal corporation elections, the BSP professedly controlled the 'agenda to defeat' by '(allowing) tactical voting by the Dalits' and forcing Muslims to switch their political loyalty away from the SP to the Congress. In this way, the BSP decided the outcome of the elections by ensuring the 'victory of Congress and (even) BJP candidates' who were themselves surprised by the election results. Certain instances would highlight the intent of the political game plan of the BSP to confuse and marginalize the SP. Muslims openly supported Congress mayoral candidates at Bareilly, where the leader of the Barelvi sect Maulana Mannan Raza Khan supported Congress candidate Supriya Aron defeating the Muslim candidate Shagufta Yasmin of the SP. At Lucknow, the Congress candidate Mansoor received a high proportion of Muslim support defeating the SP. At Orai, there was a sharp division of votes among Barelvi Muslims who voted for the SP and 'Deobandis' who voted for the BJP. The BJP candidate won. There were other notable examples of Muslim votes being fragmented, leading to victories of the Rashtriya Janata Dal over SP candidate in Tambor in Sitapur. In Nighasan, Muslim voted for the independent candidate Kariyum Shah who defeated Deepak Shah of SP. The BJP appeared as a 'party (that) did not know what to read out of the municipal corporation elections and the way to carry it forward'. BJP's victorious candidates in the municipal elections were 'largely (decided by the BSP) due to the vote transfer by the Dalits to defeat the SP'. The 'impact of BSP's politics to transfer and to split Dalit and Muslim votes' had the necessary political impact on SP candidates in the mayoral/chairman posts on offer in the Municipal Corporation elections. Post-polls report suggested that the SP lost in the 'most pampered constituencies where it (had invested) money and electricity', such as Gunnaur (Badaun), Sambhal, Kannauj and Mainpuri represented by Mulayam Singh Yadav's brother Ram Gopal Yadav, his son Akhilesh Yadav and his nephew Dharmendra Yadav.[89]

Contextual Advantage: BSP and the Micro-Management of 'Caste' Votes

As the BSP began to explore the effectiveness of a sarvajan scheme of electoral politics, the Congress-backed Samajwadi Party government faced a dismal law and order situation in the state that overlooked some of the development initiatives undertaken by the coalition government: providing debt relief to farmers, unemployment wages to the youth and educational grant to girls. Communal riots in Mau (7th October–16th October 2005)[90] that left 12 dead and over a hundred shops and houses gutted, riots in Barabanki (October 2–4, 2006) and a series of terror attacks in Varanasi (May 7, 2006), Ayodhya and Faizabad displayed a lack of coordination exposing the inept administration of district and law enforcement agencies. Nearing the 2007 assembly election, the ghastly 'Nithari killings' (December 2006), in Greater Noida, of young children for suspected organ trade culminated in a political crisis for the SP-led government.

To counter the negative publicity of the law and order situation in the state, the SP government used the popular appeal of matinee idol Amitabh Bachchan, a one-time SP supporter, in television advertisements, to argue that UP had a 'lower crime rate' compared to other states. The media campaign read: 'Uttar Pradesh mein hain dum/yahein jurm hain kum' (Uttar Pradesh has the strength/here crime is low) which elicited political reactions within the SP. A section of party activists and leaders held the view that the advertisement 'campaign' 'was not only ineffective but counter-productive'. The popular perception of a 'jungle raj' (law of the jungle) in Uttar Pradesh was seen as 'Yadav raj' (law of the Yadavs). In 2007, UP had no police station in the state without a 'Yadav inspector', thereby creating 'virtual SP cadres within the constabulary who were (apparently) given "free rein" in districts, in many cases marginalizing the "young IAS and IPS officers" who served as District Magistrates and Superintendents of Police'. In a 'recruitment drive for constables' prior to the May 2007 assembly elections, out of 3,000 available jobs, 2,400 Yadavs were employed. In the 'Yadav-dominated pockets of Etah, Etawah and Mainpuri, local Yadavs (party activists would/were reported to) beat anyone who may have led a protest demonstration against the government'. At the tehsil and village levels, there (were) 'oral instructions to all district magistrates that if a Yadav (applied) for a gun license, he (had to) be immediately obliged'. In the year 2006–2007, Uttar Pradesh accounted for 21,899 incidents or nearly 66% of all law and order-related cases at the all-India level. In 2007, the National Human Rights Commission (NHRC) recorded '603 custodial violence deaths, 241 extra-judicial killings, encounter killings and fake encounters'. There were '995 cases of unlawful detention, 44 cases of disappearance, 2,289 cases of false implication and 862 cases of other police excesses' in the state. Caste atrocities against Dalits assumed barbaric proportions that included cutting off of tongues and 'gouging out of eyes'. The National Crime Records Bureau (NCRB) of the Ministry of Home Affairs in 2006–2007 recorded a 'total of 4,960 cases against the Dalits, including 318 cases of killing and 229 rape cases and 113 abduction cases among others'. In the first half of the year 2007, 3,782 cases of crimes committed against Dalits were recorded in the state and 158 cases involved rape of Dalit women.[91]

The SP suffered internal schisms prior to the 2007 elections as Beni Prasad Verma, a former union minister and senior leader of the party, launched a rival political outfit 'Samajwadi Kranti Dal'. On the other hand, the BJP suffered factional fights between national party president Rajnath Singh and former CM Kalyan Singh, who had re-joined the party in 2004, on the issue of ticket allocation to rival candidates. Such was the intensity of factionalism that the party leadership was forced to stop the distribution of assembly tickets allocation for many assembly seats.

For the May 2007 state polls, the BSP had a politically imaginative electoral strategy. The Party had already built strong organizational machinery at the grassroots level to collect a vast constituency-wise database of 'caste population' and 'voting blocks'. In as many as 150 seats, the party announced its candidates more than a year ago. Divided into 25 sectors, with 10 polling booths in one sector, each assembly constituency was closely monitored by senior party leaders. Each polling booth, hosting a population of approximately 1,000 voters, were made the responsibility of a 'nine-member committee', comprising of at least one woman 'party representative' to mobilize women voters.[92] Mayawati said: 'The BSP had the moral right, organizational strength and political vision' to replace the SP.[93]

In the 2007 assembly elections, the BSP emerged victorious with 206 seats and a 30.46% of the total votes polled for the party registering a 7.40% increase in its vote share since the 2002 assembly elections (see Table 5.6). For the first time in 16 years, the state witnessed a majority government.[94] The electoral victory validated Kanshiram's prophetic conclusion that he had held for the party. Almost 11 years ago, on July 30, 1996, at a political rally Kanshiram had said that the aim of the Party was to attain about '41 per cent of the vote in Uttar Pradesh'. Depending on the 'vanguard' Dalit vote, Kanshiram had stated that (the Party had) 50% of all SC votes.

Table 5.6 UP Assembly Elections 2007 and 2002: A Comparison

Assembly Elections	*2007*			*2002*		
Parties	**Cont.*	*Won*	*Vote%*	*Seats*	***G/L*	*Vote%*
Cong(I)	392	22	8.56	25	(-) 3	8.93
BJP	349	50	16.93	88	(-) 38	20.7
SP	392	97	25.45	143	(-) 46	25.45
BSP	402	206	30.46	98	(+) 108	23. 20

Election for Khaga was countermanded due to death of Congress candidate. In the Khaga by-election, BJP won.
* Contested
** Gain/Loss
Source: A.K. Verma, 'Mayawati's sandwich coalition', *Economic and Political Weekly*, 42, 22, June 2, 2007, pp. 2039–40.

If all the SCs (voted for the Party), the target (to form a majority government) would be fulfilled.[95] Fashioning electoral victories with a 'mere 35 per cent', if not lesser, was possible, that was borne by the political history of the Congress' ascent to power in various states and at the Centre in post-independent period. In the state polls, the triangular and in certain constituencies quadrangular electoral contests between BSP, BJP, SP and Congress Party significantly lowered the threshold of an electoral victory.

To analyze the factors that contributed to the victory of the BSP in the 2007 assembly elections in UP, the idea of a 'BSP stronghold' needs to be abandoned. The BSP in pre-2007 elections had displayed an even greater tendency to be drubbed in its '(political) strongholds' while expanding electoral bases in other regions of the state. In 2007, of the '30 reserved seats that the BSP won, in only 11 was the Party placed at "number two position" in 2002 assembly elections. In the rest its ranking was a lowly third, sometimes even fourth or fifth'. SC constituencies were not 'safe bets' for the BSP.[96] Further, most of the BSP MLAs who won in 2007 were 'first time ministers'. Out of 61 assembly 'tickets' given to Muslims, only 7 had been 'sitting BSP MLAs' since 2002.

The BSP did well in constituencies where there was a fragmented vote share with a winning margin as low as 20%, where a swing of 1% decided the election result. In a number of assembly constituencies across the state, it was not uncommon where a win or a loss was so delicately balanced. In sum, the BSP lost a number of 'constituencies' in closely fought contest, either to SP or to the BJP. If the BSP lost narrowly at Sarsaul, it won close political victories at Ghatampur, Bhognipur, Bilhaur (SC), Derapur, Auraiya, Gauriganj, and Mahoba by only a few thousand votes. The BSP was successful in consolidating the Muslim vote, with Dalit and OBC support, to vote for its candidates in constituencies where the Muslim community could influence the poll results. Thus, in Hasanpur, Bahjoi, Kunderki, Afzalgarh, Bisalpur, Moradabad (West), Bareilly Cantonment, Laharpur, Nanpara, Domariaganj, Sandila, Shahbad and Gopalpur, the BSP won. In Gopalpur, the BSP ensured that a non-Muslim candidate won with a successful transfer of Muslim votes. Interestingly, at Thakurdwara, the 'Yadav plus Muslim support' consolidated behind BSP at the cost of the SP. The Party had made inroads into the Muslim base of SP. Muslim support for SP till 2002 stood at 51% but fell by 7% in the 2007 elections. Conversely, the BSP benefited increasing its overall Muslim support from 10% to 17%. The Congress, despite being an indirect recipient of an enhanced Muslim support (from 10% in 2002 to 14% in 2007), suffered in the assembly elections. For instance, at Bhinga, Muslim vote did not split between the Congress and the BSP, but went to the BSP. It was one more instance of the Muslim voters opting for a candidate who could win to defeat the BJP. Out of 61 'election tickets' given to Muslim candidates by the BSP, 29 won. The Milli Council which in the past surveyed each constituency to guide the Muslim community did not 'issue a checklist' to avoid confusion about the

BSP or any other party. But the All India Muslim Majlis-e-Mushawarat[97] posed two objectives before the Muslim voters: one, to defeat the BJP, and two, to raise Muslim representation in the UP Legislative Assembly. The Mushawarat even issued a 'list of 98 Muslim constituencies and endorsed (deserving) candidates. The Mushawarat stated that if 'no suitable Muslim candidate was found, the Muslims (were to) vote for a non-Muslim candidate of a secular party'.[98] The BSP figured prominently in such an electoral calculation.

The BSP performed well in the SC reserved constituencies winning 62 out of 89 seats. In the assembly elections, the participation of the Chamars as the dominant SC group in the state rose to 85%. Non-Chamar SC support for the party registered a marginal increase up from 69% in 2002 to 72% in 2007. The impressive turnout of the SC population was complemented by Brahmin support for the BSP's SC candidates in reserved constituencies such as Hargaon, Sidhauli, Siddhaur, Khalilabad and Bawan. BSP's electoral victories across 'reserved constituencies' indicated that Brahmins voted for BSP's SC candidates that highlighted the success of Dalit-Brahmin bhaichara committees.

A detailed analysis of caste affiliation of elected members revealed that the BSP support base among the OBC had increased. Contrary to political expectations, 51 OBC BSP candidates won that included a number of low-caste backwards, including 'four Yadavs'. On the other hand, the SP had 27 OBC MLAs out of which 17 winning candidates were Yadavs. This indicated that non-Yadav OBC vote had shifted to the BSP from the OBC-dominated Mulayam Singh's 'Yadav Party'. The BJP which secured 50 seats in the state assembly had 12 OBC MLAs.[99] BSP's support among the lower backwards vindicated through 'bhaichara caste samitis' that led to the endorsement of prospective lower backward 'political leaders' who became the Party's winning candidates in the 2007 elections by a combination of 'own caste' and transferable Dalit-Bahujan and Muslims votes. Such a voting pattern based on an expansive inter-grouping of castes was witnessed across numerous assembly constituencies. At Dataganj, a Shakya won; at Katehari and Pipraich, a Nishad; at Akbarpur, a 'BSP stronghold', a Rajbhar. Other notable 'winner MBC groups' were the Kushwaha, Maurya, Jaiswal, Dhimar, Patel, Saini, Kanwaria and Pal. The increased number of winning MBC candidates ensured that the BSP doubled its political base of MBC from 15% in 2002 to 30% in the 2007 assembly elections. During the same period, the SP's MBC vote bank fell from 18% to 11%, while the BJP's MBC vote share fell from 21% to 17%.

The BSP won a number of 'defector case' assembly constituencies. At Dhampur, the BJP candidate's political base was undermined by the RLD, who since then defected to the BSP before the 2007 elections and won. At Faridpur (SC), Milkipur and Nawabganj, BJP candidates defected to the BSP and won. At Captainganj, the 'flip-flop of political defection' ultimately gave the BSP an electoral victory. Here a SP candidate defected to the BSP, then to BJP and back to BSP. At Masauli, the SP 'suffered due to the Beni Prasad Verma factor', whose 'revolt' damaged the party's electoral prospects. The BSP consolidated Muslim-Dalit-MBC votes in this constituency and won.

The success of the Brahmin jodo sammelan and Dalit-Brahmin caste samitis ensured the victory of 34 Brahmin BSP candidates[100] out of a total of 86 assembly tickets which were allocated to the community by the party. Brahmin candidates won close contests with SC support in numerous assembly constituencies such as Sadabad, Dhaurehra, Mahoba, Bilgram, Bilhaur, Auraiya, Machhlishahr, Barsathi, Karchana, Chillupur and Atraulia and significantly in two out of three seats in Agra and Allahabad. Mayawati's 'axis of bhaichara politics', whereby the Brahmin BSP candidates would ensure the support of 2–3% of upper-caste votes where they were demographically between 10% and 15%, was a 'political clincher'. A different facet of caste politics translated into electoral victories for BSP candidates in Balrampur, Chitrakoot and Sonabhadra. The basis of the political victories was the Ahir-Yadav support. It highlighted that the party was able to use its expanding political network to nurture Kurmi factional leaders as divisive political actors to vote for Ahir-Yadav BSP candidates. The political split in the Kurmi caste monolith enacted by factional leaders ensured that Sonelal Patel, the founder of Apna Dal, lost his prominence in the 'Kurmi dominant' constituencies.

In the state polls, the BSP allocated 38 tickets to the Thakur and Rajput communities to ensure that the party benefited from 'en bloc community' voting preference for the Party candidate whose electoral victory could be assured by transferable Dalit-MBC vote. Out of 38 BSP Thakur candidates, 18 were elected to the state legislative assembly. The victory of Thakur and even Bania BSP candidates were ensured by the 'Thakur-Bania divide' in the BJP and SP's mishandling of the contemporaneous 'Raja Bhaiyya episode'. The BSP did not post political victories in urban centres of Lucknow, Mathura, and Kanpur but won the North, South and West Allahabad assembly constituencies.[101]

A Sarvajan Emblem to a 'Bahujan Government'

Forming the first 'Dalit' government in post-independent India in the most populous state of Uttar Pradesh, the BSP chief Mayawati stated that her priority would be to 'establish an injustice-free, fear-free, crime-free, corruption-free and development-oriented government'.[102] Mayawati's patronizing way of asserting Dalit leadership became apparent in the party's new slogan to behave with 'shistachaar' (respect) towards Brahmins, considered the key political constituency in BSP's quest for political power in Uttar Pradesh.[103]

In an article written for *The Hindu* newspaper to commemorate India's 60 years of independence in August 2007, Mayawati wrote:

> (The) 'precipitous arrival' of the BSP in Uttar Pradesh signified a 'positive progressive sign', a shashan mantra (motto of ruling) based on sarvajan hitaye sarvajan sukhaye (progress and prosperity for all) and the creation of a 'samta-mulak samaj' (equality-based society) based on 'proportionate' social empowerment; that governance and administration were critical to the welfare of the people because the people (were) more concerned with how law (was) administered.

After becoming the Chief Minister of Uttar Pradesh, Mayawati clarified that all transfer and postings below the ranks of Additional General and Principal Secretary would be conducted at the level of the Service Establishment Board, putting an end to the reviled 'business of transfer industry' in UP. Consequently, state administration would run without the political interference of the BSP government. It was the first real impact of the sarvajan ideology on BSP's politics. Mayawati stated: that the 'social impact of her political design of sarva samaj' would seek to enhance social harmony in rural and urban Uttar Pradesh, which would fulfil her aim for uttam aur khush-hal pradesh (good and prosperous state).[104]

The caste composition of the 'sarva samaj' cabinet included eight Dalits, four Brahmins, four OBCs and one each from the Muslim, Bania, Thakur and Bhumihar communities. The ministers of state with independent charge included 11 Dalits, 7 OBC members and 4 each from the Brahmin, Thakur and Muslim communities. A Brahmin legislator said with a sense of relief:

> Though all of us joined the BSP to win the elections and become MLAs there was no certainty on the level of accommodation we would get in the government. But 'behenji' ha(d) removed all the tensions by (her) 'even-handed exercise'.[105]

In October 2007, Mayawati expanded her five-month-old ministry by allotting portfolios to a set of new lawmakers in an effort to bring about 'caste and regional balance' in the government. Notable inclusions were the induction of ten ministers — four ministers of state to cabinet rank, three Dalits, two Brahmins, two Thakurs, and a Vaishya, Yadav and Muslim each. Yet, out of a total of 29 BSP Muslim MLAs, only 4 were represented in the cabinet ministry.[106] What was rather conspicuous was the inclusion of 17 ministers with 'criminal backgrounds' contradicting Mayawati's highly publicized claim of providing a 'bhaymukt' (fear-free) and 'aparadhmukt' (crime-free) government.[107] Despite the inclusion of ministers with criminal background, a 'fear-free and crime-free' administration carried a month-long political campaign to register the complaints and FIR of people who were victimized during SP rule in the state. At the conclusion of the month-long campaign, Mayawati remarked: We had promised to 'end the jungle rule' of the 'modern kansa' (metaphor for evil) during the political campaign for assembly elections. It (was) time to act, as people have given (the BSP) a clear mandate' (and) further that the 'campaign' to restore law and order in the state would not be misused to victimize political rivals. Nevertheless, the SP accused the BSP government of implicating SP activists and leaders in fake cases. Referring to the police cases against SP workers, Amar Singh, the senior leader in SP, stated: 'Mayawati was acting like a "mafia queen" and the opposition leaders of the SP were (being) seen as gangsters'.[108]

In power, the BSP government allocated public funds and resources to expand the Party's patronage system of 'segmental' political mobilization of castes and social groups. For instance, despite lacking constitutional validity, the 'New Positive Reservation Initiative Policy' was proposed by the BSP for new social categories of Dalit-Christians, and Dalit-Muslims, religious minorities and 'economically weaker sections' among the upper castes.[109] The affirmative 'policy' was divided into three parts: the first section dealt with 'Public-Private Partnership' (PPP), the 'main component of an all-inclusive, realistic and practical economic policy of the state'. The PPP route was expected to be expanded to various sectors of the economy — power, education, infrastructure, health, medical tourism and urban development. As part of 'Urban Development', it was decided that the 'provision of job reservation' in businesses developed on PPP model would be similar to recruitment in state government, that is, 21% for the SC, 2% for the ST and 27% for the OBC. The second section dealt with reservation for SC, ST and OBC in 'outsourced jobs'. If the services rendered by the government departments and corporations, authorities and councils and other semi-government institutions or the maintenance of their establishment were substituted by outsourcing, then the contract to be executed for the said purpose would include the provision of providing 21% of the jobs to SC, 2% for the ST and 27% for the OBC. The third section elaborated the provision of 'reservation for the sarva samaj' in the projects where the government provided land, state subsidy and assets to private sector, seeking to invest in infrastructure and service sectors, or proposing to set up industrial units, educational institutions, by 'voluntary and mutual agreement with the employers'. The provision of providing reservation would be 10% to the SC, 10% to OBC including 'backwards' of religious minorities and 10% to the 'economically weak' belonging to the upper castes.[110]

The 'sarvajan' government chose to act as 'an enforcer of development schemes'. Under Dr. Ambedkar Samagra Gramin Vikas Yojna (integrated village development plan), 17,000 gram sabhas were earmarked to be developed in 'every aspect and people of all communities and castes (were) to be benefited in five years'. 'Vikas Yojna', another government-approved policy, was introduced with an allocation sum of Rs. 10,000 crore for developing rural infrastructure in 1,900 gram sabhas by selecting 4–5 gram sabhas each from every assembly constituency.[111]

For the entirety of her term in office, Mayawati became known for inaugurating 'money-spinning projects' and initiating a diverse range of sociocultural, economic and educational programmes without a timeline for their completion or fixing responsibility as to whether the desired objectives reached targeted sections of society. Mayawati's 52nd birthday in 2008 became a grand occasion for the BSP to launch a Rs. 30,000-crore mega 'public-private' collaborative Ganga Expressway Project for a 1,047 kms road project between Ballia in eastern UP and Noida in western UP. Rehabilitation and resettlement of people affected by the acquisition of land for the Ganga Expressway project were promised with 'adequate financial compensation'. The showcasing of the 'Ganga Expressway project' into an 'investment region' which would be a 'hub of business and commercial activity and townships' became the centrepiece of BSP policy to endorse the image of the Party keen on investment and infrastructural development in the state. Three major policy decisions were initiated — to construct a '8-lane expressway' from Delhi to Ghazipur in eastern UP; a 'Yamuna expressway' that would reduce the travelling time between New Delhi and Agra and a plan outlay to set up 4,000 MW Ultra-Mega Power Project at Lalitpur with the National Thermal Power Corporation to 'renovate and improve' the power distribution system in the state.[112]

Mayawati launched a variety of housing sector projects for the rural and urban poor. The Kanshiram Ji Nagar Vikas Yojna and the Kanshiram Ji Shahri Samagra Vikas Yojna (Urban Integrated Development Plan) were initiated to build 'one lakh two-room houses'. In addition, Nagar Palika Parishads (Municipal Councils) and Nagar Panchayats (Notified Area Council) would be covered in the housing scheme under the Integrated Housing and Slum Development Project. Scheduled Castes and Scheduled Tribes would be accorded priority in allotment with a special provision made for the poor among the upper castes, the 'shelter-less widows and the differently abled' living below the poverty line. Another housing project under the SC and ST Development Corporation Scheme was initiated to provide 'affordable houses' to the urban poor in Allahabad, Varanasi, Agra, Lucknow, Kanpur Nagar, Meerut and Mathura'.[113]

In the education sector, the BSP government formulated a scheme of higher education for students of Gautam Buddha University, in New Okhla Industrial Development Authority (NOIDA), Uttar Pradesh, belonging to SC, ST OBC, religious minorities and the 'upper castes' below the poverty line targeted with a 'Special Scholarship Scheme'.[114] The state government allocated Rs. 500 crores for a Backward Area Subsidy Fund to 30 backward districts of the state and instituted 'Regional Rural Employment Generation Centres' to create employment opportunities instead of providing unemployment allowances to youths.[115] Mayawati's birthday on January 15, 2009, was projected by the party as 'arthik sahyog diwas' (financial assistance day) targeted to alleviate 'special category' groups among the marginalized sections empowering young girls and boys, urban slum dwellers, manual scavengers, etc. In this regard, the Mahamaya Garib Balika Aashirwad Yojana (Mahamaya Poor Young Girls Blessing Plan) was inaugurated for girls born on or after January 15, 2009, wherein a fixed deposit would be set aside to fund her education through school years up to higher education. The Savitri Bai Phule Balika Shiksha Madad Yojana (Savitri Bai Young Girls Educational Assistance Plan) was initiated to target girls belonging to families living below the poverty line who would receive Rs. 15,000 for gaining admission to Standard XI and Rs 10,000 for admission to Standard XII in government-aided schools.[116] A project was initiated to construct a Mahamaya Girls Hostel for SC and ST students enrolled for engineering courses in colleges in Noida and Greater Noida. Ambedkar Scheduled Castes and Scheduled Tribes Boys Hostel was planned to be constructed for 500 boys at Greater Noida. This measure was a continuation of the initial steps undertaken by the BSP government in 2008 to organize special scholarship schemes for SC and ST students studying in Gautam Buddha University in Noida.[117]

The BSP government proposed the setting up of an Arabic-Persian University and formulated a Rs. 1015.70-crore package to build 964 new primary schools and 1,212 secondary schools with 100 new schools exclusively for girl students and 58 government secondary schools in 21 Muslim-dominated districts of the state; a 'Kanshiram Self-Employment Scheme' for the educated Muslim youth; a grant of Rs. 2 crores for improving the financial condition of the Waqf Boards across the state; increase the annual grant for the Urdu Academy to Rs. 3 crore and a State Advisory Council was set up under Satish Chandra Mishra to cater to the social and economic advancement of the Muslims.[118]

Before the 2009 Lok Sabha elections, the government inaugurated the ambitious long-term project 'Accelerated Power Development and Reform Project' that would cover 28 cities across the state to provide uninterrupted supply of electricity. Additionally, 'the government allocated Rs. 2,500 crores to urban projects with the purpose of upgrading major cities and towns of 'Lucknow, Faizabad-Ayodhya, Kanpur-Bithoor, Allahabad, Varanasi, Meerut and Mathura-Brindavan (which would) emerge rejuvenated (after investment in infrastructure development) in (one) years' time'.[119] The BSP government outlined its intention to initiate '158 (small to medium) development schemes' with an outlay cost of Rs. 3,000 crores for the 'all-round integrated development' of Uttar Pradesh.[120] A follow-up to earlier urban housing projects was to be complemented by the 'Sarvajan Hitay Shahri Garib Awas Malikana Haq Yojana' (Welfare of All Property Ownership Plan for the Urban Poor) for 1.40 crore population residing in urban slums who would 'get ownership right on a maximum of 30 square meters of land'. The provisions of the programme were applicable to 'slum areas' that were situated on land belonging to government, local bodies, government estates and 'nazul' (land escheated to Government).[121] The 'Sarvajan Government' made a specific effort to end the 'inhuman practice of carrying (human excrement)'. For this purpose, '2, 52, 404 toilets (pits) were identified which were to be converted to flush toilets'. The project cost of Rs. 252.40 crores were sanctioned by the Centre. BSP's 'dry latrine free-state' programme had a provision to provide employment to manual scavengers under the State SC and ST Development Corporation Schemes.[122]

The BSP government directed by the political principle of 'welfare for all' intended to enclose the 'Dalit-Bahujan' and even non-Dalit/Bahujan groups into a 'privileged' social identity, of being a part of an ongoing 'social reconstruction' agenda manifested by a plethora of development projects and programmes. In effect, the 'publicity-oriented' programmes appeared as unrealizable goals and further delay and bureaucratic logjam rendered them ineffective in two years. The delay and inconceivable nature of the programmes only served to politicize an expanding political network of bahujan caste groups desperate for accessing resources and public goods through impending development schemes and projects that would not materialize.

'Electoral Review': Imbalanced Sarvajanism

In the 2009 Lok Sabha elections[123] in UP, the BSP won 20 seats, one more than it won in the 2004 Lok Sabha elections. The party was expected to win 35–45 seats, which would have approximated the tally of seats it won in the 2007 assembly elections. The Lok Sabha elections witnessed a shift in the Muslim vote as the community distributed its voting preference to SP and Congress Party candidates in constituencies where they could win.[124]

In a general sense, sarvajan politics failed to find a balance between contentious political claims of caste and community groups across the social continuum and its programmatic objectives. Beneath the fanfare with costly development projects fundamental issues remained neglected. Dalit-Bahujan interests were abandoned as the BSP began to operate the principle of 'equality-based society' through sarvajan politics. 'Bahujan samaj', the supposed bastion of BSP's support, 'wanted a better standard of living and a greater and more visible share in the power structures which continued to be dominated by forward (Brahmin) castes'. 'Welfare Programmes' patronized through 'proclamations' and 'initiatives' failed as they lay exposed to administrative paralysis and bad governance. What led to further political alienation of the 'oppressed' classes from the party was the high financial cost[125] of Mayawati's anti-hegemony culture manifested through the 'history-making spree', of statues, memorial, parks, institutes named after Dalit personages and Mayawati's own 'giant statues' — the impact of carving an 'empowering (Dalit) history' of the Dalits that negatively affected significant sections of non-Jatav Dalits, MBCs and Muslims. 'Even Jatav-Chamar Dalits thought (Mayawati) was spending lavishly on memorials' and their political disenchantment with the BSP was exposed in the 2009 Lok Sabha elections. Even as the Lok Sabha elections were underway in the state, Mayawati was conspicuous by her prolonged absence, entering the electoral fray in Uttar Pradesh only in the fourth phase having already addressed innumerable political rallies across India. Behenji's 'Prime Ministerial' ambitions and her ability to play a significant role in national politics on the basis of a conclusive assumption of a highly fragmented Lok Sabha verdict were misplaced. The absence of Mayawati and a disappointment with the BSP's two-year governance resulted in a low turnout of Dalit voters (30%) in the first three phases of Lok Sabha election in the state.[126]

In the context of a poor electoral verdict for the BSP in the Lok Sabha elections, Mayawati '(scrapped) all MBC non-Dalit committees' and the 'much-hyped' bhaichara committees that operated at the mandal, district and constituency levels with a Dalit 'Secretary' and 'President' of a particular non-Dalit low caste which was being represented. Mayawati conceded the abject failure of Dalit-OBC committees that were supposed to 'build bridges between Dalits and OBCs' to transform '(political) support into votes' for the BSP. The political failure of Dalit-OBC committees can be indicated by the fact that, in Etah, the BSP's Shakya bhaichara committee 'head' Shyam Singh Shakya contested on 'a BJP (Lok Sabha) ticket'. A reason for the failure of the Dalit-Brahmin bhaichara committees was that it was the upper castes who got Lok Sabha tickets 'often by allegedly paying a huge price' even as the BSP organization at the constituency level was directed to politically mobilize Dalit voters for Brahmin BSP candidates. The failure to activate the 'committees' was attributed to the fact that in actuality the tenuous compact between Dalits and Brahmins had alienated the BSP's Dalit base. Local party units and non-Dalit MLAs were in a state of conflict that interfered with the party's organizational activities.[127]

Having acknowledged that it had failed to implement party-directed development programmes, the Mayawati government brought drastic changes in political appointees who acted as quasi-administrative personnel: Mayawati 'dismissed around 150 chairman, vice-chairman and directors (known) as commission chiefs of various state commissions, boards and councils'. The 'commission chiefs', mostly belonging to the upper caste, had been recruited by the BSP and given the 'status of ministers'. Apparently, these 'commission chiefs' on their part blamed bureaucrats for their own poor performance in effecting party programmes which in turn affected the party's electoral prospects in the Lok Sabha elections. The BSP identified a number of development schemes and projects which had become controversial such as the Rural Development Department, the Ambedkar Gram Vikas Yojana, Kanshiram Urban Housing Scheme, Rural Drinking Water Programme and policies related to the disbursement of pension and scholarships of the Social Welfare Department. Governance suffered as the BSP government's populist 'tehsil' and 'thana' diwas (administrative division and police station day) — a day of the week when the poor in a particular district would meet administrative and police officials with complaints — failed to address the accountability of the state administration towards the poor. Further, in pursuit of an expedient politics of 'sarvajanism', party leaders had directed local activists 'not to put (pressure) on the administration and the police; to let non-Dalit bureaucracy function independently and to not influence transfers and postings'. However, the party directive to that effect had the opposite result as BSP activists could not direct a Superintendent of Police to file an FIR in a case of an incident of Dalit atrocity which had shown a sharp increase since May 2007. Party workers were unable to fulfil the recruitment of educated SCs under the 'quota' in state public services. When administrative officials 'openly defied BSP party men' at the local level, 'what hope was there that the Dalit population could get anything done?'[128] To address poverty in the state, the Mayawati government refused to implement the nationally approved 'Below Poverty Line' (BPL) list, a rural poverty alleviation scheme of the UPA government, on the pretext that 'poorer' deserving families needed to be included in the 'category of the poor'. Mayawati decided that the 'BSP carried out its own BPL surveys,[129] spent Rs. 10 crores, did not complete it and then scrapped it'. In the process, the landless and Dalit families suffered. If they were unable to avail of the opportunity to buy cheap ration, and if such was the concern Mayawati and the BSP had for them, 'how (could) Dalit voters have the enthusiasm to turn up at the polling booth to press the elephant button'.[130]

'Dalit Prerogative' and the Crisis of Governability

After the 2009 Lok Sabha elections, 'Dalit agenda' became a 'priority-based' policy objective of the BSP. Mayawati side lined Satish Chandra Mishra, the 'Brahmin mascot'[131] of the party, who had been crucial to the successful implementation of the sarvajan scheme of electoral mobilization of upper-caste voters in the state. Rare was a moment between 2007 and 2009 when Mayawati was seen in public without the presence of Satish Chandra Mishra. Rare was a moment since 2009 when Mayawati was seen with Satish Chandra Mishra. Educated SCs began to get jobs; the landless began to own small pieces of land. A major policy thrust was initiated by the BSP in the rural and urban housing sector. In rural areas, pending AVP projects were completed. In urban towns, a policy impetus was given to 'disburse the Mahamaya Scheme monthly cash cover to 30 lakhs beneficiaries'. In rural areas, senior administrative officers were directed to 'inspect one Dalit locality every month' and monitor the extent to which beneficiaries of numerous social schemes were receiving financial assistance. Mayawati outlined measures to ensure that 'big business houses did not monopolize development and mega-infrastructure projects'. Small businesses were given a 'greater stake in development projects'. The implementation of the SC Atrocities Act became more stringent as Mayawati directed officials to submit monthly report on the action taken on the basis of complaints of the people. The complaint had to be submitted by Chief Secretary, Cabinet Secretary, Additional Cabinet Secretary, Principal Secretary of Home and Director General of Police. A policy was formulated to direct officers to ensure 'that effective action was taken upon an official complaint'.[132]

Despite the impress of a 'prerogative-based Dalit agenda', post-2009 a continual crisis of governability gripped the BSP in the remainder of its term in office. The BSP was exposed even further by corruption and bad governance. The dubious role of the 'developer' in PPP mega projects initiated in 2008–2009 and the nexus between politicians, 'dalals' (middlemen), corrupt officers and the mafia over 'contract businesses' became a notable feature of the state administration. In western UP, for instance, the Mayawati government presided over a series of mega projects in Gautam Budh Nagar and Ghaziabad. It was alleged that two 'developer' companies apparently active as 'personal firms of Mayawati' and her family handled the projects. In Noida, Greater Noida and Noida Extension development, projects were auctioned to 'dubious builders' by selling off farmers land. There were allegations that devious land deals in Noida and Ghaziabad between the Mayawati government and a 'few builders' and 'real estate agents' ran into thousands of crores of rupees.[133] 'Dalit symbolism' was highlighted by the construction of a Noida Park worth Rs. 685 crores when the money, instead, could have been spent on pressing infrastructural needs such as roads, electricity and schools. The Uttar Pradesh National Rural Health Mission was mired in a Rs. 2,500-crore scam as 30% money was diverted by a 'collusion of a political-bureaucratic nexus'. The State Teachers Eligibility Test[134] turned out to be fraud with the 'seizure of Rs. 86 lakhs by the administration in Kanpur Dehat'. The money was meant to 'pay bribes to officials in Lucknow' to get candidates through the teachers 'eligibility test'.[135] Mayawati's 'schemes', many of them announced on her birthday to dispense patronage through social programmes which were expected to provide 'direct financial gifts' to the poor failed to reach the 'beneficiaries'. For instance, the Uttar Pradesh Mukhya Mantri Mahamaya Garib Arthik Sahayata Yojana (Uttar Pradesh Chief Minister Mahamaya Economic Assistance to the Poor Plan) earmarked Rs. 300 every month to SC, ST and families headed by women. Half the population was aware of the 'scheme' and an abysmally low percentage of 8% actually benefited from it.[136] In Bundelkhand region of the state, there were a rising number of famished farmers, including debt-induced suicides, rising unemployment and a declining human index which created a perception of total political and bureaucratic apathy.[137] Accessibility to functioning schools suffered due to bad roads, and of course, getting 'routine work done in tehsil, thana and court came at a price'. Poverty alleviation remained a 'non-starter' even as CM Mayawati was charged for 'misappropriating NREGA funds'[138] that was meant to provide rural employment. Weighed in by a mismanaged (sarvajan) governance model, the impact of bad politics and governance exposed and fractured the tenuous bahujan caste-community ethnic coalitions creating resentment against the BSP government.[139] As the BSP government lurched from one political crisis to another, Mayawati became even more 'whimsical self-indulgent and inaccessible'. There were allegations that Mayawati bought a fleet of planes and choppers; her official residence renovated allegedly at a cost of Rs. 86 crores fortified and expanded on the pattern of '7 Race Course Road', the official residence of the UPA Prime Minister Manmohan Singh. When Mayawati left her residence, she was escorted by a 'fleet of 7 Prado bulletproof cars'.[140] She 'rarely interacted with her cabinet colleagues and insulated herself' with a set of bureaucrats who virtually ran the administration. Unaffected by a lack of any tangible benefits of governance and development, Mayawati spent more funds on monuments and statues, occasionally emerging from her self-imposed political hiatus by 'wearing a garland of banknotes and describing it as empowerment of the downtrodden'. According to an 'affidavit furnished by the Election Commission of India in 2012, Mayawati's personal wealth assets totalled Rs. 87.27 crores'.[141]

Sarvajan Politics Exposed

By the time the 2012 assembly elections were held, Mayawati and her 'sarvajan hitaye sarvajan sukhaye' government had been denuded of its legitimacy, riddled with corruption allegations and failed bahujan programme initiatives. Mayawati and the BSP faced a different political challenge in the form of a 'young' aspirational Akhilesh Yadav, son of SP patriarch Mulayam Singh Yadav, and the Chief Ministerial candidate of the party. Akhilesh Yadav-led SP's electoral campaign set aside emotive religious issues and the ideological contests between a 'neo-Brahminical Hindutva', 'plebeian disempowered castes' and 'minority insecurity' which had since the early 1990s been the staple mode of electoral appeal of the SP towards the vast disaggregated OBC constituency and Muslim voters of the state. The polls were all about the successful incorporation of a populist agenda – a publicity-oriented election campaign of 'development, employment and education' to be carried out by the 'new' political leadership of the SP. With the BJP not yet a political force one would reckon with it in 2014, there was a significant shift in upper-caste votes (almost 60% away from the BSP, a majority of whom, among them, Brahmins and Thakurs had voted for the party in 2007) towards the SP who did not want another five-year term of 'harijan (BSP) raj (rule)'. Brahmin and Bhumihar castes would rather have voted for the Congress or the BJP but voted for the SP to make sure that anti-BSP votes of the upper castes did not split. Mayawati's post-2009 pro-Dalit measures had consigned the privileged upper-caste accommodation within the party into one of victimhood. Irrespective of the fact that Akhilesh Yadav's 'clean image' was a decisive political advantage over Mayawati's persona and her scam-ridden term in office, a study revealed that a large cross section of Dalits and a 'young class of OBC and Muslims' responded favourably to the call of 'development'. It is to be noted that while 70% Jatavs aged between 45 and 59 voted for the BSP, 49% of younger Jatav voters (overall 20%) under the age of 30 years of age voted for SP.[142] BSP Jatav vote fell to 55% down by 27%. The non-Chamar Dalit and MBC or 'low-caste OBC' vote went down by 15% as Pasi, Sonkar, Swarnkar, Valmiki, Nishad, Jaiswal and Dhanuk voted against the BSP due to their exclusion from economic benefits in a five-year 'Dalit government'.[143] The caste-wise figures for a massive electoral victory for the SP were an unprecedented upper-caste support of 27% (with 11% Brahmins and 9% Rajputs), Yadavs 72%, non-Yadav OBCs 42%, Jatavs 20% and 33% among smaller castes.[144] For the state polls, the BSP for the first time since its inception in 1984 released a '28-page electoral manifesto'[145] that promised an array of populist welfare schemes for Dalit, MBCs and Muslim voters. Predictably, Mayawati's reactive call for 'welfare of the subaltern classes' failed to retrieve the fragmenting support base for the 2012 state polls (Thachil 2014: 184, 203). Facing democratic deficit, a poor five-year track record of governance characterized by inaccessible institutions and procedures had undeniably failed high expectations for fulfilment of material inducements of the marginalized social groups.[146] Thus, Mayawati's political sops to the bahujan masses were out of sync with a genuine sense of discontent against the party. The SP catapulted to power with 231 seats in the state assembly. It was the first indication in more than two decades that approximately 45% young voters of Uttar Pradesh of varying caste and community denominations had voted for a party around acceptable 'secular' credentials – access to urban jobs, rural market, efficient public delivery of services and goods – of development and progress as a poll programme.[147]

Defeated in the 2012 state polls, the loss of a 'Dalit vote bank' was a political setback for the BSP. Pushed back to 80 assembly seats from the 206 it won in 2007, SP's electoral victory bothered Mayawati less than the prospect of a 'gain of 100 seats' for either of the 'national parties', the Congress or the BJP, with a definite focus on the latter. In fact, Behenji assumed that the 'tables on the SP could be turned at the next election' by reworking caste politics. This was based on the premise that SP was the 'ideological and caste-opposite' – the 'other-half' of the 'oppressor-oppressed' syndrome of identity politics – of the BSP. To the BSP, UP electoral politics should, if it had to, represent a 'bi-party' political contest between the BSP and SP similar to the electoral battles between the Dravida Munnetra Kazhagam and All India Anna Dravida Munnetra Kazhagam in Tamil Nadu.

Yet in the 2014 Lok Sabha elections, the BJP would overturn this 'electoral presumption' of an alternating 'two-party system' in the state.

Rise of the 'nationalist' BJP

In the months preceding the 2014 Parliamentary elections, the BJP had led a nationwide high-decibel political campaign on a new 'narrative of (anti-corruption) development' which appeared as an exclusive ideological crusade against the 'corrupt and tainted' Indian National Congress (INC)-led United Progressive Alliance government (UPA). The UPA government was on the verge of completing two successive five-year terms. However, the Congress Party was facing a massive erosion of legitimacy aggravated by the mega-corruption scandals surrounding the Commonwealth Games of 2010. A galvanized and rejuvenated BJP armed with the talisman slogan of development for the 2014 national elections: 'Sabka Saath, Sab ka Vikas, Sabka Vishwas (Together with All, Development for All, Trust of All) based on the maxim: 'Minimum Government Maximum Governance' began to take effect across the country. It had an immediate political impact in Uttar Pradesh. It was seen by the party as the perfect electoral platform to win Parliamentary seats by appealing to the rural and urban UP voter who would be reassured of a guaranteed public delivery of targeted programmes.[148] 'Development', or rather it be viewed contextually in terms of a state-specific poll strategy, a 'Gujarat model of development' to which PM aspirant Narendra Modi belonged, was portrayed as an 'economic solution' to the crisis-ridden cash-strapped poorly governed state. As proof of what lay ahead for poverty-stricken voters of UP, 'development', as an election propaganda offensive would be spearheaded by Modi, a 'common man' ghanchi (oil presser) OBC, that would be further attested by the significant presence of a number of UP migrants sharing the dais of campaigning BJP leaders recounting their 'pleasant experiences' in Gujarat where 'girl child and social schemes worked, where fan and light never went off; where women on two-wheelers (could) safely travel at night'.[149] The Modi-led election campaign received a political momentum as 'young voters' who had supported the SP across caste and community continuum had become disillusioned with policy paralysis and government inaction that led to the failure of development promises, disapproving the reappearance of old-style 'dominant' caste politics reminiscent of the political control that SP patriarch Mulayam Singh Yadav had over the party. The more far-reaching impact of the 'development campaign' became evident post-electoral victory of the BJP in the state Lok Sabha polls. In one single stroke, the BJP successfully reworked, substituted and altered the political parameter of an entrenched identity politics played around 'core' Jatav (BSP) and Yadav (SP) votes. A consequent effect of it was that the party was also able to ideologically appropriate the social idioms, economic concerns and cultural capital of subaltern 'non(privileged) core' groups, the fleeting OBC voters of the BSP and SP, in the state, thereby comprehending the massive political mobilization of a broader spectrum of castes.

Underlined by an 'ideological alternative' of a development discourse, a meticulously managed election strategy was able to mobilize vast swathes of voters across the state.

The electoral campaign featured numerous occasions when Modi garlanded statues of Ambedkar and other local Dalit icons en route for his political rallies. On his part, Amit Shah, a long-time close associate of Modi and chief election strategist of the party in Uttar Pradesh since June 2013, consolidated the political presence of the BJP across the state. While promising

Bharat Ratna (highest Indian civilian award) to Kanshiram, the late founder of the BSP, Shah organized 200 Nyaya Sammelans (Justice Conventions) and 'street meetings' at 'Scheduled Caste localities' to create 'election committees' amongst them. In this regard, Shah was assisted by social organizations such as the Sewa Bharati Vishwa Hindu Parishad with Rashtriya Swayamsevak Sangh (RSS) linkages. Keeping in focus the mobilization of backward castes which constituted 50% of UP's population, a new nomenclature 'Extremely Backward Castes' was introduced by the BJP to represent prominent poorer OBCs such as Majhi, Dhobi, Nishad, Mallah, Prajapati caste groups. There were 'dark zones', that is, rural areas where neither TV nor newspapers were available to report, where Amit Shah in person travelled, mobilizing poor voters. Amit Shah in person participated in numerous backward caste associations meetings roping in influential leaders such as Satyendra Kushwaha, Rajveer Singh and Rameshwar Chaurasia to bolster the party's prospects. Consequently, it was this electoral strategy that was evident in Modi's 'Vijay Shankhanaad rallies' (the 'call to victory' rallies) across constituencies where he shared the podium with notable OBC political heavyweights Uma Bharti and Kalyan Singh. Much of BJP's massive mobilization of 'non-core' underprivileged groups were based upon years of RSS' service activism among Dalit and marginalized OBC castes, brought together through 'social harmony campaigns'. Besides, at the grassroots level, the RSS played a part in leveraging political strategies to forge links between subaltern groups and the BJP.[150] It must be noted that in organizing such 'fraternal' caste meetings, the BJP on its part played 'smart politics' by taking predominant 'caste correlations' out of the political equation. The party discretely politicized 'individual' social groups of peasant, artisan and Dalit castes. It was done by separating and politicizing life-worlds of analogous social groups in proximate habitat whose claims and counter-claims over each other often manifested through an advocacy to jati purana (origin tales of different castes) for a 'worthy' higher social position in society. In this way, the BJP 'beat the usual presumptuous arguments of urban experts who would have no hesitation to clubbing these caste groups together as Scheduled Castes and Other Backward Classes' and treat them as a bloc to 'share (electoral) space in the rubrics designed for political purposes.'[151] This calibrated electoral strategy was aimed at displacing the 'dominant' subaltern caste voters of the BSP and SP. Another instance of it was to exploit the misgivings of other non-Jatav SC groups, who were mobilized at the grassroot level across specific reserved constituencies, by turning their political dissatisfaction into electoral capital by exploiting their 'repulsion at Jatav dominance'. A notable example of this process was how Jatav dominance was juxtaposed by portraying Pasis as 'rakshaks' (protectors) of Hindu religion with their 'izzat' (honour) at stake. Constituency-specific 'winning combination of castes' were equally successful. For instance, Sadhvi Niranjan Jyoti from Fatehpur got the BJP the support of Kashyap and Nishad communities, while selection of Sonkar and Rawat community candidates ensured that non-Jatav votes consolidated behind the BJP. In general, the 'poor' backward caste electorate was promised reservation in education and jobs.[152] Nothing was left to chance. The election campaign was backed by a well-organized and coordinated grassroot mobilization based upon a micro-management of polling booths through the slogan: 'mera booth sabse mazboot (my election booth is the strongest) handled by an 'army of approximately 18 lakh BJP activists and volunteers'. The usage of digital communication, including 12 3D holograms in rallies, fused with approximately 40 political rallies that Modi held between late October 2013 and May 2014 across the state,[153] was intended to reach 'target' voters. The subtle message of an ideological Hindu narrative was used where required while Modi was consistently marketed and portrayed by the BJP and the RSS as a 'no-other- alternative' 'strong (OBC) leader'.

Mayawati had a standardized response for BSP's poll debacle. She blamed the Congress at the centre and its policies for BSP's electoral defeat suggesting that smaller political parties had to 'bear the brunt of people's anger' 'who wished to 'throw out the Congress in Delhi'. Mayawati perceived that in such a political scenario, 'vote for either the BSP or the SP was tantamount to a vote for the Congress as these two parties were identified with the prevailing ruling establishment' who had supported the Congress Party at 'various stages' due to their decade-long association with the Congress-led UPA government.[154]

The BSP faced a paradoxical situation: Compelled to respond to a changed dynamics of state politics, winning Lok Sabha seats required the incorporation of more and more castes into its fold and getting their votes on 'identity and caste' rather than making promises of 'development'.[155] In fact, much of the political dilemma that the BSP faced was lent by BJP's near precise organized electoral cum development campaign, that was also marked by the carving of a socio-symbolic space for majoritarian politics viewed in the context of communal riots that took place in August–September 2013 in the hinterlands of the western Uttar Pradesh city of Muzaffarnagar. With an eye on the upcoming polls post-riots, the BJP targeted Mayawati whose political indifference to the 'riots' was portrayed as pandering to 'minority' politics while 'Modi – the strongman' the 'man from Sabarmati' generated personal rapport and was there to share the grief of the riot-affected Dalits.[156] Ultimately, it came to light that the BJP had been successful to a considerable extent to mobilize the 'riot sufferers' Dalits and lower castes. Subsequently, the BJP was also able to successfully counterpose BSP Dalit cadres against 'Muslim campaign coordinators' of the party unit in western Uttar Pradesh, the region where the riots took place, to breach a section of the non-Jatav and Jatav votes in its favour. Though denied by the BSP, there were reports that couple of months before the May 2014 polls, more than 3,000 'Dalit party workers' of the party had supposedly joined the BJP.[157] In this region, the BJP achieved further political success as Jat voters voted for non-Jat BJP candidates. Unable to forge a clearly defined electoral schema to challenge the BJP, Mayawati predicted a pragmatic vote-combine of bahujan groups correctly deducing that riot-affected returnee Muslims would vote for the BSP and not the SP exposed by its failure to control the riots; a regime that increasingly became identified by poor law and order and corruption. Thus, apparently, BSP was 'the party' capable of defeating the BJP. The BSP was able to secure the Muslim vote in the region but won no seats as other bahujan groups had already distanced from the party. The fragmented bahujan vote was, then, as much a 'creation of BJP politics' as an underwhelming legacy of how sarvajan politics had halted the process of democratization of smaller subaltern Dalit groups and OBCs[158] particularly evident during the five years the party ruled the state. The old adage of a negligible 'core' vote and therefore an insignificant 'plus' vote conundrum was evident for the BSP in other regions of Uttar Pradesh, reflective of hastily concluded Dalit-Brahmin-Muslim alliances (22 Brahmins, 18 Muslims, 8 Thakurs and 17 Dalits) in select parliamentary constituencies, even providing tickets to those candidates ignored by the BJP. It is in this context that SP's frenetic electoral mobilization of MBC due to receding non-Yadav mobilization assumes political significance. A 'Mulayam Singh Yadav (not Akhilesh Yadav)-sponsored Samajik Nyaya Adhikar Rath Yatra (Journey by Chariot for the Right to Social Justice) appeared as a desperate effort by the SP to electorally mobilize receding non-Yadav MBCs such as Majhis, Nishads, Mallahs, Prajapati, etc. that had already demonstrated their electoral preference for the BJP. The BJP further exploited the internecine rivalry between Yadav sub-castes such as the Ghosis and the Kamariya, the latter sub-caste to which the SP leader Mulayam Singh Yadav belonged.[159]

The BJP won a record 71 Lok Sabha seats (and a total of 73 seats with its ally Apna Dal which won 2 seats) in the state and in the process wiped out the BSP.

Assembly Elections 2017: Development Goals and Consolidation of Political Space

Since 2014, the BJP's electoral strategy has grown exponentially in Uttar Pradesh. The state government till 2017, the assembly election year, was still being effectively run by a decrepit SP. As the state elections neared, SP leader Akhilesh Yadav's irresponsible remark: 'kam bolta hai' (work speaks for itself) effectively summed up the party's defiant mood to mull over a state experiencing growing discontent. Significantly thereafter the suitably termed but electorally disastrous 'UP ke ladke' (boys of UP) pre-poll coalition pact between Akhilesh Yadav and Rahul Gandhi, not between the two parties, with the SP seemingly 'carrying the burden' of the Congress Party, contrived to hand the party an electoral disaster (Shakil 2017).[160] In contradistinction Modi-led BJP at the Centre and through its Lok Sabha MP's in Uttar Pradesh were in a continuous 'informal' campaign mode for the 2017 assembly polls. The thrust of PM Modi and state MPs were the numerous central government-assisted development schemes for the state. Of particular interest were a set of mega target-oriented goals such as the 'electrification of 1,400 villages', 'round the clock' delivery of 'Ujjwala' cooking gas connections through the Pradhan Mantri Ujjwala Yojana (PMUY), Swachh Bharata Abhiyan (health and sanitation), Pradhan Mantri Awas Yojana-Gramin (PMAY-G) (affordable housing) and 'beti bachao, beti padhao' (save girl child, teach girl) campaign for education among others. By March 31, 2017, a few weeks before the state polls, 55 lakh gas cylinders, 25 lakh toilets and 4.7 lakh rural houses had been delivered to 'poor' backward castes and Dalits (Upadhyay 2019). At the level of electoral politics, BJP's rollicking party machinery divided the state into '82 districts', 1,463 mandals (local administrative units) and 9,933 sectors'. 'Parivartan Yatras' (transformation journeys) were undertaken in '75 districts in 403 constituencies covering 8,138 kms'. There were '233 small and large meetings and 2,537 welcome meetings'. In all, '5 million people took part'. Modi addressed '24 rallies while Amit Shah spoke at 150 rallies'. Hundreds of other senior leaders also participated in these rallies. 'Video vans and Parivartan Sandesh (transformation messages) bikers were organized'. The BJP party manifesto received '3 million tweet' suggestions. suggestions.[161] The party held 200 Pichda Varg Sammelan (Backward Caste Conclaves), even arguing the case for the inclusion of 17 OBC castes in the 'SC category'. Influential backward caste leaders such as Keshav Prasad Maurya, a Kushwaha, was made the 'state party president' as 40% of party posts went to OBC candidates. Dissident leaders from the BSP such as Swami Prasad Maurya, O.P. Rajbhar and Sanjay Rajbhar were included and given a larger role in local-level electoral management and political campaigns.[162] Anupriya Patel, a Kurmi and daughter of Sonelal Patel, the founder of Apna Dal and a BJP ally since the 2014 state Lok Sabha polls, was appointed as a union minister.[163] The BJP gave a larger role to OBC caste leaders in its organization and campaigning. To mobilize the simmering identity backlash among the non-Jatav Dalits such as the Pasi (16%), Dhobi, Kori, Balmiki (15%), Amit Shah formulated a winning strategy by organizing 1.28 lakh 'booths' out of 1.47 lakh polling stations across the state. An 'army' of 13 lakh party workers 'micro-managed' the election booths. About 40% of party posts went to the OBC and 20% to the SC which was accurately reflected in the distribution of election tickets.[164]

The BSP's preparation for the state polls was affected by intra-party discord as 'influential leaders' such as S.P. Maurya, Nasimuddin Siddique, Brajesh Pathak and notable others left the party. The BSP chief was accused by her party leaders of 'demanding cash for giving party tickets to prospective candidates'. It was a contentious issue that assumed prominence in the aftermath of the BJP-led National Democratic Alliance government's decision to 'demonetize the Indian economy' in early November 2016 which coincided with a strong assertion of the claim that the BSP had stored huge amounts of unaccounted cash by means of donation to be used for purposes of the upcoming assembly elections. Thus, post-demonetization of old currency, the party was supposedly left with little resources to 'fund' its electoral campaign. Therefore, when Mayawati spoke against demonetization, many took it as a confirmation of the allegation levelled by her political opponents, notably BJP, about the party stashing unaccounted money.[165]

Irrespective of the fact that demonetization ostensibly meant to combat black money, counterfeit currency, terror financing and facilitate an increase in the volume of digital payments it appeared to be a misjudged policy which could have negative and disruptive effects on the economy. Politically, it had a signalling value for Modi and the BJP. Announced in the background of approaching assembly elections in five states, with a focus on Uttar Pradesh, Modi was personally able to identify himself with demonetization as a crusade against corruption; a PM trying to reform a system, in which, the poor, used to daily economic hardship received a 'grievance redressal': that the 'rich and the powerful had to comply and were in fact inconvenienced by it'. Through demonetization, whose economic impact began to be felt immediately across the country, Modi achieved political success portraying himself and the BJP as moving away from a 'defunct' caste-based sectarian vote politics of SP and BSP. Demonetization was interpreted as one that highlighted the class-based bipolarity of the rich and the poor by seemingly coopting, adopting and representing the voice of the poor. Together with vikas (development) politics and the implied assumptions of demonetization, the BJP successfully outlined the electoral campaign plan for Uttar Pradesh.[166]

The immediate political importance of state polls indicated that the BSP was worse off. A much-lowered Dalit vote was enervated by a split in Muslim vote across Uttar Pradesh. In western UP, the 'votes' went to the SP-Congress alliance while in certain constituencies of central and eastern UP despite knitting Jatav and Muslim votes together, BSP's vote share was not enough to win seats to make an electoral impact. Already at a disadvantage with a receding non-Jatav Dalit votes, it made little sense to focus on the 'electoral potential' of the Muslim vote. In fact, affected by the 'politics of revenge' between the SP and BSP, each going their way to garner 'Muslim' votes, as the 2017 assembly elections unfolded, it became clear that the Muslims did not vote unitedly or in 'larger numbers' for either of the two state parties. For the BSP, the fragmented Muslim vote count was 36% across the state while it was 55% for the SP.[167] In sum, the 2017 state polls were yet another poll disaster for the BSP as it was reduced to a paltry 19 seats in the state assembly.

On the other hand, the BJP's electoral campaign showed that Muslim votes did not count for much or to any extent significantly impacted the fate of their 'all non-Muslim' candidates in assembly constituencies where Muslim vote was sizeable and could influence the electoral prospects of a candidate. The BJP won the Uttar Pradesh assembly elections with a record number of 312 seats in the backdrop of a weak and divided political opposition.

Lok Sabha Elections 2019: Cultural-National Politics over Identity Politics

Two years later, the political stage in Uttar Pradesh was set for an electoral contest that would pit the BJP against the 'mahagathbandhan' (MGB) of the SP and the BSP, though Ajit Singh-led Rashtriya Lok Dal (RLD), a marginal political party in western Uttar Pradesh, also joined the 'alliance'. The RLD claimed the support of 'non-Yadav Jat voters'. Irrespective of a number of optimistic pre-poll political surveys, there were valid reasons for the 'SP-BSP coalition front' to firm up for the state Lok Sabha polls. The Adityanath government was mired in state-level issues: the effect of demonetization and agrarian distress indicative of the collapse in prices, drought dues for sugarcane farmers and potato farmers and the nuisance of stray cattle etc. The state government was also criticized for 'running a savarna (upper-caste) type' government.

The 'grand' alliance was precluded by a political experiment in vote mobilization in the Gorakhpur, Phulpur and Kairana Lok Sabha by-polls in May 2018 where BJP's vote share of more than 50% went much below as opposition parties vote share went up. For instance, in the Gorakhpur seat, the stronghold of the current UP CM Yogi Adityanath, the logic of 'your party my candidate' ensured that the candidate of the locally influential Nishad Party won by contesting on an SP ticket. In another instance, the Kairana by-poll SP leader Tabassum Hasan joined RLD just days before contesting the election and won.

Fuelled by the political success of by-poll victories, the rudiments of the MGB were laid out. A significant feature of the poll alliance was that in all of the Lok Sabha seats, the two parties competed they did not overlap? In five out of six regions in the state 'seats', as was claimed, had been immaculately distributed so as to ensure that there was no split in votes against the BJP candidate and neither intra-party rebellion that could affect the SP-BSP pact for the polls. Much of the conclusive electoral agreements reached between Akhilesh Yadav and Mayawati had been about reworking and assessing the performance of the parties since the 2014 national elections in UP. The BSP won no seat but came second in 34 out of 80 seats while the SP won 5 seats and likewise accounted for a second position in 31 seats.[168] Both the parties in numerous pre-election meetings had engaged in preparing constituencies upon each party's strength by building on 'second placed' seats inasmuch as consolidating vote transfer formulae to marginalize the BJP vote base.

For the election, the SP and BSP finalized their seat allocation at 37 and 38 seats, respectively. As part of the 'alliance', two seats in Mathura and Baghpat for the Jat-dominant RLD were left for their leaders Ajit Singh and Jayant Chaudhry. It was believed that if the 'pact' worked, sizeable Jat presence could help the BSP win a number of seats in western Uttar Pradesh.[169] On the other hand, Amethi and the Rae Bareli seats were left to the Congress Party. The SP-BSP pact had for tactical reasons left the

Congress out of the political equation to forge a united anti-BJP alliance. The two parties perceived the Congress Party as '(eating) up much (political) space in (any) alliance'. In the 2017 assembly elections, the SP gave the Congress one-fourth of the assembly seats and the latter would have possibly demanded 15–20 seats in the 2019 Lok Sabha elections which appeared impossible to accommodate. The 'pact' would have been unwieldy with the BSP and RLD as part of the alliance.[170] In recent elections, the Congress vote share in UP has dipped to 'single-digit figures'. With a negligible vote base (11.2% in 2012 to 7.5% in 2014 and further to 6% in the 2017 assembly elections),[171] the only suitable way in which the INC could play a part in defeating the BJP in Uttar Pradesh was by being 'vote-katua' (cutting vote share) of BJP votes, by putting up candidates belonging to those castes that were likely to vote for the BJP.[172] The MGB was supposedly to have a larger political ramification for opposition politics against the BJP: It was to be seen as a 'successful' pact offering important considerations to other strong regional leaders across states to follow by keeping out the Congress Party; that there was no need for a 'national (Congress) alternative'. Rather, it was possible (as the MGB was expected to fulfil the role in Uttar Pradesh) to tie down the BJP to almost 'insurmountable state-level contests'. The BJP would be forced to fight different alliances on separate issues from one state to another and find it difficult to get into a singular contest.[173]

However, the question that was expected to be critical to the political success of the 'pact' was that whether the two political parties, down to their core voters, would transfer vote for the other party on the instruction of their leaders.[174] In fact, it was felt that in the polls the alliance might benefit in certain seats by a division in existing Congress votes howsoever marginal it may be. For the same reason, a section of Congress voters could shift to the BJP which might enable the party to retain slightly more than half the Lok Sabha seats it won in the 2014 national elections in the state.[175]

The 'mahagathbandhan' (MGB) of Akhilesh Yadav and Mayawati was 'pushed, celebrated and touted' as the perfect electoral alliance to check BJP's political dominance in the state since 2014 and was expected to do well. There were high expectations from the 'alliance' as was evident at the MGBs joint political rallies all over the state which drew huge crowds; with even Mayawati campaigning for Mulayam Singh Yadav at Mainpuri, a Yadav-stronghold, asking Jatavs to forget past political bitterness. In fact, such was Mayawati's confidence on the strength of the MGB that at an election rally in Ambedkarnagar, the BSP chief introspecting the prospect of her prime ministerial ambition said: If all goes well, I may seek election from here because the road to national politics passes through Ambedkarnagar.[176]

In the 2019 state Lok Sabha polls, the BJP not only put on a stunning electoral performance winning 62 seats and together with its alliance partner Apna Dal (S) (2 seats), a total of 64 seats, but also increased its vote share to almost 50%, an improvement of as much as 8% since 2014 Lok Sabha elections in the state. The SP won five seats and the BSP ten seats.

A post-poll introspection suggests that Mayawati failed to ensure that the core BSP votes transferred to the 'gathbandhan' SP candidate. The SP had been weakened by infighting in the Mulayam Singh Yadav clan and Shivpal Yadav's rebellion, poor distribution of 'tickets' and the fact that 'SP got a tougher lot of seats'. Yet, it was clear to the SP that its poor performance was due to a 'shabby vote transfer' from the BSP. Could it possibly be that Mayawati's own Jatav caste vote had shrunk significantly and that it was no longer a 'bloc' like it was in the 1990s? The 2012 assembly elections and 2014 Lok Sabha elections in the state had shown that younger Jatavs no longer supported the BSP. Thus, there is a justification that probably, despite her efforts, she was 'fighting a depleting Jatav vote base' in her party; that BSP was no longer a 'Dalit Party' but 'overwhelmingly supported by Jatavs and not all of them'. Another plausible reason could be that the BSP campaign for the alliance SP candidate failed to mitigate the Jatavs social distrust towards the Yadavs.[177]

Throughout the election campaign, the Congress Party kept hinting that it was trying to indirectly help the MGB by swaying votes away from the BJP. It was felt that Congress would help defeat BJP stealing away upper-caste votes. However, the Congress Party cornered 11% of the Muslim vote share (73% approximately voted for the alliance) rather than the upper-caste voters which led to a fairly large number of defeats of SP candidates compared to BSP candidates. As Shafiq Rehman Barq, the winning SP candidate from Sambhal Lok Sabha constituency said: 'They (Congress) hurt us on many seats and cut our votes'.[178]

If Mayawati had been unable to influence Jatav voters, in particular 'SP constituencies' to vote for the MGB, the Yadavs who were assumed to be less inclined to vote for BSP alliance candidates 'displayed much better rate of transfer of votes than the Jatavs contrary to popular perceptions. Yadavs voted for the alliance with a sense of ownership'.[179] Perceptions differed as Barq stated that in 'some constituencies Yadav support did not come and (instead) Muslim and Jatavs voted (including his constituency)'.[180] The core vote share of respective political parties to the MGB also varied. While BSP was able to hold on to its core Jatav votes as 75% approximately voted for the 'BSP' MGB candidates, the SP's Yadav vote share that consolidated behind the alliance was not as strong as it should have been. While 60% approximately did vote for the alliance, it was lower than the percentage of Yadav votes polled in the 2017 assembly election when over 75% voted for the SP-Congress alliance.[181] Arithmetically, the MGB made a lot of sense based on voting patterns of Yadavs, Jatavs and consolidation of Muslim votes deduced from 2014 polls. However, the major partners of the alliance were aware that a complete transfer of votes would not happen, that is, in this context, 'neither from the Congress to the MGB or among partners for the alliance'.[182] A favourable estimate for the MGB in the pre-election analysis expected 40–45 seats for the SP-BSP alliance. The alliance was also riddled with contradictions as it gave more space to upper castes (20 candidates), a doubtful proposition considering that upper-caste voters in the preceding two elections in 2014 and 2017 had shown a high level of political mobilization under the BJP considered as their 'parent' political party. In spite of running a political campaign for social justice, non-Yadav OBCs (19 candidates) got less than upper castes. The alliance also had just three Jat candidates of which two of them from the Rashtriya Lok Dal's ruling family.[183] In a number of seats 'local politics hurt the "gathbandhan" candidate as (local) leaders were denied tickets due to alliance seat-division which worked at cross-purposes'.[184] Preoccupation with 'seat allocation' and 'vote transfer' also put paid to sound logic of the SP-BSP pact. For instance, in the Phulpur by-poll elections held in March 2018, a tacit understanding between the SP and the BSP and the consequent vote mobilization against the BJP candidate ensured the victory of the SP 'Kurmi' candidate. However, the Kurmi MP was replaced in the ensuing 'alliance' seat distribution by a Yadav candidate. A seat traditionally dominated by the Kurmis, the BJP Kurmi candidate won comfortably with a margin of 1.71 lakhs votes.[185]

A survey undertaken by Lokniti – Centre for the Study of Developing Societies (CSDS) shows that 75% Jatavs, 42% non-Jatav Dalits, 60% Yadavs and 73% Muslims voted for the 'alliance' as compared to 68% Jatavs, 42% non-Jatav Dalits which supported the BSP and 53% Yadavs that supported the SP with the Muslim vote split in 2014 Lok Sabha polls in the state. The Lokniti-CSDS survey concluded that the alliance consolidated the social base of its constituencies better than what each could achieve on its own in the 2014 Lok Sabha elections in the state.[186] However, it was evident that the alliance needed to actively mobilize the non-Jatav Dalits and non-Yadav OBC to stem a possible shortfall in core vote transfer to 'joint' SP/BSP candidates. Evidently, a hurriedly negotiated 'alliance of January 2019' of the two state parties had left little time for respective party coordinators to direct local party workers to impart political education to respective 'core' voters to tactically defeat the BJP.

In comparison to the BJP's well-oiled electoral machinery to mobilize 'non-core' voters of the state, even a satisfactory transfer of votes, an evaluation based upon post-poll study of caste vote preferences across constituencies by the MGB constituents, turned out to be ineffectual. The upper-caste candidates were divided into 14 each for Brahmin and Thakur castes. Non-Yadav OBCs received 28 'tickets' of which 8 were Kurmis, 5 Jats, 4 Lodhs, 4 Mauryas/Sainis, 4 Mallahs and 2 Gujjars. The reserved seats went to 2 Jatavs, 15 non-Jatav Dalits which included 6 Pasis, 3 Khatiks, one each Dhanuk, Valmiki, Kol, Dhangar, Gond and Koeri castes.[187] The caste-wise distribution of the 2019 Lok Sabha elections in UP for the BJP was Brahmin 82%, Rajput 89%, Vaishya 70%, Jat 91% (a political rout for RLD candidates in Baghpat and Muzaffarnagar, the latter the centre of riots in 2013), other upper castes 84%, non-Yadav OBCs 72% non-Jatav SCs 48% Kurmis and Koeris 80% which was ahead of the mahagathbandhan core support of

Yadav 60%, Jatav 75%, Muslim 73%, non-Jatav SCs 42%.[188] In fact, the BJP gained support among all major castes since the 2014 Lok Sabha polls — Brahmin 11%, Rajput 7%, other upper castes 9%, Yadav 8%, Kurmi and Koeri 16%, other OBCs 8%, Jatav 2%, other Dalits 4%, Muslims 11% and other smaller castes 10%.[189]

BJP that won the 2019 polls in the state with more than 50% vote share was inclusive of a 43% vote of the youth for Modi who they thought was better placed to create jobs. The BJP also had a higher percentage of female voters who were a 'loyal base' for the party riding on increased 'female literacy, welfare services and awareness' and also due to the overall success of the mega-development projects launched by the PM in the state over five years.

The 'combined votes' of the MGB which was 37% in the 2019 state polls was 5% less than the 'combined' total percentage of votes secured by BSP and the SP (as political contestants) in the 2014 state Lok Sabha polls. In the 'first past the post system' where every vote count, the BJP won over the[190] 'bua-bhatija' pact ('aunt-nephew' indicative of a close personal relationship of Mayawati and Akhilesh Yadav) which lost.

Post declaration of election results, addressing the media, Behenji made a terse remark indicative of her changed political stance. She said: 'Yadav samaj (in the UP Lok Sabha election) had shifted its vote from Yadav strongholds' (such as Kannauj and Badaun, where despite a marginal decrease in vote percent since 2014, Dimple and Dharampal, prominent members of the Mulayam Singh Yadav family, lost the election) and that the 'Yadav-led SP was (therefore) no longer an 'effective (political) party'. This remark was indicative of Mayawati's decision to maintain a political distance, a 'cooling off', short of a formal split from the largely 'ineffective alliance' which failed to win an expected 40–45 seats in the 2019 state Parliamentary polls. Mayawati's logic of expedient politics became clear as the political implications towards building a new electoral equation with the 'Muslim samaj (community)' began to gain ground whose political support for the MGB was impressive during the state Lok Sabha polls. Second, post-poll survey by the BSP also suggested the reason behind a favourable electoral result for the party in western UP where it won a cluster of seven seats. It was symptomatic of a 'plus 75% turn-out of Jatav votes' polled in its 'electoral stronghold' as part of a larger electoral support for MGB 'BSP' candidates in the 38 out of 80 seats, the party contested as part of a seat-sharing agreement with the SP. A summation of a new possibility of a coalition convinced Mayawati to forge a (Jatav) Dalit-Muslim (DM) alliance for future elections in Uttar Pradesh. Certainly, if Mayawati is to be believed, a 'window of opportunity' has arisen for the party that had been on a steady downswing since the state polls of 2012.[191]

Realistically, how sure can the BSP be with alliance formation among 'castes' and 'samaj(s)', considering that in recent times BSP's Dalit, OBC and Muslim groups have not consolidated as reliable voting blocs for the party. Therefore, it comes as a major political surprise that the BSP has suddenly found political comfort in a Jatav-Muslim base, whose combined voting strength in the recent Lok Sabha elections in the state is a 'product of MGB' and not the sole organizational effort of the party. Can this vote combine be readily available as 'vote guarantors' for the BSP that wishes to pose a constituency-wise political opposition to the Bharatiya Janata Party? Professedly, it appears that the DM alliance can work effectively only in western Uttar Pradesh. Despite the fact that the two social groups constitute nearly 50% of the electorate in some assembly seats and more than 40% in nearly half the Lok Sabha constituencies, it remains a contentious issue as to whether an en bloc shift of Muslim voters would gravitate towards the BSP. A post-2007 sarvajan government had posted no calculable benefits for the community which could hamper Mayawati's strategy of a broader social alliance between Dalits and Muslims. The other challenge that confronts BSP is that while constructing a Muslim electoral base as part of an anti-BJP narrative, the party has to take into consideration the SP and the INC having a common electoral capital in it, thereby immensely complicating a strategy to mobilize Muslims in a wider social coalition across the state. With the BSP drawing a blank in the recently concluded October 2019 by-poll elections in the state and the party not seeing much hope in mobilizing 'non-core' voters – the 60% vote capital of the BJP – the 2022 assembly election in Uttar Pradesh is going to be the big political test for the BSP. However, the party has already declared that it would contest the 2022 assembly polls for the 'No. 2 position'. Is it a clear indication of a foregone BJP win?

A question that surely requires a precise answer is: if the BSP is upbeat about its newly founded alliance of two impoverished subaltern groups, why has it already forfeited a future 'assembly' electoral contest? Is it possible that the BSP leadership is aware of the immense organizational skills required to outline effective electoral strategies for a voter outreach of subaltern groups, that is made more complex due to the party's inability to comprehend how 'ethnic vote mobilization' is being rendered ineffective in an altered paradigm of state politics? It might also be that the BSP would like to believe that settling for a realistic 'lesser (electoral) result' is a practical outcome that emerges from a political assessment of the party's present electoral and organizational capacity in the state. Yet, in actuality, there is a greater chance that BSP may perform badly in the 2022 state polls.

Notes

1 Andrew Wyatt, 'The limitations on coalition in India: the case of electoral politics in Uttar Pradesh', *Journal of Commonwealth and Comparative Politics,* No. 2, July 1999, pp. 1; *The Hindu,* New Delhi edition, October 20, 2008.
2 Thomas Blom Hansen and Christophe Jaffrelot (Eds.), *The BJP and the Compulsions of Politics,* New Delhi: Oxford University Press, 1998, pp. 78–81.
3 Vidya Subramanium, *Voters Disenchantment*, pp. 52–56; 'Message from the states', *Frontline,* 15, 6, March 21–April 3, 1998, pp. 33–36

4 Schwecke, *Rationality in Politics*, p. 19; 'It's Gupta Period', *Outlook,* 15, 20, May 29, 2000, p. 18; 'Writing on the wall', *Outlook,* 5, 19, May 24, 1999, pp. 10–14.
5 A paradoxical verdict', *Frontline,* 16, 28, November 6–19, 1999, p. 42.
6 Venkitesh Ramakrishnan, 'Continuing crisis in UP', *Frontline,* 16, 11, May 22–June 4, 1999, pp. 33–34; Bhaumik, 'Caste no bar', *Outlook,* 15, 34, September 4, 2000, pp. 24–26.
7 Bhaumik, 'Caste no bar', *Outlook,* 15, 34, September 4, 2000, pp. 24–26.
8 'Distress signals', *Frontline,* 17, 14, July 21, 2000, p. 22.
9 Purnima Tripathi, 'A new calculation in Uttar Pradesh, *Frontline,* 18, 19, September 15–28, 2001, pp. 40–41.
10 Purnima Tripathi, 'A feud in Uttar Pradesh', *Frontline,* 10, 25, December 8–21, 2001, pp. 37–39.
11 Sohini Guha, 'Asymmetric representation and the BSP in UP, *Seminar,* 571, March 2007, pp. 57, 58.
12 Verma, *Reverse Osmosis,* p. 818.
13 In the 1996 assembly elections in UP, the BSP gave 28% of tickets to SC, 24% to OBC, 18% to the Muslims and 16.6% to upper-caste candidates. The party tried to gain support of the MBCs, giving 51 members of this community tickets of whom 16 won, a better performance than that of the upper castes. Some upper-caste BSP candidates won, voted by the Dalits, as the Party lived up to its reputation of a party that could transfer en bloc votes to candidates of its choice.
Vidya Subramanium, *Voters Disenchantment*, pp. 55, 56.
14 Sudha Pai, *Dalit Assertion*, pp. 180–81; Kanchan Chandra, *Why Ethnic Parties Succeed?* pp. 217, 226, 235.
15 Sudha Pai, *Dalit Assertion*, pp. 180–81; Kanchan Chandra, *Why Ethnic Parties Succeed?*, pp. 217, 226, 235.
16 Sudha Pai, *Dalit Assertion*, pp. 180–81; Kanchan Chandra, *Why Ethnic Parties Succeed*, pp. 217, 226, 235.
17 The BJP secured 3 seats in Punjab, 1 seat in Haryana, but did extremely well in Gujarat, where the party secured 19 seats, in Karnataka 13 seats, in Bihar 20 seats and in Madhya Pradesh 30 seats.
URL: http//www.eci.gov.in/KR_KeyHighlights/LS_1998/vol_1_LS_98.pdf (accessed March 1, 2008).
Vivek Kumar, 'BSP and dalit aspirations', *Economic and Political Weekly,* 39, 18, May 1–7, 2004, p. 1779; 'Umbrella of the oppressed', *Outlook,* 5, 36, September 20, 1999, p. 33.
18 Sudha Pai, *Dalit Assertion,* p. 179.
19 Verma, *Reverse Osmosis,* pp. 818, 819.
20 'Umbrella for the oppressed', *Outlook,* 5, 36, September 20, 1999, p. 33.
21 Sudha Pai, 'Elections 1999 Uttar Pradesh: BSP's New electoral strategy pays off', *Economic and Political Weekly,* 34, 44, October 30, 1999, pp. 3099–100; Sudha Pai, *Dalit Assertion,* p. 182; Sudha Pai, *Political Process in Uttar Pradesh*, p. 229.
22 Mayawati reminded the Muslims of BSP's 'volte-face' in Parliament that led to the dismissal of the 13-day BJP government at the Centre in 1996, ostensibly to protect and secure Muslim interests.
'Umbrella of the oppressed', *Outlook,* 5, 36, September 20, 1999, p. 33.
23 Sanjay Kumar, 'The prospects', *Seminar,* March 2007, No. 571, pp. 67–68; Purnima Tripathi, 'The churning in Uttar Pradesh', *Frontline,* 19, 4, February 16–March 1, 2002, pp. 28, 29, 30.
24 Sudha Pai, *Dalit Assertion,* pp. 184–85; Vivek Kumar, *Dalit Aspirations,* p. 1779.

25 URL: http://www.eci.gov.in/Statistical Reports/LS_1999/Vol_I_LS_99.pdf (accessed March 1, 2008); H.D. Singh, *Faces in India,* pp. 254–87; Aggarwal and Chowdhry, *Elections in India,* pp. 232–37.

26 'Consolidation in Uttar Pradesh', *Frontline,* 16, 22, October 23–November 5, 1999, p. 114; Sudha Pai, *Political Process in Uttar Pradesh,* p. 232.

27 Sohini Guha, *Asymmetric Representation,* pp. 59, 60.

28 Verma, *Reverse Osmosis,* p. 819; Verma, *Elusive Samajwad,* p. 43; 'Uttar Pradesh: uneasy outcome', *Economic and Political Weekly,* 37, 9, March 9, 2002, p. 815; Mr. Brajesh Pathak, a one-time BSP MP from Unnao (2004) considered the term 'social engineering' as wrong. He said that it was an invention of the press. Instead, 'bhaichara' or fraternization was the correct approximation of the electoral strategies pursued by the BSP.

Interview with Brajesh Pathak, March 21, 2009.

In August 2016, he joined the BJP hours after he was expelled from the BSP for anti-party activities.

29 Ranjit Bhushan, 'The deep rising', *Outlook,* 42, 9, March 11, 2002, pp. 18–20.

30 In the 2002 assembly elections in UP, it became evident that the BJP could not strike a balance between the MBC and the upper-caste aspirants in the run-up to the polls.

Source: Verma, *Elusive Samajwad,* p. 46.

Uttar Pradesh: Uneasy Outcome, p. 815.

31 Ibid.

32 Sanjay Kumar, 'The prospects', *Seminar,* 571, March 2007, p. 67.

33 Upadhyay, *Verdict UP*

34 In a bid to fight the anti-incumbency factor, Rajnath Singh, the incumbent Chief Minister, launched the 'chalo gaon ki ore (let's go to the village)' drive. BJP leaders and workers participated in this ambitious programme of approaching over 50,000 gram sabhas and nearly 8,815 nyaya panchayats (*lit.* system of dispute resolution at the village level) in the state. 'Dalit utthan' (upliftment) rallies were organized in November 2001 just as in early 2002, Rajnath Singh was also seen at a Muslim Jagran Sanmelan (*lit.* Muslim awareness conference) in Varanasi. It was to no avail as the BJP lost votes among all four major constituent sections of the UP population – upper caste, OBC, Muslim and dalits.

Kalyan Singh's Lodh-based Rashtriya Kranti Party (RKP), which won only 4 out of 333 seats contested, damaged the electoral prospects of the BJP in several constituencies and dented the OBC support base of the party. In western UP, the swing away from the BJP was kept down to 6% largely due to the Party's alliance with Ajit Singh's Rashtriya Lok Dal (RLD) which eventually won 14 out of 38 seats contested. However, any benefits of the 'Ajit Singh factor' were set off by Kalyan Singh's RKP, Chautala's Indian National Lok Dal (INLD) and by political heavyweights like D.P. Mishra and D.P. Yadav, who continued to have traditional support in certain pockets in western UP. In Rohilkhand, the BJP faced a threat from another ally – Maneka Gandhi's Shakti Dal that put up candidates in 13 constituencies.

Uttar Pradesh: *Uneasy Outcome*, p. 815; Purnima Tripathi, 'In a cleft stick', *Frontline*, 19, 2 January 19–February 1, 2002, p. 34; Purnima Tripathi, 'Desperate measures in Uttar Pradesh', *Frontline*, 18, 17, August 18–31, 2002, pp. 124, 125; 'Uttar Pradesh: uneasy outcome, *Economic and Political Weekly*, 37, 9, March 9, 2002, p. 815; Purnima Tripathi, 'Desperate measures in UP', *Frontline*, 18, 17, August 18–31, 2001, p.; Purnima Tripathi, 'An uphill task', *Frontline*, 18, 12, June 9–22, 2001, p. 43; Verma, *Caste Dominates Ideology*, p. 1976; Sudha Pai, *Political Process in Uttar Pradesh,* pp. 176, 180; A.K.Verma, 'UP Assembly elections: caste dominates ideology', *Economic and Political Weekly,* 37, 21, May 25–31, 2002, pp. 1977, 1978.

35 *Uttar Pradesh: Uneasy Outcome*, p. 815; Upadhyay, *Verdict UP*.
36 Sudha Pai, *Political Process in Uttar Pradesh*, p. 286; Sanjay Kumar, *Prospects*, p. 67.
37 The main reason for Congress' disinclination to lend political support to the SP was 'its new-found confidence' that the party was indeed on a 'comeback trail', following good electoral performance in the assembly elections in Punjab and Uttaranchal. In these states, the Congress wrested power from the BJP and its National Democratic Alliance (NDA) allies. Any support to SP at this juncture in UP, where the Congress was reduced to a mere 25 seats and only about 9% vote share, would mean 'frittering away the minority vote in the state, which was, apparently, coming its way'. The SP's attempt to woo a substantial section of the BSP Muslim MLAs too came to nothing.

    Purnima Tripathi, 'The Uttar Pradesh tangle', *Frontline,* 19, 7, March 30-April 12, 2002, pp. 35, 36.
38 Platts, *Digital Dictionary*, p. 542; Saba Naqvi Bhowmik, Sutapa Mukherjee, 'Big hit on Chhota Raja', *Outlook*, 43, 5, February 10, 2003, pp. 10, 11; Purnima Tripathi, 'The great game', *Frontline,* 19, 10, May 11–24, 2002, p. 21.

    On its part, the BSP supported the BJP to sail through the vote on Gujarat, in the wake of the Godhra carnage, in the Lok Sabha on April 30, 2002.

    'UP: survival arrangement', *Economic and Political Weekly*, 37, 9, May 11, 2002, p. 1773.

    The expression 'Coalition Dharma' was used by former Prime Minister Atal Bihari Vajpayee as a convenient expression explicitly conveying 'illusions of sanctity to cloak unprincipled compromises and accommodations' arrived at by leaders of coalition governments desperate to cling to power and its perquisites.

    Kamal Kant Jaswal, 'From coalition dharma to governance dharma' *Common Cause*, Vol. XXIX, No. 4, October–December 2010 URL: http//www.commoncause.in/publication_details.php (accessed July 7, 2019).
39 'UP: survival arrangement', *Economic and Political Weekly,* 37, 9, May 11, 2002, p. 1773; *Hindustan Times,* New Delhi edition, June 29, 2002; *Amar Ujala,* Lucknow edition, April 15, 2002.
40 Saba Naqvi Bhowmik, Sutapa Mukherjee, 'Big hit on Chhota Raja', *Outlook,* 43, 5, February 10, 2003, pp. 10–11; Purnima Tripathi, 'The great game', *Frontline,* 19, 10, May 11–24, 2002, p. 21.
41 *Hindustan Times,* New Delhi edition, May 7, 2002.
42 'Adventures in wonderland', *Outlook,* 43, 35, September 8, 2003, p. 30; 'Kanshiram: BSP will fight the polls on its own', *Frontline,* 18, 9, April 28–May 11, 2001, p. 43.
43 By rejecting BJP's demand for the post of Deputy CM, Mayawati made it known to the BJP that it was the junior partner in the coalition.

    Purnima Tripathi, 'The great game', *Frontline,* 19, 10, May 11–24, 2002, p. 21.
44 Purnima Tripathi, 'The great game', *Frontline,* 19, 10, May 11–24, 2002, p. 21.
45 Purnima Tripathi, 'The great game', *Frontline,* 19, 10, May 11–24, 2002, pp. 21–22.
46 *Amar Ujala,* Lucknow edition, 26 June, 2002 and 30 June, 2002; *The Hindu*, New Delhi edition, October 14, 2008.
47 For further elaboration on 'Madrasa', refer to Platts, *Digital Dictionary*, p. 1015.

    Amar Ujala, Lucknow edition, 26 June, 2002 and 30 June, 2002; *The Hindu*, New Delhi edition, October 14, 2008.
48 *The Pioneer,* New Delhi edition, October 11, 2002 and October 12, 2002.
49 *Amar Ujala,* Lucknow edition, September 28, 2002; Purnima Tripathi, All for Bahujan Samaj, *Frontline,* 19, 21, October 12–25, 2002, pp. 43, 44.

50 Purnima Tripathi, 'All for Bahujan Samaj', *Frontline,* 19, 21, October 12–25, 2002, pp. 43, 44; Uttar Pradesh: Politics over Governance, *Economic and Political Weekly,* 37, 42, October 19, 2002, p. 4253.

51 *The Statesman*, New Delhi edition, March 12, 2003.

52 *The Pioneer,* New Delhi edition, January 25, 2003.

53 *Amar Ujala*, Lucknow edition, October 28, 2002, December 23, 2002, January 11, 2003 and February 25, 2002; *Amar Ujala*, Lucknow edition, February 20, 2003.

54 Raghuraj Pratap Singh was arrested under Prevention of Terrorist Activities (POTA) in January 2003 for keeping AK-56 rifles, three dozen cartridges and wireless sets.

Mulayam Singh Yadav's efforts to weaken the government was dealt a blow as 8 out of 23 Congress MLAs split engineered by a top BSP leader. The breakaway Congress MLAs formed the Akhil Bharatiya Congress Dal (ABCD), and subsequently 4 ABCD ministers were inducted in the BSP ministry.

The Pioneer, New Delhi edition, October 24, 2002, November 11, 2002, January 29, 2003, and February 5, 2003.

55 Mulayam Singh Yadav's efforts to weaken the government was dealt a blow as 8 out of 23 Congress MLAs split engineered by a top BSP leader. The breakaway Congress MLAs formed the Akhil Bharatiya Congress Dal (ABCD), and subsequently 4 ABCD ministers were inducted in the BSP ministry.

The *Pioneer*, New Delhi edition, October 24, 2002, November 11, 2002, January 29, 2003, and February 5, 2003.

56 The war of attrition between the SP and the BSP continued with the SP publicizing the infamous 'tape scam' that alleged to have contained a recorded voice of Mayawati 'urging money for favours'. Mayawati lodged 135 cases against Mulayam Singh Yadav 'spread over 40 districts', primarily on grounds of misappropriation of funds. It was a charge that was specifically levelled for the misuse of discretionary funds from the state treasury, bringing into question the role of the Governor Motilal Vora. A case was lodged against Mulayam Singh Yadav and his associates for 'falsely implicating Mayawati' in the 'farji' (*lit.* fake) 'CD case'. The Mayawati government further indicted Mulayam Singh Yadav in '600 cases'.

Amar Ujala, Lucknow edition, April 15, 2003.

57 Venkaiah Naidu spelt out the intentions of the BJP. He said the 'alliance was essential if the BJP (wanted) to continue (to be in power) in New Delhi'.

Amar Ujala, Lucknow edition, April 15, 2003; Poornima Joshi, 'A few sharp dog bytes', *Outlook,* 43, 15, April 21, 2003, pp. 22–23; *The Pioneer,* New Delhi edition, February 16, 2003 and February 15, 2003; *The Statesman,* New Delhi edition, June 16, 2003; *The Pioneer,* Lucknow edition, February 15, 2003.

58 *Amar Ujala,* Lucknow edition, May 20, 2002; Sutapa Mukherjee, 'Shifting sands', *Outlook,* 42, 28, July 22, 2002, p. 16; *Hindustan Times,* New Delhi edition, May 9, 2002; *The Statesman,* New Delhi edition, April 15, 2003.

59 *Hindustan Times,* New Delhi edition, July 7, 2002.

60 Subsequently, the BSP took a decision to allot 10 acres of land in front of Apna Bazaar in Vibhuti Khand of Gomtinagar for the Indira Gandhi Pratishthan, instead of land adjacent to Ambedkar Park which has been taken over to extend Ambedkar complex, to end the spat between the Congress and BSP.

URL: http://timesofindia.indiatimes.com/articleshow/23009224.cms (accessed July 16, 2008).

The Statesman, New Delhi edition, September 13, 2002, and September 17, 2002.

61 *Unki Disha: Hamare Prayas, Vartaman Uttar Pradesh Sarkar ki Ek Saal Ki Uplabdhiyan* [Her Vision: Our Efforts, Completion of One Year Achievements of Uttar Pradesh Government], published by the Department of Information and Public Relations, Lucknow, UP, May 2003, pp. 4, 6, 7, 10, 11, 12, 18, 19, 22, 39, 41, 46; *The Statesman,* New Delhi edition, September 13, 2002 and September 17, 2002.

62 According to Archaeological Survey of India (ASI), no construction within 500 meters of the prohibited area around Taj Mahal can be carried out. The Mayawati government appeared to have violated the guidelines.

Yogesh Mishra, Sutapa Mukherjee, 'A tag on the Taj', *Outlook*, 43, 31, August 11, 2003, p. 23; *The Statesman*, New Delhi edition, July 4, 2003.

63 Sudha Pai, 'Choices before the BSP', *Seminar,* No. 534, February 2004, pp. 12–15; *Hindustan Times,* New Delhi edition, September 9, 2003; A.K. Verma, 'BSP's strategy in Uttar Pradesh: wooing the Brahmins for a new alliance', *Economic and Political Weekly,* 40, 26, June 25, 2005, p. 2647; Shivam Vij, (28.04.07) 'Behenji's Brahmin gamble', URL: http//www. shivamvij.com /2007/04/behenji% E2% 80% 99s brahmin-gamble.html (accessed August 24, 2007); *The Pioneer,* New Delhi edition, September 6, 2003; 'BSP-BJP alliance', *Economic and Political Weekly,* 37, 23, June 8, 2002, p. 2204.

Out of power in UP, the BSP focused on weakening the electoral prospects of the BJP in the four assembly elections – Chhattisgarh, Madhya Pradesh, Rajasthan and Delhi – that were held in December 2003. For the second time in the 1990s, the BSPs lack of political influence outside UP was exposed. The 'BSP factor' in the four states, where it claimed to support candidates in a position to defeat the BJP was negligible. In the December 2003 assembly elections to the four states, the BJP formed government in Chhattisgarh, Rajasthan and Madhya Pradesh, while in Delhi the Congress(I) won. In the 1998 assembly elections in Madhya Pradesh, the party had secured 11 assembly seats and in Rajasthan won 2 seats. Yet, in sum, if 1998 assembly elections and 1999 Lok Sabha elections are any indication, they point to the negligible vote share of the political party. Thus, in Madhya Pradesh, it was 6.15% and 5.23%, in Rajasthan 2.17% and 2.76% and in Delhi 3.09% and 2.24%.

Poornima Joshi, 'Baby elephant walk', *Outlook*, 43, 45, November 17, 2003, pp. 30, 31; 'The BSP factor', *Outlook*, 43, 45, November 17, 2003, pp. 30, 31.

64 Mayawati accused the coalition government headed by Mulayam Singh Yadav of 'misleading the (Muslim) minority community' and criticized the state government for 'disbandment of four commissionaires and nine districts created by Mayawati during her three previous regimes in coalition with the BJP'. Mulayam Singh Yadav was careful 'not to [touch] areas like Kannauj, Baghpat and Hardoi to safeguard the interests of his son Akhilesh Singh Yadav and RLD leader Ajit Singh'. Mayawati summed up her opposition to the SP by stating that 'she intended to wipe out the SP in the 2004 Lok Sabha polls in the state'.

The Times of India, Lucknow edition, April 26, 2004, and March 14, 2004; *The Times of India,* Lucknow edition, May 1, 2004, and January 14, 2003.

65 *The Times of India,* Lucknow edition, April 27, 2004; A.K. Verma, 'Uttar Pradesh: will BSP and Congress gain?', *Economic and Political Weekly,* 39, 15, May 1, 2004, p. 1775; *The Times of India,* New Delhi edition, March 19, 2004.

66 *The Times of India,* Lucknow edition, March 18, 2004 and April 27, 2004.

67 *The Times of India,* New Delhi edition, April 23, 2004; Verma, *Uttar Pradesh,* p. 1776; Purnima Tripathi, 'Feel good wearing thin', *Frontline,* 21, 9, April 24–May 7, 2004, pp. 14–16.

68 Purnima Tripathi, 'Decisive defeat for Hindutva', *Frontline* 21, 11, May 22–June 4, 2004, pp. 19–20.

69 According to Manoj Mishra, a BJP-affiliated psephologist during the 2004 election campaign, the BJP was under the impression that it had a 'copyright on the Brahmin and Thakur voters', but in reality, 'the Brahmins were so upset with the BJP for ignoring them that they have gone back to the Congress, while Thakurs, angered by the 'Raja bhaiyya' episode and its handling by the BSP-BJP government and the (political) isolation of the community within the party, went to the SP'. On the other hand, the emergence of Amar Singh, a Thakur leader, became SP's focal point in this election to mobilize the Thakur community. Thakurs who constitute nearly 9% of the state's population constituted 19% of the total vote share of the SP across parliamentary constituencies in the 2004 Lok Sabha elections.

Purnima Tripathi, 'Decisive defeat for Hindutva', *Frontline* 21, 11, May 22–June 4, 2004, pp. 19, 20; A.K. Verma, 'BSP's strategy in Uttar Pradesh: wooing the Brahmins for a new alliance', *Economic and Political Weekly,* 40, 26, June 25, 2005, p. 2647; Venkitesh Ramakrishnan, 'The battle for UP', *Frontline,* 21, 10, May 8–21, 2004, pp. 4–5.

70 Sanjay Kumar *The Prospects,* p. 67.

Ilyas Azmi, an MP from Shahabad, UP, seeking re-election in 2009, had incidentally left BSP to join SP before defecting back to the BSP. He did not divulge on the reasons for rejoining the BSP except that the Party provided security and partnership to the Muslim samaj. Similarly, Mitrasen Yadav, a BSP MP from Faizabad in the 2004 Lok Sabha elections has defected back to his parent party SP prior to the 2009 Lok Sabha elections. Ramesh Dube, a Brahmin MP of the BSP fought the 2009 Lok Sabha elections on a Congress ticket.

Interview with Ilyas Azmi, Shahabad, UP, 05.04.09.

In Chandrauli Rajput voters were of immense political value to the BSP's winning candidate.

71 URL: http://www.indian-election.com/uttarpradesh/index.html#cont (accessed October 24, 2007); H.D. Singh, *Faces in India,* pp. 254–287; Aggarwal and Chowdhury, *Elections in India,* pp. 232–37; Ramashray Roy and Paul Wallace (Eds.), *Indian Politics and the 1998 Elections: Regionalism, Hindutva and State Politics,* New Delhi: Sage Publications, 1999, p. 62.

72 'Being Mayawati' (12.05.07) URL: http://www.indianmuslims info/news/2007/may/12/impt/-being-mayawati.html (accessed December 22, 2007).

73 'Mayawati revolution', *Economic and Political Weekly,* 42, 20, May 19, 2007, p. 1795, 1796; Shivam Vij, 'The elephant paradox' (10.03.07) URL: http://www.shivamvij.com/2007/03/the-elephant-paradox.html (accessed on 25.08.2007); Venkitesh Ramakrishnan, 'A new caste formula', *Frontline,* 22, 13, June 18–July 1, 2005, pp. 27, 28; Gupta and Kumar, *'Caste Calculus'*, p. 3389.

74 *The Hindu,* New Delhi edition, June 16, 2005.

75 Ramakrishnan, 'A new caste formula', *Frontline,* 22, 13, June 18–July 1, 2005, 27, 28; T.V.R. Shenoy, (11.05.07), 'The victory of caste arithmetic' URL: http://www.in.rediff.com/news/2007/may/11 flip.htm (accessed August 25, 2007); Anand Teltumbde, 'A 'Mayawi' revolution', *Economic and Political Weekly,* 42, 23, June 9, 2007, p. 2148.

76 *The Hindu,* New Delhi edition, May 12, 2007; Vivek Kumar, 'Behind the BSP victory', *Economic and Political Weekly,* 42, 24, June 16, 2007, p. 2238.

77 A.K. Verma, 'Mayawati's sandwich coalition', *Economic and Political Weekly,* 42, 22, June 2, 2007, p. 2040.

A discussion on Parashuram appears in a 'Commentary' written by A.M. Shah, 'Parashuram: icon of new Brahmism', *Economic and Political Weekly,* 41, 51, February 4, 2006.

78 Ramakrishnan, 'A new caste formula', *Frontline*, 22, 13, June 18–July 1, 2005, 27, 28.

79 Badri Narayan, *The Making of the Dalit Public in North India: Uttar Pradesh, 1950–Present*, New Delhi: Oxford University Press, 2011, pp. 116, 117; Mukul Sharma, *Caste and Nature: Dalits and Indian Environmental Politics*, New Delhi: Oxford University Press, 2017, p. xv.

In addition, Badri Narayan adds that the 'Kendra' uses images of Dalit heroes, the physical size of the buildings magnificence to rethink their self-esteem, pride and place in the world and to bring newly aroused aspirations firmly to the BSP's political agenda. Other notable monuments such as the Kanshiram Memorial, Shahuji Maharaj Shodh Evam Parikshan Sansthan, Dr. Bhimrao Ambedkar Samajik Parivartan Dwar, Samtamoolak Chowk, Bauddha Vihar Shanti Upvan, Bhikshu Niwas, Ramabai Park and Antarrashtriya Bauddha Addhyan Kendra were erected by the BSP during the post-2009 period.

Badri Narayan, *Dalit Public*, p. 117.

80 Pradeep Kapoor, (14.11.07), 'Brahmins, BSP's new found love' URL: www.hardnewsmedia.com/2007/11/1809 (accessed on 18.12.2007); *The Times of India,* Lucknow edition, May 24, 2005; Ramakrishnan, 'A new caste formula', *Frontline,* 22, 13, June 18–July 1, 2005, 27, 28; Sudha Pai, *Political Process in Uttar Pradesh,* p. 265; Interview with Brajesh Pathak, BSP MP from Unnao, UP; Bahujan Samaj Party, *CD-ROM*, Vols. I and II, Lucknow, UP, 2005.

81 Niranjan Pandey and Devendra Mishra, belonging to the Brahmin community, stated at the June 9, 2005, Lucknow rally that 'in the last couple of years, only [Mayawati's] party had come to [their] rescue when faced attacks from communities, such as Thakurs and Yadavs'. Devendra Mishra added that 'the BSP leader Mayawati enhanced the dignity of Brahmins by appointing them to high positions in her party'.

Ramakrishnan, 'A new caste formula', *Frontline*, 22, 13, June 18–July 1, 2005, pp. 27, 28; Pradeep Kapoor, Brahmins, BSP's new found love (accessed December 18, 2007).

82 Rahuraj Pratap Singh alias Raja bhaiyya who was jailed under the Prevention of Terrorism Act (POTA) along with his father Uday Pratap Singh, of SP, is a Thakur; Amarmani Tripathi dropped as a minister in Mayawati's government (2002–2003) after he was held for the murder of young poet Madhumita Shukla, and who was shortly thereafter accepted into the SP, is a Brahmin; and Mau's notorious 'don' Mukhtar Ansari and Allahabad's equally well-known gangster Atiq Khan, long patronized by the SP, both are Muslims.

For more details on 'Yadav offenders', see Smita Gupta, 'Does law and order matter?', *Seminar,* March 2007.

Gupta and Kumar, *'Caste Calculus',* p. 3393; Smita Gupta, 'Does law and order matter?', *Seminar*, 571, March 2007, pp. 16–20.

83 Verma, *BSP's Strategy in Uttar Pradesh,* pp. 2247, 2248; Venkitesh Ramakrishnan, 'For a winning formula', *Frontline*, 24, 6, March 24, 2007, pp. 121, 122; Venkitesh Ramakrishnan, 'The new behenji', *Frontline*, 24, 8, April 21, 2007, pp. 11, 12, 13

84 Verma, *BSP's Strategy in Uttar Pradesh,* pp. 2247, 2248; Venkitesh Ramakrishnan, 'For a winning formula', *Frontline*, 24, 6, March 24, 2007, pp. 121, 122; Venkitesh Ramakrishnan, 'The new behenji', *Frontline*, 24, 8, April 21, 2007, pp. 11, 12, 13; Shivam Vij, 'The elephant paradox' (accessed August 25, 2007); 'Change in ideology puts BSP in power for 5 years' (12.05.07), URL: http//www.news.speeple.com/instablogs.com/2007/05/12/change-in-ideology-puts-BSP-in-power-for-5-tears-in-UP.htm (accessed August 24, 2007); Interview with Brajesh Pathak, BSP MP from Unnao, UP.

85 Suhas Palshikhar, 'Beyond Uttar Pradesh: new implications for party politics', *Economic and Political Weekly,* 42, 21, May 26, 2007, pp. 1892, 1891; 'Mayawati's revolution', *Economic and Political Weekly,* 42, 20, May 19, 2007, p. 1796.

The Pal community, an intermediate backward caste in UP, was effectively mobilized by Sobran Pal, during the 2007 assembly elections in UP. He was the architect of 'Pal-Baghel samaj', one of the hundreds of caste-based associations across India. The Pals and Baghels are numerous in UP and adjoining state of Madhya Pradesh. Sobran Pal was the first 'caste' leader of the Pals who was from the district of Jhansi in Madhya Pradesh.

Source: Tehelka, New Delhi edition, April 7, 2009.

86 Vivek Kumar, Behind the BSP victory, p. 2238; The *Hindu*, New Delhi edition, May 3, 2007; Palshikhar, *Beyond Uttar Pradesh*, p. 1892; *Hindustan Times*, New Delhi edition, May 25, 2009.

Siddiqui was a former Environment Minister in the 2002–2003 BSP government and National General Secretary and President of the Youth Wing of the BSP. He was found guilty along with Mayawati in the Taj Corridor scam. His name was also associated with a 'land scam' in Unnao. He had been a cabinet minister a number of times (March 1997–September 1997, September 1997–October 1999, May 2002–August 2003) and was an influential leader closely associated with the BSP government between 2007 and 2012.

'Naseemuddin Siddiqui: Muslim face of the BSP' (13.05.07) URL: http://www.twocircles.net/2007, May 13/naseemuddin-siddiqui-muslim-face-bsp.html (accessed August 24, 2007).

In the days leading to the May 2017 assembly elections, he was expelled from the party by Mayawati.

87 Vivek Kumar, *Behind the BSP Victory*, p. 2238; Palshikhar, *Beyond Uttar Pradesh*, p. 1891; Verma, *Sandwich Coalition*, p. 2040; Pratap Somvanshi, 'King Mayawati', *Himal*, June 2007, p. 18; *Hindustan Times,* New Delhi edition, 8.12.07; Naseemuddin Siddiqui: Muslim face of the BSP (accessed August 24, 2007).

88 Ramakrishnan, 'The new behenji', *Frontline*, 24, 8, April 21, 2007, pp. 11, 12, 13.

89 A.K. Verma, 'Municipal elections in Uttar Pradesh', *Economic and Political Weekly,* 41, 51, December 23, 2006, pp. 5218–5221.

90 The incident flared up due to a clash over a ritualistic procession honouring Bharata (second brother of Lord Ram) by Bharata Milap (embracement of Bharata), a local Hindu outfit and the Hindu Yuva Vahini (Hindu Youth Armed Force) and roza (fasting) rituals performed by the Muslims.

V. Ramakrishnan, 'Heat and dust', *Frontline*, 24, 8, April 21, 2007, pp. 4–7; V. Ramakrishnan, 'Stoking the communal fire', *Frontline*, 22, 23, November 5, 2005, pp. 36–37; Smita Gupta, *'Does Law and Order Matter?,* pp. 16–20; India Events of 2005, Human Rights Watch (World Report 2006) URL: https://www.hrw.org/world-report/2006/country-chapters (accessed May 13, 2018), *The Times of India*, New Delhi edition, September 22, 2008; Ramakrishnan, 'For a winning formula', *Frontline,* pp. 121, 122; V. Ramakrishnan, 'Conquering style', *Frontline,* 24, 8, April 21, 2007, pp. 8, 9.

91 Beni Prasad Verma left the SP because he was kept out of the candidate selection process even in his own constituency of Kaiserganj. Verma decided to contest the assembly polls independently, though he remained a SP member in the Lok Sabha.

Kalyan Singh joined the SP briefly in 2007. This angered the Muslims and in 2007, the SP registered a significant drop in Muslim votes.

The BJP released a 'communally sensitive CD during the campaign and later officially withdrew for fear of getting into trouble with the Election Commission'.

V. Ramakrishnan, 'Heat and dust', *Frontline,* 24, 8, April 21, 2007, pp. 4–7; V. Ramakrishnan, 'Stoking the communal fire', *Frontline,* 22, 23, November 5, 2005, pp. 36, 37; Smita Gupta, 'Does law and order matter?, pp. 16–20; *Times of India,* New Delhi edition, September 22, 2008; Ramakrishnan, 'For a winning formula', *Frontline,* pp. 121, 122; V. Ramakrishnan, 'Conquering style', *Frontline,* 24, 8, April 21, 2007, pp. 8, 9.

92 Ramakrishnan, 'For a winning formula', *Frontline,* 24, 6, March 24, 2007, pp. 121, 122; Ramakrishnan, 'The new behenji', *Frontline,* 24, 8, April 21, 2007, pp. 11, 12, 13.

It was widely rumoured that assembly tickets had been sold two years in advance for a sum ranging from '25 lakhs to one crore'.

Shivam Vij, 'The elephant charge' (26.05.07) URL: https://www.india.eu.org/spip.php?article7686 (accessed March 13, 2009).

93 Mayawati remarked that UP was being ruled by a 'corrupt government which had ruined all systems of governance. ... The (SP) government had to go if the state (was) to turn ... (for the better)'. The BSP leader stated that the 'BJP had showed no vision beyond Hindu communalism and the Congress had done nothing for the poor and the downtrodden despite ruling the state and the country for many years'; that the Congress helped the SP government 'survive for three years' (2003–2007) and the 'BJP had a secret understanding with the SP' for the 2007 assembly elections in UP. Mayawati urged the party rank and file to ensure that anti-SP votes are not split, especially among 'insincere parties' like the Congress and the BJP, as well as smaller non-serious political players like V.P. Singh-led Jan Morcha and Beni Prasad Verma-led breakaway Samajwadi Kranti Dal.

Ramakrishnan, 'The new behenji', *Frontline*, 24, 8, April 21, 2007, pp. 11, 12, 13.

94 Election Commission of India URL: http://www.eci.gov.in/Statistical Reports/SE_2007/StatReport AS 2007_UTTAR _PRADESH.pdf (accessed April 21, 2008); Sanjay Kumar, *The Prospects,* pp. 66–69.

95 K. Chandra, *Why Ethnic Parties Succeed?,* p. 236.

96 Gupta and Kumar, *Caste Calculus,* pp. 3393, 3394.

97 Platts, *Digital Dictionary,* pp. 1003, 1037.

98 *Hindustan Times,* New Delhi edition, May 13, 2007; Syed Shahbuddin, 'Muslim and UP assembly elections – 2007: some gains and guidelines for the future', *Muslim India Monthly, Journal of Reference, Research and Documentation,* 24, 276, June 2007, p. 27.

99 *Hindustan Times,* New Delhi edition, May 13, 2007.

Pathak added that the Dalit-Brahmin alliance accounted for 104 of 206 seats the BSP won in the May 2007 assembly elections. He further suggested that the 'social alliance' would work successfully in 90% of constituencies (probably Lok Sabha constituencies) across the country. This was hard to believe considering the complete lack of organizational presence of the BSP in other states. Was Pathak suggesting that the BSP would intensely focus on a handful of Lok Sabha constituencies per state across the country based on the success of this caste equation which would require Mayawati and other influential BSP leaders to merely address from the dais and rally support?

Interview with Brajesh Pathak, BSP MP, Unnao, UP on January 28, 2009.

100 In the run-up to the assembly elections, most of the upper caste mostly Brahmin and Thakur candidates, about 68 in all, dissatisfied with BJP and SP ticket distribution, defected to the BSP which fielded them in the assembly elections.

Interview with Ambeth Rajan, New Delhi, January 21, 2009.

101 In the 2007 assembly elections, the BSP displayed an upward swing of support among the Rajputs and Thakurs (12%), Banias, and Kayasthas (13%), Jats (11%), Yadavs and Ahirs (8%), Kurmis (15%) and Lodhs (19%).

Schwecke, *Rationality in Politics,* p. 20.

102 *The Telegraph*, Kolkata edition, May 18, 2007; 'BSP sweeps UP polls', *NDTV English News,* 11. 05. 07, [5.40 PM-6.04 PM]; *The Hindu,* New Delhi edition, May 14, 2007.

103 *The Hindu*, New Delhi edition, August 15, 2007.

104 *The Hindu,* New Delhi edition, August 15, 2007; *Deccan Herald,* Bangalore edition, May 15, 2007.

105 *The Telegraph*, Kolkata edition, May 13, 2007; V. Ramakrishnan, 'Dalit Power', *Frontline,* 24, 10, May 19, 2007, p. 9.

106 Ranganath Mishra and Anant Kumar Mishra were considered close to chief minister's confidante S.C. Mishra. The Department of Secondary Education was shifted from Thakur Jaivir Singh to Ranganath Mishra. Anant Kumar Mishra held the health and medical portfolio. Mannan, a Muslim BSP MLA, was given the portfolio of Science and Technology, and Chandra Dev Ram Yadav and Ashok Kumar were given small-scale industry and land, development and water resources, respectively. Trusted lieutenant K.K. Gautam became the Finance Minister, while Nandgopal Gupta, a Bania, became the state's trade and tax minister. Badshah Khan, an MLA with a criminal background, became the Labour Minister while Bhagwati Prasad Sagar held the portfolio of employment as Minister of State (Independent). Flood Control and Water Planning was given to Jaivir Singh, which has been taken away from Naseemuddin Siddiqui, the chief campaigner of the BSP in charge of mobilizing the Muslim samaj.

Hindustan Times, New Delhi edition, October 19, 2007.

107 For details on the Mayawati ministry in UP, see 'Kumari Mayawati mantrimandal', URL: http://www.uplegisassembly.gov.in/mayawati ministry 2007.h tm (accessed August 24, 2007).

108 *Hindustan Times,* New Delhi edition, June 23, 2007; *The Hindu,* New Delhi edition, October 9, 2007; *Times of India,* New Delhi edition, October 9, 2007.

109 *The Hindu,* New Delhi edition, May 14, 2007; *The Hindu,* New Delhi edition, February 2, 2008; *The Hindu,* New Delhi edition, October 20, 2008.

110 MBC representation either the government or in the form of being a direct beneficiary of socio-economic programmes was scarce. Out of 54 Cabinet, State and Ministers holding Independent Charge, the MBC representation was a paltry 7 members. Except being the beneficiary of the BSP government's policy of reclaiming illegally occupied land, and that too subject to the availability of landless MBCs (which would otherwise go to the Dalits) and modest benefits accrued through PPP, the MBCs were at a disadvantage in comparison to other castes and communities. Government programmes directed to benefit the OBC were systematically appropriated either by the influential and powerful landowning OBCs, or 'prime MBC beneficiaries' such as Pals. The Pal-Baghel samaj in Bundelkhand region were reaping the political success of supporting the BSP. The ideological commitment towards a more equal bahujan samaj was increasingly being adjusted to the pragmatic necessity of upholding the political value of sarvajan politics.

For more details on the PPP, see *Business Standard*, New Delhi edition, July 11, 2008; *New Positive Reservation Initiatives*, published by the UP Information and Public Relations Department, *Hindustan Times*, New Delhi edition, February 6, 2008.

111 For more details on development projects, see *Business Standard*, New Delhi edition, July 11, 2008; *New Positive Reservation Initiatives*, published by the UP Information and Public Relations Department, *Hindustan Times*, New Delhi edition, February 6, 2008.

112 The flagship Ganga Expressway Project, estimated at a mammoth Rs. 30,000 crore, was given to the diversified Jaypee Group after a bidding process. DLF and GMR had also submitted 'expression of interest' (EoIs) for the project. On May 29, 2009, a Division Bench of the Allahabad High Court restrained the Mayawati government in UP from proceeding with the mammoth Ganga Expressway Project. The Court was responding to a petition filed by a Varanasi-based social organization. The Court had ordered the state government to obtain prior environmental clearance since the 'No-Objection' certificate was obtained not in accordance with the law. Opposition to the project came from farmers facing the prospect of displacement. As against the claim of the BSP government, majority of the land (70%) is 'farm land' and not barren land. 'Sops' such as free residential plots and quotas in jobs were not successful in enlisting the support of the farmers for the project. The Yamuna Expressway Project began to make headway after the legal and administrative hurdles were cleared. The SP government inaugurated it when it came to power in 2012.

The proposed Lalitpur ultra-mega 4,000 MW power project could not make headway due to scarcity of water in the region. It is presently operating to a capacity of 1,320 MW with an additional 600 MW under construction.

Business Standard, New Delhi edition, July 11, 2008; *The Hindu*, New Delhi edition, May 30, 2009; *Hindustan Times*, New Delhi edition, May 30, 2009.*The Hindu,* New Delhi edition, January 15, 2008; 'Special Gifts for all round development of most backward areas of the state and poor families', published by UP Information and Public Relations Department, January 15, 2008; Information and Public Relation Department of Uttar Pradesh, *Outlook,* 48, 36, September 8, 2008, p. 63.

113 Special Economic Assistance Package of Rs. 9,400 crores for development of infrastructure in Poorvanchal and Rs. 4,700 crores for Bundelkhand were demanded from the UPA Government.

'Achievements during 100 days of the Government led by Kumari Mayawati, Chief Minister', published by Information and Public Relations Department, Government of Uttar Pradesh, *Times of India,* New Delhi edition, August 22, 2007; 'Uttar Pradesh seeks a development package of Rs. 80,000 crore' from Government of India, *Outlook,* 67, 39, September 24, 2007, p. 79; 'Achievements during 6 months of the Government led by Kumari Mayawati, Chief Minister, Directorate of Information and Public Relations, Uttar Pradesh, Lucknow', *The Hindu,* New Delhi edition, December 29, 2007; *The Hindu,* New Delhi edition, June 4, 2008; *Hindustan Times*, New Delhi edition, February 8, 2009.

114 *The Hindu,* New Delhi edition, July 27, 2008.

115 'Achievements during 100 days of the Government led by Kumari Mayawati, Chief Minister', published by Information and Public Relations Department, Government of Uttar Pradesh, *Times of India,* New Delhi edition, August 22, 2007; 'Uttar Pradesh seeks a development package of Rs. 80,000 crore' from Government of India, *Outlook,* 67, 39, September 24, 2007, p. 79; 'Achievements during 6 months of the Government led by Kumari Mayawati, Chief Minister', Directorate of Information and Public Relations, Uttar Pradesh, Lucknow, *The Hindu,* New Delhi edition, December 29, 2007; *The Hindu,* New Delhi edition, June 4, 2008; *Hindustan Times*, New Delhi edition, February 8, 2009.

116 SP President Shivpal Yadav underlined details suggesting that 'amounts (had been fixed) for legislators and ministers in the state government (as part of) donation for CM's birthday. 'Contribution was fixed depending upon the ministry and post enjoyed'. For instance, Yadav stated that 'Naseemuddin Siddiqui had to donate Rs. 15 crores, Nakul Dubey, a Brahmin, Rs. 5 crores, Satish Chandra Mishra, a Brahmin, Rs. 20 crores, Ram Achal Rajbhar, a MBC, Rs. 5 crores.'

'BSP MLA admits killing PWD engineer: UP Police' (02.01.09) URL: https://www.news18.com/news/politics (accessed on 16.06.2019) and http://www.hotnewsb4ublogspot.com/2008/12/up_engineer_lynched_by_bsp_mla.html (accessed January 20, 2009).

'Achievements during 100 days of the Government led by Kumari Mayawati, Chief Minister', published by Information and Public Relations Department, Government of Uttar Pradesh, *Times of India*, New Delhi edition, August 22, 2007; 'Uttar Pradesh seeks a development package of Rs. 80,000 crore from Government of India', *Outlook*, 67, 39, September 24, 2007, p. 79; 'Achievements during 6 months of the Government led by Kumari Mayawati, Chief Minister', Directorate of Information and Public Relations, Uttar Pradesh, Lucknow.

117 *The Hindu,* New Delhi edition, 16.01.09.

118 This was part of BSPs effort to ensure that the Central government accepted a scheme of Rs. 1015.70 crore for the development of 21 'Muslim' minority-dominated districts – Bijnore, Bulandshahr, Badaun, Barabanki, Bareilly, Baghpat, Bahraich, Balarampur, Ghaziabad, Jyotiba Phule Nagar, Kheri, Lucknow, Moradabad, Muzaffarnagar, Meerut, Pilibhit, Rampur, Shahjahanpur, Shravasti, Siddharthnagar and Saharanpur.

Munquad Ali, a former BSP Rajya Sabha MP, said that Muslims and Brahmins were represented equally, about 20–22% in government and administration, though he did not elucidate on the ministerial portfolios allocated to the community. Ali said that the party was not wary of SP which still has an impressive base of Muslim support. He said that in the 2009 Lok Sabha election in UP, Muslim support would register a 'phenomenal increase', though he did not quote figures. He said there were good reasons for increased Muslim representation in the party. First, the image of SP in the eyes of the Muslims with Kalyan Singh, the former BJP OBC leader joining the party; and second, Varun Gandhi's hate speech against Muslims in Pilibhit, UP. Programmatic goals for the Muslims had been modest and the BSP continued to mobilize the 'samaj' on the planks of 'security, representation and minority status'.

Interview with Munquad Ali, BSP Rajya Sabha member, Member of State Minorities Commission, UP and Director, Minority Finance Commission, Lucknow, UP, March 6, 2009. At present he is the State President of BSP, Uttar Pradesh.

The Hindu, New Delhi edition, October 14, 2008; 'Waqf', Platts, *Digital Dictionary*, p. 982.

119 *Hindustan Times*, New Delhi edition, February 24, 2009; *The Hindu*, New Delhi edition, February 23, 2009.

120 On the occasion of Kanshiram's second death anniversary, the BSP government inaugurated a number of 'awards' – Kanshiram International Sports Award, Kanshiram Award for Social Change, Kanshiram State Handloom Award, etc.

Hindustan Times, New Delhi edition, October 9, 2008.

The Hindu, New Delhi edition, October 10, 2008; *Hindustan Times*, New Delhi edition, October 9, 2008.

121 Nazul means a land that is vested with public authority for development purpose as per the stipulations of authority.

'Basic concept of Nazul' (16.02.2014) URL: https://www. lawweb.in/2014/02/basic-concept-of-nazul-land.htm (accessed January 18, 2018).

122 *Hindustan Times*, New Delhi edition, February 24, 2009; *The Hindu*, New Delhi edition, February 23, 2009.

123 More specific reason for an improved performance of the Congress in 2009 elections was the strategic shift in the vote base of the SP. The SP's pre-election pact with Kalyan Singh, the former BJP leader, was struck with the hope of achieving a Yadav-Muslim-OBC (Lodha votes) political formation in the state. However, the 'Kalyan impact' on the Muslim electorate split the Muslim vote towards the Congress, which received 25% and the BSP 18%, with virtually no change in vote share since 2007 and to Muslim political parties like the Ulema Council and the Peace Party visible in Eastern UP. The SP's Muslim base was reduced to 30% down from 47% in 2007 assembly elections. Unsure of the 'benefits' that would accrue through sarvajan politics and having found a 'surprising' political alternative in the Congress Party, large sections of the upper caste such as Brahmins (31%), Rajputs (16%) and other upper castes (31%) voted for the party. Congress also gained support among Kurmis (24%) and Koeris. Non-Jatav support increased to 16% from a mere 5% in 2007.

The BSP won in Saharanpur (from SP), Kairana (from RLD) and Muzaffarnagar among other seats in these two regions. But in central UP, eastern UP and Bundelkhand, the party suffered several defeats. The BSP won Bhadohi, Sitapur, Misrikh, Phulpur, Lalganj, Ambedkar Nagar, Basti, Sant Kabir Nagar, Ghosi, Salempur, Jaunpur, etc. in central and eastern UP. BSPs electoral performance demonstrates the inability of the Party to win constituencies in 'swathes', which would be indicative of a pattern of electoral victories for the Party. On the other hand, the Congress Party's victories were all geographically linked. The party won in 'clusters', in eastern UP, such as Shravasti, Bahraich (R), Gonda, Faizabad and Barabanki (R). Further, it also won in Kushinagar, Maharajganj and Domariaganj, Kheri, Dhaurahra and Bareilly; and in Pratapgarh, Sultanpur, Amethi, Rae Bareli, Unnao, Kanpur and Akbarpur across western, central and eastern UP. The Congress also won in Jhansi in the Bundelkhand region. The SP established its hold over a cluster of seats from Kannauj, Mainpuri, Etawah, Firozabad, Etah, in the so-called Yadav-Lodha belt in central UP. The SP did well in the Bundelkhand region winning two neighbouring reserved constituencies of Jalaun and Banda. In western UP, the SP won from Badaun and Shahjahanpur. In this election, one notable feature was also the performance of the SP in reserved constituencies. The Party won 10 reserved seats out of a total of 17 seats. In the reserved seats, the SP was a clear favourite. For instance, the Party won in Bulandshahr, Hathras, Mohanlalganj, Etawah, Jalaun, Kaushambi, Bahraich, Machchlishahr as well as all the reserved seats of Mirzapur, Chandrauli and Robertganj in the naxalite-affected region on the southern side of neighbouring central-eastern UP. Perhaps, the probable reason for the victories could be an OBC consolidation for the SP. This is also the reason as to why Mulayam Singh Yadav allied with Kalyan Singh, though at the cost of Muslim votes for the party. The stunning reverse of the BSP in the reserved constituencies can be gauged from an example: In Barabanki (R), a crucial seat, the BSP lost. 'Here it was apparent that at the ground level everything was not perfect for the party. Congress candidate P.L. Punia, a Jatav by caste, defeated BSP's Kamla Prasad Rawat, from the Pasi caste. The BSP's calculation was that Pasis would vote for the Pasi (Rawat) and Jatav's would punish behenji's enemy (the Congress)'. 'The BSP got only Dalit votes on reserved seats and other castes tactically voted to defeat it'. The reason, while Dalits vote for all BSP candidates, other castes only vote for BSP candidates belonging to their caste.

The Hindu, New Delhi edition, May 13, May 17, May 19, May 20, May 21, May 23, May 24, 2009; *The Telegraph*, Kolkata edition, May 24, 2009; *Deccan Chronicle,* Hyderabad edition, May 4, 2009; *Central Chronicle*, Madhya Pradesh edition, May 14, 2009; *Hindustan Times*, New Delhi edition, May 17, May 20, May 22, 2009; *Business Standard*, New Delhi edition, May 18, 2009; Shivam Vij, 'UP Dalits remind Mayawati: democracy is beautiful' (21.05.09) URL: http//www.kafila.online/2009/05/21/ups-dalits-remind-mayawati-democracy-is-a-beautiful-thing (accessed June 18, 2009); *Hindustan Times*, New Delhi edition, June 15, 2009; *Congress Election Manifesto* 2009, p. 8; *The Hindu*, New Delhi edition, May 26, 2009; *The Hindu,* New Delhi edition, June 5, 2009.

124 The Party got 27% of the vote in UP but elsewhere it ranged between 0.49% (Kerala) and 7.57% (Punjab). The national vote share of the party stood at 6.22%'.

Hindustan Times, New Delhi edition, June 15, 2009; *The Hindu*, New Delhi edition, May 26, 2009; *The Hindu*, New Delhi edition, June 5, 2009.

125 Harish Wankhede, 'Dalit symbolism and the democratization of secular spaces', *Mainstream*, Vol. XLVIII, No. 12, March 13, 2010, pp. 29–32.

126 In Agra (reserved) Lok Sabha constituency, a traditional stronghold of the Party Dalit turnout was consistently less than 30% across polling booths.

Hindustan Times, New Delhi edition, June 15, 2009; *The Hindu*, New Delhi edition, May 26, 2009; *The Hindu,* New Delhi edition, June 5, 2009.

127 A Dalit secretary is a necessity since the BSP is primarily identified with a 'Dalit-based party' seeking to expand to include other communities and caste groups 'on board'.

Hindustan Times, New Delhi edition, May 25, 2009; Wankhede, *Dalit Symbolism*, pp.29–32.

128 Yogendra Yadav (27.02.12), 'The more they (don't) remain the same'. URL: http://www.outlookindia.com (accessed December 16, 2014).

129 'Mayawati government to draft BPL list afresh' (08.10.07) URL: http://www.articles.economictimes-indiatimes.com/2007 (accessed June 6, 2015).

130 Atiq Khan (16.03.10), 'Mayawati sidelines Satish Chandra Mishra'. URL: http://www. the hindu.com/todays-paper (accessed on November 30., 2014).

131 Atiq Khan, 'Mayawati sidelines Satish Chandra Mishra' (accessed November 30, 2014).

132 Sharat Pradhan (04.07.09), 'Mayawati's fad for private statues puts her in tight spot'. URL: http//www. Rediff.com/news/report (accessed September 6, 2015).

133 Pradhan, 'Mayawati's fad for private statues puts her in tight spot'. URL: http//www. Rediff.com/news/report (accessed September 6, 2015).

134 'Education officer held in TET scam' (09.02.12) URL: http://www.hindustantimes.com/Lucknow/education (accessed December 04, 2015).

135 Heath and Kumar, *Why Did the Dalits Desert the BSP*, p. 46. Juned Shaikh, 'Who needs identity? Dalit studies and the politics of recognition', *India Review*, 11,3, August 2012, pp. 205, 206.

136 Heath and Kumar, *Why Did the Dalits Desert the BSP*, p. 46. Juned Shaikh, *Who Needs Identity?* pp. 205, 206.

137 'Mayawati government indifferent to Bundelkhand's miseries: Centre' (14.06.11). URL: http://www.timesofindia.indiatimes.com (accessed May 24, 2015).

138 'Five FIR against NREGA misuse during Maya's reign' (22.02.14) URL: http://www.business-standard.com/article/economy (accessed December 28, 2015).

139 Yogendra Yadav, 'The more they (don't) remain the same' (accessed December 16, 2014).

140 Sharat Pradhan (02.05.12), '200 personnel guard her, but Maya still fears for life' URL: http://www.rediff.com/news/report/(accessed December 28, 2015).

141 Shivam Vij (21.09.2009) 'UP's Dalits remind Mayawati: Democracy is a beautiful thing' URL:https://kafila.online/2009/05/21/ups-dalits-remind-mayawati-democracy-is-a-beautiful-thing (accessed on August 8, 2014); "Solve people's problems or get punished: Mayawati" (20.01.13). URL: http://www.business-standard.com/article/economy-policy (accessed April 5, 2017); S.R. Darapuri (25.03.12), 'Why Dalits have slammed Mayawati's sarvajan rule'. URL: http://www.countercurrents.org (accessed November 16, 2015); Shivam Vij (06.03.12), 'Why Mayawati's defeat is the BSP's victory'. URL: http://www.rediff.com/news/column (accessed November 16, 2015); Akash Vashishtha (08.03.12), 'Samajwadi Party to review status of projects undertaken by Mayawati government in UP'. URL: http://www.indiatoday.in/story/(accessed August 24, 2015); Oliver Heath and Sanjay Kumar, 'Why did the Dalits desert the Bahujan Samaj Party in Uttar Pradesh?', *Economic and Political Weekly*, 47, 28, July 14, 2012, pp. 44, 45.

142 Heath and Kumar, *Why did the Dalits desert the BSP?* p. 44.

143 Heath and Kumar, *Why did the Dalits desert the BSP*, p. 46; Shaikh, *Who Needs Identity?* pp. 205, 206.

144 Heath and Kumar, *Why did the Dalits desert the BSP*, p. 43; Sudha Pai, Understanding the defeat of the BSP in Uttar Pradesh: National Elections 2014 studies in Indian politics, *Studies in Indian Politics,* 2, 2, 2014, pp.161, 162.

145 Mahamaya Garib Arthik Madad Yojana (Mahamaya Economic Assistance for the Poor Plan), Savitri Bai Phule Balika Shiksha Yojana (Savitri Bai Young Girl Education Plan), Mahamaya Garib Balika Aashirwad Yojana (Mahamaya Poor Girl Blessing Plan), Mahamaya Sarvajan Awaas Yojana (Mahamaya Public Housing Plan), Kanshiram Awaas Yojana (Kanshiram Housing Plan), etc.

Heath and Kumar, *Why did the Dalits desert the BSP,* p. 42; Juned Shaikh, *Who Needs Identity?* pp. 205, 206.

146 Heath and Kumar, *Why did the Dalits desert the BSP,* p. 42; Pai, *Understanding the Defeat of the BSP*, pp.163–64,166; Tariq Thachil, *Elite Parties, Poor Voters: Social Services Wins Votes in India*, UK: Cambridge University Press, pp. 184, 203.

147 Heath and Kumar, *Why did the Dalits desert the BSP*, pp. 44–46; Juned Shaikh, *Who Needs Identity,* pp. 205, 206.

148 Pai, *Understanding the Defeat of the BSP*, pp. 162.

149 Ramseshan, R. 'Cadre and caste do the trick' (17.05.2014) URL: http://www.telegraphindia.com/india/cadre-and-caste-do-the-trick/cid/183006 (accessed December 29, 2019).

150 Narayan, B, 'The secret of BJP's success in Uttar Pradesh: winning over Dalits and OBC's and a dose of Hindutva' (23.05.2019) DNA India URL: https://www.dnaindia.com/analysis/column-the-secret-of-bjp-s-success-in-uttar-pradesh-winning-over-dalits-and-obcs-and-a-dose-of-hindutva-1990583 (accessed November 02, 2019).

151 Gupta, D (22.06.2019), 'Caste and electoral outcomes: misreading hierarchy and the illusion of numbers', *Economic and Political Weekly*, 54, 25, pp. 27.

152 Narayan, B, 'The secret of BJP's success in Uttar Pradesh: winning over Dalits and OBCs and a dose of Hindutva' (23.05.2019) DNA India URL: https://www.dnaindia.com/analysis/column-the-secret-of-bjp-s-success-in-uttar-pradesh

-winning-over-dalits-and-obcs-and-a-dose-of-hindutva-1990583 (accessed November 2, 2019).

153 Pai, *Understanding the Defeat of the BSP*, pp.162.

154 Pai, *Understanding the Defeat of BSP*, p. 162.

155 Heath and Kumar, *Why did the Dalits desert the BSP*, p. 42; Pai, Understanding the Defeat of BSP, pp. 163–64, 166; Ghatak, M, 'Demonetization was bad economics but as an act of vigilantism it served Modi politically' (13.07.2017) The Wire, URL: https://thewire.in/politics/demonetization-bad-economics-clever-politics-modi-116124 (accessed September 18, 2017).

156 Pai, *Understanding the Defeat of BSP*, p. 161.

157 Pai, *Understanding the Defeat of BSP*, p. 162.

158 Pai, *Understanding the Defeat of BSP*, pp. 163, 164,166.

159 'Mayawati dissolves all committees of BSP' (20.05.14) URL: http://www.hindustantimes.com/elections2014/election-beat/mayawati-dissolves-all-committees-of-bsp/article1–1221175.aspx (accessed May 29, 2014).

Biswajit Banerjee (16.05.14), 'Modi sweeps UP, BSP wiped out'. URL: http://www.niticentral.com/2014/05/16/modi-wave-wipes-out-bsp-crushes-sp-224132.html (accessed May 20, 2014).

Mehernaz Patel (17.05.14), 'Why despite her loss Mayawati thinks Dalits are unaffected by Narendra Modi wave'. URL: http://www.dnaindia.com/india/report-why-despite-her-loss-mayawati-still-thinks-dalits-are-unaffected-by-narendra-modi-wave-1989266 (accessed May 20, 2014).

Biswajit Banerjee (20.05.14), '2014 mandate: flimsy excuses will not help SP, BSP'. URL: http://www.niticentral.com/2014/05/20/2014-mandate-flimsy-excuses-will-not-help-sp-bsp-225182.html (accessed May 28, 2014).

'Election results: only statues proclaim Mayawati not UP voters'. (17.05.14) URL: http://timesofindia.indiatimes.com/home/lok-sabha-elections-2014/news/Election-Results-Only-statues-proclaim-Maya-not-UP-voters/articleshow/35230961.cms (accessed May 20, 2014).

Radhika Ramaseshan (17.05.14), 'Cadre and caste do the trick'. URL: http://www.telegraphindia.com/1140517/jsp/nation/story_18352434.jsp#.U3tydaO_nIU (accessed May 20, 2014).

Kashif-ul-Huda (18.05.14) 'Modi wave nullified anti-BJP Muslim voting in UP'. URL: http://twocircles.net/2014may18/modi_wave_nullified_antibjp_muslim_voting.html#.U3tzmaO_nIU (accessed May 20, 2014).

'Mayawati faces grim reality as cadres rush to join BJP' (20.05.14). URL: http://economictimes.indiatimes.com/news/politics-and-nation/mayawati-faces-grim-reality-as-cadres-rush-to-join-bjp/articleshow/35354753.cms (accessed May 25, 2014).

Piyush Srivastava (24.02.14), 'BJP castes its net in UP: how party is using Modi's background to attract OBC votes while still seeking Brahmin blessings', URL http://www.dailymail.co.uk/indiahome/indianews/article-2566926/BJP-castes-net-UP-How-party-using-Modis-background-attract-OBC-votes-seeking-Brahmin-blessings.html (accessed May 20, 2014).

160 Shakil, M., 'Why the Akhilesh-Rahul alliance lacks the punch of Nitish-Laloo combo' (13.02.2017) URL:https//www.news18.com/news/politics/why-the-akhilesh-rahul-alliance-lacks-the-punch-of-nitish-laloo-combo-1348624.html (accessed June 2, 2017).

161 Devendra Kumar (17.03.17) 'Four-pronged strategy behind BJPs Uttar Pradesh election victory' URL: www.livemint.com/Opinion (accessed June 2, 2017).

162 Narayan, B., 'Assembly elections 2017: how the BJP won and the SP, BSP lost the Dalit vote in UP.' URL: www.hindustantimes.com/assembly-elections-2017-how-the-bjp-won-and-the-sp-bsp-lost-the-dalit-vote--in-up/story-rPZmjerz0

e5figRRuKUdTP.html (accessed May 31, 2017); Kumar, S., 'BJP has edge in capturing floating non-Yadav OBC vote in UP' (12.01.2017). URL: www.newsindiaexpress.com/nation/2017/jan/12/bjp-has-edge-in-capturing-floating-non-yadav-obc-vote-in-up-1558780.html (accessed May 30, 2017).

163 Badri Narayan (12.03.17) 'Assembly elections 2017: how the BJP won and the SP, BSP lost the Dalit vote in UP' URL: www.hindustantimes.com/assembly-elections (accessed on 31.05.2017); Sajjan Kumar (21.01.17), 'BJP has edge in capturing floating non-Yadav OBC vote in UP' URL: www.newindianexpress.com/nation/2017/jan/12 (accessed May 30, 2017).

164 Kumar, U., 'UP election results: how Modi's BJP won the Dalit vote, destroyed Mayawati's BSP' (12.03.2017) URL: www.hindustantimes.com/assembly-elections/-results-how-modi-s-bjp-won-the-dalit-vote-destroyed-mayawati-s-bsp/story-U5phXLvaevGtQnd4r9m51L.html (accessed May 30, 2017).

165 Jha, S, 'UP elections 2017: Mayawati's Dalit vote base slipping away fast' (14.03.2017) *Hindustan Times* URL: http://www.hindustan.com/assembly-elections/up-elections-2017-mayawati-s-dalit-vote-base-is-slipping-away-fast/story-BmjVMSJNWEdQagefXIIBUBO.HTML (accessed June 2, 2017); Pai, *Understanding the Defeat of BSP*, pp.163, 164; Heath and Kumar, *Why Did the Dalits Desert the BSP*, p. 42; Ghatak, M, 'Demonetization was bad economics but as an act of vigilantism it served Modi politically' (13.07.2017), The Wire, URL: https://thewire.in/politics/demonetization-bad-economics-clever-politics-modi-116124 (accessed September 18, 2017); Thachil, *Elite Parties, Poor Voters,* pp. 184, 203.

166 Maitreesh Ghatak (13.03.17) 'Demonetization was bad economics but as an act of vigilantism it served Modi politically' URL: https://thewire.in/116124 (accessed June 3, 2017); Sreemoy Talukdar, UP Assembly Elections 2017 (accessed June 3, 2017); Ravish Tiwari (16.03.17) 'Results backlash against SP, BSPs identity politics' URL: https://www.pressreader.com/india/economic-times/(accessed June 1, 2017); Marya Shakil (13.02.17) 'Why the Akhilesh-Rahul alliance lacks the punch of Nitish-Lalu combo' URL: www.news18.com/news/politics (accessed June 2, 2017).

167 Jha, S, 'UP elections 2017: Mayawati's Dalit vote base slipping away fast' (14.03.2017) *Hindustan Times*. URL: http://www.hindustan.com/assembly-elections/up-elections-2017-mayawati-s-dalit-vote-base-is-slipping-away-fast/story-BmjVMSJNWEdQagefXIIBUBO.HTML (accessed June 2, 2017).

168 Shivam Vij (14.01.19) 'The BSP-SP alliance in UP is rare, formidable and perfect' URL: https://www.theprint.in/opinion/(accessed January 20, 2019).

169 Vij, SP-BSP alliance in UP (accessed January 20, 2019).

170 Aman Sharma (07.01.19) 'Congress staying out of SP-BSP alliance in UP a plus for all three' URL: https://www.economictimes.indiatimes.com (accessed January 22, 2019).

171 'SP-BSP alliance leaves 2019 prospects bleak for Congress in Uttar Pradesh: division of voters may deal blow to BJP' (14.01.19), URL: Firstpost, https://www.first-post.com/politics (accessed January 22, 2019).

172 Vij, SP-BSP alliance in UP, https://www.theprint.in/opinion (accessed January 20, 2019).

173 Mukhopadhyay, SP-BSP alliance in UP reduces options for BJP (accessed January 24, 2019).

174 Roshan Kishore, SP-BSP alliance dash BJP 2019 hopes (accessed January 23, 2019); Vij, SP-BSP alliance in UP (accessed January 20, 2019).

175 Virendra Singh Rawat (04.06.19), 'SP-BSP honeymoon over as Mayawati hints at dumping 'Mahagathbandhan' URL: https://www.business-standard.com/article/politics (accessed June 4, 2019).

176 Sanghamitra (25.05.19), 'The failure of Mahagathbandhan in UP: have voters finally discarded caste-based politics' URL: https://www.opindia.com/2019/05 (accessed May 29, 2019); BSP-SP alliance: united they fall in UP' (24.05.2019), URL: https//www.business-standard.com/article/pti-stories (accessed May 29, 2019); 'BSP biggest gainer among Mahagathbandhan constituents in UP' (24.01.19), URL: https//economictimes.indiatimes.com/news/elections/lok-sabha/uttar-pradesh (accessed January 29, 2019).
177 BSP-SP alliance: united they fall in UP (accessed on 29.05.2019); Omar Rashid, Internal contradictions (accessed May 29, 2019).
178 BSP-SP alliance, united they fall in UP (accessed May 29, 2019); Mirza Asmer Beg, Shashikant Pandey, Sudhir Kumar (26.05.19) 'Post-poll survey: why Uttar Pradesh's Mahagathbandhan failed?' URL: https://www.thehindu.com/elections/lok-sabha-2019/post-poll-survey (accessed May 29, 2019); Aman Sharma (27.05.19) 'Delayed tie-up with BSP hurt us: SP MPs' URL: https://economictimes.indiatimes.com/politics-and-nation/(accessed May 29, 2019),
179 Omar Rashid, Internal contradictions (accessed May 29, 2019).
180 Aman Sharma, Delayed tie-up with BSP (accessed May 29, 2019).
181 Mirza Asmer Beg et al., Why Uttar Pradesh's Mahagathbandhan failed? (accessed May 29, 2019).
182 Farhad Hasin (27.05.19), 'Explained: the BJP's stunning performance in Uttar Pradesh' URL: https://thewirein/politics/explained-thebjps-stunning-performance-in-uttar-pradesh (accessed May 31, 2019).
183 Omar Rashid, Internal contradictions (accessed May 29, 2019).
184 Aman Sharma, Delayed tie-up with BSP (accessed May 29, 2019).
185 Omar Rashid, Internal contradictions (accessed May 29, 2019).
186 Ajaz Ashraf, UP's Mahagathbandhan (accessed May 30,2019).
187 Similar to the Hukum Singh Committee Report of 2001 under the then Chief Minister of Uttar Pradesh Rajnath Singh, the Raghavendra Kumar Report of 2018 whose selective portions were leaked to the press in the months leading to the election, argued the case for a sub-categorization of benefits of reservation across three broad categories – backward, more backward and most backward. Following the Hukum Singh Committee Report which was not implemented, the Kumar Report on similar lines seeks end to disproportionate share of reservation benefits among Yadavs, Jatavs and a few other landholding castes such as Jats and Kurmis in the backward class category. While the administrative measures to 'equally spread' the benefits of reservation can be politically surmised as an effort to isolate Yadavs and Jatavs in the political realm, a lesser share of state resources for the Jats and Kurmis and Sonars could be politically unviable for the BJP in the state. It could lead to a consolidation of landholding caste groups, at least the non-Yadav and on its own become a constituency opposing the BJP. The Report finding if recommended and implemented could rupture the wide social (landholder) base of the party. On the other hand, there would be expectation among non-Jatav lower backward castes such as Kashyaps, Nishads, Rajbhars, etc. to make the Report public so that such benefits and access to government resources are available. The matter becomes complicated if one considers the Report findings in the backdrop of the Modi government introducing 10% reservation for Economically Weaker Section at an all-India level among social groups (primarily upper castes) outside the reservation pool.
Rawat, SP-BSP honeymoon (accessed June 4, 2019).
Ajaz Ashraf, UP's Mahagathbandhan (accessed May 30, 2019).
Omar Rashid, Internal contradictions (accessed May 29, .2019).
188 Mirza Asmer Beg, et. al. Post-Poll Survey (accessed May 29, 2019).

189 A.K. Verma et al. A saffron sweep (accessed May 29, 2019).

190 Rashid, O., 'Internal contradictions' (accessed May 29, 2019); Mirza Asmer Beg, et al. Post-poll survey (accessed May 29, 2019); Sharma, A., 'Congress staying out of SP-BSP alliance in UP a plus for all three' (07.01.2019) *Economic Times*. URL: https://www. economictimes.indiatimes.com/news/politics-and-nation/congress-staying-out-of-sp-bsp-alliance-in-up-a-plus-for-all-three/articleshow/67414009.cms?from=mdr (accessed January 22, 2019); Vij, S., 'The SP-BSP alliance in UP is rare, formidable and perfect' (2019), The Print. URL:https://www.theprint.in/opinion/the-sp-bsp-alliance-in-up-is-rare-formidable-and-perfect/177657/ (accessed January 20, 2019); Tiwari, A, 'How BJP trumped SP-BSP with Congress help in Uttar Pradesh' (26.05.2019) Bloomberg Quint, URL: https://www.bloombergquint.com/elections/how-bjp-trumped-sp-bsp-with-congress-help-in-uttar-pradesh (accessed February 9, 2020).

191 Tewari, R, 'Explained: BSP minus Samajwadi Party, between the lines' (05.06.2019), *The Indian Express*, URL: https://www.indianexpress.com/article/explained/explained-bsp-minus-sp-between-the-lines-5765433/(accessed August 8, 2019); Singh, D.K. and Samyak Pandey, 'Why Akhilesh Yadav and SP have reason to be "cheated" by Mayawati and her BSP' (29.05.2019), The Print. URL: https://theprint.in/politics/why-akhilesh-yadav-sp-have-reason-to-feel cheated-by-mayawati-her-bsp/242319 (accessed June 5, 2019); Lalchandani, N, 'Split with SP final, will fight polls on our own now: Mayawati' (25.06.2019) *Times of India*. URL: https://timesofindia.com/india/split-with-sp-final-will-fight-polls-on-our-own-now-mayawati/articleshow/69935225.cms (accessed June 27, 2019); Bhatt, V, 'Woo Muslims, fight for No. 2 spot: what three poll defeats, alliance failure taught Mayawati' (26.06.2019), News18 URL: https://www.news18.com/news/opinion/woo-muslims-fight-for-no-2-spot-what-three-poll-defeats-alliance-failure-taught-mayawati-2204295.html (accessed June 27, 2019).

Conclusions

How do we assess three decades of Bahujan Samaj Party's 'ethnic politics' in an altered socio-political landscape in Uttar Pradesh? The past decade has witnessed ideological confusion coinciding with significant electoral losses for the BSP and left it desperate to search for reasons that have rendered the party incapable of retrieving, re-asserting and appealing to vast segments of the subaltern class. Symptomatic of BSP's political drift has been the phenomenal growth of a 'new' cultural-nationalistic politics ushered in by the BJP in the aftermath of a resounding 2014 Lok Sabha electoral victory in Uttar Pradesh.

Two defining factors are identifiable in BSP's praxis of social justice: one, the pre-eminence of an evolving electoral strategy to further the prospects of a revised Dalit politics, the former considered as the only political course to empower the poor; two, the 1990s post-Mandal democratic upsurge among underprivileged social groups that provided the BSP the political and concomitantly the institutional space to leverage Dalit-Bahujan goals. It must be considered that BSP's focus on firming up electoral politics by building ethnic coalitions to ensure that people spontaneously accrete along hierarchically proximate castes is not a political outcome of the consequent political stabilization of the democratic upsurge of participation that occurred post-impact Mandal politics on the Indian polity and political parties. Ethnic caste models for electoral politics were in evidence in the late 1980s woven around a singular political goal to compete in elections and increase vote share. In the 1990s, as an alliance partner in a ruling coalition government with the BJP on three separate occasions and as a single-party majority government in power in 2007, pursuance of a heightened political value attached to expedient ethnic politics expectedly deepened political representation of disenfranchised social groups in a caste-driven polity in Uttar Pradesh but reflected a structural shortcoming of the party as socio-political aspirations of the subaltern groups became a political casualty within the party.[1] In consideration of these developments, plausible answers to two interrelated questions that feature BSP's 'party-directed' bahujan struggle is required. First, to question the party's ideological presumptions that seek to centre and problematize Dalit-Bahujan exploitative conditions in society, and secondly, to introspect the ambiguous relationship between BSP's anti-caste ideology and the ethno-electoral mobilization which restricted democratic possibilities to create viable action frameworks to secure livelihood entitlements for marginalized social groups.

BSP and Group Identity: Revising Politics?

The BSP has effected a compromise, that is, of shifting the central focus of a critical evaluation with untouchability that is symptomatic of an iniquitous exploitative lifeworld, by demonstrating no political urgency to cast Dalit subjectivity – the reinvention of the 'self' as a rebel' and the possibility of the emergence of a new/autonomous politics of social protest – within the context of a political struggle based upon 'discrimination' and 'resistance'.[2] In the course of its unfolding ideological and organizing components attuned to a Dalit-Bahujan-Sarvajan politics, the BSP has bypassed the critical relationship that must exist between social complexities of marginalization and the political path addressing a representative community experience for a new Dalit public sphere. In a manner it has transformed the socio-historical significance of an anti-untouchability struggle into electoral politics. The BSP's 'political mantra' is to selectively engage with social democracy and fraternal ideas of Ambedkar, which has provided a vantage point to the party to appear as an advocate of an 'uncompromising dedication to an equality-based society' for the subaltern classes.[3]

With the destruction of the Brahminic-savarṇa political democracy being the composite design of BSP's abrasive ideologized politics and not Dalit subjectivity, the actualization of the 'social emancipatory' project follows the familiar trope as it considers the Dalits and low-caste bahujans as 'multiple caste groups'[4] that must meaningfully crystallize within BSP's ideological-cum-electoral scheme for purposive action. Based on this assumption, the BSP political leadership has focussed on electoral politics to realize a range of interrelated goals – individual and collective – and treating other possible forms of popular democratic politics or non-electoral public/political activity as irrelevant to its goal of a samta-mulak samaj.[5] The BSP states that the potential towards 'organized (political) mobilization' solely for multiple electoral projects would empower the socially oppressed to restructure the sociopolitical order by ensuring that bahujans would 'reign'.[6] Therefore, the centre point of the struggle is 'electoral' and is focussed on changing the way the poor vote: the transformation of what routinely appears as a purported act of rebellion at the polling booth, which is translated into an ineffectual vote and 'which compound(s) feelings of inferiority by underlining the material and social subordination of the SC, and their political impotence.'[7] The BSP has claimed that since the time of its inception in the mid-1980s, the party turned elections into a 'political battleground' to leverage the goal of 'social emancipation'. This was enabled through the conversion of the 'vote of the poor' into a valuable political capital which led to increased vote share of the bahujan public, leading to the electoral victories of party candidates as state lawmakers.

Public Good as Symbolic Capital and 'Invincibility' of Political Leader

The second feature of the BSP's ethno-caste politics is that to endure a unidimensional focus on electoral politics, the party constantly needs to ensure that an 'instrumentality of an (leader-people) organic bond' must exist, which is not exposed to the risk of factionalism, to resist and overthrow the BSO. It is at this juncture that the enduring 'faith in the leader's sincerity and ability' to fulfil the aspirations for material goals of social empowerment – the disbursal of public assets and resources to the Dalit-Bahujan masses as a means to 'acquire dignity' in lifeworld – assumes political importance within the party. Kanshiram and Mayawati showcased 'their power that can be unleashed, a leader who cares, or even, pretends to care for (those), who (have been) ignored'.[8]

Third, it was of critical importance and a central principle of the party that marginalized and exploited bahujan caste groups were to be ideologically inculcated to an expansive Dalit-Bahujan iconography, to ostensibly overturn the hegemony of an iniquitous and upper-caste political sphere in place of public-political space. The political agenda of constructing a living socio-cultural history of the poor castes was indicative of engaging in building a cultural-symbolic capital necessary to convert emotional sensibilities into a faithful voting public and centrepiece Mayawati's 'transformative' leadership. Yet, the bahujan agenda was conceived differently. As Chief Minister of Uttar Pradesh, Mayawati initiated a 'culture of defiance',[9] anchoring Dalit pride not through a more difficult engagement with unifying politically the syncretic and diverse jati-purana cultural-language histories of the distinct bahujan caste groups to formulate a recognizable 'subaltern' political forum but constructing new structures of obeisance that brought a strong 'class demarcation' between the leader and the bahujan people, of 'command' and 'submission', to 'propel' a bahujan agenda on behalf of the 'people'. Cultural symbolism was typified by the iconography of parks, plazas, monuments, roads, buildings and memorial centres which would lend charisma to the 'persona' of the Dalit 'beti' (daughter) who would be or is 'on the throne in Lucknow'. Much of the anti-caste bahujan struggle of the BSP has been about Mayawati's apparent self-aggrandizement of 'supremeness' in the eyes of her political supporters, the accumulation of wealth and personal fortune, that are still considered by a significant section of the core Jatav caste as proud achievements of a Dalit political leader who possesses more wealth than her '(upper)-caste (political) adversaries', thereby conjoining her personal 'material' accomplishments as bahujan seva (service).[10] Besides that, a political hagiography has created the 'Mayawati aura' that is reverential. Special 'public events', such as birthday 'community gathering', observed with greater intensity in the immediate years leading to and during BSP's five-year term in the state, periodically recaptured the emotive sensibilities of the Dalit masses by reinforcing 'behenji's' organic political solidarity with the bahujan people. Thus, the personification of 'peoples' representative power as a matter of subjective consciousness, and not based on principles of political democracy, would leverage social dignity and emotional psychological and physical security to the 'constituency of the poor', to be realized by increased '(assembly and Parliamentary) seats' to prevail upon an unresponsive and 'caste-biased' state administration machinery. In sum, Mayawati has compiled symbolic capital, both public and personal, upon a well-crafted narrative of honour, prestige and recognition, in the context of running for political office.

However, to what extent has the effectiveness of Dalit-Bahujan empowerment politics failed even though under successive coalition governments Mayawati earmarked policies and programmes that were expected to address 'security and material welfare' of the disenfranchised groups? Political parties in India have generally not been keen to act as purveyors of structural change in society but nevertheless have advocated political agendas on social welfare policies to serve their voting constituency. Such populist pronouncements are often unrealizable poll promises made during elections and yet do initiate state-driven policy of public delivery whatever may be their desired social outcomes. In the period between 1995 and 2003, which occasioned the emergence of the BSP-BJP ruling coalition in Uttar Pradesh – leading to Mayawati becoming a 'three-time CM' – the access to public assets and services in the mould of 'Dalit empowerment policies' were conceptualized for the poor by the party. Yet, transcending ideological symbolic space of politics to the fulfilment of programmatic goals did not materialize. Mayawati's symbolic power, which coincided with 'social (empowerment) projects' 'inaugurated with fanfare' amassed resources but selectively disbursed goods and services, affected either by a defect in attending to a beneficiary target or by a debatable political will. To conscious 'Dalit-Bahujan subjects', the act of political floundering became overbearing, as it bypassed the materiality of conditions perceived as the ideological subject that needed to be addressed. Thus, prospects of material gains in terms of delivering promised 'development goals' faded.

However, the apparent political worth of patronage-driven social programmes helped Mayawati acquire a political stature as she was able to personalize her identification with the broader-level crusade against inequality and exploitation. This was noticeable during Mayawati's coalition-backed chief ministerial stints in the state. Legislations were framed to act upon 'forces of domination' in the state – 'transfer raj', SC Act, Gangster and Goonda Act – even as simultaneous 'economic plans', such as the AVP for the Dalits were launched. In 2007, when the BSP formed a majority government in Uttar Pradesh, there was an opportunity for the 'Dalit Party' to redress the flaws and comprehensively evaluate the 'policy status' and/or outline alternative programmatic options to firm up party-sponsored development-based programmes. However, the ideological reverse of a 'sarvajan' scheme of governance to reconfigure social empowerment and mainstream it to 'broad-based' politics delegitimized the 'promise' of material improvement to expectant Dalit-Bahujan groups. Upon a less than expected electoral result in 2009, it was partially corrected, not reflective in a democratic 'bhagidari' representation of the marginal groups in decision making but in a re-activation of pro-Dalit administrative legislation. However, bad governance and high proportion of mismanagement of state assets, goods and resources ensured that the due policy prerogative for social, educational and employment-specific entitlements failed. A governance model with a 'social face' would have coordinated the state-funded educative-cum-social projects evenly spaced over the full term in office rather than be known to be symptomatic of a desperation for quick disbursal of goods and resources to 'base voters' solely for electoral gains nearing end of the term. The failure of the Mayawati-led government to pursue long-term policy goals is an evidence of the overt populist character of the party leadership that heightens social expectation but fails to deliver on any conceivable front.

An analysis of BSP's fancied social programmes would highlight the 'impracticable' people-oriented policies that failed to fulfil social development goals to its bahujan voting constituencies.[11]

Examples would put matters in perspective.

BSP's much publicized and fancied 'education schemes' that promised high school, Dalit hostels, coaching centres etc., while arousing interest and expectation among the marginalized groups were in effect a limited policy measure that appeared to be directed at children who had cleared primary school while completely ignoring Dalit children who dropped out of school. The policy was oblivious of the quality of rural government schools, which is the main reason why even children who enrol dropout before they complete elementary school, as their teachers are regularly absent. The Niti Aayog figures for 2016 provide a disconcerting record of 'school dropouts' rampant in the villages and small towns of Uttar Pradesh. The figures suggested that between Class 1 and Class 5, 49.25% of boys and 55.12% girls after having enrolled did not regularly attend school. Similarly, the figures became negligible (50.51% and 66.93%) if one stretched the evaluation period between Class 1 and Class 8. The worse social indicators were recorded if one took a sample of school dropouts between Class 1 and Class 10. It was 64.00% for boys and 86.80% for girls. 'School dropouts' presents a rather contradictory picture to the overall increase in SC literacy in UP, which has risen to about 60.9%, according to the census of 2011, with SC male literacy at 55.7% and SC female literacy at 43.7%.[12] The lack of clarity that exists between school dropouts and the formal acceptance of literacy arises from the fact that states might constitute certain evaluative standards of what constitutes a literate person. Thus, a primary school 'dropout rates' (till Class 5) is the least negligible in comparison to the other two models, and the social indicator of literate schoolchildren does give us a picture of increased literacy in the state over a period of time. In India, particularly in UP, where access to education has been systematically denied to low castes, a comprehensive structural initiative to broaden the resource capability of the 'selected group(s)' is needed. 'Targeted action', aimed only at the SCs, helps when the general education system is providing quality education. If there is still exclusion for reasons of caste, religion or gender, then target-based action plan can help pull up the excluded. Despite exemplifying 'Dalit pride', the BSP avoided the political responsibility to correct (the) injustice 'of a decrepit government school (education) system' in the state.

The AVP (1995) was formulated to 'saturate predominantly Dalit-inhabited villages and habitations with 'physical and social infrastructure'. The intended objective of the scheme was to bring these areas under the ambit of other nationally sponsored anti-poverty programmes', such as the Integrated Rural Employment Programme (IREP), National Rural Employment Programme (NREP), Mahatma Gandhi National Rural Employment Guarantee Act (NREGA) etc., and thereby concentrate the benefits of all available schemes in these villages. The AVP first focused on 'revenue villages' with a majority Dalit population but the criteria were progressively relaxed and later 'hamlets' and not villages were also taken as the unit of selection. The 'programme' sought to correct the 'historical neglect of localities and villages' inhabited by Dalits. However, the 'village project', already uneconomical, became a self-serving goal of the party after it was extended to 'micro-level' habitations. It is not clear to what extent the AVP coordinated with national anti-poverty programmes even as state bureaucracy struggled to 'meet targets and beat deadlines' and targeted groups did not get the intended benefits. In general, the AVP programme actually met the aspirations of a new capitalist and entrepreneurial group that emerged among sections of the Dalits in the rural areas. In western UP, for instance, the benefits of the AVP programmes have been appropriated in its entirety by a small and already better-off section of Dalits who have taken advantage of the provision of reservation provided in the village panchayats in collusion with the local 'public' officials and the village pradhan (headman).

Since 1995, the BSP carried out a land distribution programme 'with mildly distributive overtones', which pertained to and possession of patta lands and the regularization of land that had been in de facto possession by way of encroachment by local landholding castes. Despite distributing government 'patta lands' to the landless Dalits, and only when the Dalit legal claimant was not found to the 'most backward castes', the BSP failed to generate a policy-driven 'action programme' to address problems of poverty and landlessness. For instance, the inability of the BSP to review the policy of land ceiling by way of intervening in rural land disputes over land and labour meant that Dalits in rural areas who are poorly placed in local land and labour hierarchies continued to be greatly limited in their capacity to contest and participate in local-level politics. A study in a central UP district showed that BSP's land distribution programmes had a relatively modest impact and were dwarfed by similar programmes implemented in earlier periods, especially under the 'Twenty Point Programme'.[13] Despite lakhs of landless and homeless Dalits getting a possession of pattas, irrespective of fraudulent allotments and Mayawati's dictate in 2010 directing public officials to take strict action against land mafia in illegal possession of 'land plots', no study was carried out to measure the fertility of agricultural land or security considerations for those wishing to build homes on it. The fate of low agricultural output and poor fertility in small land holdings was augmented by constant policy modifications and faulty implementation of AVP and lack of state subsidy for crop production. Such helplessness was magnified by the 'suicide cases' of farmers in the parched and dry Bundelkhand region in southern UP, consisting of Banda, Jhansi, Hamirpur, Jalaun, Chitrakoot, Lalitpur and Mahoba districts. In 2007, 12 Dalits in the Bundelkhand region and 11 Dalits in other districts of the state committed suicide, which happened in the wake of '25 hunger deaths' amongst the Dalits. In 2008, rain failure meant that farmers were without crops to sow and harvest, and Dalit agricultural labourers in possession of unviable lands were without wages. Dalits' share of woes was about 30% among 'suicides' and 70% among 'hunger deaths.' In 2008–2009, it was reported that more than 80% Dalits field labourers were on the verge of death due to hunger. The region recorded 1,351 deaths during the three-year (2007–2010) period. The grim economic situation was further aggravated as it came to light that a number of other factors also contributed to the innumerable farmer suicides in the Bundelkhand region. Greedy politicians and corrupt bureaucrats siphoned off the special financial package of Rs. 3,506 crores allocated by the central government for the region. About 31,000 farmers owed the rural banks Rs. 280 crores and another Rs. 150 crores that was borrowed under the Kisan Credit Card Scheme. Due to unseasonal rainfall and hailstorm in 2009, crops were destroyed, with the result that there was a threat of compounded interest from the banks upon the massive loans taken by the farmers. Many more committed suicides when they were simply unable to pay back money taken from 'private moneylenders', a recourse taken by farmers to bypass the compounded interest charged by banks. The private moneylenders charged a fixed interest rate of 5% on recovery of cash given to farmers. The BSP government continued to deny that 'any person had died either of hunger or committed suicide associated with agriculture'.[14]

Ideological Crossroad: From Dalit-Bahujan to Sarvajan

The BSP outlined an intersecting bahujan ideology which offered possibilities of political mobilization of the poor to experiment with an 'innovative' anti-caste electoral politics, an outcome of an expedient ideology-politics dyadic 'guru-killi' (master key) with which, supposedly, 'every lock, whether social, economic or political could be opened'. With a focus on a 'politics of the marginalized', by its mode of operation, the BSP consequently produced a political consciousness that if left unrealized materially, would exacerbate inter-caste fragmentation among the subaltern groups. An inherent part of state politics since the 1990s, the BSP attempted to organize 'Dalit castes', but in essence it was the predominant and numerous 'elite' Jatav castes. Other marginalized social groups were mobilized around the 'dominant Dalit caste', to be rendered as electoral capital apparently preserving one's own specific caste grievances and political interests within the prism of BSP's ethno-identity politics. Non-Jatav Dalit and bahujan groups despite being apprehensive about cloistered Chamar-Jatav-centric presence had gravitated towards the BSP to redress their aspirations for 'self-esteem and material development'.[15] Associative relationship with the party increased political awareness that coincided with a proliferation of caste associations. However, as it can be assessed, much of the logistic of political support was achieved and lost by BSP's incapacity to accommodate and ensure access and flow of resources to non-Dalit voting castes. Such numerous caste groups rendered themselves ready-made political resource for whichever political party that represented a political narrative of their 'suffering and social empowerment'. The shifting political preferences of the state's Most Backward Castes (MBC) or referred to in plain speak as the 'lower backwards' between the Samajwadi Party, Bahujan Samaj Party and the Bharatiya Janata Party, the latter in recent times is a case to the point.

Pretentious Sarvajan Ideology

Despite increasing its 'vote share' in the early 2000, the BSP was impaired by its inability to resolve the contentious political capital of variant 'bahujan' caste groups. In 2005, the BSP substantially re-strategized the political parameters of ethnic politics. The 'ideology of sarvajan' was crafted in a period in Uttar Pradesh politics characterized by a governance crisis of the SP-Congress coalition and a fractured state leadership of the BJP. The new sarvajan initiated political model earmarked a micro-management of diverse caste groups carrying 'electoral value' for the BSP. The ideological scheme that strategized the role of the Dalits was twofold: one, as a vital cog of BSP's sarvajan model in a social entente with the upper castes, particularly the Brahmins, in which Dalit voters were specifically directed by the party leadership through numerous Dalit-Brahmin caste 'fraternity' associations to vote for 'Brahmin candidates' so that the party won more seats in the 2007 assembly elections; two, Dalits and a myriad of bahujan caste groups had to adopt a transferable vote sharing arrangement to ensure that maximum number of BSP candidates won. To render effective the electoral plan, innumerable 'caste associations' were also created among non-Dalit bahujan sections of the society, notably among the MBC and the Muslims. The obvious reason for the Brahmins gravitating towards the BSP prior to the assembly elections was to end the 'Yadav raj' of the SP. It is worthwhile to consider, irrespective of the party's novel electoral plan to institutionalize plus votes, whether 'Brahmin support as an upper caste in the social hierarchy in essence gave legitimacy to the party and enabled diverse bahujan groups to cling together?'[16] Certainly, Brahmin votes helped to increase the inflow of diverse bahujan groups to the BSP.

The electoral success of the sarvajan model was in full political view in the state polls of 2007 as the BSP became the single largest political party and the first 'Dalit' party in modern India to form a government in Uttar Pradesh.

The sarvajan scheme was considered as a political masterstroke with an innate potential to expand BSP's political presence in other parts of the country. Yet, sarvajan ideology failed, and its failure highlighted the problematic of a prejudiced and inequitable ideology of politics. Out of political reckoning, certainly by the end of the term in 2012 if not earlier, the 'ideology for all' requires a closer introspection for the difficulties it poses for Dalit politics.

The sarvajan model is a dilution of Kanshiram's notion of 'political bhagidari' couched in bahujan phraseology, which was meant to provide representation to social groups supporting the BSP from 'within the bahujan fold' according to their demographic strength as a 'voting caste(s) unit' in a constituency. Despite legitimate claims of aggregate-based representation of diverse caste groups, the 'partnership of oppressed castes' was ineffectual as the structural alignment of the party was pointedly Chamar-Jatav. Sarvajanism appeared as an ambitious 'ideology-seeking action' representing all sections of society to ensure that the party acquired a 'national character'. With the approximation of the sarvajan model, ideologically opposed groups could form political alliances, that is the 'inclusion of their (social) oppressors', the upper castes, to create a broad-based party with a Dalit core at a political cost of diluting an ethical commitment to fighting on behalf of the marginal social groups.[17]

The sarvajan model carries a far deeper meaning – a separation of the 'ideal' from the 'instrumental' value. It was a fact that was central to the sarvajan ideology and was noted by Mayawati two years before BSP came to power in UP. Thus, the Brahmins in UP supported the BSP purely on self-interest – a passing phase of shoring up their political value at a time of 'Yadav dominance' in the state – and not because of their commitment to equality or opposition to untouchability. The support for the BSP was to oust a 'lower (than upper caste) caste' 'anti-Brahmin' SP. Furthermore, Brahmins were aware that the BJP was no longer capable of winning elections in UP. On the other, 'embracing the sarvajan ideology would give the Brahmin respite from possible humiliation' and insecurity that would have seemed a certainty except for the 'model of sarvajan'.[18]

The sarvajan model disregards caste domination and oppression, highlighting the 'unmarked universal identity of all Hindus, glossing over the difference between Puruskrut Bharat (ideal, pure India) and Bahiskrut Bharat (actual, polluting India)'. It relies on the moral legitimacy of the Dalit struggle but at the same time ignores it for the sake of caste votes. The sarvajan model is 'not a product or a source of Dalit politics because the model has already been produced for the Dalits'. This ideological product is a consequence of certain socio-historical conditions, such as the 'failure of mainstream political parties' to uphold principles of social justice and equality to deny Dalit autonomy and agency or accommodate the material aspirations of the lower castes. The sarvajan model, in effect, is a 'product of an imperfect world where structures of inequality and asymmetry are firmly established', where Dalits carry 'secondary responsibility' for producing this model through 'ideological interpellation yet play a far greater role than caste Hindus' in terms of performing an 'ideological function to leverage an egalitarian vision where it does not exist'. In fact, Dalit politics within the confines of sarvajanism acts as a medium through which the 'hagiography of Indian nationalism becomes rooted in society, as well as in the minds of succeeding generations of Dalits'.[19]

The sarvajan idea operates 'beyond the pale of caste identity or is casteless' and is used in this way by the BSP to mobilize all sections of the society. In this way, sarvajanism 'sustains itself in the public imagination of Dalits by resolving the irresolvable tension' between 'rhetorical' (respect for larger than life size images of Dalit leaders such as Ambedkar or even Mayawati) and 'substantial' (little or no respect for Dalits) recognition of Dalits.[20]

The sarvajan model is of immense benefit to Dalit leaders who reach the top, 'deftly reproducing the nationalist' egalitarian rhetoric to remain in power. They benefit from 'power seepage', which gives a 'feeling of ownership and a sense to the Dalit masses that they too are stakeholders in the system, a reassurance of a continued systemic resource'. The sarvajan model appears to be somewhat vague and ambiguous so as to 'provide space for erasure'. It is an 'intentional ambiguity to explain the durability of the concept' in the context of UP politics. Rather than fostering the 'hard politics' of aggregating the mobilization of demands, the sarvajan model outlines the benefits of participation in which people begin to 'offer allegiance to the leader who would ensure that promises are realizable political goals': that rest upon 'structures of opportunities and patronage which flow from Dalit leaders who control state institutions, whose ascendency to power is a weapon to deflect upper caste domination and discrimination'. It is natural to expect that such structures 'do not solve problems of everybody all at once but gradually.' To be a beneficiary of 'state patronage', power holders 'advocate virtues of patience, to effectively prevent the widespread expression of discontent'.[21]

The operation of the sarvajan model failed to contain the growing frustration of multiple bahujan castes or even Brahmins as it accelerated the degeneration of promises into vacuity. As doubts about the efficacy of the ideological project became an obvious political reality, sarvajanism continued to be propagated publicly, positioned as having given Dalits the perfect vision of empowerment. It was even being suggested by its apologists that the 'ideology' needed to be 'adopted by the people in other parts of the country so as to avoid the inherent flaws in the philosophies of other dominant political parties'.[22]

From Revisionism to Re-envisioning Popular Politics

Successive assembly polls of 2012 and 2017 and Lok Sabha elections of 2014 and 2019 in Uttar Pradesh have put in perspective two significant observations that impinge upon the political marginalization of the BSP in the state: one, a new era of politics ushered in by the BJP, which has emerged as a significant political force post-2014 with a phenomenal Lok Sabha victory in Uttar Pradesh, and which has extended its continued domination over state politics if 2019 polls are any political indication. Three successive electoral victories for the BJP are indicative of a major ideological push towards a different narrative of politics in the state, one that is contextualized in a socio-symbolic space of majoritarianism, micro-managed electoral mobilization of non-core voters and centrally sponsored targeted development initiatives. At the grassroots level, the organizational presence of the BJP and its connect with the concerns of poor was complemented by the narrative of development. It has indeed been an electoral game changer, appearing as a political showcasing of PM Modi-led BJP's nationwide programme of providing the poor 'contact points' with the central government to expand 'economic connections' of various kinds – electricity, housing, gas, direct monetary support, drinking water etc.[23] What began as an electoral promise to a poorly governed and cash-strapped state in 2014 began to be turned into reality in 2017 as 'development schemes' in Uttar Pradesh were persuasively expedited, which exponentially increased the number of beneficiaries. By the time the BJP won the 2019 state Lok Sabha polls, central government welfare schemes for Uttar Pradesh had reached impressive targets: such as cooking gas connection (achieved target of 1.46 crores), rural housing (achieved target of 12.4 lakhs), toilets (achieved target of 1.46 crores), 'annual pay-out' of Rs. 6,000 to poor farmers etc. that were delivered roughly to an approximated 4.25 crores population in the state. It is highly probable that 'core voters' of the BSP and SP may have also been recipient of such welfare measures.[24] Irrespective of the questions that have been raised about the estimates, figures and the success rate of the centrally assisted programmes in Uttar Pradesh, the poor are seemingly content with what they already have or will have – a guarantee that Modi has effectively conveyed: 'gas chulha, shauchalaya aur garibo ko ghar' (a gas cylinder, a toilet and a house for the poor).[25]

Two, on a different keel, the successive winning electoral formula of the BJP over the last five years has sidelined the staple 'core voter' ethnically-driven electoral model of subaltern politics in Uttar Pradesh. While addressing election rallies across Lok Sabha constituencies in the state, Modi accused the BSP and SP of pursuing identity politics that prioritized 'social differences' and 'caste rivalries' with politically closed groups. To that effect, Modi made a pointed remark: for instance, (that) the 2019 BSP-SP coalition was an excuse to 'cheat the mandate, to somehow make sure that there (was) a hung (assembly) and each (political) party got a chunk of power'. The BJP claimed that its electoral victory in the 2019 UP Lok Sabha polls vindicated 'rashtravaad' (nationalism) and 'vikas' (development).[26] Modi's election speeches in the state also successfully contrasted the BJP with the other 'national' and 'regional' political parties across India. These political parties were identified as being run by 'political elites' and being known for their 'corruption scandals', 'dynastic politics' and charges of favouring one social group or the other.[27]

The BSP certainly could not have captured founder Kanshiram's bombast that the party must have the [reverse caste politics] 'arsenals' to 'strangle the neck' (Uttar Pradesh with most number of Lok Sabha and assembly seats and considered as the 'nucleus of Brahmanism'/'upper-caste rule' in government) to render the 'rest of the limbs in the body (meaning other regions or states or 'upper-caste' dominated political parties) useless'.[28] Yet, in terms of realpolitik, for a party that has evolved since the early 1990s, to be distinctly inclined to 'territorialize power to a particular region (Uttar Pradesh)' – a fact that Kanshiram reconciled to after his failed nation-wide tour in 1993–1994 to search for viable bahujan alliances with "like-minded political parties" across the country – a decade of poor electoral performance has displaced BSP from that very 'site and stability of the location'.[29] The BSP under Mayawati is no longer a 'jeetnewala party' (a party that could win), as Kanshiram had predicted,[30] in Uttar Pradesh, that is 'efficiently capable' to ensure a steady rise in bahujan vote share and capitalize on political opportunities to leverage governmental power. In the present political environment, the party is not at all certain of holding on to its 'flock of core (bahujan) voters'. Mayawati continues to remain the unchallenged 'bahujan' leader of the three-decade-old party, but the incumbent is under pressure to deliver a good electoral verdict.

Since its inception, the BSP has used a 'top-down' strategic vision that has prioritized 'building networks between lower-caste elites with the intention to create an empowered bahujan class within the electoral arena and to create a successful alternative led by subaltern politicians'. In doing so, the BSP adopted an ethnocentric approach, and with an obvious attempt to expand its electoral constituencies, created a politics of divide between 'elite and non-elite' to a high degree and 'forced voters to think of themselves as an autonomous electoral community, challenging the vertical incorporation of these voters by existing political parties in the state'. Yet, a sharp politicization of lower-caste identities did not go with the equivalent broadening of social provisioning. In quest of power, the BSP encountered the limits of patronage, including direct cash handouts, which was a substitute of broad social empowerment programmes: of material benefits that were equated with symbolic politics and the 'politics of dignity'. It has become evident that an evaluation would suggest that despite having a social image of being an 'advocate of the disadvantaged', the party could not directly improve the material well-being of the bahujan class. This has been the primary reason for the party 'not being able to sustain a plurality of votes from any other caste electorate' despite adopting expedient electoral measures to sustain caste coalitions.[31]

Staying on the main political course which the party has followed, as a starting point of introspection, the BSP must move away from its prescriptive coalition-era mentality of a 'majboor not mazboot sarkar' (dependent not durable government), the "guru-killi" termed as the "master-key" of political power to attain social equality, as Kanshiram would suggest, which inexplicably defined an electoral-cum-anti-caste ideological politics of the party against 'brahmanvadi' (upper/dominant caste-based political parties) and middle-caste landed elites. Since this presumptive principle and the modus operandi is now being questioned and appears exposed in a post-coalition era UP politics, the logic and efficacy of a 'Bahujan State' to 'equalize oppressed castes' and 'weaken caste mindset' must also be debated. This is crucial since BSP's 'five-year sarvajan governance model' had clearly moved away from a formal adherence to a dictum of 'bahujanwad', howsoever imperfect in its operative dimensions that symbolized the politics of social justice.

Second, does the BSP leadership need a political transformation? Probably yes. Mayawati is remembered for her oligarchic control over the party and a leadership style that is neo-patrimonial and less participatory. Of increasing relevance to the BSP chief is to spin a narrative about 'what is wrong with the current situation' prevailing at the societal level and in politics; what is the vision for a better future; who can be trusted to realize the vision. For this vision to be marketed and delivered to its vote constituencies, the BSP chief must connect with below 35 years of age voters; eschew old style of political rallies where she reads out a speech. In tune with electioneering campaigns post 2014, the BSP must 'infuse technology and pompous audiovisual (social media and political advertisements) canvasing and not hesitate to throw catchy jibes at their opponents'.[32] Otherwise, the collective bahujan citizenry would continue to remain subservient to the unchanging political whims of the party leadership and its allied sociocultural assortments. Encoded in the exactitude of caste technicalities, the bahujan populace would continue to wait its turn to be recipients of social entitlements.

The predicament that the BSP faces is whether it can explore a new course of 'bahujan' politics not attempted by it in the past? The party's failed sarvajan-modelled government has been lost substantially in terms of political credibility to even rejuvenate a plausible political model to chart electoral success. Since 2012, the BSP has adopted an interlinked bahujan-cum-quasi sarvajanist model, more reactive than initiated, to appeal to Dalit-Bahujan class but has failed comprehensively. Simply put, the party is no longer an emerging political alternative for the poor in Uttar Pradesh – its style of politics having been evaluated in its manifold political avatars by bahujan voters. Thus, there are more reasons for the BSP to ideologically refashion its image of a party of the socially disenfranchised which must guide the course of politics to attain goals of social justice.

Is there a historical case that could be useful to the BSP aiding in the conceptualization of a collective subaltern consciousness?

Possibly, the social and political consciousness of the subaltern class in Kerala can hold important political lessons for the BSP. While it is impossible to transpose a 'Kerala-type' socio-economic context and the political roles/practices of the state actors in Uttar Pradesh, the BSP can comprehend and build on certain tenets gleaned from the significant role played by the Left in Kerala to ensure an autonomous and empowering politics of lower castes since independence. Suffice is to suggest that there are a set of interrelated aspects which need to be considered from the Kerala case: the sustained mobilization of politicized non-elite communities in Kerala created pressure for strong policies in the state. Peasant and worker campaigners for the Left ensured that the poor were sufficiently self-mobilized to be in a position to stage continuous agitations to sustain the pressure required to overcome considerable opposition by the local gentry to progressive land legislations. A tremendous proliferation of mass organizations by the Left in such a manner served to embed the party among the poor. The CPI (M) on its part adopted a series of pro-poor policies as the reasons for their political attachment to an expanding voter base. Self-mobilized subaltern electorate pressurized the party or the government (whether CPI (M)-led Left Democratic Front or the Congress Party-led United Democratic Front) to ensure broad and effective social services. This virtuous cycle of grassroots mobilization and social development yielded the mixture of programmatic ties and social attachments that communists appear to enjoy with subaltern communities in Kerala.[33]

For the BSP, the need to explore a genre of popular democratic politics would mean putting on hold a routine post-election 'short-term' assessment of the party's electoral performance to pursue a more challenging goal to reinvent itself. It is a goal that could clearly offer a political challenge to the established old styles of unvaried functioning of the party but also that a political makeover of such a kind may offer the BSP a renewed potential to galvanize subaltern groups towards a radically imaginative politics. If for the sake of an effective argument the Kerala experience is considered, then a possible set of prescriptive steps need to be undertaken on a certain designated trajectory of politics. BSP's schematic framework of electoral politics, which is designed as a 'plan of action and a tool of mobilization' for a 'politics of the moment (that is an approaching election)' that earmarked a constant making and unmaking of caste coalition for a best-fit electoral preparedness, should posit a decentred political approach to generate popular activism. A 'decentred' politics must 'centre' the notion of Dalit subjectivity and the associative concept of a 'bahujan samaj' that Kanshiram had once confessed as difficult to construct and a time-consuming and wasteful political deliberation in the context of achieving political power through 'expedient' Dalit politics. A distinct possibility that would be deduced from the 'Kerala experience' would be for the party to make certain the 'empowerment of representatives' of subaltern castes to assume the stature of local leaders with affixed organizational roles to develop place (locality) or ground level-based social networks; which in turn could provide a political context for the party to organize politics around a more direct and popular form of participation. The stature of local leaders must be autonomous, decoupled from the tightly institutionalized leadership and preconceived electoral schemes of 'ethnic' political alliances. Only then there could appear an autonomous 'democratic space' qua empowerment and a sociopolitical context for such grassroots 'activist' leaders to mobilize marginal groups around land rights, access to water, education, health, jobs, fair prices for poor farmers, food and other basic amenities. Such a democratically construed politics could then open the possibility for underprivileged groups to be better organized for political struggles in their specific locales and be emboldened to 'democratically resist the hierarchical pattern of material dependence that is rooted in pre-capitalist division of labour and reinforced by the severity of caste-class hierarchy and inequality'.[34]

Aided by the party, numerous self-mobilized associations could initiate popular mobilization by taking an ideological position on a critical issue: numerous incidents of anti-Dalit violence in Uttar Pradesh and beyond that have been a glaring omission in BSP's 'revised' Dalit politics till date. Addressing 'Dalit atrocities' requires a deeper political vision that is necessary to comprehend the complex sociopolitical dimensions of exploited and discriminated lives of the subaltern class embedded within the context of a modernized caste consciousness of the dominant castes. Anti-caste atrocity is a lived social reality and the possibilities of variant political mobilizations around it will certainly broaden the sphere of subaltern democratic politics. There are valid reasons for it, which require an explanation. Caste atrocities against Dalits have coincided with the weakening of the caste system in the traditional and ritualistic sense with the result that a modernized caste identity has emerged among the dominant castes. With depleted resources due to the breakdown of the traditional rural economy and the end to patron-client networks established by caste hierarchy dominant castes look with disbelief and anger at the political consolidation of lower 'service castes.' The 'lower castes' vocally express their caste pride, often armed with their respective 'jati histories' in a way they would have never dared to project in the past. Since the 1990s, caste pride and associated socio-economic grievances have been politicized and are in a continual mode of conversion into electoral capital by political parties across ideological hues to build voter constituencies. By default, claims of 'rightful' social entitlement of marginalized groups are being thrust on to the public sphere. On another plane, these supplicant castes have become aspirational and with a proliferation of reservation-based jobs on offer compete with a multitude of non-Dalit castes for state sector urban jobs. Those who have missed the 'mobility ladder' to a new social world for a variety of reasons, the steady commercialization and urbanization of the rural economy have offered newer occupational opportunities. The 'poor may not be better-off today but are certainly untied'.[35] It would not at all come as a surprise that 'servile duties' in the rural areas are being swapped for alternative 'commercial or urban-type' employable jobs which on most occasions can be low-paying and insecure. Therefore, caste atrocity as a complex relational engagement with a modernist caste identity is to be seen as a resultant desperation of dominant castes to keep the lower caste in their 'rightful places' in the social hierarchy. Performed through a range of acts, from the purely abusive denigrating behaviour to physical comportment to outright violence, caste atrocity essentially reproduces caste stigma in a modern context.[36] The moot point that emerges is that Dalit exploitation and the consequent urge to empower in all its aspects is experiential and the BSP would have to generate 'frames' of political struggles for the party. This might come from differing reference points – caste pride to urban jobs to land, education and health care rights to anti-caste violence – of a new route to a caste-class overlap-based subaltern empowerment. It would then be possible for the BSP, having experienced phases of popular struggles, to institutionalize such core objectives in electoral programmes and political campaigns and principally commit goals of social justice for the subaltern class.

Notes

1 Kailash, *The More Things Change*, p. 323; Gupta, *Caste and Electoral Outcomes*, p. 25; Norman. P. Barry, *An Introduction to Modern Political Theory* (2nd edition), London, Macmillan Publishers, 1989, p. 150; Andrew Heywood, *Key Concepts in Politics,* USA, Macmillan Publishers, 2000, p. 135; Adi. H. Doctor, *Issues in Political Theory*, New Delhi, Sterling Publishers, 1985, p. 170; Jeff Goodwin and James Jasper (Eds), *The Social Movements Reader: Cases and Concepts,* USA, Blackwell Publishers, 2003, p. 3.

2 K.C. Das, *Indian Dalits: Voices, Visions and Politics,* p. 49; Kanchan Chandra, *Why Ethnic Parties Succeed?*, p. 227.

3 Kanchan Chandra, *Why Ethnic Parties Succeed?* p. 227; Leo Anjou and John Van Male, Between Old and New: Social Movements and Cultural Change, *Mobilisation: An International Journal*, 1998, 3 (2), pp. 207–226; T.K. Oommen, *Protest and Change: Studies in Social Movements,* New Delhi, Sage Publications, 1990, p. 48.

4 Rekha Pappu, *A Question of Identity*, Seminar, 505, September 2001, 67.

5 Gregor Mc Lellan, *Marxism and the Methodologies of History,* London, Verso, 1981, p.31.

6 K.C. Das, *Indian Dalits: Voices, Visions and Politics*, p. 49.

7 Kanchan Chandra, *Why Ethnic Parties Succeed?*, p. 227.

8 Kalyani Shankar, *Gods of Power,* pp. 3, 7, 8, 13–14.

9 K.C. Das, *Indian Dalits: Voices, Visions and Politics,* pp. 238, 240; Bose, *Behenji,* p. 244.
10 Bose, *Behenji,* p. 256.
11 Zoya Hasan, What Next? *Frontline,* 24, 10, May 19, 2007, p. 20.
12 http//www.planningcommission.nic.in; http//www.censusindia.gov.in. (accessed on May 22, 2016)
13 Sudha Pai, *Political Process in Uttar Pradesh,* pp. 347–349; Santosh Mehrotra, Well Being and Caste in UP, *Economic and Political Weekly,* 2006, p. 4269; Zoya Hasan, What Next? *Frontline,* 2007, p. 20; Craig Jeffrey et al., Dalit Revolution? New Politicians in Uttar Pradesh, *The Journal of Asian Studies,* 67, 4, November 2008, p. 1374.
14 "Mayawati give land holdings to Dalits" (accessed on June 11, 2010) URL: https://economictimes,indiatimes.com/news/politics-and-nation (accessed on June 20, 2019);
URL: http://www.anti-caste.org/2008/05/mayawati-up-one-year-later.html (accessed on June 01, 2009); http//www.wap.business-standard.com/article (accessed on May 19, 2016)
15 Dipankar Gupta, *Caste and Politics,* p. 205.
16 Ajoy Bose (March 13, 2017), The fall of Mayawati: Brahmins leave the BSP building, URL: blogs.economictimes.indiatimes.com (accessed on June 01, 2017)
17 Sudha Pai, Understanding the Defeat of the BSP in Uttar Pradesh: National Election 2014, *Studies in Indian Politics,* 2, 2, 2014, pp. 161–162; Ramnarayan Rawat and K. Satyanarayana (Eds), *Dalit Studies,* Duke University Press, USA, 2016, pp. 35, 36.
18 Rawat, *Dalit Studies,* pp. 35, 36.
19 Rawat, *Dalit Studies,* pp. 40, 41, 42.
20 Rawat, *Dalit Studies,* pp. 40, 41, 42.
21 Rawat, *Dalit Studies,* pp. 42–45.
22 Rawat, *Dalit Studies,* pp. 40–45.
23 Aunindyo Chakravarty, "PM Modi's I-Day Speech: Why the Middle Class Has Reasons to Worry" (Aug. 16, 2019) The Quint URL: https://www.thequint.com/voices/opinion/indian-economy-pm-modi-independence-day-speech-middle-class-india (accessed on Aug. 17, 2019)
24 Dipankar Gupta (June 22, 2019), "Caste and Electoral Outcomes: Misreading Hierarchy and the Illusion of Numbers", *Economic and Political Weekly,* 54, 25, pp. 27, 28, 25; Upadhyay, D., "PMUY: How to avail full benefits of Ujjwala Yojana" (Sept. 14, 2019) Livemint URL: https://www.livemint.com/news/india/pmuy/-how-to-avail-full-benefits-of-ujjwala-yojana-1568387408556.html (accessed on Dec. 01, 2019); Verma, A et. al, " A saffron sweep in Uttar Pradesh" (May 23, 2019) The Hindu URL: https://www.thehindu.com/opinion/op-ed//A-saffron-sweep-in-Uttar-Pradesh/article11640731.ece (accessed on May 29, 2019); Sharma, A., "How Welfare Schemes and then speedy implementation helped BJP win big in Uttar Pradesh" (May 24, 2019) Economic Times URL: https://www.economictimes.indiatimes.com/news/elections/lok-sabha/uttar-pradesh/how-welfare-schemes-and-their-speedy-implementation-helped-bjp-win-big-in-uttar-pradesh/articleshow694743392.cms (accessed on Dec. 01, 2019)
25 "Ballia mei PM Modi ki vipaksh ko chunauti, sabit karo ki maine koi benami sampatti jutaye" [In Ballia PM Modi challenge to the Opposition: Prove that I have fictitious property] (May 14, 2019) URL: https://www.lokmatnews.in/india/lok-sabha-elections-2019-pm-narendra-modi-election-rally-in-ballia-uttar-pradesh-challenge-the/ (accessed on Dec. 29, 2019)
26 Sanghamitra, "The failure of mahagathbandhan in UP: Have voters finally discarded caste-based politics" (May 25, 2019) Opindia URL: https://www.opi

ndia.com/2019/05/the-failure-of-mahagathbandhan-in-up-have-voters-finally-discarded-caste-based-politics/ (accessed on May 29, 2019)

27 Sreemoy Talukdar, " UP assembly elections 2017: BJP's stunning win, SP-BSP rout point to the death of caste-based politics in India" (March 12, 2017) First Post URL: www.firstpost.com/politics/up-assembly-elections-2017-bjps-stunning-win-sp-bsp-rout-point-to-the-death-of-caste-based-politics-in-india-3330336.html (accessed on June 03, 2017)

28 R.K. Singh (1994), *Kanshiram aur BSP: Dalit Andolan ke Vaicharik Adhar Brahmanvad Virodh* [Kanshiram and BSP: Dalit Movement's Ideological Viewpoint Anti-Brahmanism], Allahabad, Kushwaha Book Publishers, p. 56; A.K. Dubey (1997), *Aaj ke Neta, Aalochnatmak Adhyayanmala Kanshiram* [Today's Leader Kanshiram: A Critical Study], New Delhi, Rajkamal Prakashan, p. 23; Anuj Kumar, (2000) A., *Bahujan Nayak Kanshiram ke Avismaraniya Bhashan* [Leader of the Oppressed Kanshiram's Unforgettable Speeches], Delhi, Gautam Book Centre, pp. 76, 82, 85.

29 Michael Peters, (2005), "Education, Post-Structuralism and the Difference", *Policy Futures in Education,* 3, 4, pp. 439, 440.

30 Kanchan Chandra, (2004), *Why Ethnic Parties Succeed: Patronage and Ethnic Head Counts in India*, UK, Cambridge University Press, p. 149.

31 Tariq Thachil, *Elite Parties, Poor Voters: How Social Services Win Votes in India,* Cambridge University Press, UK, 2014, pp. 197, 198, 201–204.

32 K.S. Shekhar, "As BSP celebrates Kanshiram's birth anniversary after poll debacle times ripe for it to reinvent" (March 15, 2017) URL:https://www.indiatoday.in/assembly-elections-2017/uttar-pradesh-election-2017/story/up-election-uttar-pradesh-kanshi-ram-bahujan-samaj-party-mayawati-965577-2017-3-15 (accessed on May 30, 2017)

33 Thachil, *Elite Parties, Poor Voters*, pp. 185, 191–193, 197, 198.

34 W. Nicholls, (2009), "Place, Networks and Space: Theorizing the Geographies of Social Movements Transaction", *The Institution of British Geographers*, 34, 1, p. 85; Gupta, *Caste and Electoral Outcomes*, p. 28; John Gaventa, J. (2006), "Deficit or Contestation? Deepening the Democratic Debate" IDS Working Paper 264, *Institute of Development Studies*, Brighton, UK, p. 16; N. Lakshman, N. (2011), *Patrons of the Poor: Caste and Policy Making in India*, Delhi, Oxford University Press, pp. 11, 13.

35 Gupta, *Caste and Electoral Outcomes,* pp. 26–28.

36 Anupama Rao, (2010), *The Caste Question; Dalits and Politics of Modern India*, Ranikhet, Permanent Black, p. 27.

Bibliography

Books

Ali, Aruna Asaf, *Words of Freedom: Ideas of a Nation*, London, UK, Penguin, 2010.

Barry, Norman. P., *An Introduction to Modern Political Theory* (2nd Edition), London, Macmillan, 1989, p. 150.

Banerjee-Dube, Ishita, *Themes in Indian Politics*, New Delhi, Oxford University Press.

Bayly, Susan, *Caste, Society and Politics in India from the Eighteenth Century to the Modern Age*, Cambridge, UK, Cambridge University Press, 1999, pp. 302–03.

Bhargava, Rajeev (Ed.), *Politics and Ethics of the Indian Constitution*, New Delhi, Oxford University Press, 2008.

Bose, Ajoy, *Behenji: A Political Biography of Mayawati*, New Delhi, Penguin Viking, 2008, p. 29.

Chandanshive, V.D., *Kanshiram The Crusader: A Golden Phase in Post-Ambedkarite Movement*, Nanded, Maharashtra, Blue Dawn Books, 2005, p. 27.

Chandra, Kanchan, *Why Ethnic Parties Succeed: Patronage and Ethnic Head Counts in India*, Cambridge, UK, Cambridge University Press, pp. 143–44, 145.

Chandra, Kanchan and Sangha Mittra, *Dalit Identity in the New Millennium*, Dalit Leader, Vol. 8, New Delhi, Commonwealth Publishers, 2003, pp. 167–70.

Chatterjee, Partha (Ed.), State *and Politics in India*, New Delhi, Oxford University Press, 1997.

Chatterjee, Partha, *Wages of Freedom: Fifty Years of the Indian Nation State*, New Delhi, Oxford University Press, 1998.

Corbridge, Stuart and John Hariss, *Reinventing India*, Cambridge, UK, Polity Press, 2000.

Damodaran,Vinita and Maya Unnithan-Kumar (Eds.), *Postcolonial India: History, Politics and Culture*, New Delhi, Manohar Publishers, 2000.

Doctor, Adi. H., *Issues in Political Theory*, New Delhi, Sterling Publishers, 1985, p. 170.

Frankel, Francine, M.S.A. Rao (Eds.), *Dominance and State Power in Modern India: Decline of a Social Order*, Delhi, Oxford University Press, 1990.

Gokhale, Jayashree, *From Concessions to Confrontation: The Politics of an Indian Untouchable Community*, Bombay, Popular Prakashan, 1993, p. 212.

Goodwin, Jeff and James Jasper (Eds.), *The Social Movements Reader: Cases and Concepts*, Hoboken, NJ, Blackwell, 2003, p. 3.

Gore, M.S., *The Social Context of an Ideology: Ambedkar's Political and Social Thought*, New Delhi, Sage Publications, 1993.

Gould, Harold and Sumit Ganguly (Eds.), *India Votes: Alliance Politics and Minority Governments in the Ninth and Tenth General Elections*, Boulders, CO, Westview Press, 1993, pp.15–16.

Guha Thakurta, Paranjoy, and Shankar Raghuraman, *A Time of Coalitions: Divided We Stand*, New Delhi, Sage Publications, 2004.

Gundimeda, Sambaiah, *Dalit Politics in Contemporary India*, New Delhi, Routledge, 2015, p. 116.

Hansen, Thomas Blom and Christophe Jaffrelot (Eds.), *The BJP and the Compulsions of Politics*, New Delhi, Oxford University Press, 1998, pp. 78–81.

Hasan, Zoya (Ed.), *Parties and Party Politics in India*, New Delhi, Oxford University Press, 2002.

Heywood, Andrew, *Key Concepts in Politics*, New York, Macmillan Publishers, 2000, p. 135.

Jaffrelot, Christophe, *Dr. Ambedkar and Untouchability: Fighting the Indian Caste System*, New York, Columbia University Press, 2005.

Jaffrelot, Christophe, *India's Silent Revolution: The Rise of Lower Castes in North India*, New Delhi, Permanent Black, 2003.

Jaffrelot, Christophe, *Religion, Caste and Politics in India*, London, Hurst and Company, 2011, p. 503.

Jaffrelot, Christophe and Sanjay Kumar, *Rise of the Plebeians? The Changing Face of Indian Legislative Assembly*, New Delhi, Routledge, 2009.

Jana, Arun and Bhupen Sarmah (Eds.), *Class, Ideology and Political Parties in India*, New Delhi, South Asian Publishers, 2002, pp. 244–245.

Jayal, Neerja Gopal, *Democracy and the State*, New Delhi, Oxford University Press, 1999.

Jogdand, Prahlad Gangaram, *Dalit Movement in Maharashtra*, New Delhi, Kanak Publications, 1991, p. 70.

Kolenda, Pauline, *Caste in Contemporary India: Beyond Organic Solidarity*, California, Benjamin/Cummings Publishing Company Incorporated, 1978.

Kumar, Arun, *Elections in India: Nehru to Vajpayee*, New Delhi, Gyan Publishing House, 2001, p. 311.

Kumar,Vivek, *India's Roaring Revolution: Dalit Assertions and New Horizons*, Delhi, Kalpaz Publications, 2006, p.130.

Kumar, Vivek and Uday Sinha, *Dalit Assertion and Bahujan Samaj Party: A Perspective from Below*, Lucknow, Bahujan Sahitya Sansthan, 2001, p. 70.

Lakshman, N., *Patrons of the Poor: Caste and Policy Making in India*, Delhi, Oxford University Press, 2011, pp. 11, 13.

Loshitsky, Yoshefa, *Identity Politics on the Israeli Screen*, Texas, USA, University of Texas Press, 2002, p. 1.

Mani, Braj Ranjan, *Debrahminising History: History, Dominance and Resistance in Indian Society*, New Delhi, Manohar, 2005.

Mc Lellan, Gregor, *Marxism and the Methodologies of History*, London, Verso, 1981, p. 31.

Mendelsohn, Oliver and Upendra Baxi (Ed.), *Rights of Subordinated People*, New Delhi, Oxford University Press, 1994.

Michelutti, Lucia, *The Vernacularization of Democracy: Politics, Caste and Religion in India*, Routledge, 2008, pp. 19, 5–6, 1.

Mishra, Jitendra, *Equality Versus Justice: The Problem of Reservation for Backward Classes*, New Delhi, Deep and Deep Publications, 1996.

Murugkar, Lata, *Dalit Panther Movement in Maharashtra: A Sociological Appraisal*, Bombay, Popular Prakashan, 1991, pp. 42, 114–115.

Narayan, Badri, *Kanshiram; Leader of the Dalits*, New Delhi, Penguin Viking, 2014, pp. 12–13.

Narayan, Badri, *The Making of the Dalit Public in North India: Uttar Pradesh, 1950-Present*, Oxford University Press, New Delhi, 2011, pp. 116–117.

Nayak, Radhakanta (Ed.), The *Fourth World: Appraisal and Aspirations*, New Delhi, Manohar Publishers, 1997.

Omvedt, Gail, *Dalit and the Democratic Revolution: Dr. Ambedkar and the Dalit Movement in Colonial India*, New Delhi, Sage, 1994.

Omvedt, Gail, *Reinventing Revolution*, Armonk, New York, M.E. Sharpe Incorporated, 1993, p. 67.

Oommen, T.K., *Protest and Change: Studies in Social Movements*, New Delhi, Sage, 1990, p. 48.

Pai, Sudha, *Dalit Assertion and the Unfinished Democratic Revolution: The Bahujan Samaj Party in Uttar Pradesh*, New Delhi, Sage, 2002, p.118.

Pai, Sudha, *Political Process in Uttar Pradesh: Identity, Economic Reforms and Governance*, New Delhi, Pearson Longmans, 2003, pp. 195–196.

Pai, Sudha, *Political Process in Uttar Pradesh: Identity, Economic Reforms and Governance*, New Delhi, Pearson Longmans, 2007, pp. 195–196.

Pai, Sudha, *State, Politics: New Dimensions (Party System, Liberalisation and Politics of Identity)*, Delhi, Shipra Publications, 2000, p. 125.

Pantham, Thomas and Kenneth Deutsch (Eds.), *Political Thought in Modern India*, New Delhi, Sage, 1986.

Parashar, Archana and Amita Dhanda, *Redefining Family Law in India*, New Delhi, Routledge, 2008.

Pathy, K.S. and Jayashree Mahapatra, *Reservation Policy in India*, New Delhi, Ashish Publishing House, 1988.

Rao, Anupama, *The Caste Question; Dalits and Politics of Modern India*, Ranikhet, Permanent Black, 2010, p. 27.

Rawat, Ramnarayan and K. Satyanarayana (Eds.), *Dalit Studies*, Durham, NC, Duke University Press, 2016, pp. 35–36.

Rodrigues, Valerian, *Dalit-Bahujan Discourse*, New Delhi, Critical Quest, 2008, pp. 17, 27, 29, 30.

Rodrigues, Valerian, *The Essential Writings of B.R.Ambedkar,* New Delhi, Oxford University Press, 2002, p. 362.

Rothbart, Daniel, *State Domination and the Psycho-Politics of Conflict: Power, Conflict and Humiliation*, London, UK, Routledge, 2019.

Roy, Ramashray and Paul Wallace (Eds.), *Indian Politics and the 1998 Elections: Regionalism, Hindutva and State Politics*, New Delhi, Sage Publications, 1999, p. 62.

Sandanshiv, D.N., *Reservations for Social Justice: A Socio-Constitutional Approach*, Bombay, Current Law Publishers, 1986.

Sathyamurthy, T.V. (Ed.), *Region, Religion, Caste, Gender and Culture in Contemporary India*, New Delhi, Oxford University Press, 1996.

Searle-Chatterjee, Mary and Ursula Sharma, *Contextualising Caste: Post Dumontian Approaches*, Jaipur, Rawat Publications, 2003.

Shah, Ghanshyam, *Caste and Democratic Politics in India*, New Delhi, Permanent Black, 2002, p. 271.

Shah, Ghanshyam, *Dalit Identity and Politics: Cultural Subordination and Dalit Challenge*, Vol. 2, New Delhi, Sage Publications, 2001, p.149.

Shankar, Kalyani, *Gods of Power: Personality Cult and Indian Democracy*, New Delhi, Macmillan, 2002, pp. 7–8.

Sivaramakrishnan, Arvind (Ed.), *Short on Democracy: Issues facing Indian Political Parties*, Haryana, Imprint One, 2007, pp. 109–110.

Subramanian, Narendra, *Ethnicity and Populist Mobilisation: Political Parties, Citizens and Democracy in South India*, New Delhi, Oxford University Press, 1999.

Thachil, Tariq, *Elite Parties, Poor Voters: How Social Services Win Votes in India*, Cambridge, UK, Cambridge University Press, 2014, pp. 197–198, 201–204.

Vora, Rajendra and Suhas Palshikhar (Eds.), *Indian Democracy: Meaning and Practices*, New Delhi, Sage Publications, 2004, pp. 273–274.

Yadav, K.C. (Ed.), *From Periphery to Centre Stage: Ambedkar, Ambedkarism and Dalit Future*, New Delhi, Manohar Publishers, 2000, pp. 135-136.

Hindi books

Akela, A.R, *Kanshiram ke Sakshatkar* [Kanshiram's interviews], Delhi, Manak Publications, 2007, p.162.

Devkar, S.T., *BSP Supremo Mananiya Kanshiram: Bhashan evam Sakshatkar*, [In Gratitude of Mr. Kanshiram : Speeches and Interviews], Aurangabad, Maharashtra, Daulat Prakashan, 2005.

Dubey, Abhay Kumar, *Aaj ka Neta, Aalochnatmak Adhyayanmala: Kanshiram* [Today's Leader Kanshiram: A Critical Study], New Delhi, Rajkamal Prakashan, 1997, p. 58.

Kanshiram, *Chamcha Yug* [An Era of Stooges], Hindi Edition, Bombay, Samta Prakashan, 1998, p. 94.

Kumar, Anuj A., *Bahujan Nayak Kanshiram ke Avismaraniya Bhashan* [Leader of the Oppressed Kanshiram's Unforgettable Speeches], Delhi, Gautam Book Centre, 2000, pp. 76, 82, 85.

Kumari Mayawati, *Mere Sangharshmay Jeevan Evam Bahujan Movement Ka Safarnama*, Part 1 [My Struggle in Life and the Travelogue of the Bahujan Movement], New Delhi, Bahujan Samaj Party, 2006, p. 278.

Namishray, Mohandass, *Bahujan Samaj*, Delhi, Neelkanth Prakashan, 2005, p. 23; Duncan, Dalits and Politics, p. 40.

Pathak, Shivmurti, *Rashtra Nayak Kanshiram*, Allahabad, Shekhar Prakashan, 1995, pp. 17, 18, 19, 27, 53.

Singh, R.K., *Kanshiram aur BSP: Dalit Andolan ke Vaicharik Adhar Brahmanvad Virodh* [Kanshiram and BSP: Dalit Movement's Ideological Viewpoint of Anti-Brahmanism], Allahabad, Kushwaha Book Publishers, 1994, p. 31.

Singh, Satnam, *Bahujan Nayak Kanshiram* [Bahujan Hero Kanshiram], New Delhi, Samyak Prakashan, 2005, p. 65.

Articles

'BSP-BJP Alliance', *Economic and Political Weekly*, 37, 23, June 8, 2002, p. 2204.

Chandhoke, Neera, 'Three Myths about Reservation', *Economic and Political Weekly*, 41, 23, June 10, pp. 2289–2290.

Chandra, Kanchan, *Elite Incorporation in Multi-Ethnic Societies*, Working Paper in Department of Political Science, Massachusetts Institute of Technology, 2000, p. 25 (The Paper was subsequently published in the Asian Survey in September/ October 2000).

'Commentary' written by A.M. Shah, 'Parashuram: Icon of New Brahminism', *Economic and Political Weekly*, 41, 51, February 4, 2006.

Duncan, Ian, 'Dalits and Politics in Rural North India: The Bahujan Samaj Party in Uttar Pradesh', *Journal of Peasant Studies*, 27, 1, October 1999, p. 36.

Gatade, Subhash, 'Subverting the Shudra-Ati-Shudra Revolution: A Close Look at the Complex Interplay of Hindutva and Bahujanwad in UP', *Mainstream*, XLI, I, December 27, 2003, p. 70.

Gaventa, J., *Deficit or Contestation? Deepening the Democratic Debate*, IDS Working Paper 264, Institute of Development Studies, Brighton, UK, 2006, p. 16.

Guha, Sohini, 'Asymmetric Representation and the BSP in UP', *Seminar*, 571, March 2007, pp. 57–58.

Gupta, D., 'Caste and Electoral Outcomes: Misreading Hierarchy and the Illusion of Numbers', *Economic and Political Weekly*, 54, 25, June 22, 2019, p. 27.

Gupta, D., 'Peasant "Unionism" in Uttar Pradesh: Against the Rural Mentality Thesis', *Journal of Contemporary Asia*, 61, 22, 2, 1992, p. 165.

Gupta, Smita, 'Does law and order matter?', *Seminar*, 571, March 2007, pp. 16–20.

Hasan, Zoya, 'Transfer of Power: Politics of Mass Mobilization in UP', *Economic and Political Weekly*, 36, 46 and 47, November 24, 2001, p. 4404.

Heath, Oliver and Sanjay Kumar, 'Why did the Dalits desert the Bahujan Samaj Party in Uttar Pradesh?', *Economic and Political Weekly*, 47, 28, July 14, 2012, pp. 44–45.

Jayal, Niraja Gopal, 'Affirmative Action in India: Before and After the Neo-Liberal Turn', *Cultural Dynamics*, 27, 1, 2015, p. 126.

Jeffrey, Craig, et al. 'Dalit Revolution? New Politicians in Uttar Pradesh', *Journal of Asian Studies*, 67, 4, November 2008, p. 1370.

Jenkins, Rob, 'International Development Institutions and National Economic Contests: Neo Liberalism Encounters India's Indigenous Political Traditions', *Economy and Society*, 32, 4, 2003, p. 590.

Kailash, K.K, 'The More Things Change, the More They Stay the Same in India: The Bahujan and the Paradox of the Democratic Upsurge', *Asian Survey*, 52, 2, March/April 2012, p. 322.

Khan, Mohammad Mujtaba, 'Muslim and Electoral Politics', *Seminar*, 571, March 2007, pp. 37–42.

Kumar, Sanjay, 'The Prospects', *Seminar*, 571, March 2007, pp. 67–68.

Kumar, Vivek, 'BSP and Dalit Aspirations', *Economic and Political Weekly*, 39, 18, May 1–7, 2004, p. 1779.

Kumar, Vivek, 'Uttar Pradesh: Politics of Change', *Economic and Political Weekly*, 38, 37, September 13, 2003, p. 3870.

Lerche, Jens, 'New Wine in Old Bottle: Caste, Local Action, Social Movements and General Elections: Scheduled Caste Agricultural Workers in Uttar Pradesh, *India*', CDR Working Paper 94:12, Centre for Development Research, Copenhagen, 1994.

'Mayawati Revolution', *Economic and Political Weekly*, 42, 20, May 19, 2007, pp. 1795–1796.

Narayan, Badri, 'Demarginalization and History: Dalit Re-invention of the Past', *South Asia Research*, 28, 2, July 2008, p. 172.

Narayan, Badri, 'National Past and Political Present', *Economic and Political Weekly*, 39, 31, July 31, 2004, p. 3539.

Nicholls, Walter, 'Place, Networks and Space: Theorizing the Geographies of Social Movements Transaction', Institution of British Geographers, 34, 1, 2009, p. 85.

Noorani, A.G., 'Indira Gandhi and Indian Muslims', *Economic and Political Weekly*, 25, 44, November 3, 1990, p. 2417.

Pai, Sudha, 'Dalit Question and Political Response, Comparative Study of Uttar Pradesh and Madhya Pradesh', *Economic and Political Weekly*, 39, 11, March 11, 2004, pp. 1141–1150.

Pai, Sudha, 'Elections 1999 Uttar Pradesh: BSP's New Electoral Strategy Pays Off', *Economic and Political Weekly*, 34, 44, October 30, 1999, pp. 3099–3100.

Pai, Sudha, 'Electoral Identity Politics in Uttar Pradesh: Hung Assembly Again', *Economic and Political Weekly*, 37, 14, April 6, 2002, pp. 1334–1345.

Pai, Sudha, 'Understanding the Defeat of the BSP in Uttar Pradesh: National Elections 2014 Studies in Indian Politics', *Studies in Indian Politics*, 2, 2, 2014, pp. 161–162.

Palshikhar, Suhas, 'Beyond Uttar Pradesh: New Implications for Party Politics', *Economic and Political Weekly*, 42, 21, May 26, 2007, pp. 1891–1892.

Peters, Michael, 'Education, Post-Structuralism and the Difference', *Policy Futures in Education*, 3, 4, 2005, pp. 439–440.

Ramaseshan, Radhika, 'Dalit Politics in UP', *Seminar*, 425 (Annual), January 1995, p. 73.

Rekha Pappu, *A Question of Identity*, Seminar, 505, September 2001, 67.

Rudolph, Lloyd and Suzanne Hoeber Rudolph, 'The Political Role of India's Caste Associations', *Pacific Affairs*, 33, 1, March 1960, p. 5.

Rudolph, Suzanne Hoeber and Lloyd Rudolph, 'Caste Associations to Identity Politics: From Self Help and Democratic Representative to Goonda Raj and Beyond', *Pacific Affairs*, 85, 2, June 2012, pp. 372–374.

Satyanarayana, K., 'Dalit Reconfiguration of Caste: Representation, Identity and Politics', *Critical Quarterly*, 56, 3, 2014, p. 54.

Sheikh, Javed, 'Who Needs Identity? Dalit Studies and the Politics of Recognition', *India Review*, 11, 2, 2012, pp. 202, 204.

Sheth, D.L., 'Secularisation of Caste and the Making of New Middle Class', *Economic and Political Weekly*, 34, 34–35, August 21, 1999, pp. 2502–2510.

Subramanian, Ajantha, 'Making Merit, The Indian Institute of Technology and the Social Life of Caste', *Comparative Studies in Society and History*, 57, 2, 2015, p. 297.

Subramanium, Vidya, 'From Heady Hindutva to Voter Disenchantment', *Seminar*, 571, March 2007, pp. 52–56.

Teltumbde, Anand, 'A "Mayawi" Revolution', *Economic and Political Weekly*, 42, 23, June 9, 2007, p. 2148.

'UP: Survival Arrangement', *Economic and Political Weekly*, 37, 9, May 11, 2002, p. 1773.

Upadhyay, R., 'Verdict of the UP Assembly Elections: An Analysis', *South Asia Analysis Group*, Paper No. 419, March 4, 2002 URL: http//www. http://www .southhasiaanalysis.org/ (accessed on 11.02.2004)

'Uttar Pradesh: Politics over Governance', *Economic and Political Weekly*, 37, 42, October 19, 2002, p. 4253.

'Uttar Pradesh: Uneasy Outcome', *Economic and Political Weekly*, 37, 9, March 9, 2002, p. 815.

Verma, A.K., 'BSP's Strategy in Uttar Pradesh: Wooing the Brahmins for a New Alliance', *Economic and Political Weekly*, 40, 26, June 25, 2005, p. 2647.

Verma, A.K., 'Mayawati's Sandwich Coalition', *Economic and Political Weekly*, 42, 22, June 2, 2007, p. 2040.

Verma, A.K., 'Municipal Elections in Uttar Pradesh', Economic and Political Weekly, 41, 51, December 23, 2006, pp. 5218–5221.

Verma, A.K., 'The Elusive Samajwad', *Seminar*, 571, March 2007, p.44.

Verma, A.K., 'UP Assembly Elections: Caste dominates Ideology', *Economic and Political Weekly*, 37, 21, May 25–31, 2002, pp. 1977–1978.

Verma, A.K., 'Uttar Pradesh: Will BSP and Congress gain?', *Economic and Political Weekly*, 39, 15, May 1, 2004, p. 1775.

Waldrop, Anne, 'Dalit Politics in India and New Meaning of Caste', *Forum for Development Studies*, 31, 2, pp. 275–276.

Wankhede, Harsh, 'Dalit Symbolism and the Democratization of Secular Spaces', *Mainstream*, XLVIII, 12, March 13, 2010, pp. 29–32.

Yadav, Yogendra, 'Open Contests, Closed Options', *Seminar*, 534, February, 2004, pp. 62–63.

Magazines

FRONTLINE (December 1993 to May 2007)

'The Winning Duo, Mulayam Singh Yadav and Kanshiram', *Frontline*, 10, 25, December 17, 1993, p. 11.

'A Secular Victory in UP: Big Blow to Hindutva', *Frontline*, 10, 25, December 17, 1993, p. 10.

[1] 'With a New Mandate', *Frontline*, 10, 26, December 31, 1993, pp. 18–19.

'The Changing Scene in UP', *Frontline*, 11, 2, January 15–28, 1994, p. 5.

Praful Bidwai, 'The Backward Bandwagon: A Regressive Social Agenda Would Not Fit the Bill', *Frontline*, 11, 3, February 11, 1994, p. 98.

'Kanshiram: We'll Bring Peace', *Frontline*, 11, 5, March 11, 1994, p. 11.

'Gaining Ground', *Frontline*, 11, 13, July 1, 1994, p. 33.

'Masood Ahmad: I Have Fought Wordy Wars', *Frontline*, 11, 15, July 29, 1994, p. 14.

'Reprieve in UP', *Frontline*, 11, 15, July 29, 1994, pp. 4, 9.

'Toppling to Conquer', *Frontline*, 12, 13, June 30, 1995, p. 12.

'The Decline and Fall: Power Games Come to a Head in UP', *Frontline*, 12, 13, June 30, 1995, p. 5.

'The Decline and Fall', *Frontline*, 12, 13, June 30, 1995, p. 6.

'Lucknow Theatrics', *Frontline*, 12, 14, July 14, 1995, p. 114.

'Cracks to the Fore', *Frontline*, 12, 15, July 28, 1995, p. 25.

'State of Limbo', *Frontline*, 12, 17, August 25, 1995, p. 88.

'Falling Apart', *Frontline*, 12, 21, October 20, 1995, p. 26.

'The Rot within', *Frontline*, 11, 23, November 17, 1995, p. 128.

'UP Eludes the BJP', *Frontline*, 13, 21, November 1, 1996, pp. 4, 5, 7.

'Exploring Coalition Possibilities', *Frontline*, 13, 21, November 1, 1996, pp. 11, 14.

'A Broader Vote-Base', *Frontline*, 13, 22, November 15, 1996, p. 21.
'Shifting Alignments', *Frontline*, 13, 22, November 15, 1996, p. 16.
'BJP's Predicament', *Frontline*, 14, 1, January 24, 1997, p. 28.
Opportunism Inc', *Frontline*, 14, 6, April 18, 1997, pp. 13, 17, 18.
'Mayawati: We Have No Reason to Disbelieve the BJP', *Frontline*, 14, 6, April 18, 1997, pp. 14–15.
'Déjà vu in Uttar Pradesh', *Frontline*, 14, 9, May 16, 1997, p. 45.
'Pressures on UP Alliance', *Frontline*, 14, 11, June 13, 1997, p. 36.
'A Confrontation in Uttar Pradesh', *Frontline*, 14, 12, June 27, 1997, p. 38.
'Rallying Forces', *Frontline*, 14, 13, July 11, 1997, p. 33.
'Message from the States', *Frontline*, 15, 6, March 21–April 3, 1998, pp. 33–36.
Venkitesh Ramakrishnan, 'Continuing Crisis in UP', *Frontline*, 16, 11, May 22–June 4, 1999, pp. 33–34.
'Consolidation in Uttar Pradesh', *Frontline*, 16, 22, October 23–November 5, 1999, p. 114.
'A Paradoxical Verdict', *Frontline*, 16, 28, November 6–19, 1999, p. 42.
'Distress Signals', *Frontline*, 17, 14, July 21, 2000, p. 22.
'Kanshiram: BSP Will Fight the Polls on Its Own', *Frontline*, 18, 9, April 28–May 11, 2001, p. 43.
Purnima Tripathi, 'An Uphill Task', *Frontline*, 18, 12, June 9–22, 2001, p. 43.
Purnima Tripathi, 'A New Calculation in Uttar Pradesh', *Frontline*, 18, 19, September 15–28, 2001, pp. 40–41.
Purnima Tripathi, 'A Feud in Uttar Pradesh', *Frontline*, 10, 25, December 8–21, 2001, pp. 37–39.
Purnima Tripathi, 'In a Cleft Stick', *Frontline*, 19, January 2, 2019–February 1, 2002, p. 34.
Purnima Tripathi, 'The Churning in Uttar Pradesh', *Frontline*, 19, 4, February 16–March 1, 2002, pp. 28–30.
Purnima Tripathi, 'The Uttar Pradesh Tangle', *Frontline*, 19, 7, March 30–April 12, 2002, pp. 35–36.
Purnima Tripathi, 'The Great Game', *Frontline*, 19, 10, May 11–24, 2002, pp. 21–22.
Purnima Tripathi, 'Desperate Measures in Uttar Pradesh', *Frontline*, 18, 17, August 18–31, 2002, pp. 124–125.
Purnima Tripathi, 'All for Bahujan Samaj', *Frontline*, 19, 21, October 12–25, 2002, pp. 43–44.
Purnima Tripathi, 'Feel Good Wearing Thin', *Frontline*, 21, 9, April 24–May 7, 2004, pp. 14–16.
Venkitesh Ramakrishnan, 'The Battle for UP', *Frontline*, 21, 10, May 8–21, 2004, pp. 4–5.
Purnima Tripathi, 'Decisive Defeat for Hindutva', *Frontline* 21, 11, May 22–June 4, 2004, pp. 19–20.
Venkitesh Ramakrishnan, 'A New Caste Formula', *Frontline*, 22, 13, June 18–July 1, 2005, 27–28.
Venkitesh Ramakrishnan, 'Stoking the Communal Fire', *Frontline*, 22, 23, November 5, 2005, pp. 36–37.
Venkitesh Ramakrishnan, 'For a Winning Formula', *Frontline*, 24, 6, March 24, 2007, pp. 121–122.

Venkitesh Ramakrishnan, 'The New Behenji', *Frontline*, 24, 8, April 21, 2007, pp. 11–13.
Venkitesh Ramakrishnan, 'Heat and Dust', *Frontline*, 24, 8, April 21, 2007, pp. 4–7.
Venkitesh Ramakrishnan, 'Conquering Style', *Frontline*, 24, 8, April 21, 2007, pp. 8–9.
Venkitesh Ramakrishnan, 'Dalit Power', *Frontline*, 24, 10, May 19, 2007, p. 9.
Zoya Hasan, 'What Next?' *Frontline*, 24, 10, May 19, 2007, p. 20.
INDIA TODAY (December 1995 to November 1997)
'Mauled Mercilessly', *India Today*, December 15, 1989, p. 43.
Dilip Awasthy and Javed Ansari [Interview with Kanshiram], 'I Do Not Want a Stable Government', *India Today*, Hindi Edition, December 31, 1993, p. 65.
'Allies of Convenience', *India Today*, June 30, 1995, pp. 47, 52, 54–55.
'It's No Alliance', India Today, June 30, 1995, p. 52.
'Living on the Edge', *India Today*, July 15, 1995, p.50.
'Convenience to Confrontation', *India Today*, September 30, 1995, p.88.
Going Their Own Ways', *India Today*, November 15, 1995, p. 61.
'Mayawati: Wait and See How Our Market Goes Up', *India Today*, November 15, 1995, p. 62.
'Uneasy Partners', *India Today*, April 15, 1997, p. 42.
'Divide and Rule', *India Today*, May 31, 1997, pp. 74–75.
'Collision Course', *India Today*, June 16, 1997, p. 32.
'Rally versus Rally, *India Today*, June 30, 1997, p. 33.
'Statue Symbols', *India Today*, July 28, 1997, pp. 38–39.
'Mayawati: I'll Definitely Hand over Charge to the BJP', *India Today*, August 11, 1997, p. 55.
'A Captive Legacy', *India Today*, September 1, 1997, p. 47.
'Double Speak Duo', *India Today*, September 22, 1997, pp. 24–25.
'Lonely at the Top', *India Today*, October 6, 1997, p. 44.
'Uttar Pradesh: Shame or Sham', *India Today*, November 3, 1997, pp. 28, 30.
'Advantage Kalyan', *India Today*, November 3, 1997, p. 18.
'Stooping to Conquer', *India Today*, November 10, 1997, p. 34.
OUTLOOK (June 1995 to November 2003)
'Kalyan Singh: The BJP Has Installed a Dalit Woman as the CM of the Country's Most Populous state', *Outlook*, 22, 25, June 18–24, 1995, pp. 30–31.
'Kanshiram: Congress Is Reduced to a C-Team Now', *Outlook*, 2, 28, July 10, 1996, pp. 4–5.
'Kanshi's One-Point Plan', *Outlook*, 2, 33, August 14, 1996, pp. 20–21.
'Kanshiram: A Helpless Congress Will Toe Our Line', *Outlook*, 2, 37, September 11, 1996, pp. 10–12.
'Together Again', *Outlook*, 3, 14, April 2, 1997, pp. 6–12.
'Fractured Legacy', *Outlook*,3, 31, July 30, 1997, p. 27.
Gatade, Shudra Ati-Shudra, 'Fractured Legacy', *Outlook*, 3, 31, July 30, 1997, pp. 24–31, 70.
'The Reign of Pawnbrokers', *Outlook*, 3, 40, September 29, 1997, pp. 8–9.
[1] 'The Mandir Spillover', *Outlook*, 3, 41, October 6, 1997, p. 8.
'Writing on the Wall', *Outlook*, 5, 19, May 24, 1999, pp. 10–14.
'Umbrella of the Oppressed', *Outlook*, 5, 36, September 20, 1999, p. 33.
'It's Gupta, Period', *Outlook*, 15, 20, May 29, 2000, p. 18.

Saba Naqvi Bhaumik, 'Caste No Bar', *Outlook*, 15, 34, September 4, 2000, pp. 24–26.
Ranjit Bhushan, 'The Deep Rising', *Outlook*, 42, 9, March 11, 2002, pp. 18–20.
Sutapa Mukherjee, 'Shifting Sands', *Outlook*, 42, 28, July 22, 2002, p. 16.
Saba Naqvi Bhowmik Bhaumik, Sutapa Mukherjee, 'Big Hit on Chhota Raja', *Outlook*, 43, 5, February 10, 2003, pp. 10–11.
Poornima Joshi, 'A Few Sharp Dog Bytes', *Outlook*, 43, 15, April 21, 2003, pp. 22–23.
Yogesh Mishra, Sutapa Mukherjee, 'A Tag on the Taj', *Outlook*, 43, 31, August 11, 2003, p. 23.
'Adventures in Wonderland', *Outlook*, 43, 35, September 8, 2003, p. 30.
Poornima Joshi, 'Baby Elephant Walk', *Outlook*, 43, 45, November 17, 2003, pp. 30–31.
SUNDAY (November 1989 to June 1995)
'On the Road with Rajiv', *Sunday*, 16, 20, November 19, 1989, p. 31.
'Going Places', *Sunday*, 18, 24, June 1991, pp. 37–38.
'Kanshiram: My Ultimate Goal is Delhi', *Sunday*, 20, 48, December 5–11, 1993, p. 38.
'Ram Was Not Enough', *Sunday*, 20, 48, December 5–11, 1993, p. 31.
'Man of the Year', *Sunday*, 20, 51, December 26–January 1, 1994, p. 29.
'Enter Kanshiram', *Sunday*, 21, 4, January 23–29, 1994, p. 37.
'Caste Conscious', *Sunday*, 21, 7, February 13–19, 1994, pp. 26–27.
'Kanshiram: My Fight is against Brahminism', *Sunday*, 21, 7, February, 13–19, 1994.
'States of Play', *Sunday*, 21, 7, February 13–19, 1994, pp. 34–37.
'Dalits vs the OBC's', *Sunday*, 21, 9, February 27–March 5, 1994, p. 13.
'The Atrocities against Dalits Continue, Despite Kanshiram', *Sunday*, 21, 7, February 13–19, 1994, p. 28, 32.
'Maya Memsahib' *Sunday*, 21, 28, July 10–16, 1994, pp. 25–26.
'Against all Odds', *Sunday*, 22, 7, February 12–18, 1995, p. 37.
'Soft Target', *Sunday*, 21, 31, July 31–August 6, 1994, p. 47.
'Where Might Is Right', *Sunday*, 22, 2, January 8–14, 1995, p. 27.
'Enough is Enough', *Sunday*, 22, 23, June 4–10, 1995, p. 41.
'A Topsy-Turvy Tenure', *Sunday*, 22, 1, January 1–7, 1995, p. 44.
'The Great Fall', *Sunday*, 22, 24, June 11–17, 1995, p. 37.
'Maya Memsahib', *Sunday*, 21, 28, July 10–16, 1994, p. 24.
'The Great Fall', *Sunday*, 22, 24, June 11–17, 1995, pp. 37–41.
'Mayawati: I Am Not Merely the Leader of the Bahujan Samaj', *Sunday*, 22, 25, June 18–24, 1995, pp. 22–23

Newspapers

The Times of India

The Times of India, Bombay Edition, March18, 1987. NMML, Acc. No. 418, R. 6779.
The Times of India, Bombay Edition, March 19, 1987, NMML, Acc. No. 418, R. 6779.
The Times of India, Bombay Edition, March 28, 1987. NMML, Acc. No. 418, R. 6779.
'V.P. Upstaged by Congress', *The Times of India*, Bombay Edition, May 24, 1988, NMML, Microfilm, Acc. No. 436, R. 6797.

The Times of India, Bombay Edition, May 25, 1988, NMML, Microfilm, Acc. No. 436, R. 6797.
The Times of India, Bombay Edition, November 29, 1989.
The Times of India, Bombay Edition, July 2, 1997, NMML, Microfilm, Acc. No. 600, R. 9130.
The Times of India, Lucknow Edition, May 1, 2004 and January 14, 2003.
The Times of India, New Delhi Edition, March 19, 2004.
The Times of India, Lucknow Edition, April 26, 2004 and March 14, 2004.
The Times of India, Lucknow Edition, March 18, 2004 and April 27, 2004.
The Times of India, New Delhi Edition, April 23, 2004.
The Times of India, Lucknow Edition, April 27, 2004.
The Times of India, New Delhi Edition, October 9, 2007.
'Achievements during 100 Days of the Government Led by Kumari Mayawati, Chief Minister, Published by *Information and Public Relations Department, Government of Uttar Pradesh*', *The Times of India,* New Delhi Edition, August 22, 2007.
The Times of India, New Delhi Edition, September 22, 2008.

Hindustan Times

Hindustan Times, New Delhi Edition, May 28, 1988, NMML, Microfilm, Acc. No. 454, R. 6197.
Hindustan Times, New Delhi Edition, June 10, 1988, NMML, Microfilm, Acc. No. 456, R. 6199.
The Hindustan Times, New Delhi Edition, September 10, 1995, NMML, Microfilm, Acc. No. 459, R. 6202.
Hindustan Times, New Delhi Edition, October 18, 1995, NMML, Microfilm, Acc. No. 567, R. 7556.
Hindustan Times, New Delhi Edition, May 9, 2002.
Hindustan Times, New Delhi Edition, June 29, 2002.
Hindustan Times, New Delhi Edition, July7, 2002.
Hindustan Times, New Delhi Edition, September 9, 2003.
Hindustan Times, New Delhi Edition, June 23, 2007.
Hindustan Times, New Delhi Edition, October 19, 2007.
Hindustan Times, New Delhi Edition, December 8, 2007.
'New Positive Reservation Initiatives, Published by the *UP Information and Public Relations Department*', *Hindustan Times*, New Delhi Edition, February 6, 2008.
Hindustan Times, New Delhi Edition, October 9, 2008.
Hindustan Times, New Delhi Edition, February 8, 2009.
Hindustan Times, *New Delhi Edition*, February 24, 2009.
Hindustan Times, New Delhi Edition, May 17, May 20, May 22, 2009.
Hindustan Times, New Delhi Edition, May 25, 2009.
Hindustan Times, New Delhi Edition, June 15, 2009.

The Hindu

The Hindu, Madras Edition, December 15, 1985, Nehru Memorial Museum and Library (NMML), Microfilm, Acc. No. 362, R. 8707.

The Hindu, New Delhi Edition, June 16, 2005.
The Hindu, New Delhi Edition, May 3, 2007.
The Hindu, New Delhi Edition, May 12, 2007.
The Hindu, New Delhi Edition, May 14, 2007.
The Hindu, New Delhi Edition, August 15, 2007.
The Hindu, New Delhi Edition, October 9, 2007.
The Hindu, New Delhi Edition, December 29, 2007.
The Hindu, New Delhi Edition, June 4, 2008.
The Hindu, New Delhi Edition, July 27, 2008.
The Hindu, New Delhi Edition, October 10, 2008.
The Hindu, New Delhi Edition, October 14, 2008.
The Hindu, New Delhi Edition, October 20, 2008.
The Hindu, New Delhi Edition, January 15, 2008.
The Hindu, New Delhi Edition, January 16, 2009.
The Hindu, New Delhi Edition, February 23, 2009.
The Hindu, New Delhi Edition, May 13, May 17, May 19, May 20, May 21, May 23, May 24, 2009.
The Hindu, New Delhi Edition, May 26, 2009.
The Hindu, New Delhi Edition, May 30, 2009.
The Hindu, New Delhi Edition, June 5, 2009.

Indian Express

Indian Express, New Delhi Edition, December 15, 1985.
Indian Express, Bombay Edition, March 20, 1987. NMML, Acc. No. 418, R. 6779.
Indian Express, New Delhi Edition, March 29, 1987.
Indian Express, New Delhi Edition, August 3, 1988.

The Statesman

'Odd Controversies in Allahabad', *Statesman*, New Delhi Edition, May 30, 1988, NMML, Microfilm, Acc. No. 291, R. 6965.
The Statesman, New Delhi Edition, March 12, 2003.
The Statesman, New Delhi Edition, June 16, 2003.
The Statesman, New Delhi Edition, April 15, 2003.
The Statesman, New Delhi Edition, July 4, 2003.

Business Standard, The Telegraph, Patriot, Deccan Chronicle, Central Chronicle, Deccan Herald, Tehelka

Business Standard, New Delhi Edition, July 11, 2008.
Business Standard, New Delhi Edition, May 18, 2009.
The Telegraph, Kolkata Edition, May 13, 2007.
The Telegraph, Kolkata Edition, May 18, 2007.
The Telegraph, Kolkata Edition, May 24, 2009.
Patriot, New Delhi Edition, May 25, 1988.
Deccan Chronicle, Hyderabad Edition, May 4, 2009.
Central Chronicle, Madhya Pradesh Edition, May 14, 2009.

Deccan Herald, Bangalore Edition, May 15, 2007.
Tehelka, New Delhi Edition, April 7, 2009.

Navbharat Times and Amar Ujala

Agnihotri, 'Mulayam ko che mahiney tak parkhenge' (*lit.* 'We Will Observe Mulayam for Six Months')', *Navbharat Times,* New Delhi Edition, November 12, 1993.
Amar Ujala, Lucknow Edition, April 15, 2002.
Amar Ujala, Lucknow Edition, May 20, 2002.
Amar Ujala, Lucknow Edition, 26 June, 2002 and 30 June, 2002.
Amar Ujala, Lucknow Edition, September 28, 2002.
Amar Ujala, Lucknow Edition, October 28, 2002, December 23, 2002, January 11, 2003 and February 25, 2002.
Amar Ujala, Lucknow Edition, February 20, 2003.
Amar Ujala, Lucknow Edition, April 15, 2003.

The Tribune

The Tribune, Chandigarh Edition, March 20, 1997, NMML, Microfilm, Acc. No. 521, R. 11170.
The Tribune, Chandigarh Edition, March 21, 1997, NMML, Microfilm, Acc. No. 521, R. 11170.
The Tribune, Chandigarh Edition, March 22, 1997, NMML, Microfilm, Acc. No. 521, R. 11170.
The Tribune, Chandigarh Edition, March 26, 1997, NMML, Microfilm, Acc. No. 521, R. 11170.
The Tribune, Chandigarh Edition, March 28, 1997, NMML, Microfilm, Acc. No. 521, R. 11170.
The Tribune, Chandigarh Edition, May 10, 1997, NMML, Microfilm, Acc. No. 523, R. 11172.
The Tribune, Chandigarh Edition, May 15, 1997, NMML, Microfilm, Acc. No. 523, R. 11172.
The Tribune, Chandigarh Edition, May 30, 1997, NMML, Microfilm, Acc. No. 524, R. 11173.

The Pioneer

The Pioneer, Lucknow Edition, June 4, 1995, NMML, Microfilm, Acc. No. 600, R. 8767.
The Pioneer, Lucknow Edition, June 2, 1995, NMML, Microfilm, Acc. No. 600, R.8767.
The Pioneer, Lucknow Edition, June 21, 1995, NMML, Microfilm, Acc. No. 600, R. 8767.
The Pioneer, Lucknow Edition, June 26, 1995, NMML, Microfilm, Acc. No. 600, R. 8767.
The Pioneer, Lucknow Edition, June 29, 1995, NMML, Microfilm, Acc. No. 600, R. 8767.

The Pioneer, Lucknow Edition, June 7, 1995, NMML, Microfilm, Acc. No. 600, R. 8767.

The Pioneer, Lucknow Edition, June 12, 1995, NMML, Microfilm, Acc. No. 600, R. 8767.

The Pioneer, Lucknow Edition, June 10, 1995, NMML, Microfilm, Acc. No. 600, R. 8767.

The Pioneer, Lucknow Edition, August 3, 1997, NMML, Microfilm, Acc. No. 525, R. 11174.

The Pioneer, Lucknow Edition, July 28, 1997, NMML, Microfilm, Acc. No. 526, R. 11174.

The Pioneer, New Delhi Edition, October 11, 2002 and October 12, 2002.

The Pioneer, New Delhi Edition, January 25, 2003.

The Pioneer, New Delhi Edition, October 24, 2002, November 11, 2002, January 29, 2003 and February 5, 2003.

The Pioneer, New Delhi Edition, February 16, 2003 and February 15, 2003.

The Pioneer, Lucknow Edition, February 15, 2003.

Official Government Notifications

Sushri Mayawati, *Bahujan Samaj Party ki sarkar ke sadey char mah ki safaltayein aur uplabdhiyan* [lit. Four and a half months of the success and achievements of the Government of Bahujan Samaj Party], 1995.

Unki Disha: Hamare Prayas, Vartaman Uttar Pradesh Sarkar ki Ek Saal Ki Uplabdhiyan [Her Vision: Our Efforts, Completion of One Year Achievements of Uttar Pradesh Government], published by the Department of Information and Public Relations, Lucknow, UP, May 2003, pp. 4, 6, 7, 10–12, 18–19, 22, 39, 41, 46; *The Statesman,* New Delhi Edition, September 13, 2002 and September 17, 2002.

'*Bahujan Samaj Party dwara Bahujan Samaj Prerna Kendra sthapana diwas par behen Mayawati Ji ka bhasan*', [Under the auspices of the Bahujan Samaj Party a speech by Ms. Mayawati on the occasion of the founding of the Bahujan Samaj Center for Inspiration], June 3, 2005, CD-ROM, I & II, Lucknow, Uttar Pradesh, 2005.

'Achievements during 6 months of the Government led by Kumari Mayawati, Chief Minister, Directorate *of Information and Public Relations*, Uttar Pradesh, Lucknow', *The Times of India,* New Delhi Edition, August 22, 2007.

'Achievements during 100 days of the Government led by Kumari Mayawati, Chief Minister, Published by *Information and Public Relations Department, Government of Uttar Pradesh*', *The Times of India,* New Delhi Edition, August 22, 2007.

'Special Gifts for All Round Development of Most Backward Areas of the State and Poor Families', Published by *UP Information and Public Relations Department*, January 15, 2008.

'New Positive Reservation Initiatives, Published by the *UP Information and Public Relations Department*', *Hindustan Times*, New Delhi Edition, February 6, 2008.

Mahamaya Garib Arthik Madad Yojana (Mahamaya Economic Assistance for the Poor Plan), Savitri Bai Phule Balika Shiksha Yojana (Savitri Bai Young Girl Education Plan), Mahamaya Garib Balika Aashirwad Yojana (Mahamaya Poor

Girl Blessing Plan), Mahamaya Sarvajan Awaas Yojana (Mahamaya Public Housing Plan), Kanshiram Awaas Yojana (Kanshiram Housing Plan), 2009.

URLs

'Ballia mei PM Modi ki vipaksh ko chunauti, sabit karo ki maine koi benami sampatti jutaye' [In Ballia PM Modi Challenge to the Opposition: Prove that I Have Fictitious Property] (14.05.2019) URL: https://www.lokmatnews.in/india/lok-sabha-elections-2019-pm-narendra-modi-election-rally-in-ballia-uttar-pradesh-challenge-the/ (accessed on 29.12.2019).

'Basic Concept of Nazul' (16.02.2014) URL: https://www. lawweb.in/2014/02/basic-concept-of-nazul-land.htm (accessed on 18.01.2018).

Beg, Mirza Asmer, Shashikant Pandey, and Sudhir Kumar (26.05.2019) 'Post-Poll Survey: Why Uttar Pradesh's Mahagathbandhan failed?' URL: https://www.thehindu.com/elections/lok-sabha-2019/post-poll-survey (accessed on 29.05.2019).

'Being Mayawati' (12.05.2007) URL: http://www.indianmuslims info/news/2007/may/12/impt/-being-mayawati.html (accessed on 22.12.2007).

URL: http://www.indian-election.com/uttarpradesh/index.html#cont (accessed on 24.10.2007).

Bhatt, V. (26.06.2019) 'Woo Muslims, Fight for No.2 Spot: What Three Poll Defeats, Alliance Failure Taught Mayawati' News18 URL: https://www.news18.com/news/opinion/woo-muslims-fight-for-no-2-spot-what-three-poll-defeats-alliance-failure-taught-mayawati-2204295.html (accessed on 27.06.2019).

Banerjee, Biswajit (16.05.2014) 'Modi Sweeps UP, BSP Wiped out' URL: http://www.niticentral.com/2014/05/16/modi-wave-wipes-out-bsp-crushes-sp-224132.html (accessed on 20.05. 2014).

Banerjee. Biswajit (20.05.2014) '2014 Mandate: Flimsy Excuses Will Not Help SP, BSP' URL: http://www.niticentral.com/2014/05/20/2014-mandate-flimsy-excuses-will-not-help-sp-bsp-225182.html (accessed 28.05. 2014).

'BSP MLA Admits Killing PWD Engineer: UP Police' (02.01.2009) URL: https://www.news18.com/news/politics (accessed on 16.06.2019) and http://www.hotnewsb4ublogspot.com/2008/12/up_engineer_lynched_by_bsp_mla.html (accessed on 20.01.2009).

'BSP-SP Alliance: United They Fall in UP' (24.05.2019), URL: https//www.business-standard.com/article/pti-stories (accessed on 29. 05.2019); 'BSP Biggest Gainer among Mahagathbandhan Constituents in UP' (24.01.2019), URL: https//economictimes.indiatimes.com/news/elections/lok-sabha/uttar-pradesh (accessed on 29.01.2019).

URL: http//www.ceri-sciencespo.com/archive/Sept04/arty.pdf (accessed on 24.05.2007).

Chakravarty, Aunindyo (16.08.2019) 'PM Modi's I-Day Speech: Why the Middle Class Has Reasons to Worry', *The Quint*, URL: https://www.thequint.com/voices/opinion/indian-economy-pm-modi-independence-day-speech-middle-class-india (accessed on 17.08.2019).

Combaz, Emilio, and Claire McLoughlin (August, 2014) 'Voice, Empowerment and Accountability', URL: http//www. gsdrc.org/topic-guides/voice-empowerment-and-accountability (accessed on 23.06.2018).

Darapuri, S.R. (25.03.2012) 'Why Dalits Have Slammed Mayawati's Sarvajan Rule', URL: http://www.countercurrents.org (accessed on 16.11. 2015).

'Education Officer Held in TET Scam' (09.02.2012) URL: http://www.hindustan times.com/Lucknow/education (accessed on 04.12. 2015).

'Election Results: Only Statues Proclaim Mayawati Not UP Voters' (17.05.2014) URL: http://timesofindia.indiatimes.com/home/lok-sabha-elections-2014/news/Election-Results-Only-statues-proclaim-Maya-not-UP-voters/articleshow/35230961.cms (accessed on 20.05.2014).

'Five FIR against NREGA Misuse during Maya's Reign' (22.02.2014) URL: http://www.business-standard.com/article/economy (accessed on 28.12.2015).

Ghatak, Maitreesh (13.07.2017) 'Demonetization Was Bad Economics but As an Act of Vigilantism It Served Modi Politically', *The Wire*, URL: https://thewire.in/politics/demonetization-bad-economics-clever-politics-modi-116124 (accessed on 18.09.2017).

Gupta, Smita, 'Does Law and Order Matter?', pp. 16–20, India Events of 2005, Human Rights Watch (World Report 2006) URL: https://www.hrw.org/world-report/2006/country-chapters (accessed on 13.05.2018).

Hasin, Farhad (27.05.2019) 'Explained: The BJP's Stunning Performance in Uttar Pradesh', URL: https://thewirein/politics/explained-thebjps-stunning-performance-in-uttar-pradesh (accessed on 31.05.2019).

Huda, Kashif-ul (18.05.2014) 'Modi Wave Nullified Anti- BJP Muslim Voting in UP', URL: http://twocircles.net/2014may18/modi_wave_nullified_antibjp_muslim_voting.html#.U3tzmaO_nIU (accessed on 20.05.2014).

Jaswal, Kamal Kant, 'From Coalition Dharma to Governance Dharma', *Common Cause*, XXIX, 4, October–December 2010, URL: http//www.commoncause.in/publication_details.php (accessed on 07.07.2019).

Jha, S. (14.03.2017) 'UP Elections 2017: Mayawati's Dalit Vote Base Slipping Away Fast', *Hindustan Times*, URL: http://www.hindustan.com/assembly-elections/up-elections-2017-mayawati-s-dalit-vote-base-is-slipping-away-fast/story-BmjVMSJNWEdQagefXIIBUBO.HTML (accessed on 02.06.2017).

Kang, Bhavdeep (05.01.1998) 'Villain No. 7 Romesh Bhandari', URL: https://www.outlookindia.com (accessed on 05.07.2017).

Khan, Atiq (16.03.2010) 'Mayawati Sidelines Satish Chandra Mishra', URL: http://www. the hindu.com/todays-paper (accessed on 30.11.2014).

Kumar, Devendra (17.03.2017) 'Four-Pronged Strategy behind BJPs Uttar Pradesh Election Victory', URL: www.livemint.com/Opinion (accessed on 02.06.2017).

Kumar, Sajjan (12.01.2017) 'BJP Has Edge in Capturing Floating Non-Yadav OBC Vote in UP', URL: www.newsindiaexpress.com/nation/2017/jan/12/bjp-has-edge-in-capturing-floating-non-yadav-obc-vote-in-up-1558780.html (accessed on 30.05.2017).

Lalchandani, Neha (25.06.2019) 'Split with SP Final, Will Fight Polls on Our Own Now: Mayawati', *The Times of India*, URL: https://timesofindia.com/india/split-with-sp-final-will-fight-polls-on-our-own-now-mayawati/articleshow/69935225.cms (accessed on 27.06.2019).

'Mayawati Government to Draft BPL List Afresh' (08.10.2007), URL: http://www.articles.economictimes-indiatimes.com/2007 (accessed on 06.09.2015).

'Mayawati Give Land Holdings to Dalits' (11.06.2010), URL: https://economictimes,indiatimes.com/news/politics-and-nation (accessed on 20.06.2019).

URL: http://www.anti-caste.org/2008/05/mayawati-up-one-year-later.html (accessed on 01.06.2009); http//www.wap.business-standard.com/article (accessed on 19.05.2016).

'Mayawati Government Indifferent to Bundelkhand's Miseries: Centre' (14.06.2011), URL: http://www.timesofindia.indiatimes.com (accessed on 24.05.2015).

'Mayawati Dissolves all Committees of BSP' (20.05.2014), URL: http://www.hindustantimes.com/elections2014/election-beat/mayawati-dissolves-all-committees-of-bsp/article1-1221175.aspx (accessed on 29.05. 2014).

'Mayawati Faces Grim Reality as Cadres Rush to Join BJP' (20.05.2014), URL: http://economictimes.indiatimes.com/news/politics-and-nation/mayawati-faces-grim-reality-as-cadres-rush-to-join-bjp/articleshow/35354753.cms (accessed on 25.05.2014).

Narayan, Badri (23.05.2019) 'The Secret of BJP's Success in Uttar Pradesh: Winning over Dalits and OBC's and a Dose of Hindutva', *DNA India*, URL: https://www.dnaindia.com/analysis/column-the-secret-of-bjp-s-success-in-uttar-pradesh-winning-over-dalits-and-obcs-and-a-dose-of-hindutva-1990583 (accessed on 02.11.2019).

'Naseemuddin Siddiqui: Muslim Face of the BSP' (13.05.2007), URL: http://www.twocircles.net/2007,May 13/naseemuddin-siddiqui-muslim-face-bsp.html (accessed on 24.08.2007).

Pradhan, Sharat (02.05.2012) '200 Personnel Guard Her, but Maya Still Fears for Life', URL: http://www.rediff.com/news/report/ (accessed on 28.12.2015).

Ramseshan, Radhika (17.05.2014) 'Cadre and Caste Do the Trick', URL: http://www.telegraphindia.com/india/cadre-and-caste-do-the-trick/cid/183006 (accessed on 29.12.2019).

Rawat, Virendra Singh (04.06.2019) 'SP-BSP Honeymoon over as Mayawati Hints at Dumping "Mahagathbandhan"', URL: https://www.business-standard.com/article/politics (accessed on 04.06.2019).

Sanghamitra (25.05.2019) 'The Failure of Mahagathbandhan in UP: Have Voters Finally Discarded Caste-based Politics', *Opindia*, URL: https://www.opindia.com/2019/05/the-failure-of-mahagathbandhan-in-up-have-voters-finally-discarded-caste-based-politics/ (accessed on 29.05.2019).

Shakil, Marya (13.02.2017) 'Why the Akhilesh-Rahul Alliance Lacks the Punch of Nitish-Laloo Combo'. URL:https//www.news18.com/news/politics/why-the-akhilesh-rahul-alliance-lacks-the-punch-of-nitish-laloo-combo-1348624.html (accessed on 02.06.2017).

Sharma, Aman (24.05.2019) 'How Welfare Schemes and Then Speedy Implementation Helped BJP Win Big in Uttar Pradesh', *Economic Times*, URL: https://www.economictimes.indiatimes.com/news/elections/lok-sabha/uttar-pradesh/how-welfare-schemes-and-their-speedy-implementation-helped-bjp-win-big-in-uttar-pradesh/articleshow694743392.cms (accessed on 01.12.2019).

Sharma, Aman (07.01.2019) 'Congress Staying out of SP-BSP Alliance in UP a Plus for All Three', *Economic Times*, URL: https://www. economictimes.indiatimes.com/news/politics-and-nation/congress-staying-out-of-sp-bsp-alliance-in-up-a-plus-for-all-three/articleshow/67414009.cms?from=mdr (accessed on 22.01.2019).

Sharma, Aman (27.05.2019) 'Delayed Tie-up with BSP Hurt Us: SP MPs', URL: https://economictimes.indiatimes.com/politics-and-nation/ (accessed on 29.05.2019).

Shekhar, K.S. (15.03.2017) 'As BSP Celebrates Kanshiram's Birth Anniversary after Poll Debacle Times Ripe for It to Reinvent', URL:https://www.indiatoday.in/assembly-elections-2017/uttar-pradesh-election-2017/story/up-election-uttar-pradesh-k anshi-ram-bahujan-samaj-party-mayawati. Aman Sharma, 'Congress Staying out of SP-BSP Alliance in UP' (accessed on 22.01.2019).

Shenoy, T.V.R. (11.05.2007) 'The Victory of Caste Arithmetic', URL: http://www.in.rediff.com/news/2007/may/11 flip.htm (accessed on 25.08.2007).

Singh, D.K., and Samyak Pandey (29.05.2019) 'Why Akhilesh Yadav and SP Have Reason to be 'Cheated' by Mayawati and Her BSP', *The Print*, URL: https://theprint.in/politics/why-akhilesh-yadav-sp-have-reason-to-feel cheated-by-mayawati-her-bsp/242319 (accessed on 05.06.2019).

'SP-BSP Alliance Leaves 2019 Prospects Bleak for Congress in Uttar Pradesh: Division of Voters May Deal Blow to BJP' (14.01.2019), URL: *First Post*, https://www.first-post.com/politics (accessed on 22.01.2019).

Srivastava, Piyush (24.02.2014) 'BJP Castes Its Net in UP: How Party Is Using Modi's Background to Attract OBC Votes while Still Seeking Brahmin Blessings', URL: http://www.dailymail.co.uk/indiahome/indianews/article-2566926/BJP-castes-net-UP-How-party-using-Modis-background-attract-OBC-votes-seeking-Brahmin-blessings.html (accessed on 20 May 2014).

Talukdar, Sreemoy (12.03.2017) 'UP Assembly Elections 2017: BJP's Stunning Win, SP-BSP Rout Point to the Death of Caste Based Politics in India', *First Post*, URL: www.firstpost.com/politics/up-assembly-elections-2017-bjps-stunning-win-sp-bsp-rout-point-to-the-death-of-caste-based-politics-in-india-3330336.html (accessed on 03.06.2017).

Tewari, R (05.06.2019) 'Explained: BSP Minus Samajwadi Party, between the Lines', *Indian Express*, URL: https://www.indianexpress.com/article/explained/explained-bsp-minus-sp-between-the-lines-5765433/ (accessed on 08.08.2019).

'1979-The Mandal Commission: Stirring the Caste Cauldron' (24.12.2009) URL: https://www.indiatoday.in/magazine/cover-story/story/20091228-1979-the-mandal-commission-stirring-the-caste-cauldron-741610-2009-12-24 (accessed on 08.06.2014).

Tiwari, A. (16.03.2017) 'Results Backlash against SP, BSPs Identity Politics', URL: https://www.pressreader.com/india/economic-times/ (accessed on 01.06.2017).

Tiwari, A. (26.05.2019) 'How BJP Trumped SP-BSP with Congress Help in Uttar Pradesh', *Bloomberg Quint*, URL: https://www.bloombergquint.com/elections/how-bjp-trumped-sp-bsp-with-congress-help-in-uttar-pradesh (accessed on 09.02.2020).

Upadhyay, D. (14.09.2019) 'PMUY: How to Avail Full Benefits of Ujjwala Yojana', Livemint URL: https://www.livemint.com/news/india/pmuy/-how-to-avail-full-benefits-of-ujjwala-yojana-1568387408556.html (accessed on 01.12.2019).

Vashishtha, Akash (08.03.2012) 'Samajwadi Party to Review Status of Projects Undertaken by Mayawati Government in UP', URL: http://www.indiatoday.in/story/ (accessed on 24.08.2015).

Verma, A. et al (23.05.2019) 'A Saffron Sweep in Uttar Pradesh', *The Hindu*, URL: https://www.thehindu.com/opinion/op-ed//A-saffron-sweep-in-Uttar-Pradesh/article11640731.ece (accessed on 29.05.2019).

Vij, Shivam (10.03.2007) 'The Elephant Paradox', URL: http://www. shivamvij.com/2007/03/ the-elephant-paradox.html (accessed on 25.08.2007).

Vij, Shivam (26.05.2007) 'The Elephant Charge', URL: https://www.india.eu.org/spip.php?article7686 (accessed on 13.03.2009).

Vij, Shivam (21.05.2009) 'UP Dalits Remind Mayawati: Democracy is Beautiful', URL: http//www.kafila.online/2009/05/21/ups-dalits-remind-mayawati-democracy-is-a-beautiful-thing (accessed on 18.06.2009).

Vij, Shivam (06.03.2012) 'Why Mayawati's Defeat Is the BSP's Victory', URL: http://www.rediff.com/news/column (accessed on 16.11.2015).

Vij, Shivam (20.01.2013) 'UP's Dalits Remind Mayawati: Democracy is a Beautiful Thing'; 'Solve People's Problems or Get Punished: Mayawati', URL: http://www.business-standard.com/article/economy-policy (accessed on 05.04.2017).

Vij, Shivam (14.01.2019) 'The SP-BSP Alliance in UP Is Rare, Formidable and Perfect' (2019) *The Print*, URL: https://www.theprint.in/opinion/the-sp-bsp-alliance-in-up-is-rare-formidable-and-perfect/177657/ (accessed on 20.01.2019).

Yadav, Yogendra (27.02.2012) 'The More They (Don't) Remain the Same', URL: http://www.outlookindia.com (accessed on 16.12.2014).

URLs of Statistical Election Data

URL: http://www.eci.gov.in/SR_key Highlights/ SE_1983/ Statistical Report Delhi_83.pdf (accessed on 20.06.2007).

URL: http//www. eci.gov.in/SR_ Key Highlights/ SE_ 1985/Statistical_Report_Uttar Pradesh_1985. pdf (accessed on 10.06. 2007).

URL: http//www. eci.gov.in/Bye Election/bye_election.asp (accessed on 10.06.2007).

URL: http//www. eci.gov.in/Bye Elections/bye-elections. Asp (accessed on 21.07.2007).

URL: http//www. eci.gov.in/SR_KeyHighlights/ SE_ 1989/ Statistical_Report_%20 UP_1989. pdf (accessed on 02.08.2007).

URL: http//www. eci.gov.in/SR_KeyHighlights/SE_1989/Statistical_Report_%20 UP_ 1989.pdf (accessed on 21.08.2007).

URL: http//www. eci.gov.in/SR_KeyHighlights/SE_1991/Stat_Rep_UP_91. pdf (accessed on 21.08.2007).

URL: http//www. archive. eci. gov. in/GE 2004 /pollup/pc/states/partycomp 01. htm; http//www.eci.gov.in/Statistical Reports/ LS_1991/vol_II_91. pdf (accessed on 24.08.2007).

URL: http//www.eci.gov.in/Statistical Report/LS_1991/Vol_II_91.pdf (accessed on 28.08.2007).

URL: http//www.eci.gov.in/Statistical Report/LS_1991/Vol_II_91.pdf (accessed on 28.08.2007).

[1]URL: http://www.eci.gov.in/KeyHighlights/SE_1994/StatisticalReport_AP94.pdf.

URL: http://www. eci.gov.in/KeyHighlights/SE_1994/StatisticalReport_KT94.pdf.

URL: http://www.eci.gov.in/KeyHighlights/SE_1996/StatisticalReport_TN96.pdf.

URL: http://www.eci.gov.in/KeyHighlights/SE_1996/StatisticalReport_KA96.pdf.

URL: http://www.eci.gov.in/KeyHighlights/SE_1995/StatisticalReport_MAH95.pdf.

URL: http://www. eci.gov.in/KeyHighlights/SE_1996/Statistical Report_WB95.pdf (all accessed on 10.08.2008).

URL: http//www.eci.gov.in/KR_KeyHighlights/LS_1998/vol_1_LS_98.pdf (accessed on 01.03.2008).

URL: htp://www.eci.gov.in/Statistical Reports/ LS_1999/ Vol_I_LS_99.pdf (accessed on 01.03.2008).

Election Commission of India, URL: http://www.eci.gov.in/Statistical Reports/SE_2007/StatReport AS 2007_UTTAR _PRADESH.pdf (accessed on 21.04.2008).

Index